Harvard Studies in Business History XXXV

Edited by Alfred D. Chandler, Jr.
Isidor Straus Professor of Business History
Graduate School of Business Administration
George F. Baker Foundation
Harvard University

Kikkoman

Company, Clan, and Community

W. MARK FRUIN

Harvard University Press
Cambridge, Massachusetts
and London, England   1983

This book is printed on acid-free paper, and its binding materials
have been chosen for strength and durability.

Library of Congress Cataloging in Publication Data
Fruin, W. Mark, 1943–
    Kikkoman : company, clan, and community.

    (Harvard studies in business history ; 35)
    Includes index.
    1. Kikkoman Shōyu Kabushiki Kaisha—History.
I. Title. II. Series.
HD9330.S653J319   1983   338.7′66454   82-25848
ISBN 0-674-50340-6

For

Carolyn, Noah, and Nathan

Editor's Introduction

MARK FRUIN'S STUDY of Kikkoman is, I believe, the first business history of a major Japanese enterprise based on its archives written by an American. The story begins in the seventeenth century and is carried to the present. It provides a detailed picture of the business of manufacturing in the Tokugawa era—activities that were carried out in strikingly different ways than they were in the West. Of particular value is Professor Fruin's description and analysis of the transformation of the enterprise in the years after the Meiji Restoration. This metamorphosis of a traditional small family Japanese business into a modern corporation by way of a trade association or cartel involved the introduction of new mass-production technologies, new legal and financial forms, new management methods, and the recruitment of a much larger semi-skilled and unskilled labor force. I know of no other study in English that provides such detailed analysis of the beginnings of a modern large Japanese enterprise or one that throws more light on the beginnings of Japanese business and industrial practices that are under such scrutiny today. The final chapter tells of the continuing evolution of the enterprise after World War II into the giant managerial, diversified, multinational corporation that Kikkoman is today. Here, Professor Fruin provides new and detailed information on the ways in which the war, the American occupation, the rapid expansion of domestic and international markets, and the increasing urbanization and modernization of Japanese society altered the enterprise, its strategy and its structure, the make-up of its workers and managers, and even the motivations, values, and ideologies that held the enterprise together.

This study is business history as it should be written. It deals not only with all aspects of operating the enterprise, but also with the changing relationships between the managers and the owners (and in

Japan the separation of ownership and management came long before it did in the West); between owners and managers and workers, foremen, labor recruiters, and union officials; between managers and their suppliers and distributors; and finally the relationships between the enterprise and its competitors. Professor Fruin goes beyond business and economic developments into defining the context in which these changing relationships occurred. He sets them in the larger social and cultural milieu; in the local community in which the company operated so long and then in the broader Japanese society where an isolated and homogeneous past brought a strong commitment to shared attitudes and values.

Such a detailed story, carefully drawn from a variety of sources besides the archives of the enterprise, thus reveals much about the institutional, social, and ideological bonds that permitted the Japanese to create in a remarkably short period of time a modern technologically advanced industrial economy out of an agrarian, commercial, and relatively poor one based on traditional techniques of production and distribution. The story suggests how the Japanese industrialists used their past social and cultural homogeneity to hasten the process of modernization and to attempt to lighten its burden. In this way Mark Fruin's history of Kikkoman not only helps to explain the "miracle" of Japanese economic recovery after World War II, but also why this small underdeveloped nation became in less than a century such a dynamic industrial world power.

Alfred D. Chandler, Jr.

Acknowledgments

No one can write a book without acquiring numerous debts and obligations, but to acknowledge all of these would be tedious and monotonous, and so I will mention only the most obvious. First, I want to remember the aid of many friends at Kikkoman, in particular, Mogi Kenzaburō of the Kashiwa house and Nakano Takeo. The scholarship of Ichiyama Morio, long an employee of Kikkoman and editor of three large volumes on the company's history, has proven invaluable. I have been blessed with many fine research assistants along the way, including Hikino Takashi, Ishigami Fumimasa, and especially Inouye Mariko. I have benefited as well from institutional help: The Japan Foundation funded a trip to Japan in 1976 that proved to be the genesis of the study and the American Philosophical Society financed a follow-up visit in 1979.

California State University, Hayward, and the Harvard Graduate School of Business Administration contributed in major ways to the completion of the work. CSU Hayward allowed me to research and write the book while on leave at Harvard. The Harvard Graduate School of Business Administration supported this and other research for nearly two years, first by awarding me the Harvard/Newcomen Postdoctoral Fellowship for research in business and economic history and by supporting me for most of a year as a Senior Research Associate. The Word Processing Center and the Division of Research of the Harvard Graduate School of Business Administration were particularly instrumental in speeding along the preparation and completion of the manuscript. I would like to thank Patricia Murphy of the Business School, who typed most of the manuscript in one or another version and who assisted me part-time with various secretarial skills for most of a year. Cynthia Rose and Helen Frey Rochlin, both of Cambridge,

Massachusetts, through subsidies provided by the Division of Research, were immensely helpful in improving the style and organization of the original manuscript. William Shurtleff, Director of the Soyfoods Center in Lafayette, California, read the entire manuscript carefully and gave freely of his expert knowledge on the history of shōyu manufacture and on the biochemical aspects of shōyu fermentation. Akiko Aoyagi, co-author and collaborator with Bill on many soyfood writings, supported my work with enthusiasm and home-cooked vegetarian meals.

Parts of the book have appeared earlier in different journals, although all of these sections have been rewritten. A portion of the Introduction appeared in "The Family as a Firm and the Firm as a Family in Japan: The Case of Kikkoman Shōyu Co., Ltd.," *The Journal of Family History*, 5 (Winter 1980), 432–449; copyright 1980 by the National Council on Family Relations and reprinted with permission. Much of the rest of this article appears as Appendix A. The section in Chapter 2 that treats the charitable and philanthropic activities of the Noda shōyu cartel is a summary of a longer discussion of this matter which appeared as "From Philanthropy to Paternalism in the Noda Soy Sauce Industry: Pre-Corporate and Corporate Charity in Japan," *Business History Review*, 61 (Summer 1982), 168–191; reprinted with permission. In Chapter 7 some of the information on personnel policies and practices at Kikkoman first appeared in "The Japanese Company Controversy— Ideology and Organization in a Historical Perspective," *The Journal of Japanese Studies*, 4 (Summer 1978), 267–300; reprinted with permission.

Finally, I wish to thank the two historians who have done more than anyone else to shape my work and career. Thomas C. Smith taught me Japanese history among many other things, and Alfred D. Chandler, Jr., brought me to Harvard, tutored me in business history, and encouraged me in this project. Two finer scholars I have not met, nor do I expect to. I would also like to acknowledge a son's special indebtedness to his parents, Dr. Richard L. Fruin and Gertrude Winter Fruin, and to express my gratitude and love to Carolyn, Noah, and Nathan, who put up with a lot in order that this book might be completed.

Contents

ILLUSTRATIONS

FIGURES

TABLES

Kikkoman

Introduction

THE KIKKOMAN CORPORATION, including its antecedent undertakings, is the oldest continuous enterprise among the two hundred largest industrial firms in Japan. Takanashi Hyōzaemon XIX, whose descendants help manage Kikkoman today, began brewing *shōyu*, or natural soy sauce, in 1661 in the town of Noda, ninety minutes from Tokyo by modern train.[1] Since the seventeenth century one cannot say shōyu without thinking of Noda, and one cannot reflect on Noda without calling to mind the Takanashi and Mogi family members who have dominated the Japanese shōyu industry from Noda for at least two centuries.

More than simply old, Kikkoman shōyu is the only traditional Japanese manufacture to succeed internationally, a success achieved in spite of a formidable array of entrenched condiments, seasonings, and sauces. In fiscal 1980 Kikkoman's sales in Japan exceeded $600 million; in the United States alone sales reached $27 million. The story of the Kikkoman Corporation is a Japanese success story in which an old and rather traditional product has been transformed into an international best-seller through the efforts of a company, clan, and community. Through their common enterprise shōyu has become the best known and most widely used soyfood in the world.

This book is a history of three inseparable entities: the Kikkoman Corporation, the Mogi-Takanashi families, and the city of Noda. It shows how over several centuries a manufacturing enterprise came to dominate a town and a clan, and how in more recent times changes in the composition of the community and in the conception of the family have forced a far-reaching transformation of business practices. The history of Kikkoman and of the events, places, and persons surrounding the firm may be divided into four epochs or phases.

Phase I: Seventeenth Century to 1887

The first and longest phase, which lasted from the late seventeenth century through the nineteenth, was characterized by nearly complete separation of ownership and management in Noda shōyu breweries under the control of local entrepreneurial families. Such a separation, together with a high level of specialization in functions, is usually considered to be a unique feature of modern managerial capitalism. During much of this premodern era, overall management was divided among separate spheres of ownership: general management (sales, finance, and purchasing), operations management (the production process), and labor management (the hiring and contractual conditions of workers). In effect, four different kinds of authority existed—one financial (capital investment) and three managerial—each distinct and relatively independent of the others (see figure 1). This complex managerial system evolved in the eighteenth and nineteenth centuries when the sizes of various facilities producing shōyu were small, on the order of several hundred full- and part-time workers per factory, and when they were not very sophisticated in operation.[2] Yet they were large and sophisticated enough to be beyond the managerial capacities of a single, well-to-do householder and to require the specialized services of a variety of functional experts.

The separation and specialization of functions such as sales, personnel, and production had less to do with size of enterprise or even speed of production than with the failure of owners to manage. Owners did not operate or even oversee their production facilities. By custom, they entered their plants no more than twice a year, in full ceremonial dress, and ritually inspected the soy sauce brew in various stages of fermentation. Otherwise, they stayed out of the way.

Owners did little more than finance the operation and "supervise" the front office. They could, if they wished, inspect the books, but such records as there were constituted only listings of what goods were bought and sold by *bantō,* the office managers and personal retainers of the owning families. It was not possible to calculate costs of unit production, profit margins, or any other refined measure of efficiency or profitability from such records. To consolidate what information was available could prove difficult, for owners would have to petition their bantō, *tōji* (factory foremen), and *oyakata* (labor recruiters) to pull their lists, journals, and notebooks together. Such an effort on the part of owners would have been entirely out of character.

With so little direct involvement on the part of owners and so many separate yet equal spheres of management, workers suffered. Oyakata did not involve themselves with workers but benefited mainly by fees

FIGURE 1. THE KIKKOMAN CORPORATION: ORGANIZATIONAL CHANGE AND ENTERPRISE DEVELOPMENT

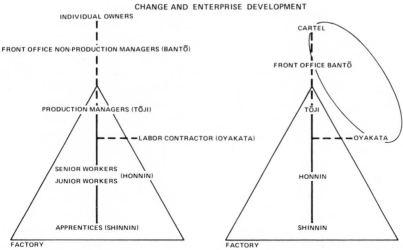

I. 17th CENTURY TO 1887

II. 1887 TO 1917

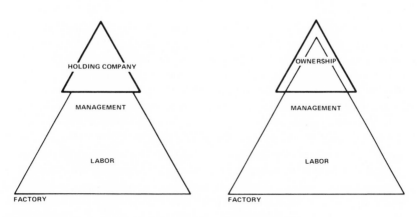

III. 1918 TO 1946

IV. 1947 TO PRESENT

paid for placing workers; tōji concerned themselves with technique, not industrial relations; and bantō were in the front office where they were not involved with workers' welfare. The only trace of worker identification with the brewery came through association with a production plant based on a particular patrilineal organization. Because no one assumed overall responsibility for enterprise management, the sense of association felt by workers rarely matured into an identification with family and enterprise. At this point of precorporate development the vaunted "family feeling" so often used to describe Japanese enterprise would not characterize an endeavor so fragmented and divided.

Phase II: 1887 to 1917

A second phase of Kikkoman's growth began with the banding together of a dozen or so owners in order to reduce risk and uncertainty. Diverse and separately owned enterprises, numbering as many as nineteen different production facilities, were joined together for the purchase of raw materials, standardization of wages, and distribution and shipping of finished goods. In 1887 the owners, in effect, formed a cartel, the Noda Shōyu Brewers' Association. During the next thirty years they met regularly twice a year—and irregularly more often—to buy raw materials and to fix price and shipping schedules.[3] The regularly scheduled meetings, on January 8 and June 20, roughly coincided with the traditional dates of ritualized inspection of factory facilities. Although the tour of the breweries was largely ceremonial, the cartel meetings were not. The January meeting was concerned with fixing wage rates and estimating production levels; the June assembly set the amount and cost of raw material purchases.

The Association carried out the classic functions of a cartel, and it made no attempt to combine and rationalize processes internal to the enterprise (see figure 1). The reasons for collaboration were almost all external to the actual manufacture of shōyu. The functions of the bantō, tōji, and oyakata did not change as a result of cartelization. The chasm between owners and workers remained vast, and it was not alleviated by paternal concern. Workers lacked job security, and their wages were arbitrarily set by cartel agreement. When prices fell, so did wages. Wage manipulation, in fact, was one of the most obvious means of controlling costs, and owners took full advantage of it. Owners did not yet enter their factories, except on the New Year's and All Souls' celebrations, and they continued to leave day-to-day management to others. Thus, even though enterprise-owning families were collaborating to a degree, family operations remained differentiated in what counted the most: internal costs of production.

The formation of a cartel represented, in an important sense, the institutionalization by communal regulation of an already existing competition over production costs and production levels between individual shōyu makers. Competition in these areas the cartel left alone. What it did was to combine the separate factories, family-owned breweries, into a collective network to fix some of their shared costs, thereby mitigating although not eliminating the competitive struggle. At long last, cartelization forced families of owners to begin to assume some managerial functions: purchasing raw materials, setting wages, sorting out distribution and shipping channels, and determining marketing territories in the countryside but not in the cities. (The last was left to the *tonya*, urban wholesaling specialists, for determination.) In short, in this phase, although families began to cooperate in certain important aspects, they remained somewhat competitive and were not yet completely involved in the internal operation of their own enterprises. As a consequence, the families of owners were still quite distinct in organization and operation from the shōyu plants and the men who labored in them.

Phase III: 1918 to 1946

In 1918 a third phase of enterprise development unfolded. That year a joint-stock company was formed through the merger of some of the cartel members and their assets. Eight, and then nine, families joined to form the Noda Shōyu Company, Limited, named for the town in Chiba Prefecture where most of the facilities were located. All nine families were related through descent or marriage, and previously all had been independent manufacturers of shōyu, *miso*, or *sake*, products made from fermented soybeans or rice. For the first time, owners became managers. They constituted the majority of senior company officers and members of the board of directors. Through the mechanism of a holding company, actual ownership of the firm remained somewhat distinct from the operation of the enterprise, yet ownership and management were merged as never before, and the disarray of managerial interests was finally put in order and entrenched in the firm's structure (see figure 1). Although it would be misleading to suggest that the new structure was joined easily, given the longstanding tradition of independent organization and operation on the part of the families concerned, within a decade consolidation and coordination characterized the management of the greatly enlarged enterprise.

At this point the association of family with firm, so often employed as an analogue in describing Japanese enterprise, begins to be noteworthy. Most top managers were "family"—members of the firm's founding families—and many middle-managers, who had been the bantō of individual entrepreneurs in prior phases, now came into the newly assembled corporation along with their family enterprise heads as "lifetime employees."[4] Accordingly, the appropriateness of the firm-family analogy at this point is mainly biological, or perhaps genealogical, in view of the importance of adoption among the shōyu-brewing families. Family members constituted 85 percent of the board of directors, and 63 percent of the first eighty managerial employees came to the company tied to individual family members on the board.

Of course it was possible for the firm-family analogy to be valid without Noda Shōyu's genealogical underpinning. Especially in joint-stock companies, which were independent of any zaibatsu association, it was rather common to have both dispersed ownership and paternalistic management. The lack of concentrated ownership in such cases probably inclined professional managers toward paternalistic management as a means of securing worker compliance. The best examples of this sort of firm-family analogy come from the textile industry, where firms like Kanebo and Toyobo Spinning were well known for paternalistic management (of a largely female work force) and widely dispersed stock ownership. In the early twentieth century it was possible to have a paternalistic firm with a "family style" but without family management or even closely held ownership. Such firms were more the exception than the rule, however, in view of the prevalence of family-owned and closely held enterprises in prewar Japan.

In the case of Noda Shōyu, the suitability of the analogy in the genealogical sense faded rapidly as the firm grew in size and nonkinsmen came to outnumber kinsmen in management. Within a decade of incorporation the number of employees had doubled from one to two thousand. Then an extraordinary event made the firm-family analogy even more appropriate than before. In 1927–28 a 218-day strike, the longest labor strike in prewar Japan, erupted at Noda Shōyu Company. The strike was not only long but also bitter and politically motivated, and it received national attention. An appeal to the emperor himself, among others, was required to bring it to settlement.[5] In the end, 1,100 employees were fired, although one-third of them eventually came back, and the company was faced with the need to rebuild its public image and its internal morale. The firm-family analogy was employed to these ends.

The first public announcement of the firm-family *ideology* by the company that I have been able to find occurred within weeks following the strike settlement. The company began a campaign of employee education that preached that all employees, from board members to shop sweepers, were members of one "family" (*ikka*), united in a spirit of industry and common purpose. For Kikkoman, spiritual kinship, as symbolized by the firm-family analogy, was the road to company rejuvenation following the Great Strike of 1927–28.

The transmutation of a biological or genealogical relationship into an ideological one at Kikkoman was not an isolated event. It happened commonly in other companies, as well as in the country in general. Kikkoman's transformation coincided with efforts of the Japanese government to instill in all citizens the belief that Japan was a patriarchal state, whose people were related to one another and to the emperor, the supreme father of the nation. The theory of the patriarchal state with the emperor as father is usually known as *kokutai*, and it became the central belief of modern Japanese ideology from the late 1880s until 1945. The philosophy of Hozumi Yatsuka (1860–1912), who is credited with being the chief architect of the state-as-household ideology, was simple and direct; the state is the household magnified; the household is the state in microcosm; they differ only in size, and they are made one through the medium of ancestor worship.[6]

That part of the kokutai theory concerned with the identity of state and household was known as *kokka*. This concept stressed the equivalence of state and household in a biological as well as an ideological sense. Officially the correspondence of state and household needed no intermediary institution; nevertheless, firms such as Kikkoman sought to juxtapose themselves between the state and household with the following construction: state = firm = household. In spite of the attempts of many enterprises to provide a bridge between state and household through programs of employee education and socialization, the state never sanctioned such efforts, and many right-wing groups were publicly critical of them. But the concepts of kokka and kokutai were extremely useful to enterprise owners and managers in their efforts to secure the loyalty of employees: the idea of a family firm allowed the company to make greater claims on the labor of its employees than would have been otherwise possible.

Insofar as businessmen were effective in their use of the firm-family analogy, it was largely because officials at all levels of society were employing the ideas of kokka and kokutai to counter the growing political and economic unrest that disturbed Japan in the first decades of the twentieth century. In 1906 the government began its "Every Village a Family" campaign to consolidate the deities worshiped on the local level into one shrine. About the same time slogans like *"kigyo-ikka"* (the enterprise as family) became widely current. Kikkoman's employee education program in the aftermath of the Great Noda Strike was representative of a national effort to enshrine the family ideologically.[7] But unlike biology or even genealogy, ideology is symbolic rather than substantive. This accounts in part for the enthusiasm with which Japanese leaders pressed such family-based analogies and policies on their own, as well as on colonial peoples, before and during the Pacific War period.

The flexibility of the firm-as-a-family ideology allowed the company to extend corporate membership to anyone with whom it had regular association. As a result, during the interwar period, when the work force doubled and new company buildings greatly altered the silhouette of the town, relations between the company and community of Noda were at their best. The material as well as the social fabric of corporate and communal relations allowed company and community to become like one family; the flexibility of the analogy fostered the development of a paternalistic spirit that was indeed familylike.

Phase IV: Postwar Democracy

Since World War II Kikkoman has entered a fourth phase in which the legal, ideological, and even genealogical foundations of the firm-family analogy have disappeared (see figure 1). Holding companies, which concentrated and protected family ownership in the firm, have been legally abolished. The emperor, who provided the essential element in the ideological analogy, has been demythologized. The household, the *ie*, is no longer a legal entity, and its head has been stripped of power and authority. A new egalitarian and democratic ethos underlies the traditional patriarchal policies. It coexists surprisingly well with the host of paternalistic benefits that Japanese firms provide for their regular employees. But such benefits as medical plans, housing subsidies, annual pay increases, and job security should not be misunderstood. They derive from postwar employee rights, not prewar patriarchal privilege or even paternalistic gratuity, and they are as much in evidence in large American and European companies as they are in Japanese firms.[8]

Though large companies may continue to espouse managerial ideologies that speak vaguely of "the firm as a family," the old legal, political, and biological-genealogical scaffolding is gone. Without formal underpinning, the firm-family analogy no longer demands respect or even lip service. Yet, as a cultural ideal and a characterization of the flexibility in ie or stem family structure and membership, the analogy remains viable. A genealogical basis for it is still found in the prevalence of family-based enterprises in Japan today. Ninety-eight percent of Japanese firms, by absolute number, are classified as small- and medium-sized enterprises. They continue the tradition of family identification with enterprise, since the core of self-employed and nonpaid family members in such operations amounts to 15 percent of all gainfully employed Japanese.[9] In these firms, size, control, and management make the firm-family analogy as appropriate as it was in the earliest days at Kikkoman following incorporation.

For Kikkoman today, however, its 4,000 employees, who perform mostly specialized and skilled jobs, make even an unofficial and informal use of the firm-family analogy inappropriate. Firms such as Kikkoman are too large and too specialized to be termed "family firms." Although family members may continue to play important ownership and management roles, they do so without the legal advantages granted ie and holding companies in the prewar era. As a result, it is increasingly unlikely that the finite resources of one or a number of families will be able to continue to supply the business talent needed to run a large modern corporation.

Yet, because of the size and business sophistication of large firms, problems of interpersonal relations and organizational behavior are more salient there. These firms must devote a far larger share of their earnings to employee socialization and corporate welfare programs than do small firms. They can of course more easily afford to do so, but size of enterprise rather than per-capita cost seems to determine the necessity of such efforts. Paradoxically, therefore, the firm-family analogy has the greatest urgency in large rather than small Japanese firms today. In practice, it is less an analogy than a simile: the prewar analogy of genealogical and ideological equivalence of firm and family has been transformed into a postwar simile of organizational culture. The firm resembles a family socially in that employees, with the encouragement of their employers, tend to identify themselves psychologically as well as intellectually with their firms or, even more, with their workmates. This is more evident in firms that provide more extensive in-company training and fringe benefits. To use the language of sociology, the Japanese display a cultural preference for affective as well as instrumental work commitment, an attitude that large firms can more easily take advantage of through emphasis on corporate welfare and paternalism. But when paternalism is institutionalized in large firms, as in Kikkoman, it is no longer "personal" and loses much of its affect. Large firms must strive even harder—and must add even more programs and activities— to maintain the motivation and camaraderie of their work forces. In this cultural sense, the firm *as* a family, when used to describe the spirit or feeling within a firm, has a certain validity in postwar Japan.[10]

The satisfaction of this preference for affective as well as instrumental commitment to work is of recent origin. The study of Kikkoman reveals, and studies of other large Japanese companies confirm, that before the 1920s and 1930s Japanese industrial workers were not especially loyal, hard-working, or dedicated. The creation of new material and psychological incentives for motivating workers—many under the guise of "family" commitment—since then has resulted in the gradual formation of a committed and productive labor force.

Family and Firm in Japanese Business and Economic History.

The close association of family and firm in Japan before World War II was quite understandable, if often misinterpreted. Industrialization there began later than in the West; as a result, the largest prewar Japanese firms tended to be smaller than their Western counterparts. Family firms predominate among smaller enterprises in all countries. Thus, because of the relatively late start of industrialization and the consequent smaller size of Japanese industrial enterprises, prewar Japanese companies were most often family-owned and frequently family-managed.

The flexibility of the Japanese stem family or ie helped guarantee continuity and ability in family-owned and managed firms. Because of the overriding importance of household preservation and success, the focus of family members in such enterprises was more institutional than personal. Institutional performance was far more important than individual power, privilege, and success; the cliché of riches-to-rags in three generations did not as frequently afflict family firms in Japan as in the West. Rather, individuals were taught to be restrained in their personal lives and to seek achievement and satisfaction within the context of the family enterprise.

The predominance of family firms and their successful maintenance over many generations were related as well to the Japanese preference for debt rather than equity financing of their industrial ventures. Unlike the United States, where Wall Street and other large and well-managed securities markets appeared by the late nineteenth century, Japan's financial markets have attained stability and major status only in the recent postwar years. When firms sought outside funds in Japan before the war they often were forced to turn to banks for loans rather than to equity markets, with the result that firms, especially family firms, came to prefer loans to lessening control by selling shares. Accordingly, family control has not been as diluted in Japan as it has been in the United States by a steady reduction in the proportion of company shares that are closely held. Shares have commonly remained closely held in Japan, even if one or several banks have become influential at the level of the board of directors in family firms.

Another reason for the prevalence and persistence of family firms in Japan has been the effectiveness of cartels. Since the character of cartelization is to promote compromise and cooperation among economic actors, individual companies were less compelled to devise independent managerial strategies and the corporate structures to implement them. The Noda shōyu cartel from 1887 to 1917 allowed at least a dozen families and family-run breweries with finite managerial and financial wherewithal to continue to manufacture, whereas in the United States, at almost the same time, comparable cartels could not be enforced in courts of law and in 1890 became illegal. Such loose federations of entrepreneurial firms often gave way to managerial firms with their large, multiunit, diversified, and integrated hierarchical organizations.

Cartels and the small family firms that composed them lasted much longer in Japan than in the United States for cultural reasons as well. Cultural or political bias against combinations, cartels, and other monopolistic forms of economic organization, evident in the United States since the Sherman Anti-Trust Laws of 1890, accelerated the movement away from family firms to managerial firms in the modern industrial enterprises. The absence of such laws in Japan, as well as the absence of other distinctive features of the American corporate environment—the size of the market and therefore the size of the firm to match those markets, the availability of equity as opposed to debt capital—when coupled with a later onset of industrialization and the flexibility of the ie form of economic organization, help account for the greater frequency of family firms in prewar Japan.

Since the end of World War II and the Allied Occupation of Japan, however, most of the ideological and institutional features that distinguished prewar Japanese family firms from their Western counterparts have disappeared. Although some legacy may linger, they are no longer buttressed by legal, political, economic, and social approbation. Family and firm are not as closely associated as before, and the analogy is no longer appropriate in most cases. When family and firm do overlap, it is under certain circumstances and for certain periods of time; family-firm analogies that ignore those conditions remain unconvincing. Such analogies have often been historically inaccurate when applied to Kikkoman, and they are equally misleading and misinformed when aimed at other large, mature, diversified, and internationally minded firms that characterize Japanese enterprise today.

1.

Factories in the Fields

JAPAN'S NINETEENTH-CENTURY INDUSTRIALIZATION occurred in the countryside; its character and composition differed noticeably from the more urban-centered industrialization of Western Europe and North America. These differences were apparent in the nature of industrial organization and behavior, the structure of work and the workplace, the method of labor recruitment and compensation, the approach to product sales and distribution, and the style of industrial supervision and managerial philosophy.

Rural-Centered Industrialization

More than two-thirds of Japan's population lived in rural areas until World War I, which allowed the majority of working and investment capital and of production capacity and know-how to be concentrated in the countryside. In the United States, by contrast, half of the population resided in cities by 1900, less than a century after Lewis and Clark blazed the Western wilderness. The concentration of people in the countryside was not the sole reason for Japan's rural-centered industrialization. Throughout the eighteenth and nineteenth centuries the countryside had grown rich at the expense of the cities. Not only did the rural population increase more than the urban-based population, it also developed and retained new sources of agricultural and nonagricultural income that urban lords and institutions were not able to interfere with. Aggregate and per capita income increased more rapidly in the countryside as a result, and rural standards of living improved proportionately. Japan's advantages—a highly monetized, commercialized, and diversified rural economy and a work-disciplined rural population—were fully exploited in the course of its nineteenth-century industrialization, producing a preponderance of rural capital, production, and entrepreneurship that contrasted strongly with the Western industrial model.[1]

Japan's rural-centered industrialization encompassed not only the expansion of traditional, long-established manufactures such as shōyu, miso (fermented bean paste), sake (traditional spirits distilled from rice), *igusa* (reed for matting), and pottery, but also the development of new manufactures such as cotton spinning, hosiery, and brush and wire implements. Its early economic success had been based on products like tea and silk, which were closely tied to the agricultural cycle, and later on textiles and sugar refining. This linkage allowed precious time for later-developing urban industries such as shipbuilding, chemicals, and metal fabrication to borrow foreign technology, train workers in new production methods and routines, and work out the problems and inefficiencies that plague nascent industries.

Rural-centered enterprises allowed economic development to occur with a minimum of disruption. Enlarging plant capacity and increasing plant utilization in the countryside did not require that traditional values and ways of doing things be discarded. Step-by-step changes in product and process in the course of rural industrialization added up to considerable improvements in productivity and performance without serious social dislocation. Rural industries well illustrate what Professor Akira Hayami of Keio University has called Japan's industrious rather than industrial revolution. People worked harder, better, and more effectively, without radical change in their livelihood or lifestyle. Where industrialization resulted in radical shifts in production technique as well as lifestyle, Japanese workers, like their counterparts worldwide, were not especially responsive or productive.

But change, however gradual, comes at a cost, and the cost of Japan's rural-centered industrialization has been twofold: not only did the countryside carry a much heavier per capita burden of the expenses of modernizing the country in the nineteenth century, but, since then, the countryside has benefited far less than urban areas from Japan's institutional progress and economic development. The land tax on agricultural holdings reputedly paid for 80 percent of the country's nation-building programs to create a "rich country and strong army" before the turn of the century. This burden fell most heavily, almost exclusively, on rural residents. Furthermore, the export industries—the capital-earning industries—in the nineteenth century were located in the countryside. Thus, the capital raised through taxation and export earnings there provided benefits mainly in the cities, in the form of roads, schools, navies, jobs, and better living conditions.

The gradual transfer of rural wealth to cities in the form of taxes and export products as well as immigrants resulted not only in higher wages and higher standards of living there but in the intensification of investment as well. This allowed an upgrading of production methods and organization which resulted in a cycle of greater earnings on investment, more product innovation, and more economic opportunity. Before long the countryside that had provided the capital for modernization fell behind the cities in investment, output, and development. This produced social strains, economic disincentives, and political problems which became only too apparent after World War I.

Japan's rural-centered industrialization constituted a crucial yet largely unsung aspect of the country's economic growth and performance in the nineteenth century. Without an understanding of this, the subsequent course and success of Japan's development in the twentieth century is difficult to understand and appreciate. Rural-centered enterprises laid the cornerstone on which modern industrial enterprises and a modern economy were erected.

The Origins of Shōyu

The production of shōyu, one of the traditional products manufactured in the countryside, grew enormously during the Tokugawa Period (1603–1867) because of a dramatic increase in its market, primarily urban residents. Whereas before the seventeenth century only 1 or 2 percent of the Japanese population lived in cities, by 1725 roughly 20 percent did so. The increased demand for shōyu was met primarily through an increase in capacity based on the entrance of new producers and the expansion of established brewers. In the latter case, rather than expand the size of a shōyu factory beyond what were considered the managerial and physical limits of the day, branch households, established by sons, adopted sons, or sons-in-law, were formed for the purpose of increasing shōyu production in associated yet autonomous operations. The increase in production during this period was also related to the rapid diffusion of soy fermentation technology during the fourteenth to seventeenth centuries.

The forerunner of modern shōyu appears to have been *miso tamari*, the liquid that forms during the process of fermenting rice or soybeans to make a soft, cheeselike product. The most popular and likely story of shōyu's origins relates how Kakushin, a Japanese Zen priest who had studied at the Kinzanji Temple in China, returned to Japan in the middle of the thirteenth century and began preparing a type of miso that became a well-known local specialty of Yuasa, the town near Kakushin's temple in the province of Kii (today's Wakayama prefecture).[2] By the end of the thirteenth century the liquid had come to be called

tamari and was sold commercially along with the miso. From such beginnings, a great variety of experimentation with the ingredients and
methods of tamari fermentation was launched. Although tamari probably found favor initially in Buddhist monasteries as a condiment for a
vegetarian diet, the popularity of tamari-type seasonings was related
more to the prevalence of battlefields than of meditation halls during
the period of civil wars that raged across Japan from the thirteenth to
sixteenth centuries. Soldiers apparently found the versatility and trans-
portability of the seasonings to their liking. Shōyu, which evolved from
these tamari seasonings by adding wheat to the fermentation mash, appeared during the sixteenth century.

The first soy sauce made in the area of modern Noda was brewed in
about 1560 by Iida Ichirōbei and respectfully presented as tribute taxes
to the local warrior family in the following year.[3] The Iida family,
ostensibly fleeing the carnage and confusion of the Ōnin Wars
(1467-1477) in the Home Provinces around Kyoto, arrived in the area
of Noda early in the sixteenth century and by mid-century were engaged, among other pursuits, in the manufacture of tamari, a type of
soy sauce that by now was made entirely from soy beans. The Iidas are
thought to have come originally from an aristocratic background, as
evidenced by a description written in the late sixteenth century of their
play of kemari, a kind of soccer popular among courtier families in the
capital of Kyoto.

Iida's first brew was closer to tamari than shōyu in consistency, taste,
and aroma. Whereas tamari is a flavoring made entirely of soy beans,
salt, and water, shōyu uses wheat to enrich the aroma and lighten the
color and taste of tamari. The fermentation period of shōyu manufacture is generally longer as well, so that the addition of wheat and longer
fermentation produce a considerably milder and more alcoholic seasoning. The widespread use of either tamari or shōyu since the Muro-
machi Period (1338-1573) indicates that the Japanese acquired about
half of their daily intake requirement of 15 to 20 grams of salt in liquid
rather than solid form.

In Eastern Japan the manufacture of a shōyu rather than tamari soy
sauce like Iida's seems to have originated in or near the town of Chōshi
at the mouth of the Tone River on the northeastern tip of the Bōsō
Peninsula, which guards the entrance to Tokyo Bay like an extended
crab's claw. The Hamaguchi families of Chōshi originated as branch
households of the main Hamaguchi house of Hiromura village in Kii,
not surprisingly the same province where Kinzanji miso and miso-ta-
mari appeared and where the Hamaguchi of Hiromura were among the
earliest commercial brewers of shōyu in Japan.

The Hamaguchi transplants in Chōshi, along with Tanaka Genba and his descendants, began the manufacture of shōyu early in the seventeenth century. Higeta shōyu was first produced here in 1616, Yamajō in 1630, and Yamasa in 1645. In addition, the Eastern branch of the Hamaguchi family in Chōshi, headed by Hamaguchi Kichiemon, opened a store in Edo for the sale and distribution of shōyu and marine food products from Chōshi in the same year (1645) that Yamasa began production.[4]

Noda Soy Sauce

It was not until the latter half of the seventeenth century, however, that Noda followed Chōshi in the manufacture of a soy sauce that was closer to shōyu than the thick, dark tamari was. In 1661 Takanashi Hyōzaemon XIX began brewing shōyu in Noda; using a work force of twenty that included fifteen contract laborers, he produced 3,000 gallons his first year.[5] The next year Mogi Shichizaemon I started with the manufacture of miso, the rice or soybean paste product similar to shōyu in fermentation technology. Miso was used as a soup base, a pickling base for vegetables, and an all-purpose seasoning in many recipes. At first, both shōyu and miso production probably were agricultural by-employments for Takanashi Hyōzaemon and Mogi Shichizaemon; they used the slack labor and excess production of the agricultural cycle to their advantage. In the case of shōyu manufacture, the mash made with grains harvested in the fall was brewed and stored between October and December, while the fermented mash of the previous year was processed and pressed from January to March. The entire cycle of production was confined to the nonagricultural months between October and March.

Those with a little wealth and land could begin to make soy sauce or engage in some other handicraft industry as a means of diversifying their risk and of fully employing their capital—human as well as material. Rural entrepreneurs like the Takanashi and Mogi families undoubtedly engaged in a variety of pursuits, including agriculture, money-lending, land speculation, and handicraft industries such as the manufacture of shōyu, miso, and sake, or the operation of lumber yards and fishing boats.

But as Edo (modern Tokyo), the military and political capital during the Tokugawa Period, grew and access to its market improved, by-employments became full-employments, although it required several centuries for this process to be completed. The government in Edo must be credited with providing an early if indirect incentive for the manufacture of shōyu as well as other commercial goods in Noda. In 1640 the Tone River, which flows on the east side of Noda, was partially diverted into a rechanneled Edo River on Noda's west side, thereby scissoring Noda between two good navigable waterways and making it a major entrepôt where Chiba, Saitama, and Ibaragi prefectures join on the northeastern Tokyo Plain. Subsequent projects, funded by the central government, improved river access to Edo; as a consequence, not only could Noda shōyu reach Edo in just one day by the late seventeenth century but also many of the agricultural and nonagricultural products of the land now passed Noda on the way to and from market. Specialized products of other areas used in shōyu manufacture, such as Aizu wheat and Kansai salt, could be easily purchased in Edo and loaded on Noda-bound boats for the return trip home after they had carried their shōyu, miso, and other goods to market. Noda's central location and superb inland water transportation practically assured its growth along with the development of Edo, which was perhaps the world's largest city in the eighteenth century, and of the Kantō or Tokyo area, the largest rice-growing plain in Japan.[6]

In addition to a growing market, differentiation in taste, between the *usu-kuchi* or light-colored shōyu of the Kansai or Kyoto-Osaka region of Japan and the *koi-kuchi* or dark shōyu of the Tokyo area, from the late seventeenth and early eighteenth centuries meant that shōyu brewers in Eastern Japan had a chance to displace the traditional product of the Western region with their own merchandise. In fact, Tokyo shōyu was the only manufactured good used widely in Japan during the Tokugawa or Edo period that overtook in value and amount of sales the already established product of Western Japan. (Actually, the nomenclature of light and dark is somewhat misleading as it refers not only to the color of the soy sauce but also to its salt content. Usu-kuchi shōyu is clearer in color and thinner in consistency but slightly saltier; koi-kuchi is darker and with more body but less salt.) By the mid-eighteenth century the population of Tokyo had burgeoned to more than a million, and Tokyo-style dark shōyu had captured the major share of the Edo and Eastern markets. By 1821, according to an Edo wholesaler's notes, all but 20,000 of the 1,250,000 barrels of shōyu shipped into the city were koi-kuchi shōyu of Eastern manufacture.[7]

The supremacy of Eastern shōyu was recognized officially by the Tokugawa shogunate itself when seven Eastern brands, but no others, were exempted from government price controls during the tempestuous Tempō Period (1830–1843). Then, in order to lessen popular unrest over increases in the cost-of-living and inflation, the government proposed a 40-percent price reduction in food and food-related products, including shōyu. Shōyu brewers countered by petitioning the government with claims that they could not maintain quality of product in the face of such a drastic reduction in price. They backed their petition with production cost figures as well as with samples of their product. The government finally exempted these seven Eastern brands from price controls, and, once singled out, they became the acknowledged leaders in a market that was characterized by oversupply and limited brand identification. The government's exemption became a sort of unofficial seal of approval, much to the benefit of the four Chōshi (Higeta, Yamasa, Yamajō, and Jigamisa) and three Noda (Kihaku, Jōjū, Kikkoman) brands.

Mogi Domination of the Market

The growing market and changing demand for Eastern shōyu account for the increasing involvement of the Mogi family in Noda in the manufacture of shōyu from the middle to late eighteenth century. Although the Takanashi family and several others—notably, the Otsukas, Kawanos, and Kodas—moved into shōyu manufacture about the same time, they did not persist in the business as the Mogis did. In 1764 the eldest son of Takanashi Hyōzaemon, now the XXII, married the daughter of Mogi Shichizaemon V. As was often the case when marriage was tied to business, he married into her family, assuming her family's name and occupation. In the year of their marriage, 1764, the adopted son-in-law (*muko-yōshi*) and his bride established a shōyu factory on the advice and with the financial support of the bridegroom's natural family, the Takanashis, who had been making shōyu in Noda since 1661. This was the first Mogi family to venture into shōyu manufacture, but two years later, in 1766, the bride's father, Mogi Shichizaemon, whose ancestors had established the first Mogi household in Noda in 1630, added the manufacture of shōyu to the manufacture of miso, which his family had begun in 1662. Horikiri Monjirō, from nearby Nagareyama, began making shōyu the same year. His wife was the second daughter of Mogi Saheiji III, who would himself begin soy sauce brewing in a few more years.

By 1768 the first in this series of marriage-business alliances, that of Takanashi Hyōzaemon's son to Mogi Shichizaemon's daughter, was recognized as a separate branch household in the Mogi line. By 1772 Mogi Shichirōuemon, head of the newly formed Kashiwa household, had accumulated enough know-how, experience, and capital to disassociate himself formally from his paternal household and establish himself as an independent householder and shōyu brewer. By 1781, therefore, when a shōyu manufacturing guild was established in Noda, two of the original seven members were Mogis (Shichizaemon and Shichirōuemon); by 1782, one year later, Mogi Saheiji, head of the oldest branch household in the Mogi line, had added shōyu fermentation to his already established ventures in grain sales and miso manufacture, making the Mogi's proportion of representation in the guild three out of seven. By 1822 two more Mogi families had been added, and a Mogi majority within the guild was secured. Japanese guilds, such as this one and those in Europe at the same time, were associations of persons with the same trade or interests who worked together to protect property and privilege for their common benefit. The shōyu guild in Noda was founded about the same time that tonya or wholesaler territories were determined in Tokyo, or about the middle of the eighteenth century. (The tonya system is discussed in the next chapter.)

The entrance of five Mogi households into shōyu production between 1764 and 1822, a sixth in 1855, a seventh in 1872, and an eighth in 1877 fundamentally reformed the nature of shōyu manufacture in Noda. For although ten non-Mogi families had opened shōyu breweries in Noda during the same period, few stayed in the business more than a generation; as a consequence, they failed to link kinship to shōyu manufacture as the Mogis did. Even the Takanashi lineage, which managed to have three households in the business in the late nineteenth century, failed to pass the breweries from father to son successfully, except in the main household of Takanashi Hyōzaemon. The Otsuka and Koda families had two households each in shōyu manufacture in the mid-eighteenth century, but they too failed to transfer the properties between generations. By the end of the eighteenth century even the main Otsuka and Koda households had abandoned shōyu production. Only the Mogi clan, represented by a main household and eventually seven branch households, succeeded in establishing and fostering a manufacturing base in shōyu, backed by a growing and diversified network of family businesses related to shōyu production. This process of family division and enterprise initiation within the Mogi lineage took place over more than a century, beginning in the Temmei Period (1781–1788) and ending by 1900.

The ability to wed kinship to entrepreneurship rested on a social innovation of considerable daring and accounts for the success of the Mogi lineage where others had failed. The Mogis chose to use household branching as a device to expand capacity in the same industry within the same town. It had been common practice either to diversify into other lines of work if a branch household remained local or to carry on the same trade in another town, thereby minimizing competition between head and branch families. In Noda, however, the Mogis chose to concentrate talent, production, knowledge, and experience in one industry, one town, and one kinship group. This became the basis for their entrepreneurial success in the nineteenth and twentieth centuries.

Such institutionalized cooperation was buttressed by a code—in this case a written family constitution. Its age is uncertain, but it probably dates from the late eighteenth and early nineteenth centuries or from the time when the move of the Mogi family into shōyu manufacture had become conspicuous. The constitution reads:

Sincerity first and profits will follow. Neglect neither.

Take care to preserve the harmony and unity of the household.

Avoid luxury and cultivate simplicity and earnestness.

Avoid matters not connected with family business.

Learn to make money and not to lose it.

Competition makes for progress, but avoid reckless competition.

Attend to your health. Eat simple foods no different from that taken by your employees.

Economize on personal expenses and give what remains to charity, taking care to preserve a sufficient estate for your successors.

Cultivate a positive attitude toward making money and be cautious in times of uncertainty.

Twice a year call a family assembly; praise family members according to their character, not according to their profits.[8]

Not every Mogi household, by any means, went into shōyu manufacture; of those that did, certain households concentrated more resources and directed more offspring into shōyu brewing than others did. The Kashiwa branch household, for example, invested far more in shōyu manufacture than did the Mogi-sa branch family (descendants of Mogi Saheiji), although both cleaved from the main household of Mogi Shichizaemon. The timing of their branchings certainly shaped the degree of involvement in shōyu manufacture. The Mogi-sa branch was established first, in 1688, at a time when shōyu manufacture was just beginning in Noda. Takanashi Hyōzaemon had not begun to make shōyu until 1661, barely a generation earlier, and its manufacture was only one of a number of family ventures. The Kashiwa branch, however, was founded in 1768, and its greater involvement in shōyu manufacture was understandable: it was founded by the adopted son-in-law of the oldest shōyu maker in Noda, and his natural family backed the marriage and business venture with capital, experience, and connections. Most important, by the late eighteenth century the shōyu market, particularly for Eastern-style shōyu, was already well developed and growing, and the timing of the Kashiwa branch's entry into the industry enabled the branch to capitalize on the market.

Other Mogis and Takanashis stayed entirely out of shōyu production. Some of them specialized in ancillary food fermentation industries, like miso, vinegar, and sake manufacture, or in the procurement of the raw materials for and in the marketing of the finished products of these businesses. Still others went into entirely different endeavors. Mogi Sōemon, for example, in 1743 started to make sliding partitions constructed from light wood and paper. His descendants carry on the work today.

Mogi Kishichi and his offspring illustrate another side of the connection between kinship and enterprise. This household, along with Mogi Saheiji's, constituted the first two branch households (bunke) of the head Mogi household of Mogi Shichizaemon, the II, in the eighteenth century. Both Kishichi and Saheiji started off in cereal wholesaling, but Saheiji switched to miso manufacture in 1756 and to shōyu manufacture in 1782, while Kishichi remained a komeya, or grain merchant, for many of the Noda miso and shōyu brewers during most of the Tokugawa Period.

In about 1840 or 1850 (the date is not exactly clear) Mogi Kishichi's family business passed to the Shoda family in Tatebayashi, Gumma Prefecture, who were long experienced in the trade. Once the connection to the Mogi and Takanashi families in Noda had been made, the Shoda family was not content simply to supply grains and soon diversified its efforts into shōyu manufacture as well. With a detailed plan provided by Mogi Fusagorō in 1873, shortly after the Meiji Restoration of 1868, the Tatebayashi Shodas produced an insignificant 700 koku (33,320 gallons) of shōyu in 1874. (See Appendix B for Mogi Fusagorō's instructions and cost calculations for making shōyu.) In 1887 the Noda shōyu cartel was established, and after this Shoda Bunuemon, the Shoda family patriarch, joined the Noda Shōyu Manufacturing Cartel for a brief period. By 1917 Shoda shōyu production had grown twentyfold to 14,000 koku (666,400 gallons). More important, the Shodas had realized other uses for the grains they brokered. The main Shoda family, now specialists in grain sales and shōyu fermentation, had established a branch household to concentrate on grain and cereal milling. Wheat, not surprisingly, was a basic ingredient of shōyu. This branch, headed by Shoda Teiichirō, an adopted son, founded the Nisshin Flour Milling Company, one of the two largest flour milling companies in Japan. Shoda Teiichirō sat for several years in the 1920s on the board of directors of the Noda Shōyu Company, the successor to the Noda Shōyu Manufacturing Cartel of which Shoda Bunuemon had been a member.

The Shodas in Tatebayashi were able to do what the Mogi Kishichis in Noda had not: move a family enterprise backward into manufacturing from grain sales and brokering. This was because avenues for family diversification into shōyu manufacture in Noda closed down after a certain point, while this was not the case in Tatebayashi. Admittedly, the Shodas could not have accomplished their diversification without the help of the Mogis, particularly Mogi Fusagorō, but their efforts in Tatebayashi were not a direct threat to anyone in Noda, and this freedom of action allowed them the opportunity to diversify from grain sales into grain milling and shōyu brewing.

In Noda, however, the density of Mogi kinsmen and their specialization over time in certain fields tended to restrict the possibilities of further diversification into fields that might prove potentially threatening to already established kinsmen. Once Mogi Kishichi restricted his family's role to that of komeya, cereals broker, for his relatives, it became difficult thereafter to make what might be perceived as a natural move into shōyu manufacture since, in the meantime, both Mogi Saheiji and Shichirōuemon and their families, descendants, and branch households had established claims in that business.

From the late eighteenth to early twentieth centuries all Mogi entrants into soy sauce brewing were branch households of families already entrenched in this business; they did not move from ancillary businesses, like cereal merchandising. As numerous families established themselves in certain lines of work, and as these patterns of family enterprise became fixed, it became difficult to switch fields of business activity. Family entrepreneurship was influenced by the boundaries of family descent and family business tradition. In this way, the emerging Mogi family network, a stimulus to diversification in the seventeenth and eighteenth centuries, by the nineteenth century had become a barrier to new families entering soy sauce manufacture. The only exceptions occurred when new enterprises did not conflict with established fields of family specialization: for example, in 1864 Takanashi Kōuemon founded a facility largely for the purpose of recovering and processing shōyu oil. Diversification into related but not competitive ventures within the already established network of shōyu breweries was possible, but new shōyu manufacturing efforts were not likely to succeed.

As opportunities for work in shōyu manufacture and even in related businesses decreased by the late nineteenth century, members of the Mogi family not yet involved in such endeavors turned toward education as an important avenue of local advancement for themselves and their families. By the late nineteenth and early twentieth century many positions in the fields of teaching, medicine, dentistry, and optometry were monopolized by its members. These new professionals joined established Mogis whose families had branched off from the main households earlier and gone into various commercial rather than manufacturing ventures. The only profession that the Mogis seem to have consciously eschewed was politics. Although an occasional Mogi held a political post, the position was often ceremonial in character and not commonly held for long. As a result of these combined efforts in industry, commerce, and higher education, many positions of wealth and influence in the community came to be dominated by members of the family in the early twentieth century, and they continued their hegemony until perhaps two decades after World War II.

Their degree of dominance and the timing of its expression, however, were related perhaps more to technology than to any other element. Technology not only regulated ease of communication and speed of information flow, it also decided in large measure the nature of work and, as a result, the pace and meaning of life for most residents of the town. Noda remained an agricultural community, overwhelmingly so, until sometime between the Russo-Japanese War of 1904–05 and World War I. After that, the technology of shōyu manufacture became modern in the sense that its processes were based on new scientific knowledge of fermentation and on new sources of energy, the introduction of steam boilers, electrical elevators and conveyors, and hydraulic presses, and the linking of products by a national railway network.

All of this resulted in greatly expanded industrial production and employment in Noda. Thus, in the early twentieth century Noda and Japan experienced the beginnings of modern industrialization—a process begun in the United States, Germany, and France in the 1850s and even earlier in Great Britain. Accordingly, the principal occupation in Noda shifted from farming to factory work. Until these developments, however, the limitations of the traditional technology had kept manufacturing from outranking farming as a source of employment and at the same time also prevented the owners of the shōyu plants and their relatives from dominating the town. Technology, rather than dynastic ambitions, proved more powerful in separating town and industry—until the recent past.

Fermentation Technology

Although the steps in shōyu manufacture are few and simple enough, the fermentation process itself is a wonder of complicated mycological and biochemical transformations. The stages of production involve the mixing of roasted wheat and steamed soybeans; setting of this mixture aside for molding; the addition of salt water to the mixture; and allowing it twelve to twenty-four months for fermentation; and, finally, the extraction of the liquid (shōyu) from the lees. This production se-

Preparing soybeans for culturing: unwrapping, sorting, weighing, soaking, mixing

Culturing: setting out of mixed soy beans and wheat (kōji)

FIGURE 2. SHŌYU MANUFACTURE
OLD METHOD

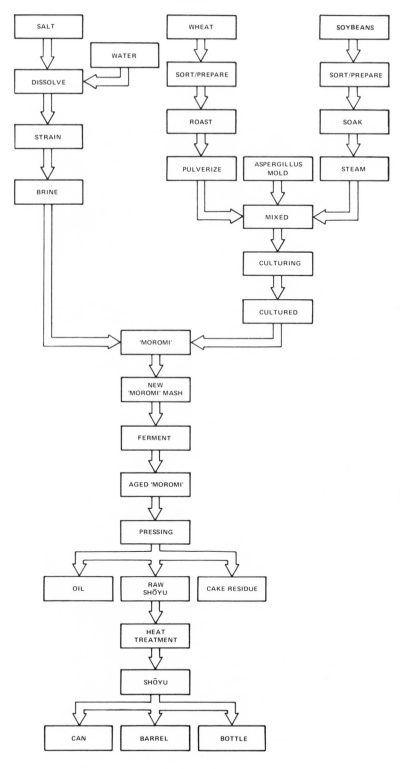

quence, only five steps when described in this way, contains three essential biochemical steps: grain starches are broken down into sugars by the action of enzymes when the mixture of roasted wheat and steamed soybeans are set aside for molding by the action of *aspergillus oryzae* molds; this molded mixture, known as the *kōji*, when mixed with brine (now known as the *moromi*) and allowed to ferment continues to be worked on by these molds and various bacteria resulting in the buildup of lactic acids and other compounds; these, in turn, are acted upon by yeasts to develop alcoholic and other aromatic compounds that give shōyu its characteristic aroma and flavor (see figure 2).[9]

Although the steps in the production process are simple, the variations on the theme are not. Literally hundreds of recipes existed in the Edo Period that specified not only what kind of soybeans, wheat, and salt to use but also what the exact proportions among them should be. Moreover, before the twentieth century many farm households substituted barley for wheat; even more often, the two were used together in the same recipe. There were variations as to the degree and length of heat treatment of the grains, the amount and salinity of the brine, the kind and amount of mold culture, the length of fermentation, and the methods of extraction, quality control, and storage. In short, production was not standardized, and wide variation in product was tolerated, even prized. All of these variations made for brand differentiation, but since consistency of product was not guaranteed, the highly variable product differences made it difficult to develop a wider market.

The degree of local variation is shown in the following three recipes taken from the *Shōyu Shusetsu*, published in 1877.[10]

Ingredients:

(1)	barley	18.0 liters
	wheat	5.4 liters
	soybeans	18.0 liters
or, (2)	soybeans	18.0 liters
	barley	5.4 liters
	wheat	12.6 liters
or, (3)	soybeans	18.0 liters

Grind & roast until brown.

Combine:

salt	16.2 liters
molded rice	36.0 liters
water	36.0 liters

Steam, allow to cool, and then add the soybean mixture.

The manual continued with the following instructions concerning the brewing and sauce extraction process:

Fermentation: Use good quality salt, like Akō salt. Untie the straw wrapping, and soak the salt in a tub for five to seven months. Remove the salt scum, place the liquid in a kettle and fill to the brim with water. Bring to a boil and then allow to cool in a separate container. Remove the scum once again and infuse the remainder into the soybean and grain kōji. Take care to disturb the kōji as little as possible. Thereafter, stir the mixture daily with a wooden paddle during the winter, and two or three times daily during the summer to fall months.

Allow the shōyu to ferment from fifteen to twenty months, or even twenty to thirty months, in small vats and during this period, stir the mixture two to four times a month.

Extraction: Put the fermented mash into cotton sacks and apply pressure to a number of these stacked on top of the other. Remove any scum or sediment from the extracted sauce and boil what is left in a kettle. Take this and put it in oak vats to cool for four or five days. Drain it by means of a small pipe stem, once again removing sediment, and place the remainder in small barrels for shipping.

The variations in fermentation technology and product were reflected in numerous shōyu recipe books from the Tokugawa Period. Figures 2 and 3 capture the principal stages in the preparation of materials, their fermentation, eventual processing, and main by-products. An early example of this technology, the *Shōyu Denjuki*, written the fifth year of Temmei (1785), gives detailed directions as to the preparation of kōji and moromi. Such manuals of technique and theory, widely read and applied in the countryside by the second half of the Edo Period, not only covered subjects directly and indirectly related to agriculture but dealt with matters that were more philosophically didactic as well.[11]

The widespread knowledge of shōyu fermentation technology that such books provided, the ready availability of the raw materials for brewing, and the daily need for the product indicate that shōyu manufacture flourished throughout rural Japan by the end of the eighteenth century. Fourteen thousand makers of shōyu, large and small, paid taxes on their production in 1910.[12] Perhaps three-fourths of these were essentially household producers with marginal effect on the commercial market. Volume production was for the cities that grew rapidly before and after the Meiji Restoration. The countryside, where local handicrafts and by-employment industries were so developed as to dissuade locals from investing time and energy in fermenting a homemade soy sauce, provided an additional if scattered market.

FIGURE 3. SHŌYU MANUFACTURE
NEW METHOD (ABBREVIATED)

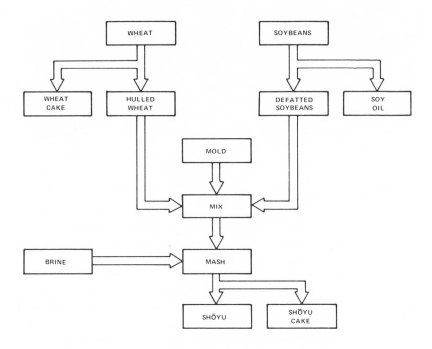

These recipes exemplified the traditional process for shōyu manufacture, which continued until the last half of the nineteenth century. Of course individual brewmasters varied the steps and added special touches of their own, but production techniques were more or less the same everywhere—whether in a factory or at home. Where the process differed between factory and home, it was likely to do so in details and for obvious reasons evident in the specialized tools or more formalized production routines of the factory.

A brewery probably had a separate room for storing and sorting wheat, soybeans, and other grains. Breweries were likely to have specialized equipment for grading and sorting grains before moving them on for processing. The wheat, for example, was hulled by a piece of foot-powered equipment, called a *jigara*, after which it was cracked by a hand- or foot-powered millstone. Grading, sorting, and grinding became more mechanized as well as standardized with the introduction of internal combustion and electric motors after 1910.

Traditionally soybeans were sorted by a bamboo-mesh screen and washed by hand in tubs, in amounts of about 360 liters; pebbles, dirt, and scum were removed. The soybeans were then vigorously agitated in water and suspended in bamboo baskets, used like wire cages, for a final cleansing before being steamed in large kettles. After about 1911 the final scrubbing was combined with the boiling via steam-pressure cooking in large earthenware or cast-iron cisterns.

After the soybeans were washed, they were either allowed to stand in water for four to five hours or steamed in a large kettle for a shorter period of time. Some plants let the beans soak in cool water in the summer and warm water in the winter, but whether this was for the benefit of the beans or the handlers is unclear. The traditional steps of washing and steaming soybeans were greatly simplified once various mechanical devices were introduced in the late nineteenth century. Steam boiling, for example, was a necessary but highly inefficient step in the premechanical period. Steaming was needed both to soften the beans and to impregnate them with water before they were coated with wheat flakes and made into kōji. Without steaming, soybeans remained hard and brittle, which considerably retarded the rate of molding and eventual fermentation.

Before the twentieth century, steaming soybeans under pressure was accomplished by use of large metal kettles sheathed in wood, called *shikakegama*. These were about four feet high with a 360-gallon capacity. A raised platform supported the shikakegama, the bottom half of which was directly exposed to a fire chamber below. The top half could be closed by a lid that was bolted down to the platform. In this way, heat could be relatively effectively applied, and with the lid bolted down considerable steam pressure could build up within the kettle. Still, the use of shikakegama left a lot to be desired. The firing process, utilizing wood and later charcoal to heat the kettle, was slow. It was cumbersome and time-consuming to bolt down and then release the kettle lid by hand. By the early twentieth century, ceramic and all-metal boilers of great capacity with more efficient heating and steaming characteristics were gradually introduced, and thereafter the critical step of steaming soybeans was much more efficiently handled.

Preparation of Wheat for Kōji

The preparation of wheat for kōji has always been a more complicated process than that required for soybeans, because wheat is cut, shredded, or otherwise cracked into small particles before and during roasting, thereby increasing the risk of overcooking or undercooking. Until the end of the nineteenth century, the normal method of roasting wheat employed an open cast-iron kettle with low sides and broad bottom. It was deeper in the middle than on the sides, a shape similar to that of a Chinese cooking wok. Once the wheat had been cracked, it was roasted in these cast-iron kettles and constantly turned with large wooden paddles; when done, it was scooped off into a low-lying trough on the side. The man who did this, the *mugi-iri*, or wheat roaster, was a prized employee in shōyu breweries, since not every one had the patience and skill to roast large amounts of wheat evenly and efficiently day after day. (A measure of his stature may be seen in the use of his title mugi-iri, signifying someone of foreman's rank in the factories.) Once roasted, the wheat kernels were allowed to cool for an evening and then were further reduced in size by crushing until the original kernels were broken down into at least three or four pieces.

Preparation of the Brine Solution

The preparation of salt and the mixing of the brine solution was simply an elaboration of the technique discussed earlier under household shōyu manufacture. The difficulty with preparing salt for shōyu manufacture was not in the steaming or roasting processes. Rather, the salt of the day required a complicated process of cooking to rid it of bitterness.

In Noda the traditional technique was to add slightly more than 270 gallons of water to 270 gallons of salt and to let this cook down in huge cauldrons for two to three hours. After the mixture was stirred, it was allowed to drain out through a sievelike trap made of horse hair that collected the impurities and scum; the mixture was then poured into large wooden vats and the cooking and purifying steps were repeated again. In 1880 Mogi Shichirōuemon, in the course of experimenting at home in his makeshift laboratory, developed a technique for slowly sinking and thereby saturating small amounts of salt in large tubs of water. After immersion and stirring, the salt solution was run into a separate vat. Various improvements were made to this basic apparatus with time, but the technique remained the same: to saturate and stir small amounts of salt in a water solution. Even though this technique could handle only small amounts of salt at one time, it was a vast improvement over the old method of boiling more than 500 gallons of combined water and salt. The speed that the newer process promised, however, could be realized only by using high-quality salt whose impurities did not have to be leached or boiled out.

Culturing of the Wheat and Soybeans

The preparation of the soybeans, wheat, kōji, and brine for fermentation was not overly complicated, but it was involved and labor-intensive, requiring a good deal of fetching, stirring, draining, and hauling from one stage of preparation to another. The labor-intensive side of traditional shōyu manufacture was nowhere more evident than in the culturing of the wheat and soybeans to make kōji. Traditionally mold cultures were grown anew every year, and since shōyu manufacture was seasonal, before the mid-nineteenth century no effort was made to preserve and improve cultures.

The usual method of growing a culture involved mixing the steamed soybeans and roasted wheat (actually the soybeans, which were hydrated in water, were coated with roasted wheat particles) and letting the mixture cool out-of-doors in light, low-sided wooden trays made of cedar. Once dried, the wheat-coated soybeans were moved inside to a room so constructed that wind and temperature conditions could be controlled. These culture rooms were usually basementlike halls of wood with earthen walls, half-sunk into the ground. Roofs were built in such a manner that aeration was easily accomplished. In Noda the danger was more often too high rather than too low a temperature, and in the summer months it was common to halt production temporarily for fear that the culturing kōji would become too hot. The ideal temperature was around 28° Celsius (82° Fahrenheit), and in the winter or summer heating or cooling devices were employed to keep the kōji close to the ideal temperature. Twice a day, usually in the morning and evening, the mixture would be lightly agitated, the trays repositioned, and often the door left ajar, to allow for temperature adjustment and equal growth of the culture throughout the kōji. After three days, another batch would be introduced into the kōji inoculation rooms; by the fourth day, when the first batch was completely molded and ready for removal, the second was dry, warm, and beginning to mold. This process would continue until all the soybeans and wheat had been used up.

By the early twentieth century new techniques that allowed the simultaneous culturing of increasingly larger batches of kōji had been developed, but these required considerable investment in new plant and equipment. By this time, too, considerable effort had been invested in the development and improvement of mold cultures for producing a more rapid and complete kōji. This work proceeded rapidly after the construction of a modern research laboratory in 1904.

Process of Fermentation

The kōji was mixed a little at a time into the brine solution to produce a moromi mash. The mash was placed in large cedar tubs, where it had to be stirred frequently and vigorously by hand in order to facilitate fermentation. Fortunately, as fermentation advanced, the escaping oxygen stirred the brew naturally, obviating the need for hand-mixing. By the early twentieth century air-pressure machines built directly into the fermentation vats took care of the mixing, but until such mechanical conveniences became available, mixing by hand was a grueling, muscle-straining necessity. Moromi-stirring required considerable strength and balance, since a worker was perched over the brew on a narrow board, vigorously agitating the brew in vats that were wider and deeper than he was tall. This was required once every couple of days in the winter and two or three times a day in the summer.

Without some kind of acceleration, chemical or otherwise, complete fermentation would require 18 to 36 months, depending on climatic conditions at the site of the brewery. In Noda complete fermentation in the premechanical days took 20 to 22 months. In Chōshi it was somewhat shorter, from 18 to 20 months. An investment in shōyu manufac-

Fermentation room: wooden vats holding fermenting soy sauce; note the planks on which the moromi-stirrer would stand to perform his task

turing, therefore, required not only a considerable outlay in plant and equipment but necessitated a two-year time lag between the initial preparation of ingredients and the final maturation of the soy sauce. One measure of the investment required can be seen in the size of the fermentation vats and buildings that housed them. The traditional wooden vats held between 900 and 3,000 gallons, and a medium-to-large-size plant might have a hundred of them. The structures housing such equipment were probably the largest in premodern Japan, rivaled only by official halls and religious shrines.

By the time a harvest of soy beans and wheat had been made into kōji, cultured, and processed as mash, the New Year would be fast approaching. At Noda it was traditional during the New Year holidays for the owners to inspect each vat to see how far fermentation had proceeded, judging the color, smelling the bouquet, and tasting the flavor. This practice continues even today, although after the company was incorporated in 1917 the inspections, now semi-annual, became more ceremonial than functional, since continuous monitoring of the fermentation process became part of daily management during the 1920s.

Extraction or Pressing

Once fermentation was completed and the brew inspected and approved, the next stage was the extraction or pressing operation. Traditionally this was not only time-consuming but back-breaking as well because in view of the muscle-power expended, the methods were inefficient. Extraction usually required the application of great weight, directly or indirectly (by means of a lever), to the moromi, which was in a box, wooden tub, or barrel with a perforated bottom. The liquid was thus forced out through strainer holes by a combination of human strength and mechanical leverage.

By the middle of the nineteenth century two developments greatly raised the efficiency of the extraction process. The first was substitution of porous cloth sacks for porous tub bottoms. Sacks were easier to move, clean, and repair, and they clogged less frequently than buckets or barrels because they could exude sauce in every direction rather than only out the bottom. The repair and restitching of these sacks, most of which were made across the Edo River in Ibaragi and Gumma Prefectures, became a household industry in the Noda area. Individually, sacks held less than buckets or barrels, but they could be stacked one on top of the other in a wooden pressing chamber, called a *fune* or boat, and then squeezed, considerably increasing the amount of shōyu that could be extracted at one time as compared to methods employing buckets and barrels. This was especially true when another innovation, in the early twentieth century, took the form of more efficient mechanical presses, which applied great force, through steam or hydraulic power, to the sacks. This greatly increased the pressure and therefore the speed and thoroughness of extraction.

Once the shōyu had been separated from the lees, some manufacturers would blend the fresh shōyu with shōyu that had been allowed to age for up to five years. Two-year-old shōyu was reputed to have the best taste, three-year-old the deepest color. Blending was an art and as such its practice was highly variable. By the middle of the twentieth century most manufacturers, even the local ones, had discontinued the practice.

Shōyu cake (*kasu*) and shōyu oil (*shōyu abura*) are by-products of the extraction process. Kasu is the compacted residue that remains after the sauce has been squeezed out of the porous sacks or barrel bottoms. Initially it was discarded as a waste product, but by the late eighteenth

Extraction and pressing: a windless type of device for applying pressure to a porous-bottom box (age-fune) in order to separate sauce from lees

century it found almost universal use as an agricultural fertilizer when mixed with other biodegradable refuse. In 1839 Noda brewers sold 1,855 bales, about 3,324 barrels, of kasu to farmers. Today the cake is more commonly used as feed for livestock. Shōyu oil was separated from the extracted soy sauce by heating, which forced the lighter oil to rise to the top where it was skimmed off or otherwise removed.

During the Tempo Period (1830–1843) the market for shōyu cake and oil expanded significantly. With encouragement from the shōgunate, Noda became a center for research and experimentation in the recovery and processing of both by-products; as a result, shōyu oil became one of the most widely used illuminants at the end of the Tokugawa Period. For a short time, 1864 to 1894, Takanashi Kōuemon's branch household in Noda specialized in shōyu oil processing and sales and was one of the leading shōyu oil producers in Japan. But in the 1880s shōyu oil was displaced by kerosene (a new Western product) as the primary illuminant, and Takanashi Kōuemon was ultimately forced to discontinue operation of his factory. During the twentieth century shōyu oil has been used as a machine oil and for the manufacture of cheap soaps and cosmetics.

After the by-products were removed, shōyu was shipped to market. Traditionally it was distributed in kegs (*taru*) produced by local coopers in Noda, who worked in family-centered shops of a half-dozen to a dozen workers. At the end of the Tokugawa Period the standard keg held nine *shō*, four and one-third gallons, which was said to be the amount of shōyu the average adult consumed in a year. The size of the keg was of little actual consequence in the retail market, however, for neighborhood vendors would sell any amount of shōyu to customers supplying their own containers.[13]

Production and Scheduling

Aside from complex biochemical aspects, the traditional methods of shōyu manufacture were not mechanically complicated; but they were time-consuming, in that coordination among many different steps of production was required, and demanding in terms of the degree of labor intensiveness and, to a lesser extent, the level of labor skill needed. Even if the ancillary industries associated with shōyu brewing are ignored—such as the sewing of sacks for pressing, the making of taru for shipping, the shipping itself, and the processing and sale of cake—the initial fermentation of shōyu by traditional methods involved a minimum of twenty distinct steps and took from 18 to 36 months, requiring at the least some workers with strength, diligence, and experience.

For most of the Tokugawa Period shōyu manufacture never entirely lost its seasonal character; raw materials were purchased in the fall (the exact time depending on availability and price) and processed as moromi by the winter. As a result of this cyclical character, there were high and low periods of employment. During the peak season for shōyu production, the off-season for agriculture, the number of workers in the soy sauce industry probably doubled. Temporary, unskilled laborers did most of the manual labor—the hand-carrying, loading, sorting, and hauling. From what is known of seasonal or casual labor migrants elsewhere, most temporary workers were young men from farms, between the ages of 17 and 25, employed by the day or week.[14]

By the middle of the nineteenth century, however, the nature of production—and therefore of work organization and coordination—in a few breweries began to change. The larger breweries, such as those of Mogi Saheiji, Mogi Shichirōuemon, and Takanashi Hyōzaemon, began year-round or nearly year-round rather than seasonal manufacture. (Because it was difficult to control the kōji-making process during the summer, work was often suspended in July and August.) In 1844, for example, these three brewery owners were each producing around 200,000 gallons of shōyu—three to ten times more than the other makers in town. Manufacturing in these large amounts required more formalized production routines as well as more intensive supervision of the fermentation process and of production workers.

The Dual Employment System

The shift from seasonal to full-time manufacture by a few brewers in Noda produced a sort of dual employment system, and by the middle of the nineteenth century a double structure of manufacturing began to emerge. The smaller makers, with more seasonal operation, employed fewer workers, used them more casually, and produced less per worker than the larger brewers, which had less slack in their operation, more specialized workers in their employ, and a higher output per employee. Shoda Bunuemon's factory, for example, produced 34,966 gallons of shōyu in 1875 with 38 workers, a ratio of 920 gallons per worker, while Tanaka Genba's larger facility had an output of 149,856 gallons in 1867 with 80 workers, or 1,873 gallons per worker.[15] Both brewers, however, depended at least in part on casual (seasonal or part-time) workers, although there might be a noticeable difference in the efficiency of part-time workers depending on the degree of supervision they received and the quality of equipment used. Here larger brewers, with a larger staff, better equipment, and more continuous operation, were likely to benefit more by casual labor.

The importance of casual workers for the development of industrial relations in the Noda soy sauce industry and in other traditional industries in Japan should not be underestimated. The practice of dividing a work force between regular employees, with the expectation of year-round work and of a certain amount of employer paternalism, and irregular or temporary workers without rights or expectations is a feature of contemporary Japanese labor relations. Its roots may go back to the circumstances of labor that characterized many nineteenth-century rural enterprises. Depending on the type of industry and enterprise today, anywhere from 15 to 20 percent of its workers might be temporary. This flexibility in size of work force and, therefore, in labor overhead, allows an enterprise to budget substantial fringe benefits for some and deny them to others. In the nineteenth century most workers were apt to be casual rather than regular employees simply because neither technology nor the market could support full-time work for many. Whether in the nineteenth or twentieth centuries, casual workers have provided marginal labor for low-skilled jobs to which employers are reluctant to assign regular workers and have supplied additional labor so that slack utilization in production may be taken up as demand increases.

A detailed ledger of temporary workers in the Noda shōyu industry during a four-month period from March through June 1885 gives us a precise portrait of casual workers. During this period 631 seasonal workers or *nagaremono*, literally "floating-people," as the ledger calls them, were employed in 36 different factories, warehouses, shipping docks, or other facilities in the Noda brewing industry. Seventy-five percent of these, or 472 persons, were engaged by the eleven largest factories; they stayed, on the average, between one and five days. They were overwhelmingly young—in their twenties, for the most part—and generally local, with 78 percent coming from Tokyo or the six prefectures that constitute the Tokyo Plain. Most—60 percent, to be exact—came from villages within walking distance of Noda, which suggests that farm youths simply took off for a couple of days' work at Noda. Because there was a daily need for casual workers to push, pull, carry, and clean, one could almost be guaranteed a few days' work there. Casuals could be assured of more. All workers, regular and irregular, stayed in the *hiroshiki*, a kind of worker dormitory, where hot food and drink were available all day and night. In sum, the ledger suggests that from four to six laborers drifted daily into Noda, that they were evenly distributed throughout the four-month period in question, and that a couple of dozen were in town on any given day or week.[16]

In spite of the name given to them, nagaremono should be distinguished from the "floaters" of Western Europe and North America who roamed from one factory site to the next in search of work in the late nineteenth century. Unlike the Noda migrants, they were typically without property, home, or family, a kind of industrial flotsam, drifting on a sea of temporary jobs and faceless flophouses. Casual workers in Noda were generally local laborers who returned home to village, family, and the agricultural work cycle from which they had stolen brief relief.

The fairly large number of casual laborers at the end of the nineteenth century suggests that most of the work in shōyu manufacture was still largely unspecialized although labor-intensive. Unfortunately the number of workers and the proportion of regular as opposed to temporary laborers in any exact year before 1900 is not known, but it is possible to estimate what the ratio might have been by working back from 1900 data. That year the nine largest breweries employed 685 workers, exclusive of members of the brewers' families, their bantō, and those employed in various subcontracting industries. In 1900 shōyu production stood at 3,221,064 gallons in Noda, while in 1885 it was about half of that. (This figure is calculated from that of 1888 when production stood at 2,192,784 gallons.) It is unlikely that a one-to-one relation in output and manpower existed at the time, but if production in 1885 was about half of what it was in 1900 when there were 685 workers, it is safe to infer that the number of regular workers in 1885 was between 400 and 500. Comparing this to the known number of casual workers, 631, in one four-month period suggests that the absolute number of casual workers on an annual basis was likely to be four to five times the number of regular workers (assuming that casual workers did not reappear in the same year). Of course the number of workhours logged by regular workers on an annual or even daily basis exceeded that of the temporary workers. Nevertheless, the heavy reliance on migrant workers during the year suggests the degree to which production depended on casual, unskilled workers.

Research on Chōshi, the other shōyu manufacturing town near Noda in Chiba Prefecture, suggests that regular workers, although more permanent than casual laborers, were not likely to stay very long themselves. In Tanaka Genba's brewery, the largest in Chōshi, most regular workers stayed no more than three years on the average, unless they were promoted to factory foremen or front-office clerks. This was true in spite of the fact that three-quarters of them came from or close by the town of Chōshi.[17] Only owners, their families, and their most trusted and well-paid employees (foremen and head clerks) stayed with the concern year after year. Most workers stayed a few days or weeks before drifting on or returning home, while a minority of locals stayed with the enterprise for several years, developing certain limited on-the-job skills.

The amount of casual labor also suggests the degree to which production organization and scheduling were run at less than capacity. Part-time workers represent slack capacity in plant utilization since they were temporary and, at best, semi-skilled workers who could not have filled in very efficiently. Their large number, nevertheless, attests to their aggregate importance in shōyu manufacture and to the labor-intensive quality of production. Noda was not unique in this regard. In Chōshi, as well, the records of Tanaka Genba reveal that he produced 134,000 gallons of shōyu in 1867 with a work force of 80. Yet, in his private diary Tanaka recorded that he had 40 persons in his employ, exclusive of family members. The figure of 40 appears to represent the number of regular—one might infer permanent—employees working in Tanaka's home as domestics (five were women) and in his factories and shops as clerks or experienced hands. The larger figure appears to be the number engaged in shōyu manufacture, presumably including some of those entered in Tanaka's diary. The larger figure was included in a report to government officials on the consumption of raw materials and the production of shōyu between March 29 and May 29, 1867, and it would seem highly unlikely that Tanaka would want to overestimate either manpower or productivity in such a document. My assumption is that the difference in reported manpower between Tanaka's private diary and his public report represents in large measure the number of part-time workers in shōyu manufacture. This would corroborate findings from Noda that the nature of work in the soy sauce industry was seasonal—labor-intensive but labor-inefficient.[18]

Production figures in Noda demonstrate the irregular nature of shōyu manufacture before the end of the nineteenth century. As table 1 shows, production did not climb to two and a half-million gallons until 1894; but after reaching that level, it never fell below it (except for 1897), as industrialization advanced and population, especially urban population, grew. Until 1894, however, for at least the preceding half-century, production varied widely between one and two million gallons, and the difference from year to year was considerable. As in all traditional and early industrializing economies, such variance was the rule rather than the exception. Before modern methods of forecasting supply and demand, establishing a market through product advertising, basing costs on volume of throughput, or of standardizing production flows, production levels had to be based on general levels of demand and of the size of the year's harvest, as well as on its quality, availability, and cost. As a result, production goals were highly variable and market conditions for the final product, nearly two years' fermentation away, were uncertain. It is understandable that labor organization and labor conditions were so unsettled when the structure of the industry was based on seasonal, slack, and uncoordinated production, tied mainly to the agriculture cycle.

TABLE 1. National and Noda Shōyu output, 1888–1973 (kiloliters[a]).

Year	National output	Noda Shōyu output	Noda Shōyu share (percent)
1887	—	7,005	—
1888	234,843	8,306	3.5
1889	222,069	9,141	4.1
1890	208,460	4,769	2.3
1891	218,459	7,011	3.2
1892	218,676	8,179	3.7
1893	230,360	8,374	3.6
1894	239,313	9,407	3.9
1895	253,784	9,740	3.8
1896	271,081	10,565	3.9
1897	275,584	8,733	3.2
1898	275,984	9,586	3.5
1899	333,963	10,873	3.3
1900	283,155	12,201	4.3
1901	310,300	12,853	4.1
1902	318,158	13,468	4.2
1903	317,500	14,178	4.5
1904	334,683	15,545	4.6
1905	316,287	17,808	5.6
1906	347,883	17,128	4.9
1907	373,443	17,991	4.8
1908	382,368	17,214	4.5
1909	395,627	20,017	5.1
1910	397,043	20,930	5.3
1911	413,840	22,904	5.5
1912	423,401	27,604	6.5
1913	430,435	26,352	6.1
1914	428,832	—	—
1915	429,920	27,200	6.3
1916	468,882	33,644	7.2
1917	465,607	—	—
1918	473,537	33,287	7.0
1919	529,277	36,782	6.9
1920	503,380	32,716	6.5
1921	578,877	38,100	6.6
1922	588,414	34,462	5.9
1923	624,764	32,020	5.1
1924	659,127	44,047	6.7
1925	633,552	54,021	8.5
1926	635,630	55,747	8.8
1927	630,824	46,172	7.3
1928	656,831	56,065	8.5
1929	653,455	61,803	9.5
1930	596,124	66,760	11.2
1931	573,980	67,638	11.8
1932	594,163	65,741	11.1

TABLE 1. (*Continued*)

Year	National output	Noda Shōyu output	Noda Shōyu share (percent)
1933	576,026	58,331	10.1
1934	584,684	79,834	13.7
1935	596,579	85,543	14.3
1936	611,259	88,931	14.5
1937	591,264	74,899	12.7
1938	609,197	83,251	13.7
1939	660,781	89,704	13.6
1940	686,696	87,590	12.8
1941	731,540	90,290	12.3
1942	723,101	79,376	11.0
1943	680,955	81,379	12.0
1944	628,091	73,761	11.7
1945	425,868	48,868	11.5
1946	399,898	31,450	7.9
1947	336,275	29,756	8.8
1948	509,459	52,406	10.3
1949	550,719	64,119	11.6
1950	689,506	69,404	10.1
1951	826,291	81,978	9.9
1952	750,754	101,867	13.6
1953	822,149	116,218	14.1
1954	919,869	127,211	13.8
1955	941,792	138,226	14.7
1956	982,667	150,103	15.3
1957	985,404	154,790	15.7
1958	977,136	159,900	16.4
1959	1,016,489	172,320	17.0
1960	1,023,622	184,401	18.0
1961	1,010,629	192,792	19.1
1962	1,014,896	202,737	20.0
1963	1,051,730	224,796	21.4
1964	1,021,758	250,333	24.5
1965	1,047,236	252,712	24.1
1966	1,056,364	273,956	25.9
1967	1,116,979	298,963	26.8
1968	1,055,873	299,900	28.4
1969	1,076,371	323,668	30.1
1970	1,125,939	347,922	30.9
1971	1,105,935	361,291	32.7
1972	1,159,009	377,783	32.6
1973	1,277,887	400,727	31.4

Source: Kikkoman Company Archives, Company Statistical Tables—1918 to 1956 (n.p., 1956), unnumbered; more recent data supplied by the Planning Department of the Kikkoman Corporation.

a. 5.55 koku = 1 kiloliter = 264 gallons

Organization of Work

In the period before incorporation, when shōyu manufacture in Noda was organized around entrepreneurial families, the functions and personnel of the factory, as opposed to what might be termed the front office, were not only distinct but different. Front-office personnel dealt with everything but production and were involved mainly in buying raw materials and selling finished products—shōyu and shōyu oil and cake. If the entrepreneurial family or others with which it was associated had invested in other ventures, such as miso or sake production, the buying for and selling of these products was coordinated in all likelihood through the same front-office.

Naturally factory workers concerned themselves with manufacturing, but this was manufacturing narrowly conceived, in the sense that factory personnel were not concerned with the amount of production, its cost, or even its scheduling. Such matters were handled by front-office employees who knew very little about the production process itself. The organization of shōyu manufacture before the twentieth century was therefore peculiarly uncoordinated. Certain entrepreneurial families were specialized in that they provided capital for shōyu production, but the actual scheduling was carried out by front-office employees who handled matters external to production, even though their actions impinged directly on it, and by factory workers who were involved in production but without direct or frequent contact with owners and managers.

The lack of coordination in the industry as a whole as well as in individually owned breweries is most clearly illustrated in a set of work rules first promulgated in 1831 by factory owners and tōji (who, at this time, functioned both as brewmasters and as plant managers). The rules reveal numerous labor problems: absenteeism, lack of orderliness and discipline, and the absence of organizational controls associated not only with the large number of temporary workers but also with the lack of coordination and routine in the entire production process. These rules were reissued in 1853, suggesting that the problems were intractable and perhaps even inherent in the structure of the workplace and the nature of work at that time.

Work Rules

1830 first statement

1853 second statement
(reaffirmed because so many tōji had turned over
during the intervening 23 years)

Lately the quality of work has fallen and workers have failed to follow instructions. This has interfered with the smooth operation of our business. Together, we have agreed upon the following regulations to overcome these abuses and to enforce our traditional ways of operation.

In accordance with the regulations established by the government, gambling is prohibited at all times and in all places.

Except for wine used during ceremonies and other formal occasions, drinking of alcoholic beverages is expressly forbidden.

Occasionally workers have failed to follow the instructions of their superiors and have refused to work, asking for time off which is not part of their work agreement. If difficulties such as these occur in the future, they will be referred to a group of brewers for deliberation and decision. We hope that this warning will prevent work from being interrupted in the future.

If work or other business detains one until late, it should be completed by 8:00 P.M. If one does not return by 8:00, some appropriate punishment will be determined by the relevant body.

With one exception, we refuse to make contributions and donations for whatever purpose. In the case of the Konpira Shrine Sect from Kyushu, we will give one combined gift from all of us [meaning the tōji group].

If an itinerant peddler—or others passing through in search of work—comes to town, he must receive a certificate of permission to stay in town. With this permission slip he is allowed to stay for only *one* night. If he stays for two nights, the reason for this, such as sickness, must be reported to the person in charge. In any event breakfast will be given to those who stayed the night but no one appearing in the morning should be fed.

If hoboes or others uninterested in working come to town, they should be refused a place to stay and food to eat, and they should in all instances be refused entry into shōyu factories. Further, they should not be allowed to hang around the factories.

From now on, workers should not ask for drinks or other favors when working. Factory foremen will determine whatever is needed by the workers, and workers need not worry themselves about such matters.

Workers who have left their previous employers without permission and who seek employment elsewhere, hoping to increase their income by concealing their past, are required to receive the permission of their previous employers before seeking work here.

Anyone who is let go for negligent or inadequate work will have his name circulated to other factories so that he will be prevented from being hired there.

If someone comes from another place to work in the shōyu factories and spends a year at one factory and then decides to change to another, that change will be allowed only after the prospective employer and the previous employer have had an opportunity to discuss and approve the matter between themselves.

The abovementioned rules were decided by the consensus of everyone present and they should be immediately enforced. If any of these regulations are not honored, then the tōji as a group should meet, discuss the matter, and decide on an appropriate punishment. Our discussion of these matters and our experience with them in the past convinces us that we have taken appropriate measures here.[19]

The characterization of Japanese enterprise and employees as being concerned with long-term performance, so often heard in recent years, would be entirely inappropriate in this one case, and I suspect most others, at least until the 1920s. Most workers were temporary and most work was dull, repetitive, and unskilled. No wonder that in 1909 many of the work quality and performance issues, first raised more than a half-century earlier, were still unsettled. Work discipline, absenteeism, and performance remained problems, and tōji appeared to be, as before, totally in charge of work organization and evaluation. Consider the following document:

1909 Wage Agreement

(1) A wage bonus will be paid only to those laborers who have worked for one year.

(2) A wage bonus will not be given to workers with poor discipline and behavior as determined by the tōji.

(3) If a person becomes ill, he must be given permission to rest or retire by the tōji.

(4) Workers who contract venereal disease must be relieved from work and treated by a physician until they are well.

(5) Workers must obey their supervisors and work conscientiously. During difficult times, they must work even harder.

The above stipulations must be met, if a worker is to be given a bonus.[20]

The same lack of coordination and specialization plagued the front office. Except that here, because of the smaller number of workers, their somewhat longer tenure, and their more direct and personal relation with owners, the absenteeism, rowdiness, and inefficiency of the factories were minimized. Even so, few front-office employees stayed long enough with an employer to be elevated to positions of authority.[21]

Until recently few workers were employed on a permanent basis in the shōyu breweries. In 1900, for example, there were only 685 permanent workers (brewery workers on an annual wage contract), in a town of over 20,000.[22] Before this time there were even fewer permanent workers because the larger breweries did not begin to lose their seasonal character until the late 1850s or 1860s. As a consequence, large-scale economies were unknown in traditional shōyu manufacture, and brewers were more likely to apportion their work by households than to concentrate it in the consolidation or coordination of production units. The seasonal nature of the industry was reflected by sizable fluctuations in production figures as well as by the large number of part-time and temporary workers.

Hierarchies of Work

The front office and factory had their own distinct hierarchies of authority and responsibility. The front office was nominally headed by an owner, a household head of one of the shōyu-brewing families in Noda; in practice it usually was managed by a number of men under the owner's authority who were known as bantō, and who were long associated, perhaps even by heredity, with the enterprise. The most senior of these might be semi-retired, in which case he was known as the *inkyo-bantō*, a title denoting his senior, somewhat inactive status. He was followed, in a typical chain of command, by a *bantō-gashira*, or office manager, who could be of senior or junior grade. In many family businesses bantō were often adopted into the owning family. In this way they perpetuated not only the ownership but the management of family enterprises as well. In Noda, however, the large number of kinsmen from the Mogi, Takanashi, and related families, many of whom were knowledgeable in one or more aspects of shōyu manufacture, apparently obviated the need to ensure continuity in entrepreneurial families through the adoption of bantō. Sufficient talent existed within brewing families to make the elevation of bantō by marriage and adoption uncommon, although women from bantō families sometimes married sons of the enterprise-owning families.

A bantō-gashira was followed by a *wakashū-gashira*, what might be termed senior clerk (following the terminology common in Western offices until the 1880s). Wakashū-gashira were responsible for various front-office functions, such as keeping track of the cost and supply of raw materials and the cost and inventory of tubs and barrels made by local coopers. They were supported by *wakashū,* a title which might be translated as junior clerk. These, in turn, were followed by apprentices, *kozō,* recruited into the front office by a brewery at about the age of puberty and who, if they remained and showed promise, might be expected to be promoted to section chief by the age of thirty and to junior bantō by thirty-five. Apprentices were recruited by owners, who relied heavily on connections with kinsmen and members of the local community for recommendations.

A similar hierarchy existed within factories. Here the factory foreman, the tōji, was primarily a technician, yet he had complete authority for all matters concerned with the production process and the production worker. Each factory had one tōji, but because there were as many as nineteen different factories in Noda at the height of factory decentralization in the nineteenth century, tōji were numerous enough to constitute a recognizable aristocracy among workers. More than just artisans of technique and form, tōji were responsible not only for the operation and organization of production but also for the quantity, quality control, and saleability of a product that was made in a highly personal manner, using mostly uncertain ingredients, and often with unskilled workmen. In addition to their duties as brewmasters, tōji were responsible for the safety of plant, equipment, and workers. They also acted as paymasters, innovators in technique and equipment, and arbiters of work rates, duties, and responsibilities.

A number of *kashira,* functional foremen, worked under tōji and supervised different facets of shōyu manufacture. They relied on wheat-roasters and kettle-tenders to oversee more detailed aspects of production. The titles of mugi-iri and kamaya symbolized their importance, not their actual position. Under them came two levels of workmen: those with experience, *honnin;* and those without, *shinnin.* Unmarried workers lived in the hiroshiki, a kind of dormitory on the grounds. The larger hiroshiki had a full-time staff to provide food for workers, to wash workclothes and bedclothes, and to clean the premises.

Specialized contractors, *oyakata,* lived and worked in the community; they handled the recruiting of workers. This method of recruiting labor appears to have evolved rather late in Noda. The first specialist appeared in 1854. The oyakata's emergence was undoubtedly related to the need for more reliable recruitment of workers as shōyu factories began to regularize manufacturing operations and began year-round rather than seasonal production. Oyakata, known also as *oyabun* in Noda, guaranteed the contractual performance of the men they recommended, promising to find replacements if the original recruits proved unsatisfactory. Oyakata arranged for the men who provisioned the factories and for those who hauled supplies and shōyu from one place to another. The first labor recruiter to work exclusively for a particular brewery was a contractor whose business (in actuality a sort of employment agency) was known as Konaya; he began to supply the Takanashi breweries with workers in 1854. The following year two Mogi families contracted with an agency, called Daishukuya, for workers. Business proved so successful for this contractor that he formed a branch household or agency. As late as 1907 Mogi Saheiji made arrangements with another agency, Yamasawai, to supply workers for his factories. By the early twentieth century these four contractors, as well as a fifth, were handling the bulk of regular workers employed in soy sauce manufacture.[23]

The development of a system of internal contracting, *naya-seido*, for labor recruitment, supervision, and compensation might seem to be a rather late occurrence in Noda. Yet its appearance in the 1850s antedates a similar sort of development in mining and shipbuilding by a generation or so. In Noda oyakata appear by the 1850s, whereas in mining and shipbuilding they appear in the 1880s. Where the naya-seido did appear, it continued apparently until at least World War I. The transition from naya-seido to a system where the enterprise directly hired and supervised workers rather than relying on independent contractors occurred swiftly in Noda in the 1920s. Its abruptness did not guarantee easy acceptance, however, for workers rebelled against the new work structure proposed by the recently formed corporate management. (This story is treated separately in Chapters 5 and 6.)

Labor contracts were negotiated between the tōji and the labor recruiter. Workers did not decide the terms of their compensation and work. They could refuse to agree to the terms, but since it was normal to pay between 50 and 70 percent of wages in advance, with the remaining balance paid semi-monthly, it was difficult to reject a contract that offered so much in prepaid wages. In Noda contracts were negotiated in January, just after the New Year; in Chōshi they were decided in December. Oyakata acted as guarantors for the satisfactory performance of workers for whom they negotiated contracts; they also served as labor arbiters should disagreements arise. Although the contract was guaranteed by the oyakata, the tōji paid the workers and decided the bonus shares for workers (if there were to be any). Oyakata and tōji usually deducted "management fees" from the wages of the men they recruited and supervised.[24]

Tōji and oyakata continued their functions in Noda until 1923. Because the Noda Shōyu Company, incorporated in 1917, was in operation by 1918, it adopted the traditional methods of labor recruitment, supervision, and compensation for the first five years of its operation. This continuity of conditions was largely responsible for the labor difficulties that plagued the company at the close of the 1920s.

Industry and Community

Since its first mention in official records in A.D. 923, Noda has been a highly successful agricultural community, with fertile alluvial soil and abundant fresh water. A millennium would pass before shōyu manufacture displaced agriculture as the main source of employment. Because agriculture predated industry, Noda cannot be considered a classic company town in the sense that the stores, schools, and lodgings were company-owned and managed. The town was not planned around a factory site, as were Hershey, Pennsylvania, Lowell, Massachusetts, and Pullman, Illinois; the ties between industry and community were more reciprocal, more subtle—and more paradoxical.

The character of these ties arose from the difference between large-scale manufacturing and small-scale farming. Although soy sauce manufacture was conceived in the countryside, it was not associated with it. The community expressed the rhythms and renewals of the agricultural cycle; and shōyu brewing after 1850 did not. Once seasonal work was replaced by year-round work in the factories, which began to occur in the middle of the nineteenth century for the largest breweries and came to characterize even the smallest factories by the 1930s, soy sauce manufacture evolved its own identity and pace. The ready association of town and industry became fitting only during the past half-century, when manufacturing replaced farming as the town's principal employment.

In spite of the close relations between community and industry since 1930, they have never been interchangeable, although they shared a great deal in common, especially between 1930 and 1960. Before that time the traditional methods of operation and production in the shōyu industry did not permit brewers to control their workers directly and, through them, the town. In the eighteenth and nineteenth centuries production was decentralized in numerous associated yet autonomous family enterprises, whose owners depended on functional specialists, such as clerks, labor contractors, and master brewers, to run the plants. These specialists, in turn, relied on local villagers and on migrant or seasonal workers to man the shōyu breweries and warehouses and to supply needed goods and services. Because laborers in breweries did not stay very long a close relationship between local residence and factory work did not develop either. This was true for locals, and even more so for outsiders.

Owners neither managed their facilities nor supervised the operation of collective facilities until the end of the nineteenth century. Even then, they cooperated only in matters external to actual production, such as purchasing, transportation, and sales. Not until the second decade of the twentieth century did owners begin to monitor and integrate the internal operations of their separate manufacturing facilities. Before that they relied on clerks for record-keeping and general "front-office" functions, on labor contractors for worker recruitment, and on brewmasters for labor management as well as for general production knowledge and experience. Owners could not control workers in any meaningful way because they were ignorant of and distant from the operation of their enterprises. They completely lacked modern notions of management regarding coordination among the functional, operational, and organizational aspects of shōyu manufacture. At most, they worked with their clerks, keeping simple records of daily and seasonal transactions, and they might occasionally consult with brewmasters and labor contractors. Their major contribution was not work but their personality, how they interacted with employees and how they related to the numerous buyers and sellers involved with shōyu manufacture and distribution. Above all, they were patriarchs of their houses (ie), responsible for maintaining the place, property, and, most important, the dignity of the families of which they were the most conspicuous current representatives. Business issues were approached first and foremost, as family interests; thus, their presence rather than performance in the front office was what mattered.

Until the twentieth century, variability in production, and extreme decentralization of control and of management in shōyu manufacture, meant that many functions and activities that would normally be carried out within a modern corporation were not, and that the town, in a general sense, functioned as a subcontractor to the industry. Except for production itself, almost every facet of operation, from the acquisition of raw materials to the shipping of finished goods, was handled indirectly through residents of the town rather than directly through workers engaged in the shōyu plants. Thus, although relatively few people worked in the breweries, many in the community were touched by their presence in Noda. Local farmers supplied rice, vegetables, and other agricultural goods. Housewives sewed and repaired the heavy cloth sacks used in squeezing out the shōyu from the fermented mash. Local artisans, such as coopers and wall masons, were not often tied contractually to factories, yet their work came in fair measure from the industry. Shippers, whether they hauled by land or by water, although not normally employees of the breweries, depended in large part on the barrels of shōyu to fill their carts and boats for market. In short, many in the community enjoyed the business the breweries provided, even though few of them actually depended on the output of the factories and fewer yet actually worked in them.

Shōyu manufacture in Noda was an important but not overwhelming fact of community life before the twentieth century. According to an 1872 partial census enumeration of what might be called central Noda, wealth was not significantly concentrated in the hands of its brewers. The enumeration listed the owners of land parcels as well as the owners and occupants of buildings in downtown Noda: 335 males, presumably heads of households or unmarried men, were listed, 29 percent of whom were classified as farmers. Besides these, 54 persons were identified as owners of land that was leased; 21 were recorded as owners of rented buildings; 12 held both land and leased buildings.

It appears that almost half of the recorded occupants of the central section of Noda—159 persons out of 335—were unlikely to be connected with the soy sauce industry; these were farmers and owners of land or buildings. Among those listed owners, names known to be associated with shōyu manufacture were not especially prominent. Of 12 owning both land and buildings, only 2 were manufacturers of shōyu; they owned 8 of 47 (17 percent) leased structures in central Noda. Of 54 persons listed as land owners in 1872, 4 had been and 5 currently were in the shōyu manufacturers; they owned 25 percent (42 out of 171) of the land parcels. Counting only those who were then active in shōyu brewing, however, would put the figure at 17 percent (29 out of 171), and more than half of these (16 out of 29) were held by one man and one family, Mogi Saheiji. The Mogi-sa family, as pointed out, had diversified less into shōyu manufacture than into various commercial and professional ventures in town, which might account for its large real estate holdings in central Noda.[25]

In sum, in 1872 in central Noda a majority of household heads did not work regularly in the shōyu industry. Shōyu manufacturers owned no more than 17 percent of the land and buildings, but this did not signify even a 17 percent exercise of control in the community, since owners were not often directly involved in their enterprises. As long as owners were not practically involved in the management and operation of their plants and as long as they did not centralize and coordinate their investments in the community, independence yet mutuality between industry and town could be maintained without a balance of power resting in the hands of either. In the early twentieth century, however, as large integrated factories requiring new methods of management were laid out along the Tone and Edo rivers, power and influence tilted decidedly in the direction of shōyu brewers, who were able thereafter to exercise their will without serious challenge for nearly half a century. But until then, mutual interests and the complementary nature of employment and residence in Noda permitted the successful growth of both the community and its major industry—farming.

Farms and Factories in Nineteenth-Century Japan

Japan's rural-centered industrialization allowed it to develop economically during the nineteenth century and to grow strong politically without serious disruption of the established social fabric. Production was expanded through the use of traditional methods of operation and traditional sources of manpower. Even so, the gains in productivity were considerable.

The leadership in establishing industries continued to come from entrepreneurial families. Such families had learned to maintain and even diversify their holdings by the judicious use of intermarriage, adoption, and household dispersion as well as by household discipline, which is evidenced in family constitutions and in the patterns of household formation. Bantō families, which provided a secondary source of permanent, experienced, and loyal employees, normally performed a number of clerical and supervisory roles for the families they served. The labor requirements for such enterprises, both in terms of amount and level of skill, could be handled either formally within the community through labor recruiters or informally through the widespread use of casual labor. Production itself, although time-consuming in terms of requirements for preparation and fermentation, and expensive in terms of the cost of plant and equipment, was not overly complicated in a technical sense (ignoring its biochemical complexity) and did not demand great knowledge (except perhaps from the brewmaster). Experience more than know-how was needed, and as long as the growth of cities and city systems provided a market, men with the necessary experience and skill to manage as well as manufacture were found.

The geographical location of the Noda shōyu industry was advantageous, since ships leaving Noda by way of the Edo River could reach Edo in one day. Tokyo was and is the largest consumer market in the country. In addition, the highly specialized division of labor there and in the surrounding Tokyo Plain meant that areas producing specialized goods for sale depended, in turn, on the specialized manufactures of other areas. Noda's advantage in transportation and in regional and local economic specialization allowed its shōyu industry to prosper. Other Tokyo-area soy sauce manufacturers, such as Yamasa and Higeta in Chōshi, had similar advantages, but they were less well located for shipping to Tokyo and for access to the highly specialized local economies surrounding that city. (Shipping time to Tokyo from Chōshi, for example, averaged five to seven days as compared to one day from Noda.)

Although Noda became the leading district for shōyu manufacture in the nineteenth century, it would be a mistake to assume that the industry had an overwhelming importance for the community. Farming remained the most important occupation until the early twentieth century, and the agricultural cycle rather than the monochromatic character of manufacturing defined the pace and rhythms of local life.

This predominance of farming was based on more than a simple tally of how many labored at which tasks. Regardless of the absolute numbers of workers in the breweries, many were temporary and casual, and few of the others remained even three years. The most direct connection between industry and town was not factory employment but informal arrangements between breweries and locals, which supplied almost everything from provisions for factory workers to sacks for separating soy sauce from lees. The indirectness of this relationship was related to the piecemeal nature of manufacturing technology. The stages of shōyu production were mostly unconnected and unmechanized; each was relatively labor-intensive, involving hauling, dragging, and carrying.

The supervision of workers in the breweries was entrusted to local specialists in the recruiting and hiring of labor and to shop-floor specialists in the disposition of labor in the manufacturing process. The entrepreneurs who established the breweries and invested in the plant and equipment to operate the breweries were surprisingly uninvolved in their creations. Ownership was disassociated from control of the workplace; control, such as it was, remained decentralized in the autonomous and independent factories. Even if an entrepreneur owned several factories there was little apparent cooperation and coordination among them.

For all these reasons—the size and impermanence of the work force, the piecemeal character of technology, the disassociation of ownership from control in manufacturing—community and industry were distinct. The community was more of an agricultural settlement than industrial town in spirit and in activity, and this would remain true until the wrenching discontinuity of World War I was felt across the land and around the world.

2.

Clan and Cartel
In Meiji Japan

THE HISTORY of industrial development in Japan is often characterized as derivative; it is charged that Japan imitated, copied or, at the very least, followed the Western world. In fact, although Japan's modern economic development began later than that of Great Britain, the United States, and France, all of which are thought to have begun industrialization well before 1870, it was nearly simultaneous with that of Germany and probably preceded that of Italy and Sweden. It would be more accurate, therefore, to characterize Japan as one of the later-developing nations.

There is one area in which the Japanese cannot be said to have been "late" at all. The growth of cartelization of Japanese industry began in the 1880s, concurrently with similar movements in the United States, Great Britain, and Germany. Cartelization represented to all these countries a universal solution to the market's failure to deal with problems of oversupply, pricing, and excessive competition among and within enterprises. That so many industries adopted this solution bears witness to its historical attractiveness, just as the large number of cartels today indicates its continuing utility.

Shōyu manufacturing in Noda was one of the first industries to be cartelized in Japan; it was also one of the first to abandon this method of organization for the more controlled and centralized corporate form in the early twentieth century. The Noda soy sauce brewers initiated both moves in response to changing market and technological opportunities. In the Meiji Period (1868–1912), they sought through a combination of local brewers to outproduce and outsell all other makers of soy sauce in the Tokyo area. Although they failed to accomplish this, they managed to control perhaps 5 to 10 percent—the largest single share—of the Tokyo market. In the Taishō Period (1912–1925), Noda brewers forged ahead with price and brand competition, which ultimately led to the undermining of their cartel and to the substitution of a new corporate structure to harness the competitive advantages inherent in mass production and distribution.

A description of the conditions that led to cartelization and the combination of brewers in manufacturing associations as the preferred form of organization at one point in history, and to incorporation and company rivalry at another time, illuminates much of the character of economic development in Japan at the turn of the twentieth century. Economic forces are only part of the story. Just as the process of cartelization altered the methods of shōyu manufacture, so too did cartelization affect the character of the families that owned and operated soy sauce breweries and their relationships to each other as well as to their community.

Cartelization ushered in a new social force in the countryside, reducing the importance of the traditional family-centered basis of social action. In its place, a new sense of community was created among shōyu manufacturers and their suppliers that was more open than the private world of family-based breweries but less public than the bureaucratic character of a joint-stock corporation. This cartel was a loose partnership, but one in which the Noda brewers developed a public or, at least a community, focus and agenda. The role the cartel played in community and charitable causes, for example, extended far beyond that of any individual brewing family. The history of the Noda Shōyu Manufacturers' Association, therefore, is a history not only of economic organization but also of social purpose and community involvement. It shows the total contribution of rural entrepreneurship to Japan's modernization.

Clan and Cartel in the Meiji Period

Before the establishment of a formal cartel in Noda in 1887 and its recognition by the governor of Chiba Prefecture in the same year, combinations of manufacturers had existed in Noda in various forms. A guild of shōyu manufacturers had been established as early as 1781, for example. At the same time, information and capital had been pooled among branches of the Mogi family, in particular, which constituted the basis for the eventual growth of the shōyu industry in Noda. Pooling within related families, on the one hand, and combining with unrelated families in guilds, on the other, provided clear precedent for the formal cartelization that occurred in 1887. Indeed as late as 1881 a shōyu sales company was established by a score of soy sauce brewers from Noda for their mutual benefit.

Formal agreements may follow informal ones logically, but they may also fail to do so historically for any number of reasons. Genealogical relatedness does not ensure economic cooperation, nor does geographical proximity. Too often one family's gain in production know-how or market share was another family's loss. Competition could be modulated but not eliminated by cooperation among kinsmen, and since the family was the unit of ownership and control in production, the degree of relatedness between families tended to govern the degree of cooperation in manufacturing. Families directly linked through branching and indirectly linked through marriage were more likely to pool information and resources than those not so bound. Head families and branch families in the same line could be expected to cooperate. The striking increase in the number of marriages, adoptions, and branchings within the Mogi and Takanashi families beginning in the late eighteenth century was directly linked to the need to pool resources among families in the development of the shōyu industry in Noda. Family growth and enterprise development were one and the same as long as the families of brewers could maintain a consensus in method, commitment, and purpose.

The transition from informal cooperation based on biological and genealogical relatedness to formal cooperation based on geographical and industrial ties was a major one—and one that took a competitive challenge to forge. Cartelization altered the cozy convenience of interfamily alliances by forcing together a large number of unrelated or weakly related families. Interfamily as well as intrafamily sharing became a requirement of participation in the Noda Shōyu Manufacturers' Association, although the sharing remained confined to matters external to the production process. The operation of individual breweries remained the concern of a single family, or perhaps of several quite closely related families that shared investment in plant and equipment. After 1887 cartel agreements set wage rates, the amount of raw material purchases and the prices paid for them, shipping schedules, and, most important, the prices of finished goods. But the cartel purposely avoided the pooling of production techniques and personnel. These were the prerogatives of individual brewers, to be shared, if at all, more in private among kinsmen than in public among associates.

The inauguration of a manufacturers' cartel in Noda in 1887 ushered in a new social and economic pact for Noda and its environs. The Association, while relying on the institutions of the old order, especially local families of influence, supplanted such traditional sources of authority and power by creating a suprafamilial group of local notables whose vision was not limited by genealogical ties and traditions. Since the cartel in its heyday could command the influence of twenty-two families of brewers in a dozen or more communities, its effect on local community life and economic conditions was far greater than that which a smaller number of close kinsmen could muster.

The advantages of cartel organization were obvious in late-nineteenth-century Japan. The number of manufacturers acting together could be readily enlarged. At a time when economies of scale in manufacture were unknown, the logical way of extending capacity, assuming such a need, was to increase the number of producers rather than the size of individual production facilities. But the process of institutionalizing more numerous and more distant brewers into an association had some unexpected consequences in view of the family's primacy as the basic, perhaps sole, institution of social and economic organization in the countryside.

As the cartel began to displace the family as the focus of economic organization and activity, it became clear, probably for the first time, that kinship and economics were distinct and distinguishable. Economic concerns could be removed from the context of kinship and family; costs, prices, and markets became public matters of cartel discussion and deliberation. Previously they had been issues to be settled in private, within a family or at family councils. After 1887 they became public business—not in the sense that decisions were made democratically or even openly, but in the sense that records were kept, issues were debated, attendance and dues were tallied. Moreover, chronic violators of cartel policy were reported to the press for public notoriety and censure (a technique of governance not commonly found in the cartels of other countries). Decisions to buy from this broker, to ship with that carrier, and to rely on a particular vendor were increasingly separated from marriage ties, descent lines, and family association. Considerations of "simple" cost displaced more complex choices of cost confused by kinship.

The separation of kinship and economics—one that proceeded gradually and continues in Noda today—did not free the cartel's economic choices from social significance. As the cartel associates grew in number, mostly by the addition of manufacturers unrelated to the dominant Mogi-Takanashi lineage group, the social and geographical borders of the cartel widened and its economic force swelled. Of the twenty-two brewers who belonged at one time or another to the association, eleven (or half) were not related to the Mogis and Takanashis; few in this group came close to producing as much shōyu as the more prosperous Mogi and Takanashi members. In total production they did not equal even the combined production of the big three—Mogi Shichirōuemon, Mogi Saheiji, and Takanashi Hyōzaemon. Nevertheless, the eleven belonged to the same organization, and their voice and concerns had to be integrated into a body that reached decisions by consensus.

Clearly, kinship alone could not constitute a basis for shared agreement in a group so unrelated not only by genealogy but also by differences in the size and sophistication of their manufacturing. Kinship was not ignored, but it no longer provided the absolute, or even the exclusive, prerequisite for joint action. The economic interests of a group of manufacturers with common residence and occupation, but without common descent, became the rallying point for consensus. Economies of scale in manufacture were not yet important, but economies of scale in shipping and purchasing were. With increasing uncertainty in the hurly-burly commodity market for bulk grains during the 1880s, these "other economies" offered powerful incentives for cooperation.

The value of economies in shipping and purchasing became manifest by the 1880s and 1890s, when the cartel turned increasingly to new foreign sources of supply, buying large lots of English and German salt and of Manchurian and Korean soybeans. Cooperative buying soon became an even more important aspect of the cartel's activities when not only the raw materials for production but also the fuel (coal) for manufacture came into Noda by bulk orders let by the cartel. The economic activities of the brewers' association became more complex and demanded more capital after 1900, as the cartel invested in new plant, equipment, and infrastructure; a railroad, a research and development laboratory, and new manufacturing equipment required more money and involvement from the cartel members than probably any of them would have foreseen and welcomed a decade earlier. In short, what had begun as a loose association of owner-brewers became by the second decade of the twentieth century a rather tight cartel. This expanded economic and managerial role would lead ultimately to a new course of social involvement that would radically alter the relationships among the shōyu brewers themselves, their institutionalized manufacturing activities, and the town and community where they lived and worked.

Government-Regulated Markets

In spite of the precedent for a cartel to be found in the formation of a shōyu manufacturing guild and in interfamily pooling, both of which occurred in Noda by the late eighteenth century, cartelization was prefigured more by what was happening outside Noda after the mid-seventeenth century than by what was occurring in the community a century later. Changes in the government-regulated marketplace, more than anything else, were to disrupt the family traditions of shōyu manufacture in Noda.

Government control of merchants and markets has a long history in Japan. Certainly by the time the country was emerging from several centuries of civil war in the late 1500s, government licensing of the marketplace and of those who traded there was commonplace. *Za* and *kabu nakama* (guild and guildlike associations) appear in the literature of Japanese economic history as early as the eleventh century.[1] The guild, like the cartel, has been a basic form of economic and business organization in Japan as well as in the West. Given the long history of such institutions, the difficulties lay in enforcing the consequences of government regulation rather than in instilling the concepts of government control. As early as 1659 the fledgling Tokugawa shogunate or central government in Edo required city merchants to be licensed, and in 1673 the Sendai domain (*han*), one of the several hundred local demesnes, established a tobacco monopoly with licensed vendors reporting sales to government officials. Following Sendai's lead, by the end of the seventeenth century practically every domain had established government licensing requirements for either merchants or merchandise. Government controls and regulations were constantly changing, however, and, as a result, were burdensome to keep up with; in the countryside, they could be occasionally, sometimes flagrantly, ignored, but in the cities rules were less easily circumvented.

In 1721 there was a major reorganization of the tonya system in Edo (Tokyo). Tonya were government-licensed middlemen who handled products coming into the city from the point of embarcation to their distribution in thousands of neighborhood stalls and shops. The shogunate established a structure whereby ten guild groups controlled most of the distribution and sales of commercial goods in that vast city. Guilds were specialized with regard to the kind of products they handled, and shōyu along with vinegar and sake were distributed by the alcohol products guild.

Distributors (tonya) handled two sorts of products: those they took on consignment and those they bought and branded themselves. Makers of the former benefited from the services the tonya provided— the distribution network, knowledge of the market, and maintenance of inventory—but they paid for these services by a markup on their product, a loss of control over pricing, and a general inability to market their own products as they saw fit. In 1834, in a move designed to remove the drawbacks but still retain the benefits of the tonya system, Mogi Shichirōuemon and Takanashi Hyōzaemon bought 450 *ryō* worth of shares in the Okugawa Tonya in Edo. Unfortunately they could not capitalize on this maneuver for long because the shogunate disbanded the tonya system in 1841, thereby deregulating the market and causing prices to escalate rapidly. Ten years later, however, as a result of mounting economic and political unrest, the shogunate reversed itself, reimposing market controls and reestablishing the tonya system.[2]

Noda Brewers Assert Themselves

Government regulation was unreliable and, worse yet, unpredictable. If producers were to maintain and improve their markets, they would have to do so on their own. From the 1840s to the 1850s, as a result of the efforts of local shōyu makers, production in Noda rose one-half, from a level of 1,047,000 gallons to an impressive 1,530,000 gallons, and in the late 1860s production even peaked for a time at over 2,000,000 gallons. Increased production did not necessarily bring increased access to the market, however, and the Noda brewers grew concerned lest they be inundated in a sea of their own soy sauce.

In 1871 the tonya merchants who handled the shōyu shipped into Tokyo by river and those who handled the road traffic decided to combine with another distribution group, the Shiba-Kanda Shōyu Associates, to form the "River-Road" Shōyu Tonya. As a result of their amalgamation, they held nearly monopolistic control over the Tokyo shōyu market. The Noda brewers became anxious at this development since their expanding production could be easily blocked from sale and distribution in Tokyo by the power of the combined group. Mogi Shichirōuemon decided to secure his own access to the Tokyo market by marrying his second son, Chōbei, into the Nakano family in Tokyo, a family not coincidentally holding vested rights in the river-road shōyu distribution tonya.

While Shichirōuemon pursued this traditional stratagem of inter-family marriage alliance, Mogi Saheiji followed another course to guarantee market access. In 1838, in a rather unusual move for the time, he petitioned for and received central government registration of the brand name Kikkoman and unknowingly began what would become a century-long crusade for brand recognition of his family's flagship shōyu, Kikkoman. Although the Mogi Saheiji family has produced other shōyu brands, Kikkoman was the pride of the family, its private label. When written longhand in Japanese characters, the brand name Kikkoman is composed of three characters: *ki*, the character for "tortoise," meaning good luck and longevity in Chinese and Japanese folklore; *ko* means "first-rate"; and *man* suggests "ten thousand" or forever. *Kikko* also means octagon, so the brand name is often written as an octagon with the character for "ten thousand" or *man* written inside the octagon.

In 1872 and 1873, shortly after the Meiji Restoration of 1868, Mogi Saheiji entered Kikkoman in two world's fairs, the first held in Amsterdam and the second in Austria. Kikkoman was awarded a letter of commendation for excellence at the Austrian fair, and following this, Mogi Saheiji redoubled his efforts to promote the brand. In 1877 Kik-

koman received a second-place medal at the All-Japan Industry Promotion Fair, and in 1879 it was registered in California as a legally recognized brand name, a move that predated the same legal protection in
Japan by six years! Finally, in the 1880s, Saheiji's efforts paid off. In
1881 Kikkoman was accorded a first-place medal in the All-Japan Industry Promotion Fair, and in 1883 Kikkoman achieved international
recognition with the award of a gold medal at the World's Fair in Amsterdam. Kikkoman's national and international reputation created demand, which was translated into higher prices in the marketplace—
higher even than the prices paid for other quality brands from Noda.[3]
Saheiji had to send off to Paris for ornate gold labels to distinguish the
true Kikkoman from its imitators, and he raised exports, especially to
California and Hawaii, where the kegs of Kikkoman were particularly
prized by the increasing number of Japanese immigrants.

Unlike Mogi Shichirōuemon or Mogi Saheiji, Takanashi Hyōzaemon, the other major brewer in Noda, did not have to initiate a proposal for marriage or dispatch products overseas in order to secure a
market outlet for his shōyu. The Takanashi family in Noda had diversified in Tokyo warehousing and wholesaling long before. In the eighteenth century, just as the Edo tonya system was taking its final form,
Takanashi Hyōzaemon XXVI had sent his third son, Chōbei, to Edo to
marry into the family of Omi Nizaburō, a shōyu tonya. Shortly thereafter, the relationship was cemented further by a series of exchanges of
sons and daughters for marriage and adoptions in the interest of maintaining the connection between manufacturing and marketing. By the
late eighteenth century Omi Nizaburō had changed surnames, becoming Takanashi Nizaburō. So when the river-road shōyu tonya group
formed in Tokyo in 1871, Takanashi Hyōzaemon could remain com-
placent, for his kinsman Takanashi Nizaburō was one of its twenty-two
charter members.[4]

The three major brewers in Noda had chosen alternative routes to
secure access to the Tokyo market. Whatever optimism they felt for the
continued sales of their products proved unwarranted, however, as
family ties came into conflict with organizational controls. In 1879 the
river-road group reorganized according to the latest government requirements, calling itself the Tokyo Shōyu Tonya. It issued a detailed
22-article covenant by which the twenty-two members of the association were bound to handle only tonya-branded merchandise or the
products of manufacturers who were willing to contract exclusively
with the association and to consign goods entirely according to the
tonya's dictates.[5]

The three Noda principals were understandably distressed. Each depended on the Tokyo market for most of his sales, even though Mogi

Shichirōuemon sold about 40 percent of his output in the highly commercialized and occupationally specialized countryside to the northeast and northwest of Tokyo. If prices and sales volume in Tokyo were to be entirely out of the hands of the major brewers in Noda, the largest producers in Japan, then there were no guarantees that returns would justify the investment in larger plants, better equipment, and more numerous workers—an investment to which they had begun individually to commit themselves from the middle of the nineteenth century.

The Noda soy sauce brewers responded by establishing the Tokyo Shōyu Company on February 12, 1881, with a founding declaration that announced, in part, "their right to protect the usurpation of their commercial rights by the Tokyo Shōyu Tonya Association." With an initial capitalization of 100,000 yen, a new building in the commercial warehouse district of Tokyo, and a membership of fourteen manufacturers (half of whom were from Noda), the Tokyo Shōyu Company set out to displace the tonya monopoly on the sale and distribution of shōyu.[6] Their efforts proved quite costly. Encouraging local retailers to accept goods not provided by their normal suppliers required both oratorical and monetary persuasion. Convincing customers to ask for certain brands by name entailed considerable advertising expense. Mogi Saheiji promoted the Kikkoman brand by sponsoring professional sumō wrestlers and storytellers as well as by having hundreds of paper lanterns and umbrellas embossed with its trademark. (These were said to have been popular in the red-light districts of Tokyo.)

Such advertising and product promotion might be viewed as an attempt to carry out a sort of minor marketing revolution wherein manufacturers attempted to handle their own distribution and to create consumer loyalty through brand identification. Unfortunately, all revolutions, however minor, are costly, and the Tokyo Shōyu Company, initially capitalized at 100,000 yen, spent fully half of that amount in just ten years pushing its wares. So much was being spent on product promotion, in fact, that the brewers who backed the company were in danger of not having enough cash to buy the raw materials to make next year's moromi.

There were compelling economic reasons for the Noda brewers to continue their attempts to gain independent access to the Tokyo market. The fall in the price index for shōyu during this period of the so-called Matsukata deflation (1881–1885) was severe. The classical response to falling prices is to limit supply, and this can be best achieved through agreements among manufacturers to limit output. Thus, the economic incentives driving the Noda brewers were twofold: to guarantee markets in a period when supply was being curtailed, and to keep marginal returns above marginal costs by controlling the prices at which their product sold. For the price index for shōyu between 1880 and 1893, see table 2.

Economic difficulties were not the only obstacles facing the Noda associates. The family alliances that crisscrossed between the Tokyo Shōyu Company and the Tokyo Shōyu Tonya Group were under great strain. Organizational secessions and defections were common. Families stopped speaking to each other, and passions that underlay years of close association erupted. The contest was bitter because the prize was considerable. Whether the power of the Noda manufacturers, who as a group probably produced as much as a tenth of the shōyu consumed in the Tokyo area, would undermine the extremely well-entrenched and long-established tonya distributors was uncertain, and as one group gained momentum or as the other improved its share, undecided contestants seesawed back and forth between rival camps.

The issues dividing the two groups involved more than control of the market, although this was the major one. A good many differences in methods of operation and finance existed as well. The following items,

TABLE 2. Base price and price index for shōyu, 1879–1893 (average price per *koku* in Tokyo).

Year	Price in yen	Price index
1879	12.31	100.00
1880	13.30	108.04
1881	15.02	122.01
1882	14.83	120.47
1883	13.39	108.77
1884	12.55	101.95
1885	10.61	86.19
1886	9.73	79.04
1887	9.62	78.15
1888	10.54	85.62
1889	10.76	87.41
1890	9.60	77.99
1891	10.72	87.08
1892	10.08	81.88
1893	9.48	76.97

Source: Kazushi Ohkawa et al., *Estimates of Long-Term Economic Statistics of Japan Since 1868—Prices*, vol. 8 (Tokyo: Tōyō Keizai Shinpōsha, 1967), pp. 138–139.

which summarize some of the operating rules and regulations of the Tokyo Shōyu Company, were in conspicuous contrast to the normal operations of the Tokyo Shōyu Tonya Association. (My comments are italicized.)

Up to 70 percent of the value of goods on deposit could be borrowed by makers; this would become effective from the first of the month after the goods were deposited in Tokyo.

The Tokyo Shōyu Company would pay the cost of transporting the goods to Tokyo, if the manufacturer was unable to do so. The transportation costs would be deducted from the sales receipts due the maker.

Monthly balances were taken and annual statements prepared by the company. Anyone with an interest in the company, that is, anyone who dealt through it and therefore owned shares in it, could inspect the books at any time. [*This was in vivid contrast to the closed and secret accounting of the tonya association.*]

Profits were distributed according to who owned how many shares in the company; books could be investigated to determine what the appropriate payout to shareholders would be. [*This was impossible to do with the tonya association.*]

The customary prohibition that prevented makers from borrowing against goods on deposit was overturned, and thus a major problem between makers and distributors was eliminated, namely, that the twice-a-year payout schedule of the tonya left makers in a poor cash flow position for most of the year.

The Tokyo Shōyu Company charged a flat 5 percent fee against sales for its services, whereas the tonya charged 5 percent for handling and distribution, 3 percent for storage (both of these charges were levied against sales), and 0.85-sen-per-barrel fee for loading and unloading, regardless of sales. [*In sum, the tonya charged nearly twice as much as the company for essentially similar services.*]

Tonya would lend money to makers for the purchase of raw materials, but they charged interest, or, in other words, gave a discount against the loan for the goods; this was in addition to other fees for handling finished goods. The company, by contrast, would not lend for raw material purchases, although it would advance up to 70 percent of the value of goods on deposit without interest charges.

The return of damaged or unsold goods to makers from distributors appears to have been a constant problem whereas, in the company, since makers were the company shareholders, these sorts of problems were minimized.[7]

The differences in methods of operation between the tonya association and the company were substantial. Each side stood to lose or gain a great deal according to the failure or success of the rival organization.

Three events that occurred during the years 1888 to 1890 decided the contest. In November 1888 the Tokyo Shōyu Association concluded a new comprehensive agreement that imposed severe penalties on manufacturers as well as distributors who associated with the Tokyo Shōyu Company. Severe organizational restraints were required because since 1881 the tonya association had seen the number of its member distributors drop from twenty-two to fifteen. The shoring up of organizational defenses on one side was matched by climatic misfortune on the other side. In 1889, during the late spring monsoon rains, the warehouse holding most of the inventory of the Tokyo Shōyu Company flooded, deluging the last assets of a company struggling to stay solvent in the face of ridiculously high advertising costs relative to sales income. The loss of inventory could not have happened at a worse time. The cost of raw materials—soybeans, wheat, and salt—had risen rapidly since 1888. In the face of the distribution barriers to their continued operation, the disastrous loss of inventory, and prohibitively high cost of getting back into production with inflated raw material costs, the Tokyo Shōyu Company declared bankruptcy in the fall of 1889.[8]

Its members then became part of the All-Kantō Shōyu Manufacturers' Union, which joined with the Tokyo Shōyu Tonya Association in 1890 to conclude a comprehensive manufacturing and marketing agreement that was to stabilize the relationship between makers and distributors for the next two decades. By the new agreement, the commission on consignment sales was fixed at 5 percent, and prior consultation was required between makers and distributors regarding the price and amount of goods to be shipped to Tokyo.[9] In spite of these incentives, the agreement was a costly failure for the brewers from Noda. They had spent the better part of 150,000 yen to break with the traditional tonya system, and in the end they still lacked direct access to the Tokyo market. Nevertheless, they had achieved something valuable: a sense of purpose and a decade of concerted action, which eroded the individualistic patterns of ownership and management of the past. Even after the disastrous 1880s, they continued to carry on as a group, recognizing the benefits of coordinated effort over independence and individuality. In 1887 a cartel of shōyu brewers was founded in Noda. This institution provided the foundation for the emergence and development of a modern shōyu industry with modern management methods.

The Noda Shōyu Manufacturers' Association

In the course of the Noda associates' efforts to link production with distribution, they turned to a classic solution—a cartel—as a means of controlling the emerging problem of oversupply. In fact, a cartel did more than that: it stabilized price, controlled supply, and guaranteed markets. But at the same time, the costs of concerted action and cartelization were substantial. The Noda brewers, as opposed to others in the Noda cartel, realized that participation in a producers' cartel would prevent them from gaining market share by taking full advantage of their strengths: their geographic advantage over their closest rivals, the Chōshi brewers, and their larger group of kinsmen and, therefore, comparative advantage in "pooling." Yet, for the time being, cartelization was beneficial because barriers to entry on the manufacturing side were still relatively minor, and until the maturing sophistication in production technology could be fully utilized in new factories, marginal producers were not at a clear disadvantage in relation to larger brewers. Better production methods and integration of these into more efficient operations would not come until the turn of the century. So, until differentiation in manufacturing efficiencies appeared, it was better to belong to a cartel where not only was supply controlled, but access to market was guaranteed as well.

Considerations such as these led to the formation of the Noda Shōyu Brewers' or Manufacturers' Association (Noda Shōyu Jōzō Kumiai) in 1887. Its structure and purpose were set forth in the articles of association (Appendix C). Because the Association was not empowered to do a great deal in the beginning, it was clearly envisioned as an intermediary between the individual brewers and the external agents, principally the tonya. It could bar from employment workers deemed undesirable (articles 8 and 9), it could collect dues from members (article 28), and it could penalize certain kinds of dishonesty (article 32) and absence (article 34). But for the early years it would be more revealing to talk about what the Association could not do rather than what it could do.

In the beginning the cartel was viewed as an institutional device to share information and to facilitate the organization and operation of individually owned breweries. In this purpose it duplicated the pooling among families that had characterized shōyu manufacture to Noda since the eighteenth century—although it probably did so more efficiently and thoroughly. Yet, with time, pooling information became secondary to coordinating information and acting upon such shared knowledge. This, in turn, required new involvement with the community, such as in the creation of local transportation and credit facilities, without which the cartel's coordinated avenues of action had little meaning. Economic necessity, in this case as in so many others, led to social action and community involvement.

A vivid illustration of the benefits of cartelization appeared in 1890, the year of initial agreement between makers and marketers of shōyu. Problems of oversupply and declining prices were so severe that the Tokyo market was chaotic. In order to stabilize prices and restore confidence to consumers, the Tokyo Shōyu Tonya recommended a 50 percent reduction in shipments of shōyu to Tokyo. The actual reduction for the Noda group was 40 percent; but in view of the high cost of raw materials, a problem that had bothered all producers since 1888, it was a drastic cutback in an era when production in Noda had been growing for most of the decade.[10]

The self-imposed controls in 1890, from the manufacturing as well as marketing side, stabilized prices and restored consumer confidence within the year. By 1891 cartel production was up 6 percent, and by 1892 the gain in Noda was 15 percent. The rewards of restraint were obvious, but the mechanisms to ensure restraint were not. Even though the Tonya Association might suggest a 50 percent reduction in shipments to Tokyo, oversupply could not be controlled unless there was effective mechanism to implement and enforce that restriction. Restraint and reduced output could be effectively enforced only if an institutional arrangement existed to monitor and legitimate cooperative manufacturing. In Tokyo the monopolistic control of the market provided by the Tonya Association maintained price and market control; the need for such coordination in the countryside sustained the life of the Noda Shōyu Brewers' Association.

Cartel and Costs

The cartel provided a classic solution to problems of erratic market demand and prices: the restriction of output or supply. This of course occurred naturally to the extent that the high cost of raw materials and the declining share of the shōyu market that the Noda association experienced between 1888 and 1890 prevented the brewers from maintaining production at previous levels. But cutting the costs of production by reducing output was only one of several cost-cutting options available to the cartel. Actually output was not lowered as much as the Tokyo Shōyu Tonya Association would have liked. The association requested a 50 percent reduction in Noda soy sauce production for 1890, although, in fact, production fell only 40 percent. The difference between these figures was considerable: almost half a million gallons (497,280 gallons). In truth, shipments to Tokyo were halved, even if production was not, because the Noda associates were able to expand the flow of their products to the highly commercialized regions northeast and northwest of Tokyo, which included parts of Chiba, Ibaragi, Saitama, and Gumma prefectures. Traditionally these areas received from one-fifth to one-third of Noda's shōyu production. In 1893, for example, 35 percent of Noda production was not directed to Tokyo but else-where—to the vast stretches of the Tokyo Plain radiating out from the concentrated population centers of the bay, or to Hokkaido, one of the most rapidly growing markets in the late nineteenth century.[11]

In spite of the efforts to redirect some of the flow of Noda shōyu away from Tokyo, the cartel could do little more than accept an abso-lute fall of 40 percent in product. With access to the principal market cut off by the tonya association, the opportunity to recoup its share by undercutting competitors was not even available. The nature of shōyu manufacture left little doubt as to where the cost reductions would have to occur: raw material and labor expenses were the only possibilities. Too great a reduction in raw material purchases would result in dimin-ished production at some point in the future, when market prospects were expected to improve. This left labor costs as the main area in which reductions would have to occur.

The fluctuation of wages with productivity and demand is a marked feature of the cost structure of shōyu manufacture in Noda during the cartel era. As prices fell, so did wages, and as prices improved, wages climbed. Adjustments to wages were made frequently—as often as every two months in some years. Because market demand was erratic, and because cartel management had not yet come to the point of trying to predict and maintain demand, workers were often and unilaterally made aware of fluctuations in price and demand. This was not a scheme to exploit workers. Rather, wages followed total output and prices; since these proved uncertain, so did compensation.[12]

Fortunately for workers their wages rose steadily, on occasion even spectacularly, during the three decades of cartel history in Noda. Im-pressive gains in productivity can be credited for this. (A lag in wage improvement following a rise in productivity was sometimes discern-ible when the two were graphed side by side, but this might be ex-pected as a result of a gap in translating knowledge into action.) Given the relation between wages and prices, the workers could have suffered far more, but the growing market for shōyu caused wage reductions to be, on the whole, temporary. Once demand improved, the market moved steadily upward with only momentary drops in production. From 1890 to 1916 Noda production increased fivefold, achieving a compound annual rate of growth of 13 percent. Thus, continuing de-mand resulted in increasing productivity and improving wages (see fig-ure 4 and table 3).

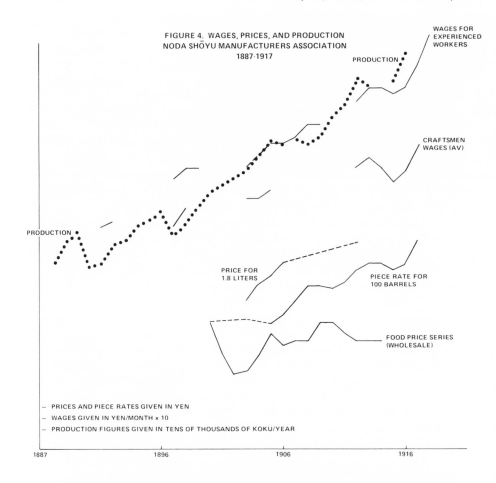

FIGURE 4. WAGES, PRICES, AND PRODUCTION
NODA SHŌYU MANUFACTURERS ASSOCIATION
1887-1917

WAGES FOR EXPERIENCED WORKERS

PRODUCTION

CRAFTSMEN WAGES (AV)

PRODUCTION

PRICE FOR 1.8 LITERS

PIECE RATE FOR 100 BARRELS

FOOD PRICE SERIES (WHOLESALE)

— PRICES AND PIECE RATES GIVEN IN YEN
— WAGES GIVEN IN YEN/MONTH x 10
— PRODUCTION FIGURES GIVEN IN TENS OF THOUSANDS OF KOKU/YEAR

1887   1896   1906   1916

All did not share equally in the cartel's success. Workers in factories were compensated at a higher rate than the artisans employed there. Although the wages of artisans varied according to their trade, in aggregate their wages ranged between one-quarter and one-third less than those of experienced factory hands, who enjoyed an additional material advantage in the form of room and board at the brewery dormitories for single workers. Perhaps this increased compensation served to lure farm boys into the factory, as compared, say, to the attraction of being an independent stonemason.

The cartel's growth in output suggests that participation in a manufacturing association did not necessarily impede growth. Although production was occasionally restricted, for the most part it climbed steadily and surely over the years. Various mechanical improvements in product flow and processing, discussed in Chapter 1, began to appear in the last two decades of the nineteenth century. They were, for the most part, minor and unrelated, since the steps of production remained discontinuous and labor-intensive. Moreover, the seasonal pattern of shōyu manufacture was not completely broken until the years between the Sino-Japanese (1894–95) and Russo-Japanese (1904–05) conflicts when Japanese industrialization accelerated noticeably. Although continuous product flow and process technology had not yet been conceived, room for improvement in the batch technology and barely mechanized production of the late nineteenth century was considerable. Within the context of such limited horizons, productivity and capacity continued to grow in Noda.

Raw material costs created several interrelated problems for the shōyu makers. Where to buy increasingly large quantities of good quality materials was the first; how to get these back to Noda, the second. In the end the solution to both was the same, but initially the acquisition of materials and their movement were conceptualized as separate and distinct issues. Take coal, for instance. As the production line converted from wood to coal as a fuel to fire boilers and steamers, local sources of firewood had to give way to more distant sources of coal. The transportation of coal proved discouragingly difficult. Not only did it have to be brought from a distance, but it was carried awkwardly—in stevedore-sized sacks, by canal and river boat. Two separate entries in cartel accounts in 1897 for 6,500 tons of coal plus expenses indicate that the amount purchased at one time was considerable and that 15 percent had to be added to the basic cost of the coal to cover its transportation to Noda.[13]

Most of the other raw materials for production were being imported by the turn of the century. Soybeans and salt, in particular, were imported in large quantities. In 1897 twice as much foreign (from England, Germany, and China) as domestic salt was used (821,000 bushels vs. 408,128 bushels), and the importation of soybeans from China and Korea became substantial after the Sino-Japanese War of 1894–95.[14] The Noda soy sauce cartel was quick to take advantage of the newly opened and nearby Chinese and Korean markets to purchase an ever-growing amount of the raw materials needed for manufacture. But because foreign supplies were generally more expensive, although of higher quality, and because they had farther to travel (adding to the cost), their use was economical only if large amounts were purchased and shipped together. The first Sino-Japanese War supplied a momentary solution to the problems of raw material availability as Manchuria and Korea became the main sources of supplies. The Russo-Japanese War, however, brought on a formidable challenge: the appearance of a maverick entrepreneur named Suzuki who sought to dominate the soy

TABLE 3. Individual and cartel production totals, 1887–1916 (kiloliters[a]).

Name	1887	1888	1889	1890	1891	1892	1893	1894	1895	1896	1897	1898	1899
Mogi Shichirōuemon	1209	1526	1558	1314	1737	1714	1831	2330	2249	2435	2285	2482	3444
Mogi Saheiji	784	965	1034	828	629	1055	1029	1116	1092	1289	900	1201	1512
Takanashi Hyōzaemon	1395	1404	1438	785	1048	1062	948	1072	1355	1340	1134	1341	1462
Mogi Fusagorō	327	495	536	551	568	700	739	860	970	1117	1165	1190	1322
Mogi Shichizaemon	510	638	720	583	643	726	849	886	922	945	975	986	1142
Yamashita Heibei	318	316	655	574	536	617	727	756	767	873	899	763	766
Mogi Yūuemon	171	203	134	119	162	163	167	179	198	257	216	279	344
Tobe Yoshirō	215	296	337	234	217	320	285	285	300	296	273	307	272
Yamashita Tomisaburō	—	—	—	—	—	—	—	—	—	—	—	—	—
Mogi Keizaburō	—	—	—	—	—	—	—	—	—	—	—	—	—
Takanashi Kōuemon	513	642	680	135	183	—	—	—	—	—	—	—	—
Takanashi Shuzō	173	183	92	24	—	—	—	—	—	—	—	—	—
Mogi Rihei	216	315	361	281	99	367	285	331	293	276	298	462	—
Akimoto Sanuemon	183	260	355	217	211	238	359	370	355	387	—	—	—
Horikiri Monjirō	377	472	618	330	210	429	531	478	360	451	—	—	—
Ishikawa Niheiji	270	314	316	315	328	313	318	321	328	358	312	289	295
Asami Heibei	182	142	194	136	144	149	146	113	162	126	—	—	—
Shimamura Katsusaburō	43	54	50	—	—	—	—	—	—	—	—	—	—
Takeuchi Kiyosaburō	112	81	62	141	180	144	162	176	131	134	—	—	—
Iwasaki Kiyoshichi	—	—	—	—	—	—	—	—	—	—	—	—	—
Shoda Bunuemon	—	—	—	—	—	—	—	—	—	—	—	—	—
Yoshida Kanuemon	—	—	—	—	—	—	—	—	—	—	—	—	—
Total output	6,999	8,306	9,141	6,569	7,011	8,179	8,374	9,407	9,740	10,565	8,733	9,586	10,873 1
Index (1887 = 100)	100	119	131	94	100	117	120	134	139	151	125	137	155

Source: Kikkoman Company Archives, *Noda Shōyu Jōzō Kumiai Shi* (n.p., 1919?).
a. 5.55 koku = 1 kiloliter = 264 gallons

sauce industry in much the same way that he already had prevailed over the world of sugar refining.

The Challenge of Suzuki Tōsaburō

In 1903 the Department of Provisions and Fodder of the Japanese Army had sought to purchase condensed or concentrated shōyu, but discovered that it was generally unavailable and, moreover, that, given the slowly changing technology of the day, it would not quickly become available. Upon learning this, Suzuki Tōsaburō, who had already had great success with sugar refining, carefully studied the fermentation process of shōyu and designed a new tank that allowed for the application of heat to fermenting mash to speed fermentation. Thus, Suzuki challenged the traditional world of soy sauce manufacture by introducing high volume, energy- and capital-intensive production methods.

In April 1904 Suzuki took out a patent on his fermentation tank de-

l	1902	1903	1904	1905	1906	1907	1908	1909	1910	1911	1912	1913	1914	1915	1916
)4	4042	4056	4116	4902	4765	4919	4792	5715	5907	5671	6755	7068	—	7329	8262
i1	2309	2331	2468	3013	3193	3737	3752	4028	4258	4383	6370	5464	—	4220	6902
i9	1584	1732	2075	2222	1735	2173	2142	2394	2774	3051	3243	3226	—	3502	4012
)2	1480	1345	1708	1859	1661	1734	1690	1977	2108	2370	2370	1816	—	2416	2712
'4	1446	1478	1557	1575	1599	1635	1593	1813	2090	2275	2348	2253	—	2528	3084
'7	1082	1024	1197	1317	1306	1223	1476	1386	1346	1350	1071	1419	—	1487	1605
i3	380	345	368	414	397	392	—	377	541	576	724	882	—	828	980
i6	347	367	418	575	538	481	89	295	322	336	335	265	—	329	324
	323	375	410	477	444	441	456	473	457	462	442	429	—	422	453
	405	477	540	627	636	688	684	810	802	882	937	916	—	1008	1115
	—	—	—	—	—	—	—	—	—	—	—	—	—	—	—
	—	—	—	—	—	—	—	—	—	—	—	—	—	—	—
	—	—	—	—	—	—	—	—	—	—	—	—	—	—	—
	—	428	299	579	504	215	205	425	—	—	—	417	—	720	486
'7	70	219	389	234	351	356	335	324	324	306	360	367	—	416	429
	—	—	—	—	—	—	—	—	—	—	—	—	—	—	—
	—	—	—	—	—	—	—	—	—	—	—	—	—	—	—
	—	—	—	—	—	—	—	—	—	1239	1243	1291	—	1391	1383
	—	—	—	—	—	—	—	—	—	—	1112	—	—	—	1264
	—	—	—	—	—	—	—	—	—	—	293	539	—	675	633
i3	13,468	14,178	15,545	17,790	17,128	17,991	17,214	20,017	20,929	22,904	27,604	26,352	—	27,200	33,644
i4	192	203	222	254	245	257	246	286	299	327	394	377	—	389	481

sign, and in 1906 he began sending samples of his new product to Hawaii for field testing. In 1907, after making various adjustments to his process based on the results of the taste sampling in Hawaii, Suzuki formed the Nihon Shōyu Jōzō Kabushiki Kaisha (Japan Shōyu Brewing Company) with a capitalization of 10 million yen, and he opened two factories, one in the Tokyo area and one in the Kyoto-Osaka area, to manufacture soy sauce by his new method. Running both factories at full capacity, he produced 300,000 koku (14,280,000 gallons) annually—three times the current capacity of the combined Noda associates! He sold his product under the brand names Plum Tree Japan, Wisteria Japan, Pinetree Japan, and Water Chestnut Japan, at four different prices, thereby blitzing the soy sauce market with his brews.[15]

Most smaller shōyu manufacturers were threatened by Suzuki's mammoth output, derived from the volume and speed of production—lessons he had learned in sugar manufacture. They had neither the size nor the resources to compete, so they seized an opportunity to strike at him when it was discovered in November 1910, during a routine government food inspection, that the shōyu produced at Suzuki's Kansai plant contained an excessive amount of saccharin. This was dramatically revealed in newspapers under the headline "EVIDENCE OF FRAUDULENT SHŌYU." According to the laboratory tests, the amount of saccharin contained in Suzuki's shōyu was several times greater than that found in soy sauce brewed in the conventional manner. In the face of the uproar and protest raised by the press and multitude of small manufacturers, Suzuki was forced to recall his shōyu, load it in boats, and dump it in Osaka Bay, where it is said to have caused the bay to turn red.

As if this were not a sufficient blow to Suzuki's enterprise, the following spring his Osaka plant caught fire and burned out of control, leaving it a total loss. By November the Japan Shōyu Brewing Company disappeared in the ignominy of bankruptcy. The ultimate irony of Suzuki's failure was that he had earlier campaigned for and succeeded in having legislation passed that forbade the addition of saccharin to sugar manufacture, only to have his excessive use of it bring failure to his shōyu manufacture.

Research and Development

Most shōyu brewers in Noda had experimented in individual and minor ways with improving production technology during the late nineteenth century. Three Mogi brewers in particular—Shichizaemon, Shichirōuemon, and Fusagorō—went about this energetically and built what might be called small research laboratories. After 1903–04, however, the cartel associates decided to cooperate in funding a research and development effort and utilizing the results for everyone's advantage. Between 1904 and 1917 the cartel spent a total of 28,406 yen in direct costs for operating a research and development laboratory—a considerable investment for its day. This figure represented, for example, nearly three times the cost of erecting a new, fully equipped elementary school (11,428 yen); sixteen times the costs of excavation and erection of a steel-rail push-cart railroad for running goods between the shōyu factories and both river banks (1,725 yen); and nearly six times the amount spent on promotion and maintenance of either the local shōyu manufacturers' association or the shōyu tonya association in Tokyo (5,000 yen each).

The cost was high, but the benefits derived were considerable. One of the first tangible fruits was a chemical analysis of the component parts, active as well as inert, of shōyu. The benefits of such an analysis were incalculable; without it there could be no quality controls and taste standards for the greatly increased production that the Noda groups sought. If the group wanted to establish and maintain itself in the consumer market, it could do so reliably only by offering consistent quality, taste, and appearance at stable prices. According to the 1905 minutes of the cartel association, the research laboratory was charged with improving soy sauce quality by analyzing the chemical composition of shōyu, providing a mold of uniform quality to member brewers, conducting analysis of chemical changes taking place during fermentation, and considering ways to improve mechanization of production.

Built in 1904, the laboratory, one of the first of its kind in Japan, had a staff of five by 1907: a college-trained chemist with a specialization in brewing and fermentation chemistry as its head, a college engineer charged with improving production equipment, and three assistants.[16] By 1909 the four major brands manufactured by the cartel—Kikkoman, Kihaku, Kamigata, and Kushigata—had been analyzed chemically (see table 4).

Apparently there were regular biweekly meetings of the brewers, their tōji, and members of the laboratory. At these meetings pure culture molds for culturing and fermentation were distributed and topics concerning production and fermentation were discussed. The minutes of a meeting held on June 20, 1912, indicate that the following were discussed: a change in the method of kōji mold distribution and an increase in the charge per box of kōji mold from 15 to 20 sen; a lecture on

TABLE 4. Chemical analysis of the major brands of the Noda Shōyu Brewers' Association, 1909.

Composition	Kikkoman	Kihaku	Kamigata	Kushigata
specific gravity	1.192	1.200	1.183	1.208
moisture	69.51	68.93	69.08	67.08
suspended solids	30.49	31.07	30.92	32.92
ash (about 90% salt)	17.73	16.93	17.54	17.75
nitrogen	1.146	1.189	1.201	1.097
protein nitrogen	0.012	1.012	1.014	0.012
ammonia nitrogen	0.153	0.200	0.135	—
sugars	5.002	5.370	4.997	5.020
paste	0.630	0.730	0.640	0.630
volatile acid	0.038	0.032	0.045	0.032
nonvolatile acid	0.960	0.940	0.940	1.004
ester	13.50	14.00	14.00	13.00

Source: Kikkoman Company Archives, *Noda Shōyu Jōzō Kumiai Shi* (n.p., 1919?), p. 160.

the chemical components that combine to form the taste of shōyu; a discussion of the need to hire three workers—two technicians and one laborer—to help in mixing the kōji; a discussion of the proposed program in training research apprentices for laboratory analysis.[17]

It is clear from these minutes that the research laboratory had come to occupy an important place in the manufacture of shōyu in Noda by the second decade of the 1900s. The laboratory distributed the kōji mold to all members of the cartel, guaranteeing its purity and uniformity; it educated brewers in the chemistry and mechanics of shōyu manufacture; and it provided information on the chemistry and quality of various brands—valuable information during a period of increased productivity. In 1921, one year for which we have a report of the laboratory's annual activities, it is recorded that 53 tests were conducted of which the results were published, a significant scientific achievement.[18] From 1904, when the research and development laboratory was established, until 1913, ten years later, production of shōyu in Noda rose 80 percent, from 4,103,880 gallons to 7,312,170 gallons. Production on this scale required constant checking for quality control, careful monitoring of equipment and of fermentation, and an attention to routine, procedure, and detail that was new in Noda.

Although the Noda laboratory apparently was the first research institution established by members of the shōyu industry, the first scientific studies of the chemical composition of shōyu as well as of the shōyu fermentation process were conducted by Westerners. During the last quarter of the nineteenth century scores of Western engineers, teachers, and advisers were hired by the Japanese government to bring Western science, jurisprudence, and education to Japan. By the end of the 1870s the first scientific investigations of the properties of fermented soyfoods in Japan were published by these scholars and resulted in an almost immediate improvement in shōyu quality and quantity. Japanese manufacturers learned how to isolate and maintain pure kōji molds and how to measure temperatures in kōji inoculation rooms with the use of thermometers. By the 1880s, when Japanese researchers had joined their Western mentors in the laboratories, the chemical compounds that appear in shōyu during different stages of fermentation and the ways in which these affect flavor and aroma had been described and analyzed. In 1905 a well-known plant physiologist at Tokyo Imperial University published the first in a series of microbiological studies on shōyu fermentation, describing in detail the active organisms that occur during it. Subsequent research showed that the three molds, two bacteria, and two yeasts active during fermentation were all salt-tolerant, osmophilic varieties; they grew in environments of high osmotic pressure resulting from dissolved salts and sugars. By the second decade of this century, 1,000-page volumes describing every chemical and microbiological aspect of shōyu fermentation were available. These greatly advanced the biochemical knowledge of shōyu manufacture in Noda and elsewhere.[19]

Distribution: The Railroad

Although research and development in Japan and Noda made possible mass production without loss of overall quality, the railroad made possible mass distribution of the ever-growing product.

By May 1911 Chiba Prefecture had financed and opened a light-rail line between Kashiwa and Noda. Built at a cost of 200,000 yen, its value to the Noda cartel was incalculable, for railroad transportation transformed that group from a large regional producer into a national manufacturer. Although water transportation was readily available, inexpensive, and one of the principal reasons for the success of the Noda soy sauce brewers in the Tokyo market, it had limitations. Riverbeds are not necessarily the most direct and convenient of transportation avenues. River traffic can be moved safely only during daylight, and, although the trip downstream from Noda to Tokyo could be relatively rapid, beating one's way upstream often took five to ten times as long. In short, rivers as compared to railroads lacked the convenience of year-round, 24-hour, continuous operation as well as the more direct routing and more continuous scheduling possibilities inherent in inland overland transportation.

Furthermore, by 1909 the waterways surrounding Noda were crowded with people and products, making it even more difficult for the cartel to assure a reliable and rapid movement of its goods. That year 383,495 horseloads of goods were hauled to and from the riverbanks that bounded Noda (see table 5). This averages 1,184 loads per day, suggesting the crowding that must have congested wharfs and loading docks. In addition to these phenomenal totals, 23,122 people boarded the riverboats going to Noda, and 18,363 sailed out of town.

Recognition of the need for alternative transportation was slow in coming. Even in the late nineteenth century, few people envisioned the congestion the next decade would bring. In 1896 Chiba Prefecture had proposed to run the Jōban railroad line through Katsushika County, placing Noda directly on the line of construction.[20] But Noda did not welcome the railroad, and the line went to Kashiwa instead. Thirteen years later, however, the town, or more correctly the shōyu manufacturers, agreed with the authorities on the need for a rail connection between Noda and Kashiwa. The reasons for this change of attitude were

TABLE 5. Movement in and out of Noda by waterway, 1909.

Product	Amount	Horseloads
Imports		
cereals	134,810 straw bags	53,924
empty barrels	220,670	22,067
lumber for barrels, tubs	146,483 pieces	24,411
coal	6,400 tons	43,439
salt	104,422 straw bags	1,393
bricks	301,831	4,643
fertilizer	4,176 straw bags	1,393
miscellaneous	123,391	25,930
		total 177,200
Exports		
shōyu	1,192,847 barrels	170,406
shōyu cake	66,123 straw bags	16,531
miso	14,767 barrels	7,383
tobacco	217,191 bundles	6,033
miscellaneous	5,335 boxes	5,942
		total 206,295

Source: Kikkoman Company Archives, *Noda Shōyu Jōzō Kumiai Shi* (n.p., 1919?), pp. 324–325.

the growth of production of soy sauce and the increased flow of other goods and persons. Production had more than doubled in the thirteen-year period, from two and three-quarters million gallons in 1896 to six million gallons in 1911; it was expected to climb even higher following the examples that Suzuki Tōsaburō and fermented food scientists had offered of research and design possibilities to enhance shōyu manufacture. Now a railroad was to be welcomed rather than spurned.

Negotiations for constructing a line from Kashiwa to Noda were conducted between the governor of Chiba, Ariyoshi Tadakazu, and the Noda Shōyu Manufacturers' Association. The initiative for constructing it apparently came from the prefectural offices, which seemed intent on developing the area around Noda and on linking Noda and Kashiwa. At an extraordinary meeting held on March 18, 1909, the cartel agreed to help underwrite the construction of the railroad with the purchase of 200,000 yen worth of prefectural bonds and to take over the management of the railroad once it was built. The cartel association allotted each member's bond purchases according to each one's level of production (see table 6).

TABLE 6. Investment shares in the Kashiwa-to-Noda railroad line, 1909.

Name	Amount
Mogi Shichirōuemon	83,000 yen
Mogi Saheiji	50,000
Takanashi Hyōzaemon	25,000
Mogi Shichizaemon	15,000
Mogi Fusagorō	14,000
Yamashita Heibei	6,000
Mogi Keizaburō	2,000
Yamashita Tomisaburō	1,000
Tobe Yoshirō	1,000
Mogi Yōuemon	1,000
Ishikawa Niheiji	2,000

Source: Kikkoman Company Archives, *Noda Shōyu Jōzō Kumiai Shi* (n.p., 1919?), p. 329.

Construction went smoothly. The line to Noda was completed by 1911, within two years of the initial negotiations between the prefecture and the brewers' association. In 1910 the cartel had decided to form a land transportation company, Marusan, to handle freight between the proposed railroad station and the cargo-handling facilities already in place (the nonmotorized railroad line constructed in 1900). That line was extended to the site of the steam locomotive station, and the three men who had operated the push-railroad line became employees of the new Marusan Transportation Company. The cartel association also constructed various storage facilities at the site of the new railroad.

The new Kashiwa-Noda line was opened in late April 1911. The manufacturers' association celebrated with a grand party—food and drink for 150 guests. The bill, including entertainment, decorations, and the impressive ceremony, came to 1,000 yen—a princely amount.[21]

In addition to the 200,000 yen used to purchase prefectural bonds to finance the railroad's construction, the Noda cartel spent an additional 4,177 yen to construct grain silos, storage facilities, scales, and boarding platforms at the railroad station. Although association expenditures were considerable, the prefecture owned the roadbed and had paid for the track and rolling stock. Its expense far outweighed the cost (but not the convenience) of the road to the Noda associates. In 1914 the cartel decided to invest in its own rolling stock so it could schedule shipments according to its own needs. Five cargo cars of seven tons each were purchased at a total cost of 4,750 yen.[22]

In the short span of five years, 1909 to 1914, the cartel association had invested 209,000 yen in railroad financing, railroad site preparation and development, and rolling stock for handling freight. This investment dwarfed any previous expenses borne by the brewers' association. It was seven times as large as the amount spent on developing and maintaining the research and development laboratory over a much longer period, and nearly four times as large as the total charitable donations and contributions made by the cartel between 1895 and 1920.

This kind of large capital expenditure was required if the cartel was to take advantage of the new possibilities in production, mechanization, and improved transportation. Ever since the cartel had begun to expend larger amounts of money for purposes not directly related to the activities of individual brewers, the financial as well as social costs had taken their toll. In 1895, when the cartel first began in a very minor way to require its members to contribute money for various causes, there were fifteen members in the association, down slightly from a high of seventeen members in 1887, the year of initial association. By 1917, after two decades of expansion of plant and equipment and investments in R&D and rolling stock, the membership had dropped to twelve regular members. Yet the benefits of continued association were real enough. The possibilities inherent in high-volume, low-cost manufacture were just beginning to be realized. Furthermore, once mass production was linked to mass distribution through the railroad, the cartel could grow from a regional association into a national enterprise.

Social Change and the Cartel

By the first decade of the twentieth century the economic future of the cartel seemed assured, but the social composition and character of the manufacturers' association were less certain. The greatly expanded financial requirements and newly emerging managerial duties that participation in the cartel came to entail after the turn of the century divided its membership. Many, accustomed to act independently, were now forced by economic circumstances to act more and more in unison. The explanation may be found in the increasingly severe requirements for successful competition in an industry on the verge of integrating large-scale production with distribution. The industry was in the middle of a transition from entrepreneurial to managerial capitalism, that is, in the process of change from individualistic, highly idiosyncratic operation of small, low-volume labor-intensive factories with low productivity to bureaucratic, routinized operations of vast size, complexity, and coordination, with high rates of throughput.

The philanthropy, social character, and economic performance of the

Noda shōyu cartel were interrelated; as one changed, all were affected, albeit sometimes indirectly. Economically, by 1911 the cartel was the acknowledged leader in soy sauce manufacture, in terms of the volume of production and of the sophistication of the production process. In its social character the cartel brought together a total of twenty-two brewers (the yearly count was less) who cooperated in numerous ways over three decades and who created, as a result, an entirely new manufacturing coalition that drew on but did not depend upon the traditional system of enterprise operation based on family and lineage organization. And philanthropically, between 1894 and 1920 the cartel gave just over 60,000 yen to patriotic, civic, and charitable causes.[23]

This amount would have been unthinkable without a fundamental change in the nature of economic organization and performance. A switch from seasonal to full-time manufacture required coordinated investment on the part of cartel members, but it brought annual increases in production in the range of 5 to 10 percent—sustained increases that were literally unimaginable during the Tokugawa Period. Such gains in output in the soy sauce and other industries resulted in a basic ideological and institutional shift in Japanese business practices noticeable at both the national and local levels. The last and first decades of the nineteenth and twentieth centuries brought a change from the purely personal capitalism of family entrepreneurship to the "public" yet private capitalism of joint-stock companies. During this transitional period, which may vary in inception depending on the type and location of the industry in question, profits were made but not justified in the name of private enterprise. Instead, a new ethic, not quite either private or public, was called forth to rationalize the place of business and businessmen in society.

In the last half of the nineteenth century, when the central government and former warriors and merchants of the Tokugawa era controlled the crucible of industrialization, they justified their preeminent political and economic place in the Meiji government with terms like "industrial patriotism" and "samurai or warrior entrepreneurship." Thus, they removed their power from criticism by investing it in the national movement for a "rich country and strong army" (*fukoku kyōhei*). Later, in the twentieth century, when commoners, not warriors and old-line merchants, grabbed the reins of industrialization, they too rationalized their role in terms of patriotism as well as in terms of humanitarianism and civic pride. It is within this changing ideological and institutional context that the charity and philanthropy of the Noda shōyu cartel should be understood. Within this context, philanthropy, economic performance, enterprise organization, and ideology were all tied together.

The Cost of Charity

The 60,626 yen given by the cartel for patriotic, civic, and charitable purposes was a great deal of money. It was enough to equal 1 percent of the total national excise taxes on the sale of sake, tobacco, sugar, shōyu, and textile fabrics, as well as on the profits from camphor, salt, and tobacco monopolies in 1890; enough to equal the entire stock of authorized joint-stock capital invested in trading companies in 1893; enough to match the total tax on alcohol in 1905; or enough to hire 170,298 carpenters for one day or 520 for one year (if you allowed for the customary two days off per month) in 1911.[24]

One is led to ask why a group of rural brewers, fairly remote from Tokyo, would give such a large amount. We might assume that prosperity alone led them to contribute. Such an assumption holds that economic motives loom large in everyone's calculation of personal and even social advantage, although one might be loath to admit and announce this calculus. Prima facie evidence of the economic well-being of the cartel is found in the steadily rising production of shōyu. Between 1887 and 1916 the production of the Noda Shōyu Manufacturers' Union grew fivefold, from 1.75 million gallons to 8.4 million gallons, an impressive growth rate of 5.6 percent compounded annually. This was accomplished in an era when continuous process technology was yet unknown, reliable and quick inland transportation was unavailable, and management of the manufacturing process in Noda was uncoordinated, being decentralized within separate family-owned and operated breweries.

Yet the figures are deceiving, for although volume of production does provide an indirect gauge of the volume of sales, it tells nothing about the costs of production, which were rather special in the case of shōyu manufacture. Making shōyu is time-consuming, often necessitating up to two years. It demands large fixed investment in plant, equipment, and raw materials. Sunk costs in the form of brewing vats, kegs, kōji rooms, grain silos, and pressing equipment were substantial, and these were all needed before the first soybeans, wheat, and salt could be purchased and processed. Fixed costs of this nature and magnitude make men cautious, so the Noda shōyu brewers never took a profit for granted, rarely lavished money on themselves or others, and constantly worried over short-term prices and long-term sales.

Moreover, with 15,000 shōyu manufacturers, excluding industrious peasants who made just enough shōyu for their own uses, there was not much of a margin left for the large brewers. Too high a markup would compel more peasants to make their own and more small-time brewers to increase their output. As a result, profits were not likely to be excessive for the Noda group, caught as they were between their large fixed costs in plant and equipment, the price-sensitive commodities of soybeans, wheat, and salt, and the thousands of diligent and efficient householders making shōyu throughout Japan.

Coincident with this double pressure on costs and with the period of greatest growth in shōyu production at Noda, the government increased the rate of taxation on shōyu by an incredible 75 percent! In November 1868 the fledgling Meiji government set a rate of 3 ryō per 100 koku (4,760 gallons) of shōyu production. This remained the rate until May 1885, when the tax rate was fixed at one yen per one koku of production, plus an annual five-yen business license tax. Small household producers escaped both levies. In February 1899 the business tax was abolished, but the tax rate was doubled to two yen per one koku of production. In 1904–1905 the tax rate on shōyu was 2.25 yen per koku. In March 1906 the tax rate was lowered to 1.75 yen per koku where it remained until April 1926, when taxes on shōyu were abolished.[25]

If the Noda associates had no use, other than personal consumption, for the profits from their obviously burgeoning venture, they might have given money for charity and philanthropy as a kind of tithing. After all, in spite of its increase over earlier levels, the rate of taxation remained fixed during the period of greatest growth in production, which came after 1898; between that year and 1912 the amount of shōyu brewed by the cartel nearly tripled, from 53,000 koku to 153,000 koku. Yet this was precisely the time when the cartel needed whatever money was available for additional investment in productive capacity and efficiency. It is unlikely, therefore, that the brewers voluntarily taxed themselves to make up for whatever real or imagined slack existed in the incidence of government taxes.

The cartel had more economic and pressing uses for 60,000 yen after 1900. At the same time that the brewers were giving away this amount, they spent more than half that sum (31,771 yen) on cartel-funded projects designed to improve the efficiency of the shōyu manufacturing process (see Appendix D). Chief among these were a research and development laboratory and a small-gauge railroad. These investments were soon dwarfed by a massive debt incurred in 1909 by taking over the prefecture-built, locomotive-powered railroad between Noda and Kashiwa. So great, in fact, were the number and amount of investments made by the cartel in direct and indirect improvements to the manufacturing plant, equipment, and infrastructure in Noda between 1898 and 1917, that these costs should refute any idea that the cartel gave money to patriotic, civic, and charitable causes in preference to productive investment.

The contributions of the brewers' association were not directly related to promotion of future profits or to public relations. Very few of their philanthropic activities could be seen as accruing to the benefit of the cartel in any direct sense. (An exception might be the expenditure of 1,667 yen in 1908 for improving local roads. But because water and later rail—but not road—transportation were important to the movement of raw materials and finished products, this cannot be taken very seriously as a motive.) The union received very little recognition for its good deeds. Letters of commendation and occasionally a set of tea or sake cups represented the extent of the public's acknowledgment of the philanthropy. It is impossible to identify and evaluate all the possible long-term economic benefits of the cartel's generosity, but the important point is that they were *long-term.* The donations were not attempts to curry favor, win political influence, or affect public policy.

There is little direct evidence supporting a hypothesis that the charity and philanthropy of the Noda Shōyu cartel can be explained solely by reference to arguments of economic rationality. This conclusion is underscored even more forcefully when shōyu production is graphed against contributions and donations during the period in question (see figure 5). There appears to be little correspondence between fluctuations in the amounts of soy sauce produced and in the amounts of contributions and donations. Whereas production levels climbed more or less steadily, giving for patriotic, civic, and charitable purposes oscillated wildly. This is explicable only if the cartel's giving was periodic and not regular.

Noneconomic Motivation

Table 7, which shows how much and for what purposes money was given by the cartel, may clarify the noneconomic motivations underlying the generosity. Four broad categories of gifts may be distinguished: patriotic/military, educational, humanitarian, and civic promotion. If the total amount given for wars, military emergencies, associated patriotic causes, and disaster relief between 1894 and 1919 is calculated, it comes to nearly 57 percent (34,551 out of 60,626 yen) of the total. This shows that a large proportion of the giving was unpredictable, occurring in response to pressing needs in the local community and to regional and national calamities. Accounting for the timing of a large share of the giving, nevertheless, still does not elucidate either the motivations or the yet unexplained three-tenths of the gifts.

Noda and Higashi-Katsushika County had not been part of any pre-Restoration domain (the area had been *tenryō* or *chokkatsuchi,* territory administered by the Tokugawa shōgun and not by some local baron) and relatively few warriors had resided there. The relative absence,

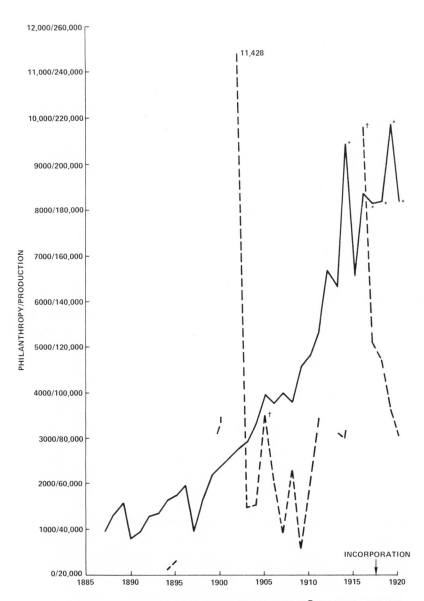

FIGURE 5. PHILANTHROPY AND PRODUCTION: NODA SHŌYU CARTEL, 1887-1920

*ESTIMATED
†INCLUDES ITEM OR ITEMS WITH EITHER 3 OR 5 YEAR PAYOUT
PHILANTHROPY IN YEN (DOTTED LINE)
PRODUCTION IN KOKU (ONE KOKU = 47.6 GALLONS)

TABLE 7. Noda charitable giving, 1894–1919.

Category	No. of gifts	Amount	Percent
patriotic/military	14	25,690 yen	42.4
educational	5	18,408	30.4
humanitarian	6	8,861	14.6
civic promotion	4	7,667	12.6
total	29	60,626	100.0

Source: Kikkoman Company Archives, *Noda Shōyu Jōzō Kumiai Shi* (n.p., 1919?), pp. 85–322.

rather than presence, of warriors, may explain what motivated the cartel associates. By the early twentieth century the Noda brewers were well-to-do and well-known in their locale. Although commoners by birth, they were considered the local elite, without direct competition from the former members of the warrior class.

Because of this prominence and the social expectations accompanying it much of the expanded social role of the cartel on the local level after 1900 may be attributed to government default: cartel members, in the perceived absence of sufficient government investment in their community, simply stepped in to take up the slack. While the national government concerned itself with plans for a "rich country and a strong army," local areas were often overlooked in the rush to erect a nation-state, whose products were located in cities and urban fringes. In lieu of national and prefectural attention, the Noda shōyu cartel filled the perceived local void remarkably well. It was the most visible and vital of local institutions, more important than whatever government offices and agencies dotted the landscape. Shōyu manufacture was the major employer, revenue generator, and paymaster as well as taxpayer, not only in Noda and Higashi-Katsushika County but in all of Chiba Prefecture. It would remain so until the eve of World War II. Not only was the cartel's economic impact direct and absolute on the wage structure and standard of living in the community, but it provided many public goods and services as well. The cartel rebuilt the local elementary school in 1902, provided the water system for the town, managed and financed the local roads and railway, and engaged extensively in charitable relief.

All of this did not happen at once. The cartel's social and economic leadership developed rather slowly, and only after the turn of the century did its new social role and expanded local station become apparent. There is no direct evidence of how cartel members viewed their expanded role or how conscious they were of it as something novel or unusual. But they must have had a sense of their local importance because nothing had prefigured such unprecedented involvement in community affairs. Although certain brewers and their families were celebrated locally for individual acts of generosity and charity during difficult times, such as the calamitous Tempō Famine (1836–1838), these were personal acts of kindness performed out of a sense of family responsibility. Charity was seemingly unrelated to feelings of social contract or of political responsibility in a direct sense, although indirectly a sense of shared livelihood and a common way of life could compel those better off to help those less fortunate within the close confines of villages and towns in the Japanese countryside.

This sense of common cause might provide the beginnings of an interpretation of the cartel's charities. While the cartel owed nothing but taxes to the community in a formal or legal sense, it could scarcely ignore the unwritten rules of reciprocity which had characterized life in Japanese villages for some centuries. If the local government could not or would not provide the resources necessary for the advancement of community and cartel interests, the cartel was forced to step in. A local school was not only a matter of civic pride but also an economic and social need in a community employing the largest concentration of workers and managers in Chiba Prefecture in the early twentieth century. Without a doubt, the improvement of local resources and the cooperation of local residents were required in the long run to accelerate and expand shōyu production. Through necessity as much as conviction, the Noda Shōyu Brewers' Association became an important source of local philanthropy in Noda after 1900.

The social involvement of the Noda brewers was not entirely accidental. These community leaders were expected to take an interest in local affairs, ensure that the town did not fall behind similar communities, and find ways to advance the cause of the locale. Social expectation and peer pressure played their part. The education and position of these men predisposed them toward a humanitarian—a Confucian—philosophy to serve all mankind, and this was realized most often by their involvement in local civic and educational affairs. (Education was the second largest category of donations.)

Whatever schooling the cartel members acquired, their basis for and general philosophy of education was found in Confucianism. Education not only shaped the social attitudes of the Noda associates but also channeled their efforts to serve society. Consider the recorded statements of Mogi Shichirōuemon, one-time director of the Noda Shōyu Brewers' Association, first president of the Noda Shōyu Company formed in 1918, and probably the most influential shōyu brewer in

Japan for the first twenty to thirty years of the twentieth century. "The prosperity of my business has nothing to do with me. It is due entirely to my ancestors' virtue and to society's abundance. My personal success must be seen in this light." And "We work in society and we are maintained by society. Everyone is dependent on each other."[26]

Mogi Shichirōuemon's words were not just decorative and self-serving. On his forty-fifth birthday, in an act of social gratitude, he founded the Noda Charitable Society and donated a great deal of money for the relief of the poor and the education of impoverished students. Furthermore, we know from the eulogy written by his executive assistant (bantō), Shinshima Jisuke, that Mogi Shichirōuemon's generosity, by his own choice, often went unrecognized. He gave frequently if anonymously to numerous benevolent associations.[27]

From Philanthropy to Paternalism

If the charity and philanthropy of the cartel were based on Confucian philosophy, then this represents a measured social gesture that was activated in response to the perceived needs of the community and engendered through education. This attitude of humanitarianism, which partakes of a Japanese sense of *ongaeshi*, of repaying one's debts to society, shares some of the meaning of social repayment evident in Andrew Carnegie's *Gospel of Wealth*. As in the lessons learned in Carnegie's famous epistle, humanitarian and charitable activities were social responsibilities of the successful. They were means whereby one's success could be repaid as well as moral duties and responsibilities that no Christian (or Confucian) could easily overlook or neglect.

In the cases of Mogi Shichirōuemon and Andrew Carnegie, the sentiment and effort to pay back society for success were conceived of abstractly, in terms of an individual acting for society in the widest possible sense. Repayment was not generally conceptualized in terms of local districts and inhabitants, except insofar as they were close at hand and thus their needs were known. The need to appease or appeal to local interests as such does not seem to have been an important part of the Noda cartel's charitable work. Rather, the community benefited from a Confucian-inspired general humanitarianism and industrial patriotism, although this was executed, more often than not, in a relatively localized geographical area.

The philanthropic activism of the cartel must be distinguished from the social and economic paternalism of the corporation that succeeded it. Whereas the cartel's philanthropy was predicated on universal principles of social expectation, economic need, humanitarian concern, and a moral imperative to return profit with kindness, not to mention a perceptible self-interest, later giving, as we shall see, grew out of attempts to quiet worker disturbances, reduce labor turnover, and increase plant efficiency. The images associated with each era differed as well. The cartel of associated entrepreneurial families, well-to-do and well-educated, gave less out of self-interest than patriotism and civic responsibility. That image contrasts sharply with the rather calculating, cool, and self-conscious efforts of the corporation to push up efficiency and hold down disaffection in the factories through paternalistic policies and programs.[28]

The narrowing of corporate concern in Noda after 1920 represents a reversal of a trend often considered synonymous or congruent with modernity: a growing emphasis on the universal rather than the particular, and on the nation-state rather than on the community. The corporation, as opposed to the cartel, represents a movement toward something concrete and private and away from the diffuse and social. Yet there was no ready-made community, no "corporate village," for the Noda associates to turn to after 1920. Relations between town and factory and owners and workers were not close, nor had they been up to this time. It would be the major task of the owner-managers of the Noda Shōyu Company to forge that identity and association between employer and employee during and after the 1920s, and this effort would become in Noda, as elsewhere in Japan, the hallmark of Japanese industrial relations in the twentieth century. Paternalism, as expressed in the creation of a "Japanese system of employment,"[29] a company town, and an ideological accord between management and labor would come only after the creation of a corporation that provided the institutional framework within which paternalism could be conceived and implemented.

The key to the philanthropic activities of the cartel era, at least in this one case and I believe in others as well, can be resolved if the changing institutional and ideological context of industrialization from the late nineteenth to early twentieth century is considered. The cartel period was not yet one of corporate primacy, but the individual family as employer had given way to the other economies of scale inherent in an association of families joined less by kinship than by ties of occupation and locale. An earlier phase of community-centered entrepreneurship in late-nineteenth-century Japan, which had been located in cities and their urban fringes and in which warriors and other holdovers from the previous regime were prominent, was considerably different from the community-centered entrepreneurship that followed. The earlier form developed in an era characterized by anxiety over the Western threat, nationalism and patriotic pride in industrial achievement, and insecurity over the entrepreneurial role that derived from Tokugawa custom.

The later phase coincided with a shift from government-initiated enterprise to more local and less conspicuous ventures. Yet in both periods private capital, that is, capital raised and invested by entrepreneurs, predominated. Thus, even though the Noda Shōyu cartel's period of community-centered entrepreneurship began late in the nineteenth century, it occurred in a period of ideological and institutional transition from family and one-man entrepreneurship, the traditional forms of business organization and operation, to the newer, more effective, more impersonal business organization found in joint-stock companies.

The cartel came in between private capital/personal enterprise and joint-stock capital/bureaucratic organization. It represented a special time when entrepreneurs imbued with Confucian values and social concerns, somewhat insecure in their local position and prominence, could look beyond personal needs, unencumbered by overriding obligations to family or to firm. It was an era when small was *still* beautiful, when economics *was* tempered by a philosophy in which people mattered and when businessmen could be, at least for a while, Confucian gentlemen and community-centered entrepreneurs.

The Transformation of Shōyu Manufacture in the Countryside

The Noda Shōyu Brewers' Association was a cartel formed in 1887 for the distribution of shōyu in the countryside and city and for stabilizing product price and market share. The prevalence of such cartels was based on three factors. First, Tokugawa tradition laid the basis for Meiji practice. Second, the industrialization of Japan was characterized by capital insufficiency; most manufacturers were small, strapped for capital, and unable to differentiate themselves by economies of scale. Finally, the tonya system of distribution through middlemen prevented manufacturers from becoming price-competitive through direct access to consumer markets. Indirect, and therefore expensive, distribution made it impossible to improve market share by passing the benefits of lower production costs to the consumer. The final pricing of products was a tonya prerogative, although, in fact, it was often determined jointly by producers and distributors. In short, the isolation of manufacturers from their markets, the insufficiency of capital investment in production, and tradition itself forced manufacturers into cartels where, at least, market share in terms of production quotas was guaranteed.

Moreover, given the minimal barriers to entry and the widely diffused character of soy fermentation technology, oversupply was always a problem in the soy sauce industry. Excess capacity made it difficult to raise prices, and the history of the Noda shōyu cartel was largely one of trying to control prices by manipulating output and reducing labor costs. Oversupply and a poorly motivated labor force, however, made it next to impossible to yield returns large enough to justify increased investment in more rationalized and mechanized production facilities. Thus, the essence of cartelized enterprise was overproduction without significant economies of scale. Price was more or less guaranteed, but only at the cost of restricted output; marginal revenue did not greatly exceed marginal costs.

With such diseconomies of scale, market share in a cartel could be expanded easily in two ways: by increasing the number of producers in one group, thereby squeezing out other cartel groups through nonprice competition (such as better transportation and scheduling arrangements for the group); and by proliferation of products so that the aggregate demand increases for the whole range of a cartel's products. Both of these options—increasing the number of producers and of products—were employed by the Noda shōyu cartel, and both were successful because of Noda's central location on the Kantō Plain and its proximity to Tokyo, with their combination of growing aggregate and per capita income and demand. (In an age when product promotion and advertising were not widespread, product proliferation was a sensible response to the variety of local taste differences and preferences.)

In spite of the barriers to expansion inherent in the distribution system and the diffuseness of the production technology, the Noda shōyu cartel's strategy of combining an increasing number of producers and products ultimately outran the capacity of the Tokyo tonya association to distribute their goods. It was not so much that the volume of the Noda group's production was astonishingly large—although it was great compared to other makers—but that the Noda group had acquired the capacity to outproduce other manufacturers *if* the tonya association accepted all the Noda group could manufacture. This, however, would upset the long-established system of sales and distribution, developed by the tonya. The Noda shōyu cartel was the first of the old manufacturers to understand the possibilities inherent in economies of scale achieved through combined manufacturing, purchasing, and marketing, yet it was not able to exploit these fully because of the entrenched position of wholesalers in urban markets.

The unique social flavor of the cartel, characterized by a Confucian-inspired philanthropy, a recognition of community responsibility, and a willingness to act in the interests of the greater good, developed indirectly. This ideological shift accompanied the more obvious economic changes which transformed the basis of enterprise structure: the traditional and rather narrow values of the family were supplanted by the needs of the industry and the community. Philanthropy was one consequence of this change in social organization and orientation.

That the Noda shōyu manufacturing cartel lasted for just three decades, from 1887 to 1917, is not surprising. The return on investment was stable, but not outstanding, although the attractiveness of other investments in the countryside was probably no better. Even if the logic of tradition recommended that the Noda manufacturers follow in their fathers' footsteps, their willingness to dismember the cartel gives credit to their vision of a better—and more profitable—way of manufacturing and distributing their products.

3.

From Cartel to Corporation and Beyond

A CORPORATION requires a nucleus for centralization and coordination—an element that was lacking in the federation of manufactuers known as the Noda Shōyu Brewers' Association. The previous method of operation for the brewers had relied merely on rough consensus, but this would not be sufficient for the future. The process of incorporation, therefore, involved great initiative on the part of the Noda brewers in creating the mechanisms for coordinating and focusing corporate resources.

The creation of such channels, difficult under any circumstances, was made even more so by the lack of precedent. The concept of a corporation was still relatively new in early-twentieth-century Japan. The first joint-stock companies had been founded in 1872, together with the establishment of a system of joint-stock banks, but this form of organization did not become commonplace among manufacturing ventures for another three or four decades. Johannes Hirschmeier and Tsunehiko Yui tell us that in 1884 there were only about ten large-scale joint-stock ventures in Japan, each with over 100,000 yen capitalization.[1] After 1893, when the commercial code was revised, joint-stock companies became more common, but sole proprietorships and partnerships, either limited or unlimited, continued to predominate until well into the twentieth century. This was especially true in the countryside where a good deal of early industry was located.

Even in the United States, where the merger of distinct business units into consolidated firms as well advanced by the turn of the century, the transition to new managerial structures was often not successful. Leslie Hannah, reporting the research of Shaw Livermore for the United States, writes:

Only half of the 328 mergers of 1888–1905 that he [Livermore] examined could be classified as successful. Fifty-three failed shortly after they were formed, and others consistently earned less than the levels of profits originally expected (on the basis of which they had been overcapitalized with watered stock). Decreased market shares for merged companies were widespread in the steel, sugar-refining, agricultural implements, leather, rubber, distilling, and car industries.[2]

Thus, consolidation of the Noda shōyu cartel interests through incorporation was neither promising nor widely precedented. There was little support for greater centralization than that already achieved by the cartel; yet various forces, among them the need for expansion, were driving the Noda associates toward some more coordinated enterprise. The major opposition to centralization came from the families of the brewers. Incorporation would unite the numerous family entrepreneurs who had been conducting their affairs independently—some for as long as several centuries. The institutional uniformity required by incorporation was anathema to the old ambitions of individual success and prestige. Manufacturers with illustrious and industrious ancestors were reluctant to subsume their family and individual identities in a corporate hierarchy. Furthermore, the traditional independence of spirit and industry on the part of so many families had spawned numerous ancient as well as contemporary jealousies and rivalries, even among closely related families.

Counterposed against traditional independence, family continuity, and even personal gain were the greatly enlarged financial and managerial requirements for expansion of the cartel's operations. A good deal of money had to be invested if the possibilities of high-volume, low-unit-cost manufacture were to be realized. Manufacture on a massive scale would make little sense without the ability to move goods quickly and widely, and this need prompted the cartel's commitment to the railroad—in spite of Noda's excellent waterway connection with Tokyo.

Recall that the cost of the railroad line from Noda to Kashiwa, not including the railroad station and storage facilities, came to 200,000 yen—a figure far in excess of the total of whatever joint investments had been made previously by the cartel. But the railroad was the key to the new business strategy since it promised a safe, dependable, year-round system of inland transportation that would enable Noda brewers to increase their sales not only in the greater Tokyo area, where they already commanded about 20 to 25 percent of the market, but throughout Japan through use of one of the world's best railroad systems. The benefits of mass manufacture and mass distribution, however, could be accrued only by additional and sizable investment in plant, equipment, and manpower in both production and transportation. This could not be accomplished within the informal and decentralized cartel structure.

The lure of the market and the availability of the technology to produce and distribute on a national basis dictated an end to the snug clubbiness of the manufacturers' association. Of course money and greed played their part as powerful solvents of tradition, but their action was more corrosive than catalytic. Something other than avarice was needed to coax a corporate phoenix from the cartel's aged yet immature form. That new element was in fact not entirely new; the embryonic company relied on that most resilient and motivating of all institutions: the family. Unlike the cartel, which had placed emphasis on locale and occupation, the new structure focused primarily on the family and less on locale and occupation. Curiously enough, family loyalty and consciousness, albeit within a greatly reduced number of families, was the means of removing the reluctance of previously independent brewers toward a more rigid and demanding corporate regime.

The creation of a joint-stock institution was both destructive and creative. The cartel was scuttled, and the interfamily cooperation that had brought nearly two dozen families together over three decades was discontinued. In its place, a corporation of nine families instead of twenty-two appeared: nine related by descent rather than twenty-two associated by common cause. Incorporation, whereby the risks of major investment and of organizational control could be minimized to tolerable levels by close family traditions, was to be confined to relatives.

Again, the Japanese stem family (ie) and genealogical descent group (dōzoku) were employed in the interest of business success. But it would be a mistake to assume that all competition and rivalry, even within this reduced family circle, had been eliminated. Such competition had existed between lineages and within sublineages before the advent of the cartel and even during the period of loose family federation, and competition over production levels and over branded product sales in the countryside would continue. The amount of production, after all, was the principal measure of family performance, lineage status, community stature, and success.

Within the cartel, and even more within the corporation, universal criteria of performance distinguished one household from another, regardless of the particularistic allegiances uniting households with common descent and occupation. Efficiency, frugality, acumen, and personality—qualities that had been elevated into virtues by Confucian and Buddhist philosophies that were adapted to support entrepreneurial activities—differentiated kinsmen and nonkinsmen alike into those who advanced the family fortune and those who did not. In spite of the uniformity and regularity demanded by incorporation, therefore, the nine families of the Noda Shōyu Company did not necessarily agree in attitude, approach, and aims. Fortunately the size of the group was large enough to ensure a kind of creative tension arising out of the historical rivalry between households.

If competition alone had characterized the group, consolidation would not have been possible. Kinship and the cooperation it engendered, as well as common residence, occupation, and history, provided the convergence for amalgamation. Both conflict and concession defined the group, and, depending on the mix of circumstances and personalities at any one time, either competition or cooperation within the kinship group could be emphasized. Certainly the culture valued cooperation within lineages, and this preference was fully exploited to encourage a mutual consciousness of common origins in order to overcome friction among families. Once cooperation, or at least coordination, was institutionalized within a corporation, the structure and process of the company—and the reliance on consensus—would smooth out a good deal of the personal variation among families.

In sum, the acceptance and implementation of a corporate form of enterprise organization, based on a maximum of mutual advantage for certain individual families making soy sauce in Noda, was a major break with the past. The process of incorporation involved three separate phases. First came a period of preparation that covered the last decade of cartelized shōyu manufacture and culminated in intensive efforts to reorganize the cartel into something more than a loose association of families. Second, there was an initial, seven-year period of incorporation during which the Noda Shōyu Company experimented with various organizational forms and devices, all designed to increase administrative and operational effectiveness. Finally, after 1925, the company was substantially reorganized in order to simultaneously amalgamate four separate companies into one operating structure and to create a new legal body, the Senshusha holding company. Its mandate was to determine and to effect an overall investment strategy for the firm and its growing number of subsidiaries.

1909 to 1918: Period of Preparation

Before the first Sino-Japanese conflict, in 1894, there were fewer than 3,000 factories in all of Japan. By 1908 that figure had increased more than tenfold.[3] Not only had the number of factories grown dramatically, the manner of production had progressed from largely hand assembly to mechanized production. Noda was one of the first shōyu manufacturing sites to employ the newer mechanized techniques. The first factory there that was designed with mechanized rather than hand production in mind was built in 1909. In that year Mogi Yūuemon and Ishikawa Niheiji formed the Noda Shōyu Gōshi Company, with a capitalization of 1 million yen. This company literally rose from the ashes of a major fire in 1908, which claimed scores of homes and several breweries, including Mogi Yūuemon's Ichiyama brewery in Noda. The following year Mogi Yūuemon and Ishikawa Niheiji formed a partnership to brew soy sauce using the latest equipment and technology, thereby reducing the fermentation period to what was considered the shortest time possible for good quality: sixteen months. Their example undoubtedly motivated others to increase their pace of production, until, by the end of the next decade, the possibilities of mass production using new machines and new technology were apparent to all.

The first brewers in Noda to talk seriously of imitating on a major scale what Mogi Yūuemon and Ishikawa Niheiji were doing on a limited basis were Mogi Fusagorō IV, Mogi Schichizaemon XI, and Takanashi Hyōzaemon XXVIII. The three met first during 1915–16 to discuss informally the possibility of their joining together to form a company. Not only did they have the 1909 example of the Noda Shōyu Gōshi Company to follow, but in 1914 three shōyu brewers from Chōshi in Chiba Prefecture had formed the Chōshi Shōyu Company. The Noda brewers had received the following letter from Chōshi in the autumn of 1914:

To: The Noda Shōyu Manufacturers' Association

It's becoming chilly. Fall must be coming. We hope everyone is fine and business is prosperous. As always, we are deeply appreciative of your continued dealings with us. This is to announce the formation of the Chōshi Soy Sauce Company Limited which combines the management of three previously independent enterprises. We hope to continue to have a good relationship with you in the future.

September 3, 1914
Hamaguchi Yoshiuemon
Fukai Yoshibei
Tanaka Genba[4]

In 1916 Mogi Fusagorō fell ill and was unable to continue with the plans for the new shōyu venture. His place was taken by his son, Fusagorō V, a graduate of Keio University. Hereafter the story becomes a bit unclear. One version (*The Twenty-Year Anniversary History of the Noda Shōyu Company*) relates that Mogi Saheiji was next approached and convinced to join the venture; after him was Mogi Keizaburō, and then Mogi Shichirōuemon.[5] Another version (*The Thirty-Five Year Anniver-*

sary History of the Noda Shōyu Company) holds that Mogi Shichirōuemon was recruited first, followed by the others. The latter version makes more sense, partly because the households of Mogi Fusagorō and Takanashi Hyōzaemon were closer traditionally to Mogi Shichirōuemon than to Saheiji (and this sort of interfamily preference was crucial in important situations such as this one), and partly because Shichirōuemon was the acknowledged leader of the brewers in the cartel.[6] Moreover, it coincides with the memory of Mogi Fusagorō V, who was a principal in the negotiations (as recorded in an interview with Tsuchiya Takao on March 7, 1968).

The inclusion of Mogi Shichirōuemon at an early date is reasonable for yet another reason: he had been planning to leave Japan for Europe and the United States in order to establish overseas marketing channels for his family's Kihaku brand. This would place Kihaku in competition with Kikkoman, which was already exported overseas by Mogi Saheiji. Such was the situation on September 28, 1917, when the heads of the five major Mogi-Takanashi families gathered at the home of Mogi Shichirōuemon to discuss amalgamation. There, before his relatives, Shichirōuemon announced that he would allow his family's principal brand name, Kihaku, to be used, without cost to the incipient shōyu company. Mogi Shichirōuemon's generosity was not accepted, however, because the family's brand was not the leading one among the Noda brewers. Kikkoman, not Kihaku, was the flagship of the Noda soy sauces; and Mogi Saheiji, the brewer of Kikkoman, was not willing to relinquish his family's brand to the company without substantial monetary compensation.

The rivalry over which brand should represent the company and would therefore receive the bulk of the money spent on advertising and distribution was a clear sign of family rivalry. It also signaled the managerial sophistication of the Mogi-Takanashi brewers, who realized that the many branded soy sauces that fragmented the market were incompatible with a business strategy based on mass production and mass distribution. Although a mass market for soy sauce already existed, one firm and one brand did not yet dominate it. To do so, brand recognition and brand loyalty were necessary, and in this regard Kikkoman had been more successful than any other Noda soy sauce. It sold no more by volume than the Kihaku brand of Mogi Shichirōuemon, but it commanded a slightly higher price per barrel than Kihaku, and 60 percent of it (as opposed to 40 percent of Kihaku) was sold in the Tokyo market. Urban markets such as Tokyo promised the greatest rewards for the heavily advertised and branded products that the founders of the Noda Shōyu Company planned on manufacturing.

Because of Kikkoman's slightly higher price and greater urban sales it was the preferred brand of the five brewers who assembled in September to negotiate the founding of the company. But Mogi Saheiji demanded an astonishing 1 million yen for the granting of his family's brand to the beginning company. This split the group into bickering factions, some backing Saheiji's brand, even at a 1-million-yen surcharge, others supporting Shichirōuemon's offer to make Kihaku the company brand without cost. The division was undoubtedly acrimonious, as witnessed by Shichirōuemon's sudden announcement on October 9 that he was leaving almost immediately for America. He had a validated passport in hand and had prepared proofs for the advertising campaign he envisioned for Kihaku in the United States.

At this point Mogi Shichizaemon, head of the senior Mogi household, visited Mogi Saheiji on October 14. There, in discussions between the Mogis Shichizaemon, Keizaburō, Saheiji, and Saheiji's bantō adviser since childhood, Uchida Hisajirō, it was agreed to lower the cost of the Kikkoman brand to 300,000 yen. Mogi Shichizaemon, along with Takanashi Hyōzaemon (two of the original three who started these talks in 1915), carried this news to Mogi Shichirōuemon, who agreed to accept that figure as one of the terms of incorporation. On October 19, at one o'clock in the afternoon, eight principals (seven Mogis and one Takanashi) gathered at the home of Mogi Shichizaemon to reach an understanding over issues of company asset determination, capitalization, and stock ownership. The most crucial part of this process was the evaluation and mutual acceptance of the size of the fixed and liquid assets—the plant, equipment, fermented and fermenting stock—of each family joining the consolidation. An inspection of all such property was conducted by November 7; within another week a final approved inventory of the property contributed by each family was drawn up (see table 8 and Appendix E).[7]

This determination was not as simple as one might think. Not only were some plant and equipment assets jointly owned by several families, but all plant and equipment were not equally valuable. Some boilers were newer than others, some mash more mature, some kegs and vats larger and better made. What is remarkable is that agreement could be reached at all, let alone within several weeks. Willingness to cooperate and compromise, once the initial disagreement over brand selection was settled, established the firm on an amicable footing from the beginning.

The speed with which the process of asset determination was accomplished had one unintended consequence. Capitalized at 7 million yen—all in the form of land, plant, equipment, fermenting mash, and other real assets—the Noda Shōyu Company soon proved to be undercapitalized when new companies were acquired or added during the 1920s. This was corrected without cost to anyone, because all shares in the original company were held within the Mogi-Takanashi group until

TABLE 8. Family assets and appointment when Noda Shōyu Company was incorporated, December 1917 (figures in yen).

Name	Fixed assets	Liquid assets	Appointment[a]	Total
Mogi Shichirōuemon	554,127	1,702,508	Director[b]	2,256,635
Mogi Saheiji	640,890	1,481,078	Director[b]	2,121,977
Takanashi Hyōzaemon	315,453	832,008	Director	1,147,461
Mogi Shichizaemon	251,743	671,668	Director	923,411
Mogi Fusagorō	177,350	502,194	Director	679,544
Noda Shōyu Gōshi K.K.[c]	72,528	159,311	Director	270,839
Mogi Keizaburō	64,151	136,269	Director	200,420
Horikiri Monjirō	42,461	63,473	Auditor	105,934
total	2,118,703	5,587,518		7,706,221

Source: Kikkoman Company Archives, Fixed and Liquid Assets at the Time of Incorporation (1917), handwritten, single page.

a. Appointment titles in Japanese are Director, *Torishimariyaku*, Auditor, *Kansayaku*.

b. In addition, Mogi Shichirōuemon was appointed President (*Shachō*) and Mogi Shichizaemon and Saheiji were made Vice Presidents (*Jōmu Torishimariyaku*). Finally, Nakano Chōbei, although not an investor in the Noda Shōyu Company, was made an Auditor along with Horikiri Monjirō. The Nakano Family was a branch household of the Mogi Shichirōuemon line.

c. Noda Shōyu Gōshi Company was a joint venture between Mogi Yūuemon and Ishikawa Niheiji formed in 1909 after Mogi Yūuemon's brewery had burned down in a fire in 1908.

the company was reorganized and refinanced in 1925, at which time the underevaluation was corrected.

During the final days before consolidation, Horikiri Monjirō, a maker of *mirin* (a sweet sake), from nearby Nagareyama, petitioned the Mogi-Takanashi brewers on November 14 to be allowed to join the amalgamation. The Horikiri family had manufactured both shōyu and sake in the past (the latter since 1766), and it had participated in the Noda Shōyu Manufacturers Association during the first decades of the twentieth century. In addition, the Horikiri and Mogi lineages were related through intermarriage and adoption. Horikiri's proposal was accepted formally one week later, so that nine and not eight families joined in the amalgamation of the Noda Shōyu Company.

Remains of the Cartel

The closing act of consolidation was the separation of the newly formalized firm from what remained of the cartel. The Mogi-Takanashi group leaving it allowed for the cartel's continuation by those families remaining in it. They were not invited to join the corporation, however, and one can only surmise that the cartel seven were excluded primarily on the basis of kinship. Yamashita Heibei, Yamashita Tomisaburō, Tobe Yoshirō, Ishikawa Niheiji (the other half along with Mogi Yūuemon of the Noda Shōyu Gōshi Company), Yoshida Jinzaemon, Shōda Bunuemon, and Iwasaki Kiyoshichi continued to meet semiannually for a period of time to set prices and negotiate rates among themselves, but they could not continue long in competition against the amalgamated leviathan of the Noda Shōyu Company, which at the time of its incorporation in 1917–18 rose to a surprisingly high seventieth place among the largest industrial companies in Japan.[8] The savings plan for accumulating investment capital within the cartel, a feature of its articles of incorporation, was discontinued after 1917, and the accumulated savings as of that time were returned to the donor families according to their proportional contributions. Those remaining in the cartel were allowed free use of the research laboratory, the railroad storage facilities, and the office space that had been the cartel headquarters, but as of 1918 all of these became the property of the Noda Shōyu Company.

The rather obvious division of the cartel properties and interests along family lines was not without precedent. In 1885, two years before the initiation of the Noda shōyu cartel, nine family heads from the Mogi lineage and one Ishikawa Yūuemon formed a mutual-aid society (*mujin-ko*) that, like the cartel, collected dues from its members in order to create a sinking fund for future investment in plant and equipment. The savings thus accrued were designed more to rebuild plant destroyed by fire and natural disaster than to invest in entirely new buildings and equipment, financing of which was left to individual families. In addition to this restorative purpose, the mutual-aid society, known as Senshusha, promoted lineage ritual and interfamily solidarity. It thus was the basis for the exclusive association along family lines that characterized the establishment and top management of the Noda Shōyu Company. The importance of the Senshusha was sustained even after 1918 and the founding of the company; and in 1925 it was reorganized as a holding company for the expanding Mogi-Takanashi business interests.

Of the seven cartel members remaining in 1918, only two have continued with shōyu manufacture into the 1980s. Yamashita Heibei's Kinoene brand has survived in Noda, although its main product now is a chemically manufactured soy sauce rather than one fermented naturally. (Hydrochloric acid is mixed with HVP, hydrolized vegetable protein, to make moromi.) Shoda Bunuemon's product, Shōda soy sauce, remains true to traditional brewing technology and continues to hold a small share of the Tokyo market. However, it has all but been eclipsed, not so much by the success of Kikkoman as by the success of its branch household, headed by Shōda Teiichirō, which established the Nisshin Flour Company, one of the largest food companies in Japan for the last fifty years.

By 1918 nonkinsmen of the Mogi-Takanashi brewers had in effect been excluded from the incorporation of the Noda Shōyu Company. In a sense, this had been happening for perhaps as long as a century. By the beginning of the nineteenth century, when most of those participating Mogi-Takanashi households were already in the business, the pooling of resources—material as well as conceptual—that characterized the commercial and social interaction between interrelated Mogi-Takanashi households assured their success as a group. This success was less at the expense of other families than in comparison with them, for the combined weight of at first eight, and later nine, families was almost impossible to compete against. Brewers unrelated to the Mogis and Takanashis could not realistically be expected to keep up—especially when the time came to coordinate efforts and to capitalize joint operations at far above what had been the traditional financial and managerial requirements—and indeed they failed to do so.

The Noda Shōyu Company

By 1918, after a decade of increasing need for coordination within the cartel, and after several years of negotiation among its Mogi-Takanashi members, a new institution with somewhat different goals from those of the brewers' union was founded. The Noda Shōyu Company, which began operations on January 1, 1918, was established not for many of the reasons normally associated with incorporation. Different types of securities, debt and equity, were not issued; a wide sale of securities was not encouraged; managerial control was not separated from ownership (in fact the opposite occurred), and the liability of stockholders was not limited since the principal officers of the corporation were also its principal stockholders. Perpetual succession of management within the firm was placed on firm ground, but this had not been a problem in Japanese entrepreneurial firms where family continuity, and therefore management continuity, was more the rule than the exception.

In truth, the Noda Shōyu Company for the first four or five decades of its history was much more like a partnership than a true joint-stock company. This would figure prominently in many aspects of the firm's development, but it was never more obvious than during the first decade of its operation.

1918 to 1927: The First Decade—Process of Incorporation

The idea of a corporation was debated and adopted during the closing months of 1917. During the next year the concept had to be translated into form and function. Although the Mogi-Takanashi brewers had long cooperated, in business as well as in family matters, nothing had prepared them for the reality of the complex problems of coordination, control, scheduling, and command that the amalgamation of some 1,000 workers, 50 managers, and scores of plants, warehouses, research units, sales offices, transportation and storage sites entailed. The Mogi-Takanashi managers were familiar with each of these operations individually of course; but being familiar with and in control of a complex of operations is quite a different matter, especially if the goal is to coordinate this maze into something at once more manageable and profitable than a simple amalgamation of independent enterprises.

Prior to incorporation, with the exception of matters external to the enterprise (purchasing, shipping, distribution, and, to a degree, pricing), all internal concerns—which is to say, production and operation—were handled independently by separate family concerns. This decentralization of production obviously decreased the need for information flow among the numerous makers of shōyu. What communication there was tended to be handled rather informally, through such institutions as the Senshusha. But in order to take full advantage of a corporation's potential for centralized planning, such a tradition of decentralization had to be renounced.

Within a decade of incorporation there would be two internal shifts, both designed to increase coordination and centralization and both requiring substantial organizational changes in order to provide channels for the flow and use of production and operation information. The first shift began almost immediately and continued for five years or so. This was a period of highly centralized planning that emphasized better scheduling of manufacturing, sales, and distribution and concentrated the decisionmaking for such improvements in a limited number of coordinating committees. These committees channeled the flow of information, which allowed for better planning of inventory levels, more timely production in accordance with market fluctuations, more success with branded product sales in specialized markets, and more effective integration of research results from the laboratory into the factories.

The second shift, which began around 1923–24, lasted for the next three or four decades. It was distinguished by a realization that all decisions could not and should not be filtered through the upper reaches of the company only to be delegated through successive lower layers of the organization. In this period, therefore, the solution to the overwhelming task of trying to coordinate everything in the corporation was once again to decentralize decisionmaking and information flow in certain functions, as in the time before incorporation, while allowing for a two-way flow of communications in other areas. In short, this phase begins an era of experimentation with arranging a balance between centralization and decentralization.

In this second, prolonged period of experimentation, the Noda Shōyu Company attempted to decentralize decisionmaking for day-to-day operations by creating a number of separate companies supervised loosely by a holding company. This strategy sought to increase information flow at the lower levels of the combined enterprise and thereby decrease the need for top managers to make a lot of nonstrategic decisions. They could now concentrate on issues of overall coordination and long-range planning. This particular phase evinced several specific manifestations of the new decentralization. Certain product lines were made autonomous, such as Manjō Mirin, a sweet sake, and Jinsen Shōyu, a soy sauce brewed in Inchon, Korea. New departments were created to handle certain issues without referring them to top management. The best examples of this were the departments of sales, personnel, architecture, and brewing, which grew out of the committee structure established during the first phase of corporate development.

1918 to 1925: From Committees to Functional Departments

One of the clearer, yet, in the long run, least permanent indications of the character of the new company as compared to the cartel was found in the keeping of an attendance ledger for managers from April to December 1918.[9] This record contained the daily activities of the thirteen top and thirty-five middle managers of the company. Their work attendance in Tokyo or Noda, their holidays, and their sick-leaves were meticulously recorded. Nothing of this sort had been attempted during the period of independent enterprise operation of course, for at that time it was essentially impossible to distinguish between corporate and personal time. Enterprise and family were synonymous as far as any issues of control and ownership were concerned, and it would have been ludicrous to keep attendance records. The early effort to keep track of managerial attendance at the Noda Shōyu Company, although short-lived (it did not survive the first year), represents one of the most striking of a variety of methods employed to regularize company routine not only for factory workers but for the owner-managers of the firm as well.

The attendance record makes it clear that the early managers of the Noda Shōyu Company considered work a duty. Mogi Shichirōuemon, the company president, Mogi Saheiji, and Takanashi Hyōzaemon—the three senior officers—worked an average of 25–26 days per month, barring illness. Their former bantō, now the middle managers of the firm, had even higher attendance, reporting for work virtually every day of the month. The same dedication to work and willingness of managers to submit to a new routine are revealed in the minutes of a number of committees established in the company in 1918–19.

These committees were designed to consider matters important to the successful operation of the new firm and to communicate suggestions to the firm's top and middle managers. The three central committees were sales, research, and managerial coordination. They were the first to consider such crucial issues as the integration of research and development with production, the coordination of production with sales and marketing, product quality control, employee compensation, and motivation. Such committees represented the first concrete attempts to establish institutional devices within the firm for the purposes of consolidating and evaluating information, coordinating the efforts of numerous units, and centralizing decisionmaking that affected the entire firm. The records of committee meetings constitute a remarkable documentation of how a newly established corporation undertakes the complex tasks of coordination, allocation, and control when fifteen different factories and as many front offices are amalgamated.

Sales Committee. The records of the Sales Committee date from February 12, 1919.[10] At its first meeting, which was attended by three Mogis and one Ishikawa as well as by those involved in local sales outside of the Tokyo area, the standardization of billing periods, practices, and paperwork was discussed. These matters did not have to be discussed relative to the urban market because at the time this area was handled by the Tokyo Shōyu Tonya Association. It was decided that outstanding accounts should be settled four times annually—in January, April, July, and October. It was noted that the company needed to respond more quickly to customers' orders and ship them within ten days. The effect of container size—the capacity of soy sauce barrels—on retail sales was discussed, and a schedule of discounts based on container size was prepared. As might be expected, the larger the container, the greater the discount. A discussion of what to do when goods spoiled in transit or while awaiting final sale was recorded.

One of the most vexing problems was that the taste and character of shōyu made in the various factories was not uniform. Until a more consistent quality could be guaranteed, it was the responsibility of those in sales to match customers' preferences for a soy sauce of a particular color, taste, and aroma with what was being produced. Most often this meant that the variety of brands brewed prior to incorporation had to be continued after incorporation as well, which was a grave deterrent to the achievement of economies of scale in production that might be realized if only one standardized brand was manufactured. The tactic of those in sales, therefore, was to try to supply customers with their former brands, while simultaneously introducing them to Kikkoman.

Although Kikkoman was the price leader among the brands made in Noda, it was only one of thirty-four brands offered at nine different prices by nine different breweries at the time of incorporation. Mogi Shichirōuemon and Takanashi Hyōzaemon had six brands each; Mogi Saheiji, Shichizaemon, and Fusagorō five each, Mogi Yūuemon boasted four, and Mogi Keizaburō, Horikiri Monjirō, and Ishikawa Niheiji produced once apiece. The price range stretched from 4.20 and 4.0 yen per barrel of Kikkoman and Kihaku respectively, all the way to 1.70 yen per barrel for six other brands. Obviously price and brand uniformity, based on product consistency and quality, was a crucial matter for the newly founded firm.

The problem had legal repercussions. At the Sales Committee meeting of May 6, 1919, it was announced that the government had determined that all trademarks in Japan had to be registered. The purpose of this was to specify clearly the nature of those trademarks and to protect them from infringement. Apparently the switching of a brand trademark of a higher-priced line to a product of lesser quality and price was fairly common, and most often Kikkoman was the Noda brand misused in this manner. Since barrels were the most commonly used containers for soy sauce, a fraudulent trademark need only be pasted on the barrels in order to deceive customers. In order to prevent this, manufacturers conceived elaborately designed trademarks and other "signatures" of their handiwork. But these too could be copied, and they were bothersome to apply in the breweries and to monitor in the marketplace.

The popularity of one brand as opposed to others impinged on the company's ability to plan production runs for its thirty-four different brands. By the sixth meeting of the Sales Committee, on August 5, 1919, it was apparent that some sort of quantitative estimates of monthly sales volume by brand were needed in order to plan overall production and to compare each month's sales performance with that of previous periods. A system of inspection was needed as well, in order to measure and evaluate the quality of each factory's output. These measures were introduced gradually, during the summer and fall of 1919. A fairly typical result of such scrutiny is revealed by an inspection on June 19, 1919, of shōyu barrels stacked at the railway station (see table 9).

The various issues touching on sales were repeatedly discussed and

TABLE 9. Barrel inspection at the Noda railway station, June 1919.

Factory of origin[a]	Production grade	Problem
2	6	barrels in poor condition
4	5	trademark not legible (5 cases), barrel seal bad (2)
5	5	no trademark (1), packing poor (1), barrel lids poorly sealed
6	6	packing rope insecure (1)
8	5	no date stamp (3)
10	6	no date stamp (1), no label (1), bottom and top seals bad (1 & 3)
11	5	no date stamp (1), barrel unclean (1), top seal bad (1), top lid insecure (1)
12	5	packing rope insecure (1), barrel in poor condition (1), barrel seals (2)
13	4	no date stamp (3), packing insecure (1), barrel in poor shape (1)
14	5	no trademark (1), barrel unclean (1), barrel seals bad (2)
15	5	no date stamp (1), no trademark (1), barrel seals in poor condition (2)

Source: Kikkoman Company Archives, Minutes of the Meetings of the Sales Committee (n.p., 1919), p. 18.

a. When the inspection occurred, there were no shipments from factories 1 and 3 on the loading docks for inspection.

debated at the meetings of the Sales Committee. It is fair to assume that a whole set of interrelated problems had to be solved more or less simultaneously if the increased potential for production and distribution that had been made possible through consolidation were to be realized. The following list, assembled from the minutes of the meetings of the Sales Committee from February 12 to November 15, 1919, demonstrates the complex linkage between sales and a variety of business functions, and the need of the Noda Shōyu Company to organize itself effectively in order to gather accurate information about its products and markets and to sell ever larger quantities of soy sauce in Japan and overseas.

Sales require:
    (1) coordination of the size of different containers with:
        (a) production levels
        (b) sales preferences for different brands in different volumes
        (c) sales performance of competitors;

(2) coordination with economic conditions, trends, and cycles;

(3) coordination of advertising strategies and campaigns;

(4) coordination of a variety of transportation schedules;

(5) coordination of production of certain brands in certain factories with estimated sales levels;

(6) coordination of inventory levels within and between various factories;

(7) coordination of various inducements to sales, such as rebates, gifts, pricing adjustments, and other sales bargaining techniques;

(8) coordination of a system of incentives and rewards for salesmen.

The coordination of each of these items or areas with sales was quite complicated, and the effort to combine and to give priority to certain ones enforced a type of planning and discipline on the fledgling firm for which it was not prepared. The members of the Sales Committee learned this lesson rapidly, however, so that by 1920 the minutes of its meetings record sophisticated debates over the merits of one kind of advertising or another. Product promotion through advertising in newspapers was contrasted with the use of posters, handbills, and postcards. Customer rebates were examined at both the wholesale and retail levels. Price competition and seasonal adjustments to prices were discussed, as was the advisability of decreasing the variety of brands offered. In the end, the strategy decided upon was to reduce the variety of brands and advertise those that remained heavily.

This decision meant that the company could designate the entire production of certain factories for certain brands on a continuing basis, thereby allowing for longer production runs that reduced the per-unit cost and prevented the confusion that resulted when production lines were switched from one brand to another. The move also allowed decisions affecting the volume and timing of production of certain brands to be decentralized to the factories that were producing them exclusively. Such decentralization of production matters allowed top executives to concentrate on matters other than the day-to-day operation of their fifteen factories.

By 1923 the original thirty-four brands of shōyu had been reduced to sixteen. Simplification of factory production in this manner allowed for better and more continuous scheduling of train transportation for the larger volume of the remaining brands. Recognizing this possibility, the company invested 413,122 yen in upgrading the Noda-Kashiwa railroad line between 1919 and 1921 in order to carry heavier and more frequent loads.

Research Committee. The work of the Research Committee, which began meeting on June 28, 1919, was to consider the firm's overall performance and to propose improvements.[11] With such a broad mandate, it is not surprising that the range of issues considered was extensive. The importance of the committee was evidenced by the regular attendance of three of the firm's top five officers: Mogi Shichizaemon, Mogi Saheiji, and Nakano Eizaburō.

The tenor of the committee was revealed early in a statement by Mogi Shichizaemon, who announced on September 28:

> I have heard that Chōshi [shōyu] has improved scientifically while Noda has improved financially in recent years. But we have no enemies in the world of soy sauce manufacture, so we are not immediately threatened. But if we depend on our capital alone and cling to old-fashioned technology, we will fall behind and eventually lose to the competition. Fortunately, scientific advances occur every day and our firm is involved continually in research to brew shōyu in new and better ways. We intend to dedicate ourselves to research as well as to sales, continuing with one research project after another, accumulating experience and practice, following the progress of the day. We will achieve the highest possible position in this business.

This ringing statement of purpose and method was not easily realized, however, for not only were the firm's established methods of manufacture sometimes antiquated, but some practices of management fell into the same category as well. Consider another statement by Mogi Shichizaemon, who had pronounced himself so decidedly in favor of shōyu manufacture by the scientific method:

> In order to maintain proper relationships between the young and the elderly, we must remind apprentices not to stand next to their superiors when walking on the road. A correct relationship between generations is the means whereby peace and order are maintained in society and this has been one of the strong points of our country. I believe that such good points need to be emphasized and that their importance needs to be taught widely.[12]

Here a potential conflict between machines and management philosophy, between the scientific method and the rule of the aged, is revealed, one that is apparent from the earliest days of the Noda Shōyu Company. These attitudes should not be singled out as exceptional at Noda, however, for most Japanese entrepreneurs willingly accepted Western machines and techniques, while rejecting most Western thoughts and customs. The early managers of the Noda Shōyu Company felt no contradiction in adopting a potentially confusing approach whereby Western science and the scientific method were drawn on, while Western ideas of individuality and equality were not—especially as they applied to the workplace.

This is not to say that the company—or, more precisely, the Research Committee—was unaware of issues and problems concerning workers. At the same meeting at which Mogi Shichizaemon spoke about enforcing seniority distinctions to maintain peace and order, the need to establish facilities to maintain worker morale as well as issues involving more pay for workers were discussed. But it is important to understand that the initiative for such changes had to come from management and not labor. For workers to suggest such reforms would be considered outside the natural order of things, improper, and, therefore, impossible to consider. In the proper manner, and at the proper time the company would decide such matters. In fact a few years later, in 1922, the company established a Personnel Department to determine on a systematic basis matters of worker compensation, training, and benefits. Yet the creation of a Personnel Department and the operation of the firm were matters entirely within the hands of the patriarchal and decidedly authoritarian owner-managers.

At the August 28, 1919, meeting the Research Committee heard a preliminary report from one of the company engineers on the feasibility and desirability of using compressed air as an aid to mixing and stirring the mash during fermentation, thereby speeding the process.[13] The committee recommended continued study of this promising innovation. At the same meeting, the advantages and disadvantages of centralizing all kōji incubation rooms were discussed. The advantages of inventory and sanitation control had to be weighed against the disadvantages of reduced access; the need for greater and more accurate information flow to coordinate the needs of numerous decentralized factories with one centralized culture room had to be assessed. This matter, too, was left for further study, although the mood of the meeting favored decentralization of the kōji rooms with more stringent controls on their operation.

A month later the important issues discussed were the need to standardize the system of emblazoning the dates of manufacture on the barrels of shōyu; the necessity of gaining the support of the factory production foremen (tōji) in coordinating the decentralization of the kōji rooms; and the desirability of establishing a keg-making facility under the direct supervision of the company. A standardized method of dating was necessary to keep track of production and inventory levels, to maintain quality control checks on each factory, and to regularize shipping and distribution. The decision to leave kōji rooms decentralized by attaching them directly to each factory evidenced the growing sophistication of the company's management, one that appreciated the advantages of decentralizing resources to the lowest level in the firm consonant with proper controls on production. At least the management was willing to attempt this approach before moving to consolidate the kōji rooms.

The decision to set up "at an appropriate time" a keg-manufacturing plant under the direct management of the company was extremely significant. Kegs were expensive to make, maintain, and store. Not only did it require great manual skill and experience to make them properly, but they had to be checked continually to ensure the integrity of their seals. When not in use they were bulky and difficult to store. The balance between the number of kegs available, the number needed, and the number in repair was a critical one. Furthermore, because kegs were bought from dozens of subcontractors (in actuality small shops of artisans), inventory control was nearly impossible, and it was difficult to reach agreement among so many parties on the standardization of keg sizes, shapes, and characteristics. Accordingly, the company began to explore the possibility of establishing its own keg-making capability, the purpose of which, at least initially, was to complement the production of the many coopers in town, not to substitute for them, and to ensure a steady flow of kegs of the proper sort.

In 1919 the company conducted a survey of cooperages in and around Noda. It discovered that there were as many as sixty shops making kegs for the company, all independent and all decentralized in their manner of operation. Each shop supported a master craftsman and an average of 8 additional workers, for a total of 565 workers in the trade. Of these, 225 were apprentices of an average sixteen years of age, while 280 were journeymen, twice the age of the apprentices on average.[14]

The large number of keg-making shops and the even larger number of coopers, all dependent to varying degrees on the Noda Shōyu Company for continued employment, proved to be a virtually intractable management problem for the company. By tradition and inclination such craftsmen were unlikely to become company employees; yet without this, the problems of standardizing and coordinating five dozen different cooperages were insurmountable. Proper containers were essential for achieving the degree of mass production and distribution for which the company was created. The company's solution—perhaps the only one available to it—was gradually to reduce its dependence on the coopers by establishing its own keg-making plant and to explore the utility of other containers, such as bottles and cans, both of which were introduced by 1922–23. Within a decade the majority of kegs used by Noda Shōyu were company-made, which freed the firm from a set of particularly vexing production and distribution problems. This solution, however, came at considerable cost to the company and community, as will be revealed when the Great Noda Strike of 1927–28 is discussed.

By the late summer of 1920 the walls of the new keg-making factory were up and workers were being hired. The recruitment of laborers for this facility had to be combined with an enlarged search for experienced and reliable workers of all kinds. As the company grew rapidly, and as multiple plants and units of the company were brought into coordination, issues of finding, keeping, training, and motivating workers began to concern management more and more. A study conducted in 1918 revealed, for example, that in one brewery, probably that of Horikiri Monjirō, most workers were paid according to a rather inflexible pay scale. Some 49 out of 68 workers were paid either 7.70 or 10.95 yen per month, corresponding in all likelihood to whether or not a laborer was classified as a honnin or shinnin worker—that is, experienced or inexperienced. The 11 who were paid less than 7.70 yen per month were either very young or old. Only 8 of 68 workers, a meager 12 percent of the total, were paid by some criterion other than those listed; among these would be found the tōji, as well as other technicians and mechanics. In other words, almost all workers received a relatively undifferentiated wage based either on age or experience.[15] Such a compensation scheme might do when the labor force was largely temporary and the work mainly unskilled, but as the production process became more or less constant and complex, a compensation schedule that both rewarded and motivated workers was needed.

At the August 28th Research Committee meeting the desirability of on-the-job training was discussed. It was agreed that ideally such training would prevent workers either from wanting to leave the company or from being hired away. It was further suggested that some sort of piecework incentive based on the volume of goods shipped by a factory might be implemented to motivate workers. At the May 28, 1921, meeting the committee decided to pay workers for attending training and educational lectures after work hours and to alter the method of paying them from one based exclusively on using tōji as go-betweens to one that achieved a greater balance between tōji and the head office. All of this was done, committee records note, in the interest of "creating a harmonious relationship between factory workers and the company."[16]

Another innovation recommended by the Research Committee was the establishment of a department of brewing that would act as an intermediary between the dozen or so brewing factories and the central research and development laboratory. A department of inspection was likewise proposed, to handle quality control sampling, taste-test comparisons, standardization of product and container, and other approaches to measuring and evaluating the production process. The need for a department of building and architecture to design new structures and remodel old ones was discussed. It would aid in the design of more efficient ways to handle the storage, flow, and processing of production line materials. When new hydraulic presses were introduced in 1922–23, for example, it was the responsibility of the architecture department to introduce and integrate them into the production line.

Many of the Research Committee's suggestions required organizational change, usually involving the addition of new, specialized departments to handle technical functions such as building and production design, quality inspection and control, and labor management and training. These changes are clearly shown in a comparison of the organization of the firm for 1918, 1920, 1923 (figures 6, 7, and 8). Not only does the organization grow larger, but it has become considerably more complex in form and function by 1923. The number of managerial appointments has jumped remarkably in the five-year period, and the

FIGURE 6. ORGANIZATIONAL STRUCTURE AND MANAGERIAL APPOINTMENTS
NODA SHŌYU COMPANY 1918

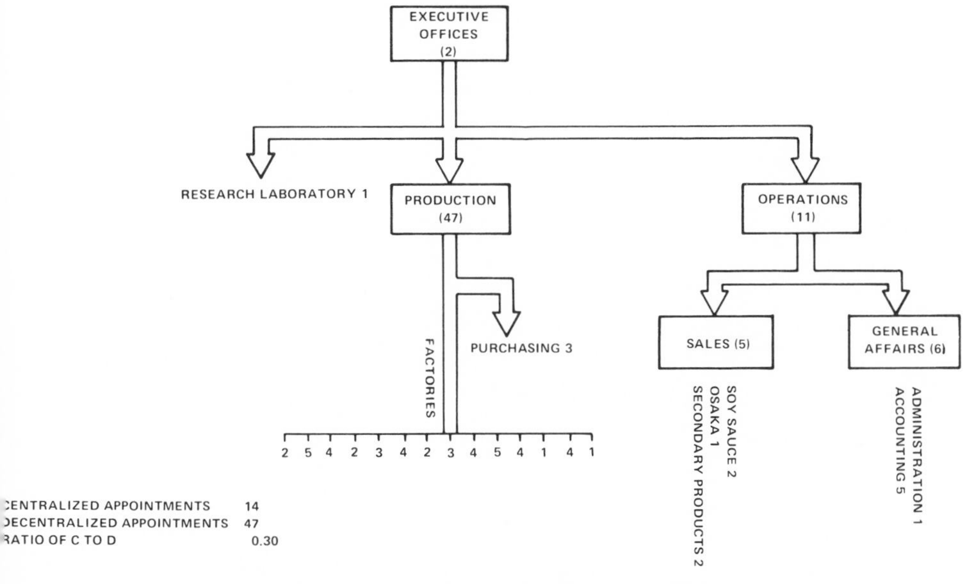

CENTRALIZED APPOINTMENTS 14
DECENTRALIZED APPOINTMENTS 47
RATIO OF C TO D 0.30

THIS FIGURE AND THE NEXT TWO WERE PREPARED BY THE AUTHOR USING THE INFORMATION CONTAINED IN THE COMPANY PERSONNEL RECORDS FOR MANAGERIAL EMPLOYEES. NUMBERS SHOWN IN BOXES OR AT THE END OF A LINE REPRESENT THE NUMBER OF MANAGERIAL APPOINTMENTS FOR THE YEAR IN THAT AREA.

112

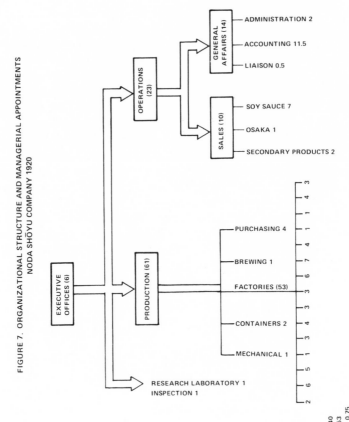

FIGURE 7. ORGANIZATIONAL STRUCTURE AND MANAGERIAL APPOINTMENTS
NODA SHŌYU COMPANY 1920

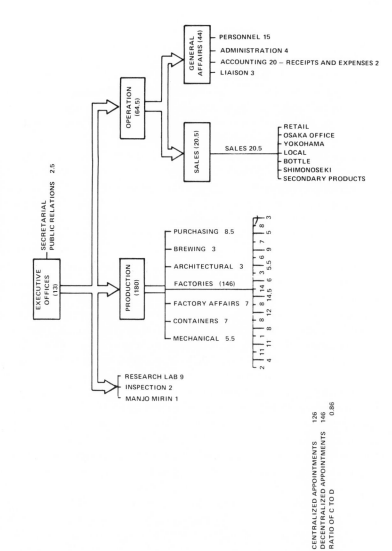

FIGURE 8. ORGANIZATIONAL STRUCTURE AND MANAGERIAL APPOINTMENTS
NODA SHŌYU COMPANY 1923

CENTRALIZED APPOINTMENTS 126
DECENTRALIZED APPOINTMENTS 146
RATIO OF C TO D 0.86

ratio of centralized to decentralized appointments—that is, the number of assignments in the head office or one of its departments as opposed to work in one of the operating plants—has changed rather noticeably as well. In 1918, out of a total of 61 managerial assignments, only 17 were centralized. The ratio of centralized to decentralized positions was 0.30, but by 1923 there were 272 managerial posts, and the ratio of centralized to decentralized slots had doubled to 0.86.[17] This reflected the corporate goals of centralization and coordination.

Second Day of the Month Committee. The minutes of the *Futsuka-kai*, the Second Day of the Month Committee, date from September 2, 1919, and reflect yet another side of the early efforts to combine, rationalize, and reorganize the company.[18] The meetings, which usually included top executives and factory managers, were designed both to deal with matters of organization and production and to encourage and motivate front-line managers with responsibility for day-to-day operations. During 1919 and 1920 a number of themes were repeated in the meetings; they constitute a sort of shorthand for the concerns of management at the operational level in the company's initial years. The need for inspection, sanitation, and efficiency in the workplace is emphasized. New methods for measuring and evaluating quality control were discussed and ultimately introduced under the aegis of the committee.

In the fall of 1919 a new system of recordkeeping designed to calculate the input of raw material at each factory site against the output of finished products was introduced. From this, it was a straightforward task to gather comparative figures and to eliminate the deficiencies of some plants while institutionalizing the methods of the most efficient factories. Before long, the gathering of statistics became one of the most important functions performed by factory managers. One purpose of the Futsuka-kai was to facilitate this function. By the end of 1919 bookkeeping and other recordkeeping procedures were unified throughout the factories and offices of Noda Shōyu.

With statistical tools and measures to guide operational management, corporate leadership had a dual purpose: the relatively easy task was to apply the tools of numerical analysis; the more difficult challenge was to encourage and motivate employees to act upon that analysis. The minutes of the meeting of November 2, 1919, reflect this duality. Mogi Shichizaemon announced the three important goals of the company: reduce the loss of raw materials; eliminate useless expenses; use everything and waste nothing.[19] Progress in these goals could be measured by the company's recently implemented recordkeeping procedures, but rather than attempt to do so in an obvious way by suggesting, say, a campaign to reduce waste by 5 percent in a six-month period, Mogi Shichizaemon chose instead to lecture to the members of the committee on a matter of morality. He did this by reminding everyone that, with the exception of those who were sick or over fifty years of age, no employees were to wear *tabi* (socks) to work until November 20th of each year. He recalled that this had long been a local custom and that it should be continued as a spiritual discipline to make everyone strong in adverse circumstances. Such discipline would have a positive effect on the operation of the company.

Shichizaemon's morality lessons continued at the meetings held on the second day of December 1919 and of April 1920. In December he reported that the performance and interpersonal relations among front-office employees were unexpectedly high and truly ideal. Accordingly, he declared:

> One should expect the same level of achievement among the factory foremen, the factory and transportation workers, as well as the coopers. This can be achieved only when a relationship based on the distinction between superior and subordinate is understood. The importance and permanency of this relationship must be taught directly as well as indirectly and must be understood by all. In this way it would become clear that the enterprise is made up of three classes: owners, office workers, and laborers, and that each of these must consider their position in relation to the others and strive to maintain harmonious relations with them. Within the factory, the factory manager should be considered as the father, the foreman as the mother, and the inspector as the successor to the father. Thus, everyone is a member of the same family and they should live together harmoniously as a result.

Shichizaemon's family analogy was not confined to the factories of Noda Shōyu. At the April 2nd meeting he asserted that:

> There appears to be a tendency toward dissatisfaction among certain workers who are influenced by unhealthy and dangerous ideologies. Remember that since the beginning of Japan, all Japanese have belonged to the nation as part of the same great family. The people are children of the emperor and the emperor is the father of the nation. Faith and filial piety are one and the same since the emperor and the nation are one. . . . Although Western nations can be a model for Japan in material matters, when it comes to morality, no other nation can serve as an example to Japan and no other nation is superior to Japan. This superiority is reflected in our company as well because it is organized by a family and is like a family. Because of the unity of superior and subordinate in our company which is based on centuries of tradition and effort, we have been able to accomplish an enviable record so far. To continue our success, we must maintain our traditions, establish loyalty and filial piety, and revere industriousness. In sum, we must commit ourselves to the country as well as to the company.[20]

Shichizaemon's sermons were not hypocritical. He and the other top executives took such Confucian and patriotic preachings seriously and attempted to incorporate them into the management philosophy of Noda Shōyu. Philosophy was combined with statistical analysis to provide managerial direction; moral examples were coupled with efficiency studies as part of the natural order of the universe. The basic message contained in the Confucian underpinning of the company, it will be seen in Chapter 4, was that all employees had their place and purpose in the firm and were expected to perform the duties associated with their position to the best of their abilities. Statistics might be a tool to pinpoint corporate shortcomings, but interpersonal harmony and mutual hard work provided the answers to such deficiencies. The responsibility to be both efficient and moral fell equally on managers and workers because each group had duties and obligations. When duties were not fully discharged, disharmony and mismanagement resulted. Moral exhortation was not intended solely for workers; as a result, managers performed their duties with a fervor second to none.

The last meeting of the Second Day of the Month Committee in 1921 provided evidence of this sense of equal burden. Mogi Shichirōuemon, the company president, opened the meeting with an apology for the fire that had broken out in Factory 15 the night of November 5. He confessed that it "was due to the lack of virtue on the part of the Board of Directors, for if they had done their duty and discharged their obligations properly, the design defects in the wheat roasting room, where the fire erupted, would have been discovered and corrected."[21]

Fortunately, the chief officers' views of company management were not confined to Confucian example and confessional breast-beating. The founding of a personnel office in 1922 and a restructuring of factory organization in 1923 offer the most concrete examples that management was aware of a need for more than familistic and exhortative models of management philosophy and practice.

Personnel Department. Created initially to provide training for workers and to rationalize the system of compensation, the Personnel Department, founded in 1922, became, as early as 1925, one of the largest departments in the company. Its establishment can be traced directly to many of the concerns raised in the meetings of the Sales, Research, and Futsuka-kai committees.

At first the department's functions were threefold: to design an equitable wage system; to develop a system for handling internal job transfers and rotations; and to house employees properly and provide for their education. Initially these functions were handled in a rather piecemeal manner and without any overall design. There was little agreement on the type of employee needed; as a result, specific skills, attitudes, and loyalties had not yet been identified as desirable or teachable. Ideas about desirable characteristics remained general rather than specific to the company. Yet, without a carefully conceived scheme of what a company employee should be, it was impossible to articulate a program that would develop the human resources needed by the firm. Such a program would come, but only after specific notions of company policy with regard to worker service and livelihood were clarified. When a refined program of human resource development and employee compensation was established in 1930, it quickly differentiated employees into two groups: regular employees, who enjoyed on-the-job training and promotion as well as off-the-job housing and cultural benefits; and temporary or part-time employees who had neither.

Although it would be accurate to suggest that the company launched itself quite early into personnel matters—particularly in the areas of proper decorum, on-the-job training, food, lodging, and extracurricular activities for employees—it is necessary to distinguish between the early and somewhat general interest in such matters and the later, rather more specific concerns with employee regulation and reward. One reason for this important distinction was that in the earliest years of the corporation—say, before 1925—its size was relatively small and many of its employees had been hired from the breweries run by Mogi-Takanashi family members in the precorporate period. Such employees were, by and large, already socialized and already accustomed to working in the close and confining world of a traditional family enterprise. They brought their years of experience in shōyu manufacture to the new company. Once the firm began to expand rapidly, however, finding new employees with skills to match changing methods of production and operation became essential. It was the responsibility of the Personnel Department after 1922 to recruit, train, motivate, and compensate such employees.

The growing significance of personnel work is manifested by the increasing size of the Personnel Department. In 1923, within a year of its establishment, there were fifteen workers in the central department and another seven in the factories assigned to an Office of Factory Affairs. By 1926 the numbers had climbed to forty-nine and eight respectively.

Factory Organization and the Office of Factory Affairs. The Office of Factory Affairs was an innovative attempt to handle the many complications resulting from a 1923 reorganization that placed managers concerned primarily with matters of personnel directly in the nearly two dozen shōyu factories now operating in Noda. This restructuring began with the methods of recruiting and supervising employees. The role of the oyabun, or labor recruiter, had been to find workers, introduce them to breweries, and negotiate their contracts. As independent contractors, oyabun worked closely with the numerous employers in town. The system remained intact in the Noda breweries until 1922. Of course some workers found employment through other channels, but until the second decade of the twentieth century, oyabun supplied the majority. After 1922 the recruitment of workers was handled by the newly created, centralized Personnel Department.

The assignment of workers after recruitment also was restructured. Heretofore they had been introduced to the tōji (factory foreman) in each factory, who had complete responsibility and authority for assigning them work and training them for it. After 1922 the tōji's responsibilities no longer extended to worker placement and education. These were now handled by the Personnel Department, whose policies and regulations were enforced in the factories by the new Office of Factory Affairs; the factory manager, as opposed to factory foreman, handled matters of assignment and training. Although managers had been in the factories with the tōji since the first days of incorporation, their role and their relationship to the tōji were not clarified until 1922. After that time tōji lost the independence and authority that they had previously enjoyed as the supreme technicians in the art of brewing soy sauce. A centralized research and development laboratory had taken much of the mystery out of brewing shōyu, and the departments of Brewing and of Inspection had ensured that each factory had received and understood the benefits of that research. Brewing, once an art, had become a science, and the traditional role of the tōji as brewmaster and plant manager was reduced to one of a simple factory foreman who ensured that the production process flowed smoothly but interfered little in it after 1923. Moreover, after 1923, when questions of production and operation arose, they were channeled through the factory manager, not the tōji, to the appropriate centralized office or department. The statistical records on which the brewing process and evaluation of that production were based were now kept by factory managers, not by the foremen.

The reorganization of the factory was part of the overall company reorganization in 1922–23. The Personnel Department and other centralized units took over their specialized functions in place of the committee system that had operated for the preceding four or five years. As this occurred, the autonomy of the oyabun and oyakata (another term for tōji in Noda) was removed, and matters of operation and production, formerly decided by the tōji in each individual factory, were now determined by the research and routine of centralized managers.

The new organization, implemented on January 1, 1923, replaced the older, more limited job demarcations in the workplace with a structure of far more complicated appointments and assignments. The hierarchy of tōji, kashira, mugi-iri, and kama-ya was supplanted by the rather elaborate form shown in figure 9.

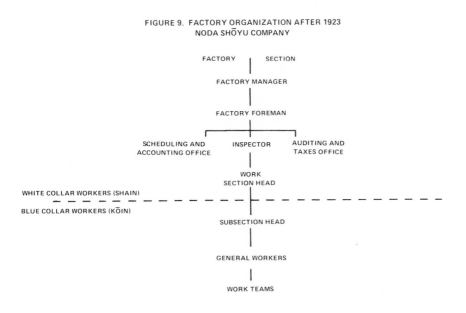

FIGURE 9. FACTORY ORGANIZATION AFTER 1923
NODA SHŌYU COMPANY

SOURCE: INTERVIEW WITH NAKANO EIZABURŌ, PAST PRESIDENT OF KIKKOMAN SHŌYU
COMPANY, ON SEPTEMBER 11, 1976.

The continued expansion of company control and coordination into
the organization of work and the livelihood of workers was increasingly
evident after the creation of the Personnel Department in 1922, as examples show. In October 1922 the first codification of company rules
and regulations was issued; this was followed in January 1923 by an attempt to define policy in the areas of employee benefits and assistance.
These written guidelines of proper company decorum, the organization
of work in different departments, and opportunities for education and
self-improvement were circulated in loose-leaf form to every department and factory, where they were bound and displayed for the
edification of all. By 1924 at least fifteen such directives dealing with
job-related medical benefits alone had been issued. They covered such
varied aspects as sick pay and hospital benefits during illness, the use of
vacation time for illnesses extending more than five days, medical coverage for injuries not incurred on the job, on-the-job medical benefits
for temporary employees, family medical coverage, and burial benefits
for full-time and part-time employees. Other directives explained company policy in matters dealing with education, retirement, savings
plans, and company-subsidized housing. It must be emphasized, however, that directives dealing with employee benefits were less numerous

than those outlining employee regulations, duties, and obligations, which were so numerous as to make their summary here impossible. In short, after 1922 the company began defining job responsibilities and job-related benefits in detail. Once this process began the company found itself increasingly deciding standards for on-the-job performance as well as off-the-job behavior.[22]

An example of an expanding area of responsibility is the dramatic reversal of housing policy in 1922. Up until this time the company had operated worker dormitories, called hiroshiki, where unmarried workers received room and board for practically no charge. The facilities were admittedly primitive, but tradition has it that workers were guaranteed their fill of rice and vegetables as well as a daily bath. Hiroshiki were abandoned after 1922 in favor of kishukusha, company-built or subsidized boardinghouses. Four-page circulars boasting of the company's history and of the newly built boardinghouses were published in March 1923 to attract new workers. The pamphlets included a map showing the location of the boardinghouses in Noda; a blueprintlike drawing of the houses detailing the size of the rooms and their relation to one another as well as to the common rooms; and an analysis of the budget for building more boardinghouses in the coming year.[23]

In addition to the company-supported education classes offered at the boardinghouses, the firm subsidized the cost of living there, so that in 1923 monthly room and board costs amounted to 40 sen per day, or 12 yen per month. If an average worker in the soy sauce plants earned about 100 yen per month at that time, room and board in the company dormitory amounted to only 12 percent of his income. Surprisingly, not enough workers were convinced initially of the attractiveness of such a relatively inexpensive cost of living, balanced against the nearly free room and board of the hiroshiki system, for the kishukusha were not filled up without considerable company encouragement.

The company could not allow the hiroshiki system to continue indefinitely, however. Not only was its extremely low cost based on a failure of the company and its antecedent breweries to control costs outside of production before 1922, but its often unsanitary and crowded conditions were not consistent with a view that labor was a corporate resource that needed to be conserved. Also, the change from hiroshiki to kishukusha allowed the company to continue its campaign of combining efficiency with morality. Now workers could live in a healthier environment, attend evening classes, eat well, and, as a result, perform better on the job. The company goal of "using everything and wasting nothing" was no longer confined to matters of production and operation. It could not be separated from the larger mission of the company: to manufacture shōyu efficiently and scientifically while retaining the traditional morality and virtue of Japan. To do this, managerial authority and routine were extended to all areas of corporate life, whether in kōji inoculation rooms or in company boardinghouses.

The restructuring of the firm was not confined to factories and to workers by any means. Every functional area was modified and reorganized, and by late 1924, when front office and factory had been reworked, top management turned its attention to the upper reaches of the corporation as well, satisfied for the moment with its accomplishments elsewhere.

1925 to 1927: Holding Company Reorganization

The 1925 reorganization was dramatic. Four operating companies were merged into one that, in turn, became the principal operating subsidiary of a holding company. The restyled Noda Shōyu Company, by far the largest soy sauce manufacturer in Japan, was an enterprise of immense size, yet it was only one part of a vast business network with overseas and domestic interests controlled by the Mogi-Takanashi brewers.

The Senshusha provided the nucleus for the transformation of the corporate superstructure. Long established as a lineage mutual-aid society, or mujin-kō, the Senshusha was reestablished on May 6, 1925, as an unlimited partnership, holding more than 60 percent of the outstanding shares of the Noda Shōyu Company as well as shares in the six other concerns. As another 30 percent of the shares was held privately by the Mogi-Takanashi-Horikiri families, over 90 percent of the company, after it was reformed in 1925, was controlled directly by the Mogi-Takanashi group through stock ownership, or indirectly through the Senshusha. Table 10 illustrates the nearly absolute control over the Noda Shōyu Company exercised by the Senshusha, the Mogi-Takanashi brewers, and their relatives. A visual representation of the chronological development and relationship of the Noda Shōyu Company and the Senshusha is shown in Figure 10.

TABLE 10. Shares in Noda Shōyu after the 1925 financial reorganization.

Shareholder	Shares	Percent of total
Senshusha Holding Company	317,882	62.0
Mogi-Takanashi-Horikiri brewing families[a]	158,520	31.0
other Mogi-Takanashi families	17,196	3.4
all others (18 individuals and enterprises)	18,760	3.6
total	512,358	100.0

Source: Ichiyama Morio, ed., *Noda Shōyu Kabushiki Kaisha Nijunenshi* (Tokyo: Toppan, 1940), pp. 663–664.

a. Includes Nakano Eizaburō.

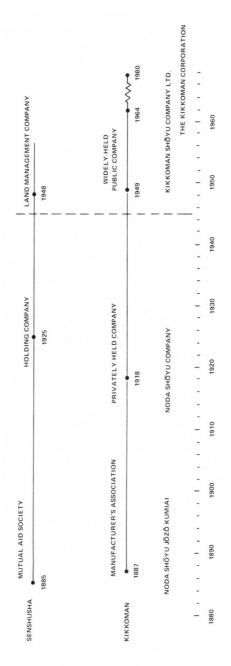

FIGURE 10. CHANGING MODES OF MANAGEMENT:
CLAN AND COMPANY – 1885 TO 1980

The formation of the new Noda Shōyu Company involved a good deal of what might be called "creative financing." When it was initially established as a 7-million-yen venture in 1917, the company's assets, particularly its landholdings, were undoubtedly undervalued. (Note the breakdown of assets by categories of holding in the property inventory at the time of incorporation: the value of the land owned by the company comes to only 2.85 percent of the total value of the company, even though the landholding, 64,347 *tsubo* [71 acres], was a large holding for Japan and included a good deal of choice riverfront and alluvial soil.) Although the firm did not acquire much more land during its first seven years, it did acquire the Yamazaki Iron Works in Noda in 1922 at a cost of approximately 165,000 yen, and accumulated retained earnings of 8,650,000 yen.[24] At the same time, a considerable if indeterminate amount was invested in plant modernization, railroad improvement, marketing research, and labor resources.

The creative financing behind the new company began on December 11, 1924, when the Noda Shōyu Brewing Company was formed with capitalization of 3,009,000 yen—a sizable sum for a company backed by nothing more than goodwill. Between its inception and March 31, 1925, nearly four months, the company neither bought nor sold any goods or conducted business of any sort. But its paper existence allowed the Mogi-Takanashi backers to correct for the undervaluation of the firm's assets in 1917. Having done so, on April 1, 1925, the assets of four companies—the Noda Shōyu Company, the Noda Shōyu Brewing Company, Horikiri Monjirō's Manjō Mirin Company, and the Nihon Shōyu Company (established in Inchon, Korea, in 1918 as an overseas arm of Noda Shōyu)—were merged, creating a mammoth firm that boasted assets of 25,000,000 yen and a capitalization of 21,250,000 yen.[25] Four months later an additional 5 million yen were paid into the firm by the Senshusha, bringing the totals to 30 million and 26.5 million yen, respectively. Five years later in 1930, the 1925 assets of the Noda Shōyu Company would still rank it among the fifty largest industrials in Japan and ninth among all food and beverage concerns in Japan.[26]

Having integrated all these companies, the Noda Shōyu Company turned to secure a manufacturing capacity and an access to market that no rival could threaten. In April 1926, Factory 17 (later known as Factory 7) began operations in Noda. This was possibly the largest factory in Japan at that time, boasting a floor space of 48,501 square meters and a production capacity of seven million gallons. The production line in Factory 17 was as mechanized as the technology of the day would allow. But in early 1929 an even larger factory was opened in Kakogawa, Hyogo Prefecture, in Western Japan. This, the Noda Shōyu Company's first plant in the Kansai district, signaled the ambition of Noda Shōyu to be a national, not just a regional, manufacturer. The sight of these mammoth plants and the thought of their truly prodigious capacity soon convinced the Chōshi soy sauce makers of Higeta shōyu, traditional rivals of the Noda brewers, that cooperation made more sense than competition.

The Chōshi brewers' desire to cooperate was reinforced by the drastic drop in the market during the summer of 1929 for agricultural commodities and for goods made from those commodities. In 1930 Noda Shōyu, along with two major producers from Chōshi in Chiba Prefecture, Yamasa and Higeta Soy Sauce companies, agreed to a quota system to limit supply in the Tokyo market and thereby prop up prices. The wholesaling and distributing firms in Tokyo agreed to abide by this quota agreement and, in turn, decided how much of each brand they should individually carry.

In order to institute these changes, two important alterations of traditional business practices were allowed. First, makers were permitted to ship directly to retailers, thereby bypassing the long-entrenched and multilayered distribution system. The reason for this change was obvious: given the depressed state of the economy and the generally restricted amount of cash flow, manufacturers could not be assured of payment under the consignment system. Second, in March 1931, after much deliberation, the three breweries decided to implement a five-year manufacturing and sales agreement that clearly defined the market

Preparation of kōji after 1927: here in Factory 17 note the steam boilers in the background and the rows of nicely turned and raked kōji in the foreground

shares allowed for each firm in the Tokyo and Eastern Japan soy sauce markets. This agreement did tend to stabilize prices and markets, but since the agreement was much more easily enforced in Tokyo than elsewhere (because of the relative ease of monitoring in Tokyo, which was true nowhere else), the agreement was honored there and overlooked elsewhere.[27]

The Making of a Rural Zaibatsu

Noda Shōyu was one of the larger and more successful companies in Japan. Yet even its size and importance fail to completely reveal the total assets controlled by the Mogi-Takanashi associates, for Noda

Extraction and pressing: an example of the kind of hydraulic press machines used to squeeze sauce from porous sacks which appeared about the time of World War I

Shōyu was the principal but by no means the only concern managed by them through their control of the Senshusha holding company. The companies directly owned by the Senshusha included the four mentioned previously, plus a fifth, the Homare Miso Company, purchased February 1, 1926. These five companies, now merged into one, manufactured a complete range of fermented rice or soybean products— shōyu, mirin, and miso—that were produced in Japan as well as in Korea and that boasted sales offices in Hotien (China), Seoul (Korea), and Tokyo, Osaka, Yokohama, and Shimonoseki (all in Japan). In addition to the five companies in the new Noda Shōyu, the Mogi-Takanashi group controlled five more firms, either through the Noda Shōyu Company itself or through stock ownership and interlocking directorates emanating from the Senshusha. These were the Marusan and Nihon Unsō Freight and Transportation companies; the Manshu Noda Shōyu Company (not formed until 1936); the Noda Shōyu Bank; and the Hokusō (later Sōbu) Railroad. Dividing them into subsidiary firms and related firms, and then combining them with the new Noda Shōyu Company makes it possible to estimate the total assets controlled directly and indirectly by the Mogi-Takanashi managers (see table 11).

If these estimates are roughly accurate, the Mogi-Takanashi brewers of Noda controlled directly or indirectly about 46 million yen during the third decade of this century. That was an enormous amount, equal to almost 70 percent of the assets controlled by the Furukawa Group, a diversified mining and manufacturing combine which was the smallest

TABLE 11. Capitalization of Noda Shōyu business group after 1936 (yen).

Main enterprise		Subsidiary enterprises		Related enterprises	
Noda Shōyu	30,000,000	Marusan[a]	150,000	Noda Shōyu Bank[b]	10,500,000
		Nihon Unsō[c]	200,000	Sōbu Railroad[d]	4,500,000
		Manshu Noda Shōyu[e]	1,000,000		
total	30,000,000		1,350,000		15,000,000

a. Ichiyama Morio, ed., *Noda Shōyu Kabushiki Kaisha Sanjugonenshi* (Tokyo: Toppan, 1955), p. 661; in 1930.

b. Deposits in 1930.

c. *Sanjugonenshi, p.* 660; in 1936.

d. Ichiyama, ed., *Noda Shōyu Kabushiki Kaisha Nijunenshi* (Tokyo: Toppan, 1940), p. 655; in 1928.

e. *Sanjugonenshi,* p. 676; in 1936.

of the so-called big seven zaibatsu groups led by Mitsui and Mitsubishi.[28] (Zaibatsu means literally "financial clique" and was the word used to describe large industrial and financial combines that formed in Japan around the turn of the twentieth century.)

After 1925 it would be correct to refer to the interrelated enterprises managed by the Mogi-Takanashi brewers as a rural zaibatsu. Three elements—family ownership, holding company control, and diversified business interests—make up the classical definition of a zaibatsu, and certainly all of these elements existed in the business empire shaped by the Noda group. But the rural site of the Noda Shōyu enterprises also gave it a special character and enabled the Mogi-Takanashi managers to enforce their control in an informal and decentralized manner. For example, because the Noda Shōyu Bank was local (situated around the corner from the headquarters of the Noda Shōyu Company), strict accounting controls on cash flow and on accounts receivable/payable were unwarranted because daily receipts, monthly balances, payroll schedules, and other corporate financial matters were all handled by the bank for the company. In one year, 1919, the financial flow between the company and the bank exceeded by eight times the total assets of the company for that year.[29] The bank, in effect, acted as a comptroller for the firm, and this was possible only in a localized setting like that of Noda. (The same was true for Dupont in Delaware during its first years following incorporation.)

The Noda Shōyu zaibatsu was a collection of a half-dozen enterprises concentrating on the manufacture of fermented grain-based products with another four enterprises in transportation and finance. This clustering of enterprises was similar in pattern to the larger, better-known zaibatsu, which likewise tended to concentrate investment in transportation and finance. But unlike them, the Mogi-Takanashi families' investments in transportation and finance grew organically, out of local needs, and were not determined by the force of outside pressure.

The larger zaibatsu's diversification into transportation and finance came, for the most part, as a result of the central government's decision to divest itself of manufacturing, transportation, and financial ventures that were begun as government-subsidized enterprises in the 1870s. These were sold in the 1880s at a fraction of their original cost to private individuals who used them as core elements in the creation of zaibatsu. This sort of grafted development resulted in rapid hothouse growth in the number and size of zaibatsu holdings—so much so that family ownership of zaibatsu assets was separated from the management of those assets. Contributing to this separation were the geographical spread of the new zaibatsu that often encompassed holdings on all of the four main islands of Japan, and the lack of an evolved logic to their hastily acquired holdings.

These features, plus the existence of holding companies that juxtaposed another bureaucratic barrier between zaibatsu families and their businesses, resulted in the formation of a new class of professional managers. These managers depended on the patronage of wealthy families like the Mitsui, yet they were employed on the basis of their business skill and acumen in the management of individual units in a zaibatsu combine. Quite often such managers had gained their experience in the very same government-financed ventures that were later sold to private enterprise. On the other hand, they might have learned the rudiments of modern management in the government agency that had sponsored the original investment. The point is the same: the urban-based zaibatsu may have been family-owned, through the device of a holding company, but they were too large, too far-flung, and too diverse to be family-managed in any significant way. This was not true of rural zaibatsu, like Noda Shōyu, which were both family-owned and managed. This difference gave them an entirely different flavor and direction of development from the urban zaibatsu.[30]

These differences were evident in the genuineness with which the family basis of ownership and management at Noda Shōyu was rationalized locally in terms of the patriarchical privilege of the Mogi and Takanashi families. The differences were also manifested in the way this local preeminence would become linked in the late 1920s and 1930s to the national ideology of family-community-nation-state-emperor. The connection between family ownership and management of the firm and the familylike national character of Japan had already been pointed out by Mogi Shichizaemon in Research Committee meetings. This theme would be elaborated and repeated even more publicly and forcefully by the firm at the close of the 1920s, in an effort to inculcate corporate loyalty and patriotism in the employees of Noda Shōyu in the aftermath of the Great Noda Strike of 1927–28. The combination of family ownership and control that distinguished the Noda zaibatsu was portrayed as a superior trait, one that ennobled the firm, in comparison to other sorts of enterprises without family honor, leadership, and emotion.

The result of the corporate reorganization at Noda Shōyu Company before and after 1925 was the creation of a modern industrial enterprise characterized, paradoxically enough, by a small group of men at the top who continued to own and actually manage an enterprise of considerable size and sophistication and by a much larger group of professional managers and highly skilled workers who administered the enterprise with methods that embodied principles of scientific management along with familial and patriotic ideals.

4.

A Loyal Retainer's Farewell

ONE OF THE SERIOUS FAILINGS in our knowledge of the history of Japanese business is a lack of understanding and appreciation of the social-psychological dimensions of corporate development. Just as organizational structure and production technology evolve, so too do attitudes and opinions about business, on the part of those engaged in it and those looking at it. During the more than two centuries of Kikkoman's history examined so far, little has been said about the beliefs and sentiments of those who initially provided the capital and later the managerial leadership for the development of the shōyu industry in Noda. The translation that follows, of a small, privately published eulogy for Mogi Shichirōuemon VI, first president of the Noda Shōyu Company, was written by his bantō, Shinshima Jisuke, in 1929.[1] It reveals the managerial thinking of merchants and manufacturers in nineteenth- and early-twentieth-century Japan about the nature of labor relations, organizational behavior, and enterprise leadership.

The reason for including this translation in what is otherwise a rather analytical work, is its effectiveness in delineating the attitudes and values of the most senior executive and most respected Mogi family member during the course of modernizing not only the legal and production-based structures of Kikkoman but also its systems of industrial and interpersonal relations. It enables us to observe the transition of an older family enterprise into a newer and more modern corporation, and to understand the response of the corporate leadership to workers as well as to the local community during the labor-management disputes of the mid-1920s, which divided the company soon after incorporation. This turn-of-the-century vignette illustrates the ideological roots underlying family and firm in Noda that helped form the social-psychological character of Kikkoman during its early corporate years.

Besides disclosing the attitudes of Shinshima toward his employer, this eulogy reveals much about the bantō's own character, for although laudatory tributes to employers, teachers, and patriarchs were and are relatively common in Japan, this one is uncommonly long, colorful, and intuitive. It is also naive. Shinshima's views of history and of Mogi Shichirōuemon are wholly uncritical, yet there is no doubt of the Confucian piety that motivated him to write, nor is there any question of the accuracy of his observations concerning the nature of shōyu manufacture in his day. Shinshima's writings show the Mogi's family enterprise was a "one man–one business" affair. The boundaries of family estate, business fortune, and personal generosity were entirely idiosyncratic, and Shichirōuemon could divide and dispose of his wealth as he and he alone saw fit to do. Incorporation, however, would change all that.

Shinshima's Views on Japanese Management

Two features of management philosophy are particularly apparent in Shinshima's work: management by example (with Mogi Shichirōuemon presented as the perfect Japanese Confucian-style manager); and the psychological or emotional quality of interpersonal relations in the work place.[2] These are interrelated aspects of what might be termed an early industrial style of management in Japan. In time, both would change; management by example giving way to management by the book (management science), while the emotional quality of interpersonal relations would be tempered by a healthy dose of scientific management.

Confucian management by example is based on the concept that whatever universal principles exist, they exist in society among men, where rules of behavior are not abstract but concrete and specific. Such rules differ according to one's status and position in society. The role of education, whether formal or informal (as by example), is to make people aware of appropriate behavior with regard to their status and to make them responsible for behaving accordingly. It is assumed that once correct behavior is understood, it will be carried out; failure to do so is the highest form of immorality in the Confucian context.

Morality is what sets man apart in the world. Yet moral behavior must be understood and acquired rationally through education. For this reason, education is the essence of Confucian culture. If all men were educated and acted accordingly, there would be no need for government: with everybody performing his duty, social harmony would be achieved. But until this felicitous state of affairs is realized, the primary duty of those in power is to uplift the moral character of others, assuming of course their own superior moral virtue. Great men educate others through their own example. Power and authority without morality are anathema, because leaders administer as much through moral example as through the rules they promulgate and enforce.

Although leadership by example and moral suasion was developed with reference to the role of the great man as a political leader, the same ideal, for lack of other models, came to characterize what was considered to be appropriate behavior for men in other leadership positions. Thus, a Japanese merchant or manufacturer schooled in the Confucian tradition would oversee his enterprise, supervise his employees, and overcome his business difficulties at least in part by use of Confucian example.

Where the Chinese and Japanese management traditions differed was in the emotional quality of that Confucian leadership. The ideal Chinese leader was thoroughly rational and extremely correct in bearing and behavior, even to the point of being aloof. The psychological quality of interpersonal relations was characteristically avoided, and even considered un-Confucian. Thus, Chinese patterns of leadership and administration typically underscore a rational, rather than an emotional commitment to men and organizations. Japanese patterning tends to emphasize a combination of rational commitment and emotional bonding to leaders and institutions. Affect is encouraged rather than discouraged in management: trust, dependency, and emotion are cultivated avidly within Japanese organizations, producing a commitment that goes well beyond the normal nine-to-five obligation.

Psychological bonding in Japanese organization often occurs within the context of pseudokinship ties. Even when there is no biological or ideological basis for describing organizational affiliation in such terms, the family-based model of organization seems to resonate with the cultural and emotional proclivities of the Japanese. Western patterns and models of interpersonal relations based on concepts of equality and individuality or on practices of non-kin-based neighborhood or occupational association, although known and understood, have made little headway in Japan. Instead, the elasticity of the concept of family, as well as its universal currency in Japanese society, have allowed notions of interpersonal trust and harmony based on the family model to be widely circulated outside of actual kin-based groups. Organizational, not genealogical, boundaries delimit the sphere within which cooperation and commitment expressed in terms of a family metaphor are encouraged and expected.

Confucianism, as it was and still is practiced in Japan, emphasizes not only the thoughts or the ideology of a leader but his emotional qualities—his charisma—as well. Emotionalism provides an additional vehicle beyond rational self-interest for imparting a sense of solidarity and identification with an organization. Company culture in Japan is distinguished by emotional appeals and exhortations; company loyalty demands total involvement, both intellectual and emotional. Feelings are not forbidden in the workplace; they are encouraged, even cultivated, and then cemented to the organization and its goals. The emotional quality of interpersonal relations has been one of the most salient and significant features of organizational behavior in Japan.

At the time in question, however, the psychological quality of interaction within the organization was notable only within the small group of personnel in Noda performing what could be called the front-office functions of buying and selling. The lack of prolonged contact by owners with factory and shop personnel meant that management by example and the psychological quality of interpersonal relations were organizational and behavioral traits confined to a small group of high-level workers within a manufacturing enterprise. Shinshima was one of these high-level workers as Shichirōuemon's personal secretary and trusted assistant. As you read his eulogy, heed Shinshima's request that you read as much with your heart as your head. Thirty-eight years old when he wrote this, Shinshima had already spent a quarter-century in the service of Mogi Shichirōuemon.

"The Master as seen by the Apprentice: Kozō kara mita Gakudō"

Preface

I first began writing this in 1924, seven years after the amalgamation of what were formerly family-based soy sauce breweries into the Noda Shōyu Company. At that time I wanted to write something to commemorate the incorporation of the company, but after doing some writing, for one reason or another the piece was not finished, and I put it away in my desk.

Then, on April 19, 1929, Mogi Shichirōuemon, first President of the company and head of the Kashiwa branch of the Mogi clan, unexpectedly fell ill and soon passed away. Of course it was tragic for his family and relatives, but as he was the first and highest officer of the newly created company to pass on, it was a misfortune for the company and town as well. As a result, the company and community were united by a frightful grief. There was a feeling of foreboding as if you had just recently but not too well rebuilt your master's castle and you feared its imminent collapse.

But as the late President always said, "The moral wisdom that we are born with is as lofty as the mountains; it's not meant to be exhausted in a lifetime." If someone could only put that teaching into practice now, as the head of the main family or a branch family of the past president, as the second president of the company, or in the Executive Offices, then the pride of the company and the fame of the town would be securely reestablished.

Because I began this work four or five years ago there are occasionally places where I would now like to make changes, but I have decided to go ahead with it as is in order to get it out as soon as possible after the President's death. Although I am not really qualified to write about the President with my limited schooling, I was nurtured by him for a long time; and as I cherished my association with him, I have undertaken this task. I will be satisfied if my readers understand my sentiments and carefully weigh my words.

Introduction

On January 1, 1918, the Noda Shōyu Company began operation. The heads of various shōyu manufacturing families became company officers and Mogi Shichirōuemon became the company President. The nucleus of the company was the Executive Officers' suite, and the axis of the suite was the desk of the company president. In order to know the company, therefore, it is first necessary to understand the President. Those of us working here in the Executive Suite came to know him well and, through him, the character of the company. We came to believe that it is important to devote ourselves not only to the President but to the company as well, and to perform our duties to the best of our abilities. We feel this will accrue to the company's benefit as well as our own.

After working closely with the President for twenty-five years, I feel that I understand him relatively well, and now it is my responsibility to make him better known in society. I have taken up pen and paper to do just that, even if there might be some self-conceit in the effort. Unhappily, however, I discovered that writing about him was not an easy task. Looking back on what I have done, I realize that it was a foolish thing to do. The President was a great man—not easily interpreted to others. He had a progressive side to his character, yet he was considered conservative. He was strong-willed yet kind. You would think him stubborn, and then find him quite accommodating. He was meticulous in his habits, and if you overlooked details, he would soon find you out. He kept track of every penny even though he dealt in sums of great substance. I'm not certain what made him great, but I automatically bowed my head whenever we met. To this day I fail to understand what hold he had over me, but I did whatever he asked.

Even though I tried to learn all that there was and all that I could about the President, I discovered how my knowledge was inadequate when I tried to write about him. It was not supposed to be like that. And so, in spite of my efforts to build him up, he somehow became smaller—an ordinary man—a president in my image—when I wrote this, and that was not at all what he was like.

Once the haiku poet Bashō was taken with the scenic beauty of Matsushima and wrote:

> Matsushima, Matsushima
> Nature singing Matsushima.

This verse has long been famous and I find myself, like Bashō, unable to express in words how I really feel. Simply thinking about the President, as I am at the moment, makes me realize that the less said about him the better. Although I did not intend to spoil what he was by writing about him, I have come this far and I cannot quit now. I've done my best even if my prose cannot capture the true essence of his personality.

The President would not have approved of this work. He disliked promoting himself. I'm not doing it for my benefit either. I simply wanted the President to be better known, and since work is the most important thing in our lives and in society, I dedicated myself to the effort, even if it is without distinction. My writing leaves a lot to be desired, but I will be grateful if in deciphering the text the unwritten meaning—the feeling in my heart—is understood.

Shinshima Jisuke

Brief Biography

Mogi Shichirōuemon was born Mogi Heianrō but became Shichirōuemon upon assuming leadership of the Kashiwa family. He retained this name until he retired, after which time he was known as Gakudō or occasionally as Nanzan [literally, "scholar" and "southern mountain"]. He was born in 1860 and studied locally at Matsuyama Academy. He showed ability early and was sent at age eleven to Kyoto for studies first at the Otsuka Tōkō Academy and later at Tanaka Academy. At fifteen he returned to Noda and entered the family business. He was elected a ward leader in Noda in 1884, when he was twenty-four, but he resigned the following year to devote himself more fully to the family enterprise. He tried to pattern his life after that of Fukuzawa Yukichi, learning economics and finance on his own and studying fermentation technology under Utsunomiya Saburō. Later he put his studies to practical use and considerably increased the family fortune.

He became head of the Kashiwa family in 1889, taking the family name of Mogi Shichirōuemon VI. Over the years, while managing family and clan affairs, he was at one time or another Director of the Noda Shōyu Manufacturers Association, Director of the Noda Commercial Bank, Director of the Senshusha—a clan holding company, President of the Noda Shōyu Company, and President of the Hokusō Railroad Company. Honest and resourceful, he concentrated on general matters, while not ignoring life's many details. He was comfortable in all situations and he never seemed to lose his composure.

For relaxation he played *Go*, wrote, and occasionally painted. Late in life he began the practice of meditation for his health. The routine of life did not discourage him, and he contributed continually, and largely anonymously, to the public welfare over his many years. In 1921 he was awarded the National Medal of Honor with blue ribbon. On April 19, 1929, he fell ill and passed away after a few days. He was sixty-nine at the time, having spent most of his life in self-cultivation and public service. On the 24th of April he was awarded posthumously the Imperial Sixth Rank, Second Order, and on the 25th thousands of mourners, including most of the town, crowded in to pay their last respects at the company funeral.

The President's Principles and Policies

The wealth presently enjoyed by the Kashiwa clan was not acquired overnight; more than half of it was inherited from past generations. But using this inheritance, the business has been steadily expanded. Business earnings have been reinvested in the family enterprise with the result that a high level of prosperity has been attained. Unlike some other family businesses, the Kashiwa lineage did not profit through speculation, such as stock and grain market manipulations; instead, the Kashiwa group has painstakingly built up its fortune over a long period of time through the honest effort of many generations and the mode of operations followed by its head, Mogi Shichirōuemon. Mogi Shichirōuemon, however, refused to recognize his unique contribution and instead attributed the success of the enterprise entirely to the virtues of his ancestors and the goodwill of society. Accordingly, to repay his ancestors and society for the continued success of the family enterprise, Mogi Shichirōuemon believed that it was his duty to make the business prosper and, in doing so, pay homage to his forebears and demonstrate his loyalty to the state.

No matter how cautious most persons are, if they are continually enticed by lucrative investment opportunities, they'll start to dream about making lots of money quickly. This never happened to the President, who had many opportunities for speculative investment but avoided them. Occasionally he would invest in state-backed enterprises or other

businesses with a secure return, but he never risked money in un-
proven ventures. Moreover, he never allowed his occasional investments in other businesses to distract him from concentrating his ener-
gies in the manufacture of shōyu. In short, the President was not greedy
and he could not bring himself to risk money thoughtlessly.

Even though the President was quite wealthy, you would not know it
to look at him. He had a bright, smiling, southern type of personality,
which is not often found among the well-to-do. He was persevering by
nature and strongly adhered to the principle of "one man-one business"; with this conservative approach he consistently expanded the
Kashiwa lineage holdings.

If he had been socially ambitious, the President might have become
an important figure in the world of Japanese business or politics. With
his money, influence, and knowledge, he could have easily accomplished such goals, and in fact he was approached with various such
offers on many occasions. But he always turned them down, explaining
that he had no talent other than brewing soy sauce. Instead of seeking
fame and fortune elsewhere, he concentrated on the development of his
inherited talent and ability. A man of true principle, he understood the
obligations of wealth, devoting himself to the state and to many charitable and voluntary activities.

The President As Businessman

As a businessman, it is natural to think that one's primary purpose is to
make a profit. But a good businessman must consider more than personal profit. He must weigh the profit and loss of society as well or risk
harming society by his single-minded devotion to profit. The President,
no matter how he felt personally and whatever the condition of the enterprise, never forgot that profit was primarily from and for society.
Manufacturing success, he felt, was totally dependent on consumer demand; consequently, he tried to supply the best quality goods at reasonable prices. A simple profit was far from the goal he set for himself
and the business. Once he remarked that "the prosperity of my business has nothing to do with me. It is due entirely to the virtue of my
ancestors and to the wealth of society; the success of our enterprise
must be seen in this light." The President saw everything in this way
and it clearly revealed his understanding of a merchant's role.

As a result of these attitudes, the President never engaged in reckless
competition, yet neither did he simply submit to current conditions. For
example, he built a research laboratory next to his home so he could
take advantage of new knowledge and improve the state of the art in
brewing technology. In setting prices for his goods, which were daily
household necessities, the President always went beyond economic

concerns. He kept shipping shōyu, for example, regardless of the market price, and as a result he sometimes lost and sometimes made substantial sums of money. But he was unconcerned about short-term market fluctuations in price because in the long run he believed that business success depended on honesty and ability. With these beliefs, we were rarely insecure in our livelihood and we could always anticipate and receive annual bonuses in our compensation. [Shinshima here seems to be speaking of all of Shichirōuemon's front-office assistants.]

The purchase of raw materials, the construction of buildings and facilities, and other business activities were all carried out on the basis of trust. Those who could not be trusted were not engaged. Trust was crucial because the President could not bring himself to profit unjustly at someone else's expense. When buying large amounts of bulk supplies, for example, he never initiated the purchases himself but waited instead for a seller's recommendation to buy. But speculation is sometimes important and necessary in business, and from time to time he was criticized for being too passive. He disregarded such comments. His response was: "If the scale of our business is small, we could take chances and speculate. Given our size, however, we require steady supplies and we cannot afford to wait for the best moment to buy. If you examine the average price paid for all our purchases, you'll find that the prices paid in individual sales do not vary that much."

With this philosophy, a lot of suppliers came to trade since we rarely turned them away and there was always a commission to be made. The President received all of them with optimism which made the trading lively and attractive. Since the spirit of the President's method was "profit for both sides," even if we did unexpectedly well, we accepted the news with equanimity and interest. Those who dealt with us regularly came to trust and depend upon the President and continued to do business with us for many years. From time to time we purchased contracts in advance or grain futures, but with uneven success. Yet as one of the traders remarked, "The President always seems to do well in such transactions. We maneuver him into buying our goods but he never fails to turn a profit." If this was true, I wonder if it was because of some business secret or was it because of the President's virtue?

Most of the real estate properties currently owned by the President, such as his paddy and dry fields or his mountain and timberlands, were not sought after and purchased by him. For the most part they were forced on him by people in financial difficulty who knew his personality, and as a result knew that he would often buy such property at more than the going market rates. Over the years, however, the trees on his mountain lots have grown and the prices of his agricultural fields have increased, so much so that he now holds quite a bit of valuable property. Needless to say, a fair proportion of his property was inherited, but as the old proverb suggests, "Where there's hidden virtue, there's good news." The great success of the Kashiwa lineage can be traced to the President's virtues of patience and perseverance.

When we returned from a business trip and reported to the President, the first thing he wanted to know was if there was any change in our customers. Next he inquired about our health, and only after this would he ask about general business matters. His preeminent concern for his customers and employees before all else rather surprised us. Furthermore, if we had made mistakes during our trips, he rarely admonished us if our errors had been honest ones. Sometimes he warned us about the future, but he never complained about the past; thus we were more often consoled than criticized. His generosity of spirit moved us not only to avoid making the same mistakes again but to pay closer attention to our duties in the future as well. Once in a while he would give us words of advice, such as, "Do not lose your soul in order to succeed in business," and "If our customers increase, the business will succeed naturally." The more I think about his advice, the better it seems.

In short, the President's moral character was always expressed in his business affairs. He respected and valued his customers, not only for the promise of future business but also for their character and personality. So, although we profited and lost at each other's expense, the President never allowed the profit motive to define relationships, either within or without the enterprise. His ideal was one of coexistence and coprosperity.

The President's Everyday Life

Some people, upon reaching a certain age, begin to spend a great deal of time contemplating nature, but the President could not be content with such a passive posture. He was constantly active, and in being so he provided us with a good model for our behavior. When he did take time from work, he often traveled for pleasure since with his money the cost of traveling was not a concern.

Although he had various hobbies, he did not pursue any of them with a passion. He enjoyed dramatic performances, sumo wrestling, and *rakugo* [storytelling]. When he attended such performances it was usually with one of our customers. For everyday enjoyment he played chess and read, especially biography. Occasionally he practiced calligraphy and composed Chinese-style poems, but his one daily pleasure that we envied most was that after a long day's work he'd return home and relax, the center of a convivial and animated family gathering.

Always frugal, the President confined his diet to soup and vegetable dishes prepared by his wife. He never showed a preference for particular foods and ate everything, remarking on how good it was. Even the soy sauce left over from flavoring the pickled cucumbers was mixed with hot water and drunk by him. What I particularly recall was how on his way home from the station, he would feed his leftovers from the train box lunches to dogs along the way. Although such behavior may appear of no account, actually it had deep meaning. His actions sprang from a conviction that "one drop of water is made in heaven and one grain of cereal is grown by the labor of multitudes." Everything should be appreciated, nothing wasted, and even the smallest scrap made useful.

Everyone in the President's family practiced frugality. Unknowing people might feel that being frugal is difficult and confining, but the President enjoyed the art of conservation. He never sought food, clothing, or housing beyond his modest needs, and he welcomed opportunities to limit his consumption. He felt that all needs were relative and ought to be controlled. The President's wife too was parsimonious, working from morning to night. Once she remarked that "even the God of Wealth rolls up his shirt sleeves in order to work."

The sash securing the President's clothes was firmly tied in the morning and was not undone until late at night. He instructed us that "when your sash is loose, your attention is wandering. Your personality is revealed in the way you tie your sash." His personality was such that he never gave the impression that his sash was undone, and because of his self-control it was impossible to take advantage of him. Many came to borrow money or to propose various business ventures, but most retreated without even offering their proposals because of his self-restraint and stern countenance. But such was his nature that he never considered himself superior to them, and he treated them with dignity and friendliness.

The President did not discriminate between his office and factory workers; he treated us all equally as members of his own family. He taught that "superiors and subordinates are members of the same body. Unless everyone—owners, office employees, and factory workers—works together with purpose and pleasure, business will not progress." Because everyone was equal, he discouraged cliques and special interest groups in the enterprise. Shortly after incorporation, for example, he called together his bantō in front of the Kashiwa headquarters and announced, "From now on your family has been increased. I will not discriminate in your behalf in the new company. I want you to understand in advance that I will treat you the same as all the others. Please work as hard for the company in the future as you have worked for me in the past. This will be our shortcut to success. I will accept greetings from you during the New Year and Midsummer celebrations, but otherwise you must act the same as all other employees." Because of such attitudes it was possible for workers from different plants to get along together; by the same token it was difficult to form groups centered around one's former employer or workplace. The President's declaration clearly indicated that we were to cooperate together and to dedicate ourselves to the new còmpany. In doing so, we discovered joy and happiness.

An Impressive Personality

Considering his total character, there is no doubt that the President was a great and even noble man. His thorough acceptance of and devotion to his ancestors' business testified to his personality, and his intelligence and greatness were obviously related to this thoroughness. It is not too much to say that these traits made his high level of accomplishment almost inevitable.

The President never exercised power and authority arbitrarily, and he did not act out of profit or insecurity. As he feared taking advantage of others, he neither plotted nor pushed. Instead, he adjusted to situations imperceptibly, almost naturally, and only insofar as circumstances forced him to change.

Although he appeared to be conservative, actually the President was quite progressive. When he took over the business from Mogi Shichirōuemon V, for example, he completely revamped the method of brewing by introducing brine much earlier into the brewing process. By this innovation and others, he raised the production of the Kashiwa family enterprise from 10,000 koku (476,000 gallons) to 50,000 koku (2,380,000 gallons) when the company began operations in 1918. He was neither restrained nor reckless in his business dealings. Instead, he was almost serene, as if he was attuned to the flow of nature; as a result, he never tried to force others into decisions so as to take advantage of them. Simply put, he did his best at all times, controlled his emotions, and accepted the course of change. He worked with composure and confidence, and in this respect he reminded one of a great politician or religious leader.

A Man of Unquestionable Character

So many people think only of their own advantage and behave like wild and greedy animals as a result. If they achieve even part of their goals, they promote and inflate themselves shamelessly. If that is what it is to be human, then the President was beyond humanity, for he was not at all selfish and self-centered. In fact, he believed that a single-minded devotion to profit only resulted in self-deception. Therefore, in whatever he did, he worked rationally without scheming and never appeared to make or lose money excessively. Most of the time he made money, but beyond that he was unconcerned with the amount of profit. Besides, much of the profit he did make was given to charity, although he often feigned no interest in charitable activities so as not to publicize his generosity. Frequently he contributed anonymously, unlike others who boasted often of their donations, making their small gifts sound like major contributions. For such self-aggrandizers, the President's behavior was incomprehensible, just as theirs was for him. In contrast to them, the President seemed afraid of becoming known in society. Consequently, I know of any number of cases where he gave money anonymously.

Ancestor Worship

The modesty of the President was strongly manifested in his attitude toward ancestor worship. Every morning at dawn he rose and bathed with spring water. Then he visited first a Shintō shrine and next a Buddhist temple where he was quietly united in meditation with his ancestors for about thirty minutes. It is said that ancestor worship is the foundation of filial piety and that filial piety is the basis for everything else. The President avidly cultivated an attitude of filial piety, and he never once missed his morning regimen in spite of his busy schedule. His devotion to his parents was beyond comparison. After their deaths he enshrined their pictures in a family altar at home and continued to revere and honor them as if they were still alive.

Since the President believed that his existence and the success of the business resulted entirely from the accumulated labors of his ancestors, he thanked his forebears daily and never admitted his part in the success of the enterprise. At the same time, he recognized the benevolence of the state and society, and he remarked more than once that "we work in society and are maintained by society. Everyone is dependent on each other." On his forty-fifth birthday, in recognition of his gratitude toward society, the President founded the Noda Charitable Society and donated a great deal of money for the relief of the poor and the education of impoverished students. His attitude of "receiving gratitude and giving gratitude" brought warmth to people and peace to the community.

The Model of Love

I recall last year when the President lost both his wife and his father. The way he so sincerely satisfied the mourning requirements left, as they say, nothing to be desired, even though it was obviously a painful duty for him. For a year after their deaths, regardless of the weather, he visited their gravesites each morning. Afterward he would sit before a small Buddhist altar in his home, remembering them and praying for them. Some people might complain that he did this for a year only, but as one who observed his morning devotions, he was the perfect model of filial piety and ancestral veneration. He overcame this difficult period in his life by quietly serving others, seeking the Way, and deepening his involvement in philanthropy.

I remember well what he said once: "Every day is precious. To spend even a day without love is such folly. Love, devotion, and diligence are the basis of life, and to realize this for even a day is far greater than spending a meaningless ten or twenty years." His exemplary behavior influenced many and he remains a local legend even today. We all wanted to model ourselves after his personality, and this was not because of his money, business success, or special circumstances, but rather because of the love he demonstrated. Without doubt his love will be reflected during and after his lifetime by his descendants, employees, and others with whom he had come in contact.

On Being What You Are

"Being what you are" was the President's teaching as well as his practice. The first step in achieving success is doing one's best, but at the same time the efforts of others must be respected. A housewife should do her best as a housewife, a domestic as a domestic, and an apprentice as an apprentice. This is what it means to "be what you are."

Sometimes it is difficult to know how to act in certain situations, whether one should be respectful or respected. Age and experience do not always define a position sufficiently; nevertheless, one should never lose sight of what one is and of one's social position. As long as a stomach acts like a stomach and a lung as a lung, our health will not be impaired; losing a sense of what one is can only lead to suffering. Some people misunderstand the meaning of being "what you are." It does not mean that a superior takes advantage of a subordinate or that a subordinate feels inferior to his superior. It means only that one must invest one's social position, whatever it is, with effort, loyalty, and all seriousness. Even former Prime Minister Lloyd of England [presumably Lloyd George, Prime Minister of Great Britain, 1916–1922] is said to have worked long, hard, and well when, as a lad, he was a shoemaker. Being faithful and loyal to one's position, regardless of what it is, is the most important thing in life; complaining about what may appear to be unsuitable work only leads to dissatisfaction, envy, and discomfort. Such an attitude inevitably poisons one's personality, making it impossible to be satisfied with and successful at work. If the great national hero

Toyotomi Hideyoshi had not immersed himself while working as a servant [*zōri-tori*] as a youth, he would not have become a great leader and later united the country. One must be content with the work one is given, understand its requirements, do one's best without complaint, and try to improve one's performance. As a consequence, work will become pleasurable and interesting and people will come to recognize your superior performance.

A poem composed by the President's father, Mogi Shichirōuemon V, expresses the attitude of "being what you are." It still provides a good example for us.

> No matter how hard you work,
> Your duty is never accomplished,
> Fulfill your duty and you will be content.

Accepting Fate

"One's fate is sealed in heaven," or so it is said; but if this is true, it can only be so with our cooperation. For although you can have either good or bad luck, luck is not accidental. Luck depends mostly on attitude and effort, although the influence of ancestors may have some effect. People who complain of bad luck usually display poor intentions and insufficient efforts. Anyone may have good luck, but there's a difference in how one uses the luck one has. One's destiny must be developed by oneself—or heaven helps those who help themselves. Work hard, observe life, and try to make your life lucky—that's the secret. The best luck is working hard and waiting for the right moment. The President was one of those who understood this and, as a result, was skilled in creating his own luck.

Happiness or unhappiness is brought about by one's own attitude and behavior. Happiness and unhappiness are a reflection of how we live our lives. Good works and self-discipline lead to happiness; their absence results in unhappiness. Happiness, like fate, is largely self-made; those who complain about their bad luck misunderstand the consequences of their own behavior.

The President's Personality as Revealed in a Game of Go

The President liked very much to play go, and even in this pastime his personality was revealed. When playing, his composure was not affected by how the game was going. He was not afraid to compete with so-called strong players, nor did he look down on those less able than himself. He played with complete attention; in a sense, playing go was more than simply playing a game, for he exercised tremendous self-discipline in the course of a match.

One day, after watching us play a game and listening to our evaluation of its outcome, the President said, "If you press too hard to win, the game will get out of hand and become unreasonable. By the same token, if you play too passively, your strategy cannot be implemented. The trick is to be careful but not too careful and to concentrate your total being on the game." I was quite impressed by these words for I felt that they manifested the President's approach to everyday life. He never forced circumstances or pressed people unnecessarily, but neither was he pushed by them. Many people get carried away with winning and, as a result, they lose easily. The President's advice should be a guide for such people.

People Rather Than Things

Before the Kashiwa enterprises were amalgamated into the firm, the President often stayed late until around nine o'clock at night at the Kashiwa business office. Then he would leave for home and have one of his clerks lock up for the night. One evening when he was ready to leave, there were just a few apprentices like myself there to help, and even though we were not familiar with what to do, he asked us—actually me—to close up. He gave me the key and I put it in the lock, turned the tumbler, pulled the key out, and was about to return it. If he did it himself, he usually checked the lock after removing the key to make sure that it was secure; since I had closed up instead of him, tonight's routine was different. A younger apprentice, realizing this, said, "May I borrow the key for a second?" I asked what he wanted it for and he answered that, "The lock was repaired today and it locks somewhat differently now, so I want to check it." I retorted, "If I turned the tumbler and the key came out, it must be locked." He persisted, however, by saying, "But it may not be locked. Give me the key, just for a second, and I'll check it." "No," I responded, "It's locked. Don't second-guess people." Just then the President walked by, with a "let's go," and disappeared into the back. I almost called after him that the lock had been fixed during the day but was all right now, but I hesitated to do so. I was embarrassed for the other apprentice and was heartened by the President's composure and trust of us. How could we disturb that calm and betray that trust? They motivated us to do whatever we could for him. They were like a fish and water: you could not have one without the other. This episode was one of the most memorable of my apprenticeship.

The President and Wine

A proverb says "a drinker resembles a cake of tofu [soybean curd]: in the beginning it's square and has shape, but it ends up shapeless, formless." If you have only one or two drinks, you're drinking wine, but if you have more, the wine is drinking you.

The President did not drink much because mostly he did not enjoy it, but he never imposed his abstinence on others. Part of the reason for his restraint, however, was the disorderliness and lack of discretion shown by those who drink too much. He felt that young people in particular should abstain from alcohol even though adults might drink—as long as the amount was not excessive. But as usual, if drinking led to disorder and a loss of personal control, he felt it better not to drink at all.

Of course drinking was not allowed on company premises and it was strictly enforced. Some considered this unjustified, but it was a simple example of why we should appreciate the company even more than we do. The company is concerned about our future and realizes that habits formed in our youth are hard to overcome; that is why the company policy is so strict about drinking. This is analogous to a parent's love for a child: if a child does not understand that love, rebellion will occur; and if an employee does not understand the company's concern, resistance and grumbling will result.

Speaking of wine, I recall something that happened on March 1, 1922. I was sent to Taiwan on a business trip and was accompanied on the first leg of that trip, from Noda to Ueno Station in Tokyo, by the President, the Master of Kakuyama, and a Mr. Minami. When we arrived at Ueno, the President looked over at me and asked if I had eaten breakfast. Before I could answer that I had, Mr. Minami broke in by interjecting, "Of course we have not." "Good," the President answered, "Let's eat together." We went to the Agedashi in Yamashita where, after we arrived, the President ordered three or four dishes with sake. I was puzzled by this because, besides myself, none of the others drank. When the wine arrived, the President poured a cup, took a sip, and passed it to the Kakuyama head and to Mr. Minami. When it came to me, the President took the bottle, filled my cup, and said, "I ordered this for you. Take your time and enjoy it." I was surprised of course that the President, a near teetotaler, would order wine for me and then invite me to drink it in the morning at breakfast. I could not immediately comprehend his intention but when the second bottle came and I began to relax and enjoy it, I began to understand—or so I thought. I finished the bottle, while the others talked and ate, and then I joined them in a pleasant completion of the meal. The President accompanied

me to Tokyo Station while the others headed for Kanda. He saw me off
on the train, as if I were his own flesh and blood, with a vigorous "Take
care." After this sincere and heartwarming send-off, he turned toward
Kurumazaka Station whence he was going by train to Koami-cho. I was
deeply moved by this incident, and I realized that the President treated
everyone equally regardless of their status. Although I might be his
subordinate, he never treated me like an inferior—more like a son. He
did these things not as a formal courtesy but as an expression of love,
and that is why they affected me so strongly. His wine and warm words
sped me on my way to Taiwan, and while on assignment there I promised myself that I would not betray the President's belief in me.

Life as a Spiritual Exercise

I entered the Kashiwa Family enterprise as an apprentice when thirteen
years old. In the beginning I did not understand the President's personality and was a constant grumbler. I felt the President was old-fash-
ioned, in words as well as behavior, and was afraid we would be left
behind by the competition. From time to time I even thought of quitting
and starting out on my own, but I continued, in spite of my complaints.
Then, unexpectedly, in the spring of my twenty-seventh year, the President proposed that I marry a local girl. Recalling it now, I am still overwhelmed by his generosity.

Only after considerable deliberation with two senior bantō, Minami
and Ito, did I decide to marry. For how was I to afford a house, clothes,
and the expense of raising a family? I considered asking my parents for
money, but because they were only agricultural tenants and not land-
owners, they did not have much themselves. And, after all, I was nearly
thirty years old at the time, and even though I had continued to borrow
pocket money from them every so often, I had not shared any of my
fifteen years of regular wages with them.

So I decided that I could no longer depend on my parents—especially for this, the most important ceremony in my life. As my wedding
day drew closer, however, and these financial problems were still unresolved, I decided to consult further with Ito, the senior bantō. Upon
meeting with him, he astonished me, saying that the Kashiwa head was
going to give me a house in reward for my many years of hard work. He
told me not to bother my parents for money, that the President was
going to take care of everything. I blushed to think that this grumbler
was going to be rewarded for his "diligence."

I was still apprehensive as the day of my wedding approached. My
parents sent me a wedding kimono, various ceremonial implements,
and anxiously advised me about protocol for the banquet following the

ceremony. The days passed and I put my trust in Ito's words, "Don't worry." I did notice that carpenters, plasterers, and cabinetmakers were hastily remodeling a house in the neighborhood, and, although no one said so directly, people were saying that it would be my home. The afternoon of the day before the wedding, I was asked to see the father of the current Kashiwa head [Shichirōuemon V] and I called upon him full of worry. "You have worked long and well for us," he said, "and as you will marry tomorrow, your life will become completely different hereafter. From now on you will live in the house of Araku and you will find that you need many things that you never needed before. But try to be frugal and persevering. Follow the example of the family head in whatever you do. Now go to your new house. Ito is waiting for you there; ask him for whatever you need."

"My own house"—I couldn't believe it! Rejoicing, I went to the house and found Ito sitting in the *tatami* room. He greeted me with "Congratulations," which quite surprised me, and during the first few moments of bewilderment and joy a gardener entered the yard and began cleaning up. "I tried to get everything that you'll need," Ito confided, "but once you move in, you'll undoubtedly find things that you want. Please let me know what they are without hesitation. Now, I'll turn the house over to you. Take good care of it and learn to work harder." After that he left, and I looked through the tatami room, the bathroom, and the kitchen. I was overcome with appreciation as I came to realize that everything was there: pots and pans, tables, cups, bowls, a tea drinking set, chopsticks, and even a bamboo pipe used for stoking the fire. I had a fine bathtub, a beautiful garden fence, as well as new tatami and *fusuma*. Everything was in such fine shape that I need not hesitate to have visitors immediately, and I sent a messenger to my parents and asked them to come over right away. Soon my father arrived, and as he listened to my story tears clouded his eyes. We slept in the new house that night—parents and son together. All we could talk about was the generosity of my boss, the Kashiwa Family head.

The next day, Mr. Okada drew up in a *jinrikisha* in front of my new home. He greeted me formally and then uncovered a vehicle crammed with wedding gifts from the Kashiwa head. These included envelopes of money, a folding fan, ceremonial paper, dried bonito, a set of clothes cabinets, and four large *furoshiki*. In the furoshiki were two new sets of bedding, summer and winter clothing, and various miscellaneous items. My name, Shinshima, was printed on the corners of the furoshiki. The cabinets were likewise filled with clothing—seasonal garments, sashes, both black and white tabi, a *hakama*. What I remember even now were the plain sashes for everyday working kimonos, a pair of gloves, and a fine set of Japanese writing paper. I had heard that the boss took care of his men as if they were his own children, but I wept with gratitude at how completely he was looking after me.

I doubted if I had really worked hard enough to deserve all this, and in fact I knew that I had not. From that moment on I decided to rededicate myself to work harder. Even now, many years later, I feel that I have not repaid the head sufficiently in spite of my years of devotion and effort, and I am still moved when I think of what he did for me and continues to do for me.

Three Great Men of Kashiwa

I would like to introduce three great men in the history of the Kashiwa enterprise: Messrs. Ito, Sano, and Nihei.

Ito was small, modest, upright, and responsible. He was especially good at breaking in new employees. Nihei was large, muscular, and incautious—a typical Mito type. He was enthusiastic about everything, thorough, and good with people. Once he became so enthusiastic and engrossed in a particular phase of product development research—I think he was working on developing a new brewing kōji—that he fainted from overexposure in the kōji fermentation room. He was always fair in his business dealings, and he treated his customers kindly; for these reasons the incense never ceases burning at his gravesite.

Sano was the serious, deep-thinking type. He was the sort who would whack a bridge with his cane to be sure that a bridge was there. He was a bit overcautious and never took any action unless he knew the results beforehand. Understandably, he did not make mistakes often and as a result he was trusted. Nihei, by contrast, was open, optimistic, and hardly listened to anyone else's opinion. He would even disagree with the President when he thought it necessary. Ito was still different. He did not express opinions readily, but he was good at listening to others and understanding their viewpoints. Even without saying much, he had the virtue of being able to smooth over differences. Sano, like Nihei, was thoroughly opinionated but, unlike Nihei, unable to differ with his superiors. He was mild and withdrawn but seemed to suffer no bad effects as a result of his timidity.

These three different personalities functioned together quite well. They had all been trained by the President since their apprenticeship as teenagers, and they had all imbibed a great deal of his personality. They were models for the other employees because they believed that once a bond of loyalty was pledged between employer and employee, it became the primary obligation of existence and must be faithfully discharged. As these three admired the President and devoted themselves so completely to their work, they rarely spent any time in leisure. They did not drink or have any regular recreations. They spent all their time working, and after forty years of devotion to the President they shone with security and contentment.

Yet their achievements were due not only to the leadership of the President but to their own developed personalities as well. All three of these men began work at the age of puberty with neither education nor social standing, but they were influenced by a great man and they developed self-discipline. As a result, they achieved a certain nobility of character and they supervised us with a concern that left us with feelings of undefinable emotion.

Is Ito Crazy?

I cannot believe that Ito is crazy, but from the age of eleven for the next fifty years, all he did was work. His sense of loyalty was so extreme that occasionally it made others uneasy. Although Ito was blessed with many children, I never saw him with them and can only assume that he actually ate, bathed, and spent time with them. He left for work shortly after rising in the morning, and he stayed at the office until nine o'clock every night. He worked in the office on holidays so that other employees could enjoy themselves with their families.

He used to tell other employees who were fathers, "Go home and be with your family. Unless you spend time with your children, love will not become strong between you, and nothing is sadder than insipid love between parent and child. Your work is important but so is your family. Don't take me as a model." Apparently he disapproved of his own single-minded devotion to work, but he seemed powerless to do anything about it. Nothing made him happier than tending to office work, which he did with enthusiasm, steadiness, and kindness. He was well liked by our customers, and it is said that our success locally was largely the result of his efforts.

Ito was a mild and conservative sort. He was advanced in years when the company was founded in 1918 and he wished to stay in the employ of the Kashiwa Family. Since this was impossible, he worked for the company as one of the supervisors of front-office employees. As the system of enterprise organization and operation changed dramatically after incorporation, however, he had difficulty adusting to the many changes, especially since he had so many employees under him. A good deal of his attention was paid to the problems of maintaining harmonious relations among employees and to maintaining proper relations between superiors and subordinates. There must have been many reasons for his illness, but his extreme sense of responsibility to his employer, coupled with his new duties at the company, undoubtedly contributed a great deal to his infirmity.

When I see Ito now, since his illness, I have difficulty controlling my emotions. He continues to wear his work sash and navy blue work apron even if he is unable to get out of bed. When we visit him and the conversation turns to the company and the President, he weeps and apologizes for letting us down. From our point of view he's the incarnation of hard work, but he thinks he's not doing enough! Although his doctor prescribes a nutritional diet, he refuses to eat anything but miso soup and vegetables, for he believes that as long as he is away from work, he should not accept better fare. Knowing his personality, this was to be expected. Looking at his life now and comparing it to what it was before he became ill, I am on the verge of tears. I want him to recover and enjoy his life as before, and I am not alone in these feelings.

Called by God

Three years ago Ito suffered a breakdown and went into seclusion at the Hokke temple in Haraki to recover. Suddenly one day he disappeared from the temple and in spite of the efforts of his relatives and acquaintances, he could not be found. I, too, had been sent out to look for him on the chief's orders. But none of us, myself included, had any luck. We searched night and day for three days without success, and finally we had to report our failure to the President. The President listened to my unsatisfactory report quietly, although it was apparent that he was as concerned as if Ito was his own brother. Finally he spoke: "Even if it takes one or two months, he must be located. Look for him until you find him. I'll get someone to take care of your work here."

Inspired by the President's solicitude for Ito—a runaway in spite of his half-century with the Kashiwa family—I redoubled my efforts to discover his whereabouts. I hit upon an idea. Although Ito himself had no particular religious affiliation, he had always admired the President's belief in Konpira, a deity of the Sanuki area in Shikoku. Without knowing why, I decided that Ito must be making a pilgrimage to the Konpira shrine. I rushed there by the first train, but the local police were unable to find him. I was desolate. I felt that I could not disappoint the President again, but I was out of ideas. I wandered up the mountain toward the shrine—and there on the path in front of me was someone who looked like Ito. I rushed up to the figure, colliding with him, and discovered with joy and surprise that it was indeed Ito. He acted as though nothing had happened, but I burst into tears. Many people felt that my running into him like that was just pure luck and coincidence. Perhaps, but I felt it was more: something unexplainable in terms of human intelligence, maybe something mysterious like divine intervention, or just simply human integrity and emotional resonance.

Everything Is One

When I recall the old days and the President, one person who always comes pleasantly to mind is Suzuki Matashichi. He was one of many whose career was influenced by the President. By occupation, Suzuki and his family were coopers, makers of wooden kegs and vats for fermentation. He came to work at Kashiwa as an apprentice when he was twelve. The coopers at that time were like a bunch of gangsters, but he was different. Suzuki was far superior to the others even though he was only twelve at the time. He did not have a bit of the so-called "apprentice-spirit," which stood for careless and lackadaisical work. He never wasted anything, whether it was his or somebody else's. He picked up discarded lumber for later use, for example, and he treated everything as if it had come from God himself. He did not act this way for praise or monetary gain; he simply regarded work and integrity in his work as human obligations. He never fought with anyone; he respected his parents, superiors, and colleagues. It could be fairly said that since adolescence, he was not at all ordinary.

I remember an interesting example of his character when he was about eighteen years old. Around that age most apprentices are interested only in having a good time, getting into fights, and generally fooling around. Even parents who rely on an emotional hold over their children have a difficult time at that age. But Suzuki was different. At the mess hall, for example, the other apprentices turned mealtime into something like a battlefield. Suzuki, however, sat alone in a corner quietly eating his meal. Here, too, he never wasted anything. If he dropped a grain of rice on the floor, he picked it up and ate it. Once the other workers made fun of him, saying, "Hey, there's some rice on the floor here. Come over and eat it." Suzuki ignored their taunts, waited till they had gone, then quietly walked over and ate the wasted rice. He was always like that. After a while the other workers stopped teasing him and came to respect his hard work and integrity. He had many qualities that they could emulate. Not surprisingly, there are many inspirational stories about Suzuki because his type is quite unusual among uneducated manual laborers. I guess people who get promoted are somehow different from the beginning.

At the age of twenty-one, Suzuki finished his apprenticeship. But as the master craftsman to whom he was apprenticed had already passed on and the master's son was still an infant, Suzuki found himself in the interim in charge of the cooperage. His unselfish efforts on behalf of his infant boss were legend. Later, when the child succeeded his father's position at the cooperage, Suzuki was asked to supervise two warehousing and shipping facilities. He did this so well that he was asked to undertake trips to purchase bamboo and other lumber materials needed in making kegs. This was the beginning of his business career.

Suzuki was gratified and inspired by the confidence placed in him, and he worked extremely hard to repay that trust. He even gave up drinking for ten years. In this way he spent his early manhood engaged in responsible and conscientious work, which was unusual for his age, and he fulfilled the trust given him.

Once when he traveled to the mountains to buy bamboo, the supply available for purchase was insufficient; not wanting to disappoint his boss, he completed the order by buying locally from retailers around Noda. The boss discovered this stratagem, however, and criticized him, calling him "sly and clever." Suzuki did not take kindly to this criticism, even from the boss, and immediately explained his actions. Once accounted for, Mogi Shichirōuemon realized that Suzuki's local purchases were not motivated by deceit, but rather were attempts to complete an order so as to not cause problems for the enterprise. After the sincerity of Suzuki's intent was clarified and once his apology was accepted, everything returned to normal, except that Suzuki was now trusted even more than previously and he carried out his responsibilities even more loyally than before, if that was possible.

Since Suzuki was employed from an early age as an apprentice, he had very little formal education. Occasionally this caused problems when he began to establish his own independent lumber brokerage business. As a result, Suzuki would sometimes ask the President to draw up contracts and write out various communications for him in order to save time and prevent misunderstanding. This helped Suzuki a great deal. Moreover, the President helped Suzuki with loans because he did not have sufficient capital at the start of his lumber business. This clearly demonstrates the meaning of the expression "trust is capital."

At that time local scrap lumber was used to make the sides of soy sauce kegs, cedar for the top and bottom. A cedar log would be split into three sections, and these in turn would be further cut up to make anywhere from ninety to one hundred tops and bottoms. Whenever Suzuki completed this milling process, he recorded the number of bottoms and tops made against the cost of the log and reported it to the President. Attention to such details established his reputation far and wide, and, as a result, he began to act as a broker of timber and bamboo materials for other breweries as well.

The growing production of the soy sauce industry in Noda finally outstripped the supply of local lumber suitable for making barrel sides and ends. Suzuki readily understood the increasing value of Akita cedar, the traditional source of our supply for tops and bottoms, but at the same time he investigated the price and quality of cedar from Kishu, another possible supply site that was occasionally used. Suzuki decided that Akita cedars were a better value, and he persuaded the President to join him in a purchase of a large supply of Akita cedar. They decided to make the purchase themselves; because they could not go all the way by train, they had to make part of the journey by foot. Six months later they returned to Noda with cedar brought from a Miyakoshi Kanbei and loaded on a vessel called *Kumamoto-Maru*. That load alone produced 36,000 kegs, 100 large vats over eight feet tall, and 100 sake vats about six feet high. The purchase attracted a lot of local attention and eventually resulted in considerable business for Suzuki's lumber concession. Although the lumber business was quite competitive, Suzuki was not bothered by it because his honesty and industriousness were his best advertisements.

Over the years Suzuki's lumber business grew as the soy sauce industry flourished in Noda. He took the President as his model, worked hard, and never indulged himself. Of course his business had its ups and downs, but by and large he was successful. His first wife passed away, leaving two small children, as did his second wife. His third wife was healthy, however, and they produced seven more children. His large family was obviously close-knit, and they were the envy of many. The success of his family, like his business, was largely the result of Suzuki's energy and integrity.

Suzuki has become a local merchant of considerable stature, grossing over a million yen a year in his lumber business. In spite of his personal success, he has forgotten neither his artisan origins nor what he had to go through to get where he is. He remains humble and hardworking. He just built himself a new house, largely with his own hands, and the President presented him with a scroll as a housewarming gift. The scroll carries the inscription "Everything is one," which I think means that all efforts are rewarded. Suzuki has it framed and hung in his new house. He regards it contentedly every day, grateful for its message of diligence and reward. Someone like Suzuki should be called a "man of willpower," for he has successfully molded his natural talents in the image of the President.

Editor's Postscript

But personal example requires personal contact, and the workmen in the shōyu plants usually came into contact with the owner just twice a year, at the ritual inspections. Although they may have admired his dignified bearing and respected his reputation for integrity, they never experienced the personal generosity and trust that bound Shinshima and his front-office colleagues so closely to Mogi Shichirōuemon. The life of dedication and modesty that gripped Shinshima's imagination failed to influence the hundreds of workers so far removed from it. Convinced as he was of his master's honorable character and good intentions, Shinshima must have been baffled by the labor unrest that burdened the Noda Shōyu Company throughout much of the 1920s.

5.

Prelude to Turmoil

THE STORY of the Great Noda Strike of 1927–28 is a tragic one. Eleven hundred men were discharged after seven months of a vitriolic and highly publicized strike. What was especially unfortunate was that the schism never should have occurred, for the differences between the Noda Shōyu Company and the resident workers in Noda were more apparent than real. Both sides agreed that the traditional system of labor contracting in town had to be discarded, but neither side could convince the other of how this should be accomplished or what should take its place.

The tragedy of the strike (or strikes, for there was more than one) was the extent of the suffering when the means rather than the ends were at issue. For six years, 1922 to 1928, labor unrest weakened both employer and employee. The lack of a means of settlement, the absence of an institutionalized structure for dialogue, allowed the difficulties to fester and cause havoc.

If any good can be said to have come of such strife it was the realization on the part of employers and workers of the need to work together for their mutual benefit. Without common interest and consent, modern manufacturing could not succeed in Noda. The lack of such common interest was never more clearly illustrated than in the celebrated murder case of 1922, which began the saga of industrial contention in Noda.

The Murder

Kimura Junichirō, a hard-drinking roustabout who worked in the breweries of the Noda Shōyu Company, was attacked by a band of some two dozen young toughs and murdered on July 13, 1922, the night of the Noda Shrine Festival. Kimura suffered multiple cuts, lacerations, and abrasions to his face, neck, limbs, and torso. The murderers fled into the festival crowd, leaving only one of their number, Aizawa Kiyoshirō, to confess to the crime.

The assassins, the police later learned, were all members of the Noda branch of the national Yūaikai (the Friendly Society), a labor union movement begun a decade earlier in Tokyo. Kimura himself had once been a member of the society, which in 1919 had been renamed the Nihon Rōdō Sōdōmei, or Japan General Federation of Labor. In fact he had been one of the two secretaries of the Noda local, along with Koizumi Shichizō. Apparently rivalry with Koizumi for union leadership had divided the men, sending Kimura out of the union and Koizumi out of the Noda Shōyu Company's employ. The two men argued frequently and in public. Kimura had accused Koizumi of embezzling union funds, and Koizumi had countered by revealing Kimura's criminal record and his connections with right-wing groups, specifically the Yamato Minrōkai. Koizumi further accused Kimura of working secretly with the company to undermine the union movement since Kimura had left the Sōdōmei.

The enmity between the men grew especially fierce a week before the murder, when the keg workers went on strike to protest the deduction of three sen from the monthly wages of each employee. Although this practice was customary, it was not contractual, and the coopers organized to protest it. Suzuki Bunshirō, a member of the Sōdōmei and one of the striking barrel-makers, enlisted the support of the union in settling the dispute. On the evening of July 20th representatives of the coopers, the bosses, the union, the company, and the local police had gathered at Izumi-ya, a teahouse in Noda, to settle the strike. In the course of the negotiations, Kimura, as was his wont, became drunk and began to criticize the union and its leaders. This incident, added to the rancor that already divided Kimura and Koizumi and Kimura and the union, was the breaking point. Two nights later a throng of about twenty union bullyboys attacked Kimura, but when sober he was no one to trifle with, and he drove them away with a dagger. The next day he sent his wife to her native village in Ibaragi and, perhaps because of her absence, stayed out late drinking after work. Intoxicated, he was rushed at the door of his house and wounded. He managed to fight his way clear and stumbled to a nearby grocery store and barber shop for help, but there he was assaulted again and mortally wounded.

The police were naturally skeptical of Aizawa's confession. Kimura's reputation alone made it doubtful that one man could take him or would even try to; with ten major wounds on Kimura's body, the police sought accomplices. In time, nineteen men were arrested and tried. All were found guilty, although on appeal by Suzuki Bunji, president of the Sōdōmei and special attorney in this case, only two were ultimately found guilty and given five years of hard labor; the others were released after more than a year in prison.[1]

The excitement surrounding the homicide eclipsed the importance of the negotiations between the striking barrel-workers and their bosses. This was unfortunate because a satisfactory resolution of this dispute had at least as much significance for labor conditions in Noda as did the personal animosity between Kimura and Koizumi and the circumstances of the union movement in town. Indeed, were it not for abuses in the traditional labor contract system—which the barrel-makers' complaints highlighted—it is doubtful that a union movement would have appeared in Noda at all. The source of most of the labor friction was not the Noda Shōyu Company but long-established abuses in the system of labor recruitment, compensation, and management, under which almost everyone, including employees of the Noda Shōyu Company, suffered.

The company, as much as anyone else, sought to correct these abuses, but its approach was not praiseworthy. Its methods were too secretive, too sudden, and too selfish. For example, in a manner that was almost imperious, it would incorporate into its structure such activities as keg- and vat-making, which were necessary to the company's development but which had previously been carried on outside the corporate structure. Also, a fatal lag of three and one-half years from the original conception of a new wage and work system to its introduction on the shop floor contributed to an attitude of suspicion and ill will between the company and its workers. The uncertainty of not knowing when or if their entire livelihood and living circumstances would be changed contributed to the workers' malaise. The company, most workers came to feel, acted in its own best interests, and, Adam Smith notwithstanding, corporate self-interest did not result in everyone's best interest in this small town of 20,000.

The company was culpable as well for removing, undermining, and generally eclipsing the traditional figures of authority for the workers, namely the labor recruiters and the brewmasters cum factory managers (oyakata and tōji). Once the company succeeded in displacing these men, it was not quick or knowledgeable enough to substitute its own men with their new programs and policies in time to prevent confrontation.

The union's approach was quite different. It sought to organize workers to combat the excesses of the traditional labor system, with the aim of improving, not overturning, the existing system. Working within the system rather than against it had been the consistent strategy of the

Yūaikai and its founder, Suzuki Bunji, since its establishment in 1912. This policy, which was enforced in the case of the Yūaikai's involvement in Noda, would be the cause of many ruptures and disaffections within the organization. Nevertheless, the appeal of this approach was demonstrated by the union's success in attracting new members.

Union Activities up to the Homicide

The records of the Noda Shōyu Company first indicate an awareness of the Yūaikai on October 28, 1921. It was noted then that about fifty workers met at the rooms of Koizumi Shichizō to discuss union issues and ideas.[2] When the Noda local of the Japan General Federation of Labor was founded six weeks later, on December 15, 1921, Koizumi claimed three hundred members. Even if this larger figure was a vainglorious gesture to impress the national organization, membership in the Noda local grew so rapidly that the union had to change its title, structure, and purpose four times during its first three years in order to accommodate new members and new goals. Although the basis of union organization shifted from that of an industrial to a craft union, then to an enterprise union, and back again to an industrial union, the organization drew on just two types of workers: those in the employ of the Noda Shōyu Company, and all others. The others, for the most part, were closely connected with the company as subcontractors, such as the coopers who made the shōyu kegs and the transportation workers who moved them to market. Workers in factories that manufactured sake, vinegar, and miso, rather than shōyu, were also likely to be attracted to a union.

The incidence of unionization—in which factories and in what industries—explains a good deal of the appeal behind Koizumi's labor association. In the Noda Shōyu Company itself, the third, fourth, seventh, and ninth factories were the first to germinate union cells.[3] Actually, factories 3 and 7 merged in 1918 and numbers 4 and 9 in 1919. Until 1925, when Factory 17 was completed, these four factories (compressed into two) were the most modern in Noda. Factory 3, rebuilt in 1919, had been the plant of Mogi Shichizaemon before the 1917 amalgamation of family enterprises into the Noda Shōyu Company. As the patriarch of all the Mogi families in Noda, Mogi Shichizaemon had taken great pride in this factory and in his family's finest soy sauce brand, Kushigata, which had been made there. He spared no expense in modernizing his plant by the installation of new machinery and the application of the latest fermentation technology. Factory 3 was the first in Noda to install all hydraulic presses to extract the shōyu from the matured moromi. In 1911, likewise, boilers were installed for the preparation of soybeans for germination. More boilers were added in 1912, 1914, and

1916. In 1921 new fermentation vats were installed, and the next year a new barrel warehouse was constructed.

Shichizaemon's efforts to lead in soy sauce manufacture were matched in Noda by only a few, and exceeded perhaps by only one. Mogi Saheiji's Kikkoman brand had been brewed in what was known since 1821 as Factory 4. He had rebuilt the plant in 1889 and again in 1910. In 1911, along with Shichizaemon, he had installed boilers to speed the preparation of the kōji. In 1912 the world's first concrete fermentation and holding vats were introduced; in 1913 new moromi- or mash-stirring and barrel-storage rooms; and in 1914, new salt and kasu (shōyu sediment cake) warehouse facilities. Saheiji's plant was so famous for its state-of-the-art technology that a picture of his factory was featured in the fifth-grade Japanese reader in geography on the section dealing with Chiba Prefecture.

Kikkoman, as noted earlier, was the first Noda brand to be exported widely. To maintain his success overseas, in 1922 Mogi Saheiji installed a new line for canning five-gallon drums of soy sauce for export. In 1924 a new kōji room was added, and in 1928 remodeled shipping facilities were in place. Since 1919 all of the new and old equipment had been linked by the use of elevators and conveyor belts to speed the manufacture and transport of shōyu.[4]

The appeal of the union, first in these two plants and later in others, appears to have been the possibility of arresting the aggressive modernization of soy sauce manufacture in Noda. Production and distribution were changing rapidly—too rapidly for many workers. New attention to detail, safety, and sanitation was required by the mechanical and chemical advances in production; new work hours, schedules, and routines were demanded of workers; and new markets were opened as the railroad network expanded. Workers who had some sense of identification with brands other than Kikkoman and with the families that produced them were called upon to work as hard or harder in the interests of a brand and family with which they had no historical association. Of course only some of the regular workers had such basic feelings of loyalty, but for these the sense of loss as the company switched more and more of its production to Saheiji's Kikkoman was real enough. For most workers, however, the issues creating dissatisfaction had to do less with the loss of tradition than with the new circumstances and conditions of work.

Traditional Wage Labor

Traditional wage bargaining in Japan was not much of a bargain from the worker's point of view because the power balance between employer and employee was tilted decidedly in the direction of the employer. Except in the newer industries and factories that appeared around World War I, industrial work was carried on most often in small shops by a dozen or perhaps several dozen workers who were indentured to a boss. Quite often, even in larger factories, workers were organized as teams subordinated to labor bosses rather than to factory owners and managers. Usually such bosses were skilled and trained their workers as apprentices. In other cases, especially where a shop was owned by someone who was not a craftsman, a boss was simply a boss—one whose authority was not supported by a proper trade. This would occur, for example, when a master craftsman died without offspring or without designating a successor.

In Noda, in such traditional crafts as barrel- or vat-making, carpentry, and stone masonry, apprentices joined a shop at the age of puberty and slowly advanced to journeyman status by the age of twentyone or so. Usually a multiyear contract specified the terms of work and the pay during this training period. After the first contractual period expired, a year-to-year contract might be negotiated. During the nineteenth century, especially, there was a tendency to shorten the contractual periods, in keeping with a widely recognized active market for wage labor.

Wage contracts specified the wages to be received, the times of payment, the conditions of work, and the length of employment. In addition to the names of the employer and employee, it was customary to find the names of persons who would act as guarantors of the worker's performance (usually a parent or guardian, sometimes a labor contractor). Contracts were written either by the parties themselves or by scriveners employed to do so.

Workers were often caught in a double bind. If they wished to maximize their wages, they sought positions of high pay and short duration. If they wished security and advancement, they accepted positions that paid less well but held the promise of promotion in a trade. An additional attraction of the latter course was that as much as 70 percent of a contract's total wages were frequently paid in advance, and if the contract was a multiyear one, the cash advance could be substantial. This is why the wage bargain resembled a system of indenture. A worker, or more likely his parents, received a substantial cash advance against which he pledged his labor for a specified period of time. During the contract period the remaining wages were paid out periodically, usually on a month-to-month basis. In addition, the employer usually was responsible for feeding, clothing, and training the worker during the contract period.

The potential abuses were obvious. Parents could, in effect, sell their offspring for the cash advance. Workers (or their families), having already received most of their wages, could be lackadaisical and uninterested in their work. Shopkeepers and master craftsmen could neglect their responsibilities to feed, clothe, and train their charges. Goodwill and trust, but not legal constraints, were the only effective controls in the traditional system of labor contracting.

A typical contract used in Noda in the 1920s read as follows:

Employment Contract[5]

Total wages ——
    to be paid in two installments: first half-year——
                       second half-year——

Employment period: from —— to ——

I agree to work until —— for the amount of money specified above and to honor the following conditions:

1. I have received —— as a loan against the wages I will receive, as written above; the remainder of my wages will be paid out monthly, as long as I continue to work; the wages will be paid directly to me or through my guarantor.

2. If I work continually and without absences, I will receive —— as a bonus when I complete my employment.

3. I promise to work earnestly and well; only military service and other unavoidable obligations will be allowed to interrupt my employment.

4. If I am ill for any extended period, I will find someone to work in my place and I will notify my guarantor immediately of my absence.

5. If, as outlined in numbers 3 & 4 above, I am unable to continue employment, I will be paid according to the total number of days that I worked. If I am not paid by my employer, the guarantor will be responsible for paying me.

6. If I am required to work more than normal due to the success of the company, I can expect to receive additional wages.

We, the undersigned, find no objection to this contract and we sign in evidence of this.

Date: _____   Principal _____
                                         Guarantor _____
                                         Witness _____
                                         (Introducer)

This sort of contract was used in both large and small enterprises. The difference between them was in the way workers were recruited for employment. Large enterprises, like the Noda Shōyu Company, utilized the services of labor contractors up to 1923 to recruit workers and to guarantee their performance. If a worker did not uphold his end of the contract, then the labor contractor, also known as the guarantor, was required to find a satisfactory replacement. Thus, wage labor performance was secured in two ways: first by the large cash advance, and next by the personalized attention of the labor contractor. Once employed, a worker in a large enterprise would have to work at least half a year to pay off the cash advance, and then, if he wished to abrogate the contract, he had to satisfy the objections of the guarantor before the balance of the year's contract could be renounced. Smaller enterprises, because of their more limited size, more informal operation, and fewer needs did not have to rely on labor contractors to find and secure workers. Their laborers came most often through personal recommendation.

Problems Associated with the Employment System

Of the many problems associated with the traditional system of labor contracting, two in particular stand out: high labor turnover, and "internal contracting."

Labor Turnover. Although this was disadvantageous for factory owners and operators, it was not at all detrimental for labor contractors. These agents derived their income by collecting fees for matching a person with a job, much like a modern placement agency does, and by taking a certain amount from the periodic wages of those whose jobs they guaranteed. In the first instance, the fees in Noda in 1923 amounted to 5.0 yen, of which 0.5 was returned if a person completed his contract without problems. The 5.0-yen fee was made up of the following charges: placement fee, 1.5 yen; guarantor's fee, 2.5 yen; office charges, 0.5 yen; earnest money, 0.5 yen (returned when work was satisfactorily completed).

The second sort of income available to labor contractors and bosses might be considered a kind of management fee: in exchange for supervising a worker's job performance, a contractor or boss deducted a small percentage of his charge's earnings off the top. This was easily accomplished because wages usually were paid indirectly through the contractor or supervisor rather than directly to the worker. Even Noda Shōyu Company, with more than one thousand workers, until 1922–23 paid its workers through the master brewers (tōji) or the labor contractors (oyakata). It is estimated that overseers and guarantors together deducted about 5 percent from the wages paid to workers.[6]

The traditional wage system did not provide continuing incentives to work. Once the cash advance was received, wages were analogous to a subsistence allowance designed to maintain but not encourage work performance. Workers had little to look forward to, except perhaps to the next year's wage bargain when they would receive another substantial advance on their services. The intermediaries (tōji and oyakata) benefited most from this arrangement. No matter what the age, experience, or initiative of the work force, they received their fees.

The dissatisfaction of workers with the traditional wage system was evident in high turnover rates, not just in Noda but nationwide. Koji Taira writes that turnover rates in 1900 and 1918, according to a government study, were on the average of 40 percent in the first year.[7] At the Noda Shōyu Company, as table 12 shows, the same high turnover among workers was evident in 1923. In other words, more than half had left in less than three years, and the remainder in another three or four years. This produced an essentially bimodal distribution of turnover and suggests two quite different sets of reasons for departure. For those who stayed less than three years the pay was low, the work mostly unskilled, and the likelihood of promotion not sufficiently attractive to remain. For those working between three and seven years the pay was a little better, the work presumably more demanding, but the future with the firm was still not compelling enough to stay on.

A number of reasons might be suggested. First, the possibility of promotion was fairly well exhausted once laborers had achieved an advancement to honnin, or experienced worker, which generally happened in the fourth year of continuous employment. Beyond that, the higher openings were those of assistant brewmaster and brewmaster, positions that possessed no clearly defined promotional steps. Selection and advancement for the experienced worker seemed uncertain and perhaps even arbitrary. Second, compensation was not necessarily

TABLE 12. Turnover among workers, 1923.

Number of years worked	Percent leaving	Cumulative total
less than 1	8.6	8.6
between 1 & 2	26.9	35.5
between 2 & 3	17.3	52.8
between 3 & 4	9.3	62.1
between 4 & 5	7.8	69.9
between 5 & 6	7.5	77.4
between 6 & 7	22.6	100.0

Source: Yoshida Tōru, "Honpō Shōyi Kōgyō," *Shakai Seisaku Jihō,* 62 (November 1925), 133.

linked to experience or skill. Wages for inexperienced workers (those who had not yet worked four years) and for experienced workers (with more than four years' service) constituted an essentially double pay scale. One received one wage or the other, regardless of the work performed, type of experience garnered, and willingness to work. There might be an occasional bonus if work was unusually heavy, but these were distributed more or less equally among all workers depending on their classification. Thus, there were no compelling monetary reasons for maintaining long service with an employer. Annual pay raises, performance incentives, pension benefits, and severance pay according to experience of seniority were unknown.

"Internal Contracting." The lack of flexibility and reward in the compensation system was tied directly to the structure of work, which was generally called "internal contracting." This was neither new nor confined to Japan. It had appeared there perhaps as early as the seventeenth century with the rise of wage labor and had grown greatly in the latter half of the eighteenth and during the whole of the nineteenth centuries as a response to problems of labor recruitment and labor management. Its attractiveness then and our disregard for it now highlight the advances of the twentieth century in the science of management. The appeal of internal contracting in the nineteenth century lay in the possibility of decentralizing the growing size and complexity of work to work gangs of manageable proportions, say, a half-dozen to several score of workers. In addition, the cost of such work groups could be calculated well in advance. Work in the shops and factories of nineteenth-century Japan, as a result, was carried out independently and without centralized coordination, in autonomous groups for which labor costs were predetermined. Once set, labor costs did not vary except when demand greatly exceeded expectation; in such cases the bonuses workers received for producing more than expected were easily financed out of increased sales.

The widespread internal contracting system was ideal for enterprises such as the soy sauce breweries in Noda. Here, before the 1920s owners did not manage their enterprises because they lacked the technical and organizational skills to run them. As a result, brewmasters or tōji determined the internal allocation of labor resources, the design and pace of the work process, and the reward and promotion of workers. Labor contractors, although "on the outside," cooperated closely with tōji to recruit workers. When a breach of labor contract occurred, the tōji and oyakata settled the matter.[8]

In short, owners contracted with brewmasters to produce a certain amount of soy sauce over a particular period, usually a year. Because the final product was blended at more or less one point in time and was so vast, measured in thousands and tens of thousands of gallons, it made little sense to determine wages in terms of a piece rate. Rather, the work was all of a single piece, and wages were paid for completion of an entire process: putting up this year's mash, pressing out last year's shōyu, and getting it into containers for distribution.

Although we have no samples of contracts between owners and tōji, they must have existed, formally or informally. Otherwise, it would make no sense for owners to supply the space, machinery, tools, raw materials, and power necessary to make soy sauce, not to mention the payment of labor. Owners could not conceivably incur such expenses without prior understanding with tōji about what the volume of production and the costs of labor were likely to be. This system, then, allowed an entrepreneur with little technical knowledge and experience to use his capital effectively by bringing together the necessary plant and equipment and by delegating managerial authority to someone who understood how to use them.

Internal contracting was not unique to Japan. It was a common practice in American industry from the middle of the nineteenth century until World War I. It worked well and was convenient, and it allowed for a growing volume and sophistication of industrial manufacture without requiring an attendant development and maturation of industrial management. Yet after World War I, internal contracting was abandoned in both countries.[9] In the United States, where it disappeared first, its elimination was associated with the appearance of scientific management. In Japan, although the eradication of internal contracting was not as closely tied to the rise of an easily identifiable new philosophy and practice of management, it nevertheless disappeared and for much the same reasons.

Oliver E. Williamson identifies eight problems associated with internal contracting: (1) a tendency for the outside owners and inside contractors to become overly concerned with the protection of their positions and privileges; (2) a tendency for inside contractors to withhold information on job conditions from labor contractors; (3) difficulty in regulating the flow of components manufactured by separate work gangs because of a lack of overall coordination; (4) too much or too little inventory at different stages of production resulting from a lack of overall coordination (related to the previous item), and a concern of each autonomous work group with minimizing its direct costs, even if this was disadvantageous for others; (5) the possibility that contractor incomes could become excessive and that they had little to do with the quality of production; (6) a likelihood that the plant and equipment, supplied but not supervised by the capitalist, were not properly cared for; (7) a tendency for contractors to be concerned with labor-saving innovations but no others; and (8) a lack of incentives for product innovation among those actually engaged in manufacturing.[10]

Internal Contracting at the Noda Shōyu Company

Many of the difficulties with internal contracting pinpointed by Williamson turned up with alarming frequency at the Noda Shōyu Company after its incorporation in 1917. As the managers of the new company began to explore the circumstances of manufacturing in various factories, they collided with the entrenched interests of tōji and others who wished to keep such information from them. A sort of diary entitled *Biroku Jūyakushitsu* (Notes from the Executive Offices), which recorded, among other things, such conflicts of interest, was kept from December 1918 to November 1919. One of its first entries (December 20, 1918) notes that the brewmaster from Factory 13 had asked for a loan of 500 yen; on January 16 and 17, tōji from Factories 5, 13, and 14 had requested money. In all likelihood the money was needed to pay advances for new workers who signed their contracts in January of each year. But another entry on January 17 states that some factory hands were refusing to work, apparently because of the presence of company inspectors. Quite clearly, the officers were responsible for paying workers but not for supervising them. On January 21 and 23, therefore, when company representatives met with bosses and contractors to negotiate new wage offers, the work to be done for the wages and the conditions under which it would be performed were apparently not discussed. The *Biroku* goes on to inform us that in February the company paid tōji and oyabun their customary fees and bonuses for recruiting and supervising the factory work force, signifying that it was business as usual.[11]

The *Biroku* continues to report incidents of tōji requesting loans. The corporation was compelled to accept such requests without too much complaint because managers were ignorant of actual conditions in the factories and, therefore, of the costs of labor inputs at different levels of production relative to other costs. To remedy this, in 1919 managers began to involve themselves more directly in factory operations and to gather statistical information from which informed cost calculations might be derived. A March 23 entry mentions the desirability of moving some surplus workers from Factory 6 to Factory 8. Two days later, the need for hiring some high school graduates to train as factory inspectors was recorded.

This year, 1919, was the one in which bookkeeping and other numerical recordkeeping procedures were unified throughout the offices and factories at Noda Shōyu. That year a numerical technique to calculate the costs of outputs against inputs for each factory was introduced and used to compare efficiency across units. Such actions were taken none too soon, as management was becoming increasingly involved in wage negotiations and this made little sense without a feel for actual working conditions.

On May 31 workers requested that their wages be temporarily raised 5 yen per month (this was the period of the rice riots in Japan, when a largely spontaneous and incendiary demonstration over extreme inflation swept the nation), and at the same time oyabun wanted to increase their placement fee to 4.5 yen per worker. To put an end to such wildcat requests, on May 31 the management of three of the breweries at Noda (none of them major brands) decided to offer together a wage proposal to their workers, regardless of the agents they worked for and the factories where they labored (see table 13).

These wages were high in comparison to the national average.[12] As the making of this scheme of wages attests, managers were increasingly forced into wage bargaining with factory workers and their agents. They also were beginning to discern the appropriateness of one wage or another relative to the contribution of labor inputs to total costs. Obviously the solution to this debacle would require that managers bypass contractors and bosses and take a more direct role in hiring, supervising, training, paying, and promoting workers.

Under the traditional labor system, workers were indentured to bosses, who sought to protect their own status at the expense of the workers and the owners. Production functions were uncoordinated,

TABLE 13. Wage proposal to workers, 1919.

Category	Level	Pay (yen)
ordinary workers	experienced	3.0 per day
	intermediate	2.5 per day
	beginners	1.5 per day
mechanics	experienced	3.0 per day
	intermediate	2.5 per day
	beginners	2.0 per day
labor contractor	factory worker	3.5 per contract
	farm worker[a]	2.5 per contract

Source: Kikkoman Company Archives, Biroku Jūyaku shitsu (n.p., 1919), p. 14.

a. Farm workers supplied produce and grains to the factory dormitories.

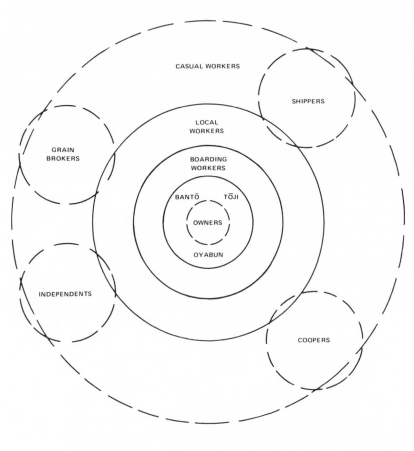

FIGURE 11. WORKERS AND MANAGERS
NODA SHŌYU COMPANY
BEFORE 1923

SOLID LINE ———————— THOSE INVOLVED DIRECTLY IN SOY SAUCE MANUFACTURE

DOTTED LINE —— —— THOSE INVOLVED INDIRECTLY IN SOY SAUCE MANUFACTURE

and, as figure 11 shows, the various stages and components of production were not well regulated or integrated. In effect, management had to be introduced to the shop floor; but this was much more easily said than done. First, tōji and oyakata would either have to be removed, ignored, or coopted. The last was the line of least resistance. In 1919, with an initial capitalization of 7,000 yen, the company established the Noda Placement Company, which brought the five labor contractors in town within their institutional control.[13] Between 1919 and 1923 the company involved the brewmasters in one new study after another emanating from the Committees on Research, Sales, and the Second Day of the Month Meeting. By 1922, when the new Personnel Department was founded, tōji had become the reluctant first line of management rather than the consummate representative of the old working classes. Tōji who could not accept the change left and retired. Second, the quality and costs of a variety of labor services would have to be carefully observed, measured, and weighed relative to the total work flow and product. Third, a fair wage system would have to be devised—one that would not only pay workers according to their marginal contribution but also motivate them to labor hard, well, and with ingenuity.

In answer to these needs, during the summer of 1919 the company began to compose new wage and work proposals. One of the earliest plans developed in Noda (and one of the earliest for Japan that I have been able to find) treats the need for a comprehensive labor policy in three broad areas: improving the circumstances of factory workers; regulations for a workers' mutual aid association; improving problem areas in the factories. This plan is reproduced in its entirety in Appendix F. In conception no less than in execution, even though it was not implemented until 1923, it was a revolutionary vision of management-labor relations in Japan in 1919. (The proposal, it is well to remember, was drawn up three years before the murder of Kimura and the beginning of labor violence in Noda.)

The delay in implementing the new work structure was crucial for the history of the labor movement in Noda for it occurred during a time of business decline and slumping demand following the boom years of World War I. Unemployment and dissatisfaction throughout Japan led to tenant and labor disputes, political protests, and the anxiety of the rice riots in 1918–19. Ideas of democracy and Marxism flooded into the country after the Great War, and political leaders in Japan, conservative and liberal alike, spoke of *kakushin* and *kaizō*, literally, reform and reconstruction. In 1920 the Japan Farmers' Union was formed, in 1922 the Japan Communist Party, and proletarian party movements peaked between 1922 and 1926. The events of 1920 put many government leaders on guard: mass meetings of nationwide proletarian groups; Yahata

Ironworks strike involving 224,000 miners; and near riotous assemblies supporting the National Universal Suffrage League, Japan Socialist League, and various anarcho-syndicalist movements. The government's response was mostly repressive, stepping up restraints, controls, emergency measures, and even arrests when needed. In Noda the intensity of political division and debate found in Tokyo was lacking, but the delay in carrying through on the new wage and work proposals, especially during the postwar political and economic upheaval, confused workers and threw into question the security and permanence of their jobs. In the meantime, the Sōdōmei was active in organizing the town.

The delay was natural. The original conception was far too simple. Increasing the levels of employment from two or three to four, for example, was insufficient: the growing complexity of the work, not only in the technology and chemistry of production but also in product scheduling and distribution, required a roster of job descriptions and job placements far more involved and detailed than could be imagined in 1919. In addition, the new wage and work proposals were tied to an effort to rationalize the entire range of production methods and routines in the factories. A scheme for worker placement and compensation had to await final agreement with regard to overall and individual job design and structure. Tōji required time and coaxing in order for them to be reliably included in the management structure rather than functioning as contractors. Although in 1922 a Personnel Department was established to handle job designation, appointment, and compensation, time was needed to implement the original conception. And time worked to the company's disadvantage and the union's benefit.

The issue was never one of technological displacement of workers in the sense of layoffs and dismissals. It meant discomfort, possible job dislocation, and probable disorientation. The entire structure and rhythm of work as well as the workplace were being altered. Although the introduction of boilers, hydraulic presses, and mechanical mills did not yet change the sequence and number of stages in the production process, the volume and rate of throughput was greatly accelerated. The potential for greater production was introduced; whether or not it would be realized depended on the cooperation and motivation of the work force.

Workers were troubled by the prospect. Tōji, the traditional sources of legitimacy and authority in the factories, were either elevated and made into factory managers, or else they were supplanted by managers who were sent into the plants as the lowest rung of a centralized managerial hierarchy. The latter represented authority, but they knew little about soy sauce brewing technology and even less about industrial relations on the shop floor.

Adding to the difficulty in convincing workers of the merits of the proposed changes was suspicion that the expected increases in productivity would accrue more to the benefit of management than to the welfare of workers. Such a fear was natural in a family-owned and operated firm where profits were equated with the owners' personal income. Indeed a good proportion of the profits did go to the owners in the form of dividends and interest. Even if this was common practice in a closely held corporation, the workers were disturbed lest their increased efforts simply benefit others and not themselves. This proved to be an unnecessary worry, although in 1919 neither management nor labor could be expected to understand that increased productivity would bring not only greater profit but expanded employment as well. Increasing productivity would require hiring more workers and assigning them to greatly elaborated tasks as compared to what they had done ten years earlier. The new work structure would require far more education, skill, and determination on the part of workers; accordingly, opportunities for promotion and pay advancement would be far greater But it is doubtful that anyone—manager, worker, or union organizer—clearly understood all the ramifications of this in 1919.

From Homicide to the 1923 Strike

The distance between the unionized workers and the managers of the company was starkly revealed in a poster, whose message I have translated. It appeared in Noda on July 25, 1922, two days after the homicide.

> TO THE PUBLIC
> TO THE WITNESSES OF THE JULY 23 INCIDENT
>
> Understand the truth of what happened and remove the fear from your minds. Here is the truth of the matter. The bourgeois class of this town is only concerned with making money. It is natural that in such an environment incidents may occur. Consider our wretched history. It is beyond description and explanation. We took this chance to uproot these evils. We are justified in our actions; our goals are based on humanity and charity. We are trying to eliminate capitalist oppression. Those of you who are aware of this oppression, listen to our cries of justice!
>
> Noda Branch (of the Sōdōmei)

This is an astonishing document. Not only was its rhetoric entirely out of character with the nature of work conditions in Noda and the surrounding countryside at that time, but so was the dialectical struggle it portrayed. Although labor and farm disputes grew dramatically in

Japan after 1918, Chiba Prefecture and Noda Township had been quiet until the homicide. In 1923 only thirteen farm disputes were recorded in all of Chiba, and some of these were insignificant.[14] Moreover, this was the highest number in any one year before 1928 in the prefecture. In spite of the tension throughout Japan between the propertied and unpropertied classes, Noda and Chiba were quiet, with little agrarian or industrial strife until 1922–23.

The appearance of the Sōdōmei in Noda undoubtedly made a great difference in the political and social fabric of the town and its major industry. From the beginning, the Sōdōmei exerted prodigious efforts to attract members and educate them in opposition to the Noda Shōyu Company. The union's opening ceremony in January 1922 was considered important enough to attract Suzuki Bunji, the president of the Sōdōmei, Matsuoka Komakichi, its head in Eastern Japan, and Azabu Hisa, another high officer, to Noda from Tokyo.[15]

The presence of such Sōdōmei notables from the inception of the Noda union movement suggests the importance with which regional and national officers viewed the developments there. The early history of the Sōdōmei in Noda was not one of obscurity and "struggle-against-all-odds," as is sometimes implied in pro-union tracts. On the contrary, from the beginning that local was one of the largest in membership, wealthiest in treasury, and most seasoned in leadership of all Sōdōmei branches in Japan. Because of the presence, almost from the start, of so many high-level union officers who were not from Noda, the branch was assured of top-flight, well-informed generalship. Whether these leaders had the best interests of the local workers foremost in their plans was another matter. Stephen S. Large has written that the Sōdōmei central committee wanted to showcase the Noda labor difficulties as a means of refuting the claims of a rival union organization (the Hyōgikai) that it was unwilling to pursue militant tactics in the interest of worker rights.[16]

The importance of the union movement in Noda rested on the significance of the food and beverage industry within Japan's industrial structure before World War II. After textiles, food and drink enterprises comprised the second most important industrial sector in Japan, accounting for more than 15 percent of the largest two hundred industrials in Japan in 1918.[17]

Like textiles, food and drink was a major employer of factory labor; but unlike textiles, most food and drink workers were not female and not particularly young. The female operatives in the textile mills typically went to work as teenagers (around age fifteen or sixteen), and stayed until early womanhood (around age twenty to twenty-two), when they married and usually returned to their native village. Furthermore, female textile operatives, because of their youth and marital status, usually were required to live in company dormitories; this effectively shielded them from union organization. Food and beverage workers, on the other hand, were generally men. They typically entered the sugar refineries, seafood canning factories, beer and shōyu industries as adults, and they might move in and out of the plants for most of their adult lives. The results of a study conducted in May 1924 at the Noda Shōyu Company provides data on the age and education of its work force (see table 14).

The food and beverage industry, and the Noda Shōyu Company in particular, offered an immense attraction to Japan's fledgling union movement. The industry was in transition, which the workers cared little for and misunderstood—even mistrusted. This was a golden opportunity for the union to organize what was for it the most critical industry in a rapidly developing Japan.

During the 1920s the union movement in Noda was directed by regional and national officers of the Sōdōmei. This was dramatically underscored by the arrival of Uchida Tomezō and Onishi Toshio from Tokyo to assume leadership of the branch after the incarceration of

TABLE 14. Age and education of workers, 1924.

Age	Male	Female	Total	Percent
under 13[a]	15	—	15	1
over 13/under 20	294	18	312	21
over 20/under 24	749	68	817	54
over 24	348	18	366	24
total	1,406	104	1,510	100

Education (years)	Brewery workers		Others		Subtotal		
	Male	Female	Male	Female	Male	Female	Percent
none	60	18	26	5	86	23	7.0
1 primary	10	—	8	—	18	—	1.0
2 primary	67	3	16	5	83	8	6.0
3 primary	70	8	33	4	103	12	8.0
4 primary	251	9	103	3	354	12	24.0
5 primary	68	7	29	1	97	8	7.0
6 primary	253	31	203	5	456	36	33.0
1 upper primary	31	3	48	2	79	5	5.6
2 upper primary	60	—	66	—	126	—	8.0
more than 8	2	—	2	—	4	—	0.3
total	872	79	534	25	1406	104	99.9

Source: Anonymous, *Honsha Sōgi Taikan* (n.p., 1928), p. 27.
a. Those under 13 years are barrel-making apprentices.

Koizumi Shichizō, Someya Sakuzō, Kaneko Kazumasa, and other local leaders for questioning with regard to the homicide in July 1922. Even Akamatsu Katsumaro, one of the so-called "radicals of Tsukishima" (a group of firebrand unionists), and a director of the Sōdōmei, was welcomed on the 27th by a double row of workers, with hats removed and heads bowed.[18] That afternoon, in a rough yet theatrical speech, he called upon the workers to wait patiently for the resolution of the homicide incident, but to resist any suggestion that connected the murder with the union.

Ultimately, the strategy of disassociating the homicide from the union was successful, but only with the intercession once again of the national leaders of the Sōdōmei: Suzuki Bunji, Matsuoka Komakichi, Akamatsu Katsumaro, and Katayama Tetsu. Through skillful trial work, all but two of the thirteen workers—Sōdōmei members to a man—were acquitted of involvement in Kimura's murder.

The homicide was not the end of industrial violence in Noda. It was more like the beginning. In less than a year, during the spring months of March and April 1923, the company and union were again in confrontation. This was almost inevitable because the interests of those involved were so dramatically opposed: the company was eager to modernize production and become the undisputed national leader in soy

1922 meeting of Yūaikai (Sōdōmei); Second General Meeting of Yūaikai, Noda Branch, in Noda; note Kimura Junichirō (3rd person from right), Akamatsu Katsumaro (6th from right), Matsuoka Komakichi (7th from right), Koizumi Shichizō (8th from right), and Okano Minoru (9th from right)

sauce manufacture; the bosses were struggling to remain independent, yet were caught between the rising expectations of managers and workers; the workers were unhappy with their lot but had no sense of how to change things; and the union was looking for ways to extend its political and economic power. Noda appeared to offer the union that opportunity.

The 1923 dispute grew out of the union's objections to the new wage and work rules, which though conceived some four years earlier were only enforced in 1922–23. The spring strike of 1923 lasted for a month. It established a pattern of dispute resolution in Noda that would be repeated often in the next five years: the union would object to company policies or activities and would counter them with a work slowdown or strike; company management, convinced of the justification of its actions, would refuse to deal with the union; and a neutral group, a mediation body of local or regional notables, would work with both sides for the ultimate resolution of the altercation.

Reorganization of Work Design and Structure

From management's point of view, the new work design inaugurated in January 1923 was implemented to accomplish three goals: to raise productivity, improve quality, and increase the welfare of workers. The most controversial of these goals was that of raising productivity, for it involved not only the reorganization of work design and routine for more efficient utilization of manpower but also a more rapid throughput of product. Workers felt that they were being asked to work harder and longer for not that much more money. Although productivity and pay were two sides of the same coin, in 1923 the crucial side of the issue was more the design and pace of work, while in 1927, as we shall see, it was more the pay than the pace of work that estranged workers from the company.

Probably the most important organizational change to occur as a result of the 1923 factory overhaul was the establishment of work sections or teams. Each team was composed of six to ten workers who were supervised by subsection heads who were, in turn, responsible to section heads. Section heads were relatively few in number, generally about five to seven in a factory of one hundred or so, and were considered to be the lowest rung of managers in the company. They were in a sense the company's front-line foremen. The subordinates, in contrast, two or three subsection heads and twenty to thirty regular workers, were considered rank-and-file or blue-collar workers. After 1923, although individual work standards were established, the measurement of performance and the assessment of productivity were always based on work sections or teams rather than on individuals. This was in part a continuation of past practice—namely, the *oyabun-kobun* (master-apprentice) pattern that obtained between tōji and their gangs or between master craftsmen and their apprentices—but it was also an innovation. The new work gangs were smaller in size, more structured in form and function, and more closely monitored to ensure their coordination with scores of other sections in a highly centralized and carefully controlled work process.[19]

The extension of managerial authority and inspection to the shop floor was new and effective: about half a dozen foremen per plant, armed with statistical and accounting controls, forged into the factories. Foremen were the obvious key to transmitting new work policies and programs since they were the source of information about actual factory conditions and performance levels. Not surprisingly, they were not popular, and their intrusion into the traditional work routine was unwelcome. Many had to be recruited from outside the Noda Shōyu Company; others, elevated from within, had to be given handsome bonuses to assume the position. After 1923 an increasingly large number of graduates from middle and technical high schools were recruited for foremen and other supervisory positions. Most came from villages and towns relatively close to Noda, although some crossed over the Edo or Tone rivers from Saitama or Ibaragi prefectures.

One week after the new system was initiated, on January 8, 1923, the company held a public meeting to explain the reasons for establishing the new system and to outline how it would alter the company's employment policies. The proposed alteration of the age and work system would institute the following:

> a new wage system with more classes and categories of compensation;
>
> a new program of fringe benefits, some general and applied equally to all employees, others tied to years of service;
>
> abandoning the internal contracting system in favor of an eight-hour day, daily wage rate;
>
> the codification and publication of company rules and regulations, specifying, among other things, grounds for employee suspension and discharge;
>
> a new program of housing workers that replaced the old dormitories attached to particular factories with company-built and subsidized boardinghouses for unmarried workers and single-family residences for married workers.[20]

Many of these items were similar to the company proposals on these matters that had been drawn up in 1919 but not implemented. In spite of the three-and-one-half-year interval, the proposals were apparently not that clear or convincing, for company workers met throughout the next day to discuss and debate the recommended changes. At eight o'clock in the evening four representatives of the workers stopped at the company headquarters with the following requests:

(1) the average daily wage should be 2 yen;

(2) bonuses should be based on seniority;

(3) discharge allowances should be calculated as one month for each year worked, and one day for each month worked;

(4) annual bonus should be paid twice a year: a summer bonus equal to forty days' wages, and a New Year's bonus equal to fifty days' wages;

(5) wages paid on all legal holidays;

(6) barrel-making apprentices working in the company factories should be recognized as company employees.

The next day, after further discussion among themselves and with company officers, the workers revised their requests. Now, the company and the workers agreed that:

(1) the average daily wage will be 2 yen, but some may be paid less according to their qualifications and experience;

(2) seniority bonus, based on years of continuous service from January 1, 1918, would be established;

(3) a separate discharge allowance is not needed if a seniority-based bonus is implemented;

(4) although the amount of a bonus will not be fixed in advance, it will be distributed so that slightly more is given at New Year and slightly less at the summer solstice;

(5) an incentive wage bonus for daily attendance will be effected;

(6) coopers hired for work within the company can become company employees.

This agreement was ratified by a vote among workers on January 15, 1923. Although records of the tally do not remain, it appears that about 60 percent of the workers voted in favor of the January 10 compromise.[21]

In terms of wages and benefits the new system was far more attractive, especially in overall terms, than what had existed previously in Noda. Table 15 highlights the improvements of the 1923 proposal.

In addition, the new system offered a 2-yen-per-month housing supplement for heads of families. For workers receiving this supplement the new wage was about 35 percent higher than the earlier wage (which had included a substantial stipend for food). Furthermore, the seniority-based annual bonus that was augmented in 1923 created a compelling economic rationale for staying with the company, as comparison of the old and new bonuses reveals (see table 16).

TABLE 15. Old and new wage and work conditions, 1923.

Item	Old	New
wages	330 yen/year	2 yen/day[a]
bonus	30 yen (once or twice a year)	21 yen 85 sen[b] plus daily attendance bonus
special increase	18 yen (for 6 months after July 1922)	n.a.
haircut & hygiene	36 yen	n.a.
miscellaneous	5 yen (once a yr.)	1 yen
holiday wages	10 yen	22 yen
food	180 yen	n.a.
total	579 yen	758 yen 85 sen
wage per calendar day	1 yen 61 sen	2 yen 11 sen
wage per work day	1 yen 73 sen	2 yen 28 sen

Source: Anonymous, *Honsha Sōgi Taikan* (n.p., 1928), pp. 23–24.
a. Average work days = 333 per year.
b. Average in 1923.

The new wage and work system provided greatly expanded medical coverage and treatment for workers and their families. Clearly the company was trying to attract and motivate employees by offering outstanding benefits. The old wage, which was not low compared to national and industry averages, appears low in comparison with the proposed revision.

Before incorporation wages were lowered or raised according to sales. Breweries would pay less for barrels delivered from coopers, or, before the use of recruiting contractors, a brewery would simply employ fewer laborers and pay them less well. The link between wages and sales was direct, although the modification of wages by sales often lagged by several months as a result of the delay in circulation of market information. The substitution of output for sales as a measure of performance and as the principal criterion of compensation was infinitely fairer yet more exacting. Production quantity and quality were easily monitored and assessed; accordingly, worker compensation could be quickly and unerringly tied to performance. The slack capacity and underutilized resources that once had characterized production could be substantially lessened, but only at the cost of greater centralization and coordination. Thus, tying compensation to production brought greater controls over production and production-line workers.

The enhanced compensation for workers under the 1923 wage and

TABLE 16. Old and new seniority bonus schemes, 1923.

Years of service	Before 1923	After 1923
1	0 yen	50 yen
2	0	70
3	0	100
4	0	120
5	10	150
6	20	180
7	30	210
8	40	240
9	50	270
10	65	300
11	80	330
12	95	360
13	110	390
14	125	420
15	150	450
16	175	480
17	200	510
18	225	540
19	250	570
20	280	600
over 20	30 yen/year	30 yen/year

Source: Anonymous, *Honsha Sōgi Taikan* (n.p., 1928), p. 25.

work revision plan required them to labor longer and more diligently. Not only could they no longer leave the factory in less than eight hours, but their compensation was tied to a certain minimum level of production. A 1922 survey had revealed that a third of the workers left the factory less than six hours after reporting for work; within another thirty minutes over half had left. Less than half of the work force stayed for eight full hours.[22] This could not continue under the new system because in order to receive the larger remuneration offered by the new wage system workers had to perform at or above a certain level of production, and that level was based on a full eight-hour day.

Table 17, which lists average daily wages for different months during 1923, illustrates wage fluctuation once compensation was tied to performance. In this, the first year of implementation of the new system, net wages for workers varied by as much as 18 percent for men and 16 percent for women.

The year 1923 was one in which output rose, although because the number of workers increased, output per worker declined (see table

TABLE 17. Daily wages calculated for selected months, 1923 (yen).

Period	Basic wage		Net wage[a]	
	Male	Female	Male	Female
January 1923	1.923	1.155	2.309	1.325
February 1923	1.893	1.116	2.098	1.301
May 1923	1.921	1.095	1.985	1.111
June 1923	1.911	1.097	2.090	1.226
November 1923	1.921	0.957	2.205	1.256
December 1923	1.932	1.047	2.317	1.182

Source: Anonymous, *Honsha Sōgi Taikan* (n.p., 1928), p. 27.
a. Includes extras.

18). Output per worker of course was the critical figure in that nominal gains in productivity were of little value if they occurred at higher per unit costs. This is what concerned the officers of the company, and what they had to impress upon the factory workers. Unfortunately there were two obstacles to management-worker accord on this matter. First, a large number of the workers—about half, according to several sources—had jobs outside the breweries. Some of these were in commercial establishments in and around Noda, but most were in farming, either on their own land, if they were so fortunate, or on leased land. As a result, about half of the men in the breweries were hard-pressed for time. Even when work began in the breweries by 6:00 A.M., as it did before 1923, a worker had to cut corners to handle two jobs successfully. After 1923, when the morning shift began at 7:00 A.M., and when eight hours of work plus various breaks during the day meant that workers could not leave the breweries until 4:00 P.M., full-time farming, especially during the planting and harvesting months, became impractical.

The displeasure of many workers with the eight-hour day was exacerbated by their concern with the pace of production-line work. By the mid-1920s the company had divided the work process into 62 different steps, not including certain operations that were continuous and had no clearly defined daily output quotas. Each step had well-defined daily performance standards. Examples of the steps include weighing, grading, and cleaning 896 gallons of wheat or soybeans; folding and stacking the sacks as they came in; tying and storing 45 bales of lees; moving 1,250 empty soy sauce kegs from the warehouse to the brewery by horse-drawn cart; filling 250 barrels or 400 bottles of soy sauce; and washing and drying 800 wooden kōji trays.[23]

TABLE 18. Output, work force, and output per worker, 1918–1930 (in koku and indexed).

Year	Output (index)		Work force (index)		Output per worker (index)	
1918	146,274	(100)	1065	(100)	137	(100)
1919	170,514	(117)	1162	(109)	147	(107)
1920	144,717	(99)	1190	(112)	121	(88)
1921	178,457	(122)	1167	(110)	153	(112)
1922	172,701	(118)	1330	(125)	130	(95)
1923	160,029	(109)	1498	(141)	107	(78)
1924	216,915	(148)	1545	(145)	140	(102)
1925	266,498	(182)	1585	(149)	168	(123)
1926	252,851	(173)	1949	(183)	130	(95)
1927	224,957	(154)	1383	(130)	163	(119)
1928	297,541	(203)	1734	(163)	172	(126)
1929	316,931	(217)	1821	(171)	174	(127)
1930	337,413	(231)	2063	(194)	164	(120)

Source: Kikkoman Company Archives, *Taishō Nananen ijō Shōkkō Genzaichō* (n.p., 1918–1940), 26 pages.

The obvious difficulty with this approach to work assignments and amounts was getting it right: too low a work standard would invite higher per unit costs and a tendency toward inattention and laxity on the part of workers; too high a level would engender anxiety, uncompleted assignments, and the possibility of antisocial and anticorporate behavior. Balance was the key to successful remuneration and motivation of workers as well as to the productivity and profitability of the firm.

The company had decided to use the six months immediately before the inauguration of the new system (July through December, 1922) as the basis for determining the work standard. This seems to have been an equitable choice. The amount of production during that period (3,864,000 gallons) was almost identical to that of the first six months of the previous year (3,873,000 gallons). The annual production for 1922 represented an 18 percent increase over production during the first year following incorporation (1918), although 1921 had been an even better year. In short, the company did not choose an artificially high level of production for setting the work standard (see table 18).

Yet as winter turned to spring in Noda in 1923, the managers and unionized workers of the Noda Shōyu Company found themselves in disagreement over the appropriateness of the latter half of 1922 as the basis for the work standard. That standard appears to have been about

15 percent higher than many workers were willing to accept. As grumbling and dissatisfaction spread, production fell. From January to the end of February it fell by a quarter. The company announced that if output remained depressed, wages would be curtailed. Not wanting to appear reluctant to back up a threat with action, it enacted across-the-board wage reductions for factory workers on February 26, 1923. Workers responded by lowering production still further. By the end of March production was off the standard by one-third.

6.

The Noda Strikes:
1923 and 1927–28

THE 1923 LABOR DISPUTE in Noda followed by the Great Strike of 1927–28 were spectacular examples of ill-advised, badly planned, and poorly executed labor actions. Because of its length (218 days) and because a number of highly placed officials, including indirectly the emperor, were involved in its settlement, the later strike has received much scholarly and journalistic attention. Nevertheless, it was not particularly meaningful in advancing the cause of the labor union movement in Japan. It presented no challenge to ownership of the soy sauce factories in Noda or, more realistically, to the authority that went along with ownership. Neither were social reform issues, like child labor laws, length of the work week, unsanitary work conditions, or the health and morals of female factory operatives in evidence.

The Great Strike was more like a maladroit comedy of errors in which large-scale dismissals of workers by the managers of the Noda Shōyu Company precipitated the local union under questionable Sōdōmei leadership into a premature political gesture, thereby losing the opportunity later to launch a well-prepared strike against the company. It could be argued in the Sōdōmei's defense that political events in Japan after ex-Army General Tanaka Giichi became premier in 1927 did not augur well for labor unions, and thus precipitated union activism. The significance of the Great Strike lies more in what it lost than in what it accomplished for the labor union movement in Noda.

The 1923 strike, although it lasted only a month, involved matters of much greater import than the seven-month strike that followed it four years later. The 1923 protest over the acceptance and terms of the new wage and work structure introduced in January 1923 was the first major confrontation between the year-old union and the company, itself only founded five years earlier. Even though the summer of 1922 had been punctuated by the dispute between the coopers and their bosses as well as by Kimura's homicide, these events were focused around the feelings of individual workers and the small, householdlike shops where they were employed. The 1923 collision, however, involved the first test of the company union, some eight hundred strong, against the resolve and tact of the management of the Noda Shōyu Company.

Worker Discontent Rises: The 1923 Protest

During March the discontent of the workers was manifested in open opposition. On March 2 hands in Factory 2 complained that their workload was heavier than that of laborers in other factories and that they had to work overtime to keep up. They lodged a formal complaint with the company and asked to negotiate the matter directly with the head of the Factory Management Section, Namiki Shigetarō. Namiki had just joined the company in January and a month later assumed the duties of works manager. He had formerly been employed in local government, rising to County Head (Gunchō) of Higashi-Katsushika County in Chiba Prefecture. Namiki's job was to see that the new wage and work system was enforced and, more important, that it worked. The company apparently reasoned—correctly as it turned out—that recruiting a high-level, local official from the civil service corps would be the best way to introduce and implement the new structure. Like most managers and bureaucrats of his day, Namiki considered unions more a hindrance than a help in the performance of his duties, although he never refused to bargain with them during his tenure as works manager. With Namiki's appointment, the business of gathering statistics, instructing workers, defining job requirements, establishing workloads, and specifying dress codes and decorum in plants—in short, the business of transforming traditional work into something standardized, measurable, and "modern"—was begun in earnest.

The complaints from Factory 2 were followed on March 5 by similar protests from workers in factories 5 and 8. By the next day about half of the plants had joined in acts of protest and attitudes of defiance. The primary complaints focused on the reputedly excessive workload, a presumed imbalance in workload distribution among the factories, and a prejudged unevenness in the quality of the newly appointed factory managers.

As accusations and disaffection spread through the rank-and-file, the company decided to suspend those workers who most flagrantly opposed company supervision. On March 9 the workers in Factory 10 and on the next day those in Factory 9 were suspended. The company threatened to turn suspensions into dismissals if the unruliness continued. In the negotiations that followed on March 10 and 11, the representatives chosen from among the workers did not attempt to generalize their dissatisfactions. Instead, specific and particular complaints about this or that work assignment or about a certain factory manager were voiced. After March 12, however, when the national and regional leaders of the Sōdōmei arrived in Noda to take over the negotiations, the dispute became focused more on the issue of the work suspension in factories 9 and 10 than on underlying specific issues of the workload standard. As before, the Sōdōmei came in force: Matsuoka Komakichi, Taguchi Kamezō, Nosaka Tetsu (Sanzō) from the Tokyo offices; Yokoishi Shinichi and Nakahara Tōji from the Sōdōmei Kantō Iron Workers Union.[1]

During a five-and-one-half-hour meeting on March 12 Taguchi, director of the Sōdōmei in Eastern Japan, berated Namiki with criticisms of the company and its management. He claimed that the Noda dispute was not primarily a local dispute, but part of a nationwide conflict between laborers and capitalists. And he charged that the dispute had become emotionally exaggerated because of the company's excessive work demands and the resulting mistrust and hostility between factory workers and managers.

Namiki argued that the workload was fair, that it had been under study for a long while prior to implementation, and that the workers had been producing close to the standard rate even before the new system was enacted. He contended that the workers were falsely complaining about the workload when in fact they had been working at or near the standard for some time.

Taguchi ignored Namiki's claims and sought to have the workload set by negotiations between workers and managers. Namiki flatly rejected this suggestion, as he did the next: that the union leaders be allowed to meet with the company's board of executives. He insisted that the issues under discussion fell entirely within the purview of the factory management section and would therefore be settled by him and no one higher in authority.

By the next day the Sōdōmei leaders had consolidated their demands and presented Namiki with the following resolutions: first, that the standard workload be mutually agreed upon; second, that certain steps in the production process be returned to the internal contracting system. The claim was made that certain steps required close and even personal supervision of individual workers by floor managers, and that this could not be accomplished within the organizational design and interpersonal relations of the new system.

During the afternoon, while these matters were being debated, Mogi Saheiji, senior board member of the company, joined the group. His presence appeared to provoke Taguchi, who attacked him verbally and threatened the company with violence. Taguchi warned that he had

told the workers to control themselves until the evening in the hope
that some sort of agreement could be reached, but he added that he was
pessimistic about the possibility. When Mogi Saheiji suggested that the
company was equally interested in resolving the conflict without violence, Taguchi called him "a fool" and asked "where his mind was."
Taunting Mogi further, Taguchi exclaimed that in twenty years of experience in labor-management issues, he had never met such an ig-
noramus as Mogi![2]

Incredibly, given their differences in status and upbringing, Mogi remained calm, although after his encounter with Taguchi one can detect
a hardening of the company's position. Thereafter, the company stead-
fastly refused to alter the structure of the new wage and work system,
although it conceded that some minor adjustments here and there
might be needed. The basic problem from the company viewpoint was
not the work design but the reinstatement of those who had been suspended.

On the afternoon of the 14th, the head factory manager from each of
the eighteen factories currently operated by the Noda Shōyu Company
met to discuss the problem of the suspended workers. They agreed that
the new work system had undercut the authority of the tōji and other
bosses and that the new factory and section managers who took their
place had not proven their value and legitimacy to the workers. Accordingly, seven—less than half of the factory managers—felt that the
suspension was too punitive and that more time was needed to change
over to the new system. Seven others felt that the suspension was justified, while four were undecided.[3]

On March 15 the executive committee of the company proposed a
compromise. It involved a new standard workload, based on output
earlier in the week (March 12 and 13, 1923), and a reinstatement of the
suspended factory workers, contingent on their public show of re-
morse. This compromise was supported by an unofficial committee of
local notables that included the mayor, vice mayor, and chief of police,
who were attempting to mediate the dispute. By evening, however, it
was evident that the union found the compromise unacceptable. It was
not satisfied with a modification of the new wage and work system and
insisted on its abrogation. Unwilling to settle for less, the union posted
a notice that evening: "as of March 16, 1923, a work boycott of the factories of the Noda Shōyu Company will begin."

The Strike of 1923

The boycott was only partially successful the first day. Most workers
reported to their factories, but little work was actually done. By March
17, however, the boycott was total. The company was forced to dis-

patch some of the clerical staff to the factories to care for the steam engines and boilers, which could not be left unattended. In an effort to win support, the company printed over a thousand handbills, which it distributed around town and to its customers, explaining that in spite of the company's efforts to modernize production and improve the workers' livelihood, the factory hands refused to accommodate themselves to the new system and persisted stubbornly in advocating the old system of internal contracting. In its closing statement the company, true to the Confucian philosophy of its founders, apologized for its lack of virtue in allowing such a deplorable situation to develop.[4]

On March 17 the workers gathered, 1,200 strong, in a show of solidarity. Some in the crowd were spectators, as indicated by their green armbands, but most were festooned with the red-ribboned headbands and armbands of protest. Speeches of dissent stirred the crowd, which strengthened its resolve throughout the day with songs of revolution and flag-waving displays.

As the boycott continued for a second week, management and labor consolidated their positions, in spite of the efforts of a town mediation committee to prevent such a stalemate. The mediation committee recognized that as long as both sides remained adamant, negotiations were futile. Although the mediation committee worked diligently to remain neutral, to a large degree Noda's many small businessmen—barbers, innkeepers, restauranteurs, and others—supported the union. Their support was colored, naturally, by their desire to continue with business as usual. Contemporary observers pointed out that the large number of shopkeepers in Noda (and their relative prosperity) depended upon the soy sauce brewery workers. A wise businessman makes the causes of his customers his own. Yet townsmen could not fail to consider the larger picture: any curtailment in the production of shōyu would soon be reflected in less money being spent. As a result, although most supported the union, almost everyone could agree that a quick end to the dispute was desirable. And, given the size, wealth, and unified management as well as ownership of the firm, it was unlikely to capitulate before the union did so.

Since both sides refused to compromise, a quick end did not seem possible. Takanashi Chūhachirō, a distant relative of Takanashi Hyōzaemon and one of the members of the town mediation committee, argued that the problem was not really the work standard itself, but the work standard within a system of centralized and depersonalized management. Supervision had become mechanical and formal; in order to overcome this, authority within the breweries would have to be decentralized. This was a prescient suggestion for its day, since it is now considered quite modern to decentralize authority to the lowest level possible in an organization consonant with an effective coordination of the work process. Takanashi Chūhachirō's plea for decentralization was an untutored yet insightful solution to a basic problem that neither management nor labor knew how to deal with effectively in 1923. Unfortunately, given the limited range of options then available to the company, Takanashi's suggestion, if acted upon, would have required at least a partial reinstatement of tōji, and this was not acceptable.

On March 22 the company drew up a policy statement for internal distribution that came as close as one could expect to answering Takanashi Chūhachirō's complaint at that time. In the section dealing with the general stance that the company should display during the strike, it was proposed that the firm make every effort to be warm-hearted and sincere and to treat workers and nonworkers alike with respect and restraint. This was the company's answer to Takanashi Chūhachirō: to be paternalistic, benevolent, and proper. Confucian philosophy was the only management ideology that the company knew, even though it had little to offer in this instance. Confucianism might mitigate the conflict, but it could not offer any fundamental resolution of the dispute.

The inadequacy of Confucianism as a philosophy of industrial management stemmed from its hierarchical view of society and of social relationships generally. The labor union, workers, and even managers needed a more egalitarian ideology, but inequality was basic to Confucianism. Confucianism was too philosophical to serve as a practical guide to management. Nor could it justify the hierarchy of work required in the modern factory system—and no wonder, for the hierarchy of Confucianism was primarily the hierarchy of the household. Confucianism had little relevance to the managerial hierarchy of nearly two dozen shōyu breweries in Noda, each with several hundred workers. Nevertheless, it was the company's only guide.

Assuming a Confucian view, then, the company should act munificently while the union should assume a posture of supplication, no matter the irrelevancy of either position. Although neither side referred explicitly to a Confucian model or example in its dealings with the other, there is no doubt that the philosophy and practice of Confucianism affected the course of the negotiations. The company could not free itself of the feeling that it should act like a forgiving father, while the union, at least its local members, never entirely lost the sheepish grin of children who have taken secret delight in upsetting their elders.

Meanwhile the union had been strengthening its recruiting efforts as well as its boycotting activities. The local was reinforced on the 25th by twenty members from Minami-Katsushika County Workers Association and thirty more from the Tokyo Shibaura Labor Union, and on that day a large rally was held at Shimizu Park near Noda under the guise of an athletic meet. On the way back to Noda, the crowd became unruly, breaking windows and pushing over fences at Factory 1 near the company headquarters. The next day the company discharged a total of 127 workers from sixteen breweries. In response, on March 27, the town formed an emergency mediation committee of five who would work for "the coexistence and coprosperity of workers, capitalists, and citizens of the town."[5]

Negotiation and Compromise

The initial compromise submitted by the emergency mediation committee on March 28 involved a recognition of most features of the new wage and work system established by the company, with certain major exceptions. The exceptions were that three steps in the traditional process were to be returned to the former internal contracting system: these were the mixing of steamed soybeans and cracked wheat for culturing (*muromae, koji katsugi*), the stirring of the moromi mash during the early stages of fermentation (*moromi-kaki*), and the making of soy sauce kegs (*taru-koshirae*). These should be excluded, according to the committee's recommendations, because they required either intensive and exhausting efforts for a few hours but not for a whole day (muromae and moromi-kaki) or highly personalized supervison of a piece-work process (taru-koshirae). These activities, the committee felt, were better served by the traditional contracting system rather than the new wage and work system.

The response of the company on March 29 to the proposal was an artful give-and-take. It put forth new, slightly reduced workload standards for the muromae and moromi-kaki steps, but it did not offer to return these or any other steps to the former contract system. It offered to compensate workers injured on the job and forced to take a leave of absence as though they had continued working without interruption. Finally, the company proposed to increase personnel supervision in the factories by adding at least one assistant manager in each factory and by fully implementing the work gang system wherein every work team had a section and subsection head. In effect, the company offered to modify the new wage and work system, but not to dismember or discontinue it.[6]

The appearance on March 29 of Honda Sadajirō, the representative from Noda's district to the Chiba Prefectural Assembly, brought a new figure into the negotiations that neither the company nor the union could choose to ignore. The prestige of his political office was matched only by his power to influence public opinion and, perhaps more important, public spending. After Honda's arrival, police authorities in

Noda increased in number, and the singing of revolutionary songs and the waving of revolutionary flags were proscribed. Honda stayed only one day on this visit, but returned three days later. The day before his return the company sent out 1,200 postcards to the boycotting workers. They said:

> Greetings. The company has been hoping you would return to work earlier, but for various reasons this has been impossible. If you will return to work now and accept the following conditions, the company is willing to reemploy you. The conditions of reemployment are that you agree to uphold the company regulations and to work diligently in your job. Moreover, the eight-hour daily wage system will not be altered even if the workload standard, for the moment, will be adjusted to the amount produced on March 12 and 13, 1923. If you agree with these conditions and would like to return to work, please return the card with your signature by April 5, 1923.[7]

On April 2 Honda Sadajirō returned with three other prefectural assemblymen. They met at 4:00 in the afternoon with the board of directors and Namiki's factory section. Honda emphasized the need for both sides in the negotiations to save face; as a consequence, the company would have to mitigate its demands. He suggested a type of bonus scheme to reward workers who were willing to change jobs and to compensate those whose work performance was better than average. He and his fellow legislators made it clear that they felt the discharged workers should be included in the company's reappointment offer.

Mogi Shichirōuemon, president of the Noda Shōyu Company, demurred on the question of rehiring the discharged workers. Clearly he did not want them back, fearing that their presence would lead to continuing conflict. But Honda's position was reinforced on April 4 when the Governor of Chiba Prefecture, Saito, and his Chief of Internal Affairs, Shiragami, arrived in Noda. They, too, stressed the desirability of reappointing the discharged workers. Shiragami argued that little would be won if the workers were forced to surrender, while much could be gained if the company and union would settle the dispute in a spirit of accord. He emphasized that goodwill was far more important than good wages in securing the livelihood of the company. Then the governor and his lieutenant played their trump card: in the interest of maintaining the nation's economy and for the sake of preserving the social order, they endorsed a compromise solution.

To understand the urgency of the governor's position, one must understand something of the circumstances of Japanese development since the mid-nineteenth century and of the unrest disturbing the country in the early twentieth century. Japanese leaders were convinced of the need for Japan to be politically and economically strong in order to protect the country against Western encroachment. On this overriding premise of defensive modernization, the country had been both militarized and industrialized in an astonishingly short period of time. The nation's leaders were not willing to see this jeopardized by political attitudes or movements that they considered to be dangerous to the country's interests. Accordingly, the governor's suggestion of a compromise in the 1923 dispute had unmistakable political and moral overtones that neither labor union organizer nor corporate officer could refuse to notice.

On April 5 additional political pressure was mustered in favor of a negotiated settlement. A request from the Home Ministry itself for a quick and equitable resolution was received by mid-morning. And while Honda and Saito maintained political pressure on the company, the Noda police made certain that union activities were constrained during this exceptionally crucial point in the mediation effort. Later on the 5th, the company's officers gathered for another meeting. There they agreed to rehire all workers, including those that had been discharged, if they admitted their transgression. The recognition of error and the realization of guilt were to be sufficient punishment. This was characteristically Confucian: attitude was just as important as action in the remediation of wrongdoing.

On April 7 representatives of the company's executive committee traveled to Chiba City to meet with the prefectural governor, where they obtained his signature and seal on the following document:

Memorandum[8]

To: Chiba Prefectural Governor Saito

From: The President of the Noda Shōyu Company, Mogi Shichirōuemon

1. As we have been promised by the Governor that he will be completely responsible for the resolution of disputes, not only the current one, but also those in the future, we propose to have all negotiations handled by the governor.
2. On any future matters concerning the treatment and disposition of the company's workers, we will consult with the governor.

This amazing document argues that the company should abdicate its managerial authority in the areas of dispute resolution and worker treatment in favor of political authority. In doing so, it discloses several important aspects of the political economy of corporate Japan in the early twentieth century. First and most obvious, the separation of business and government that characterized Western practice at this time

was not nearly so evident in Japan. Second, the absence of ready channels of communication between management and labor made it all the
easier to appeal to an outside source for mediation. This suggests quite
vividly that while the company had been successful in amalgamating
certain features of production and operation since 1919, the problems
of labor relations were still very much unsettled. The company had
very little notion of what might be called industrial relations, and it was
just as happy to leave such matters to outside authorities for settlement.
This was in part a continuation of traditional practices, namely, the delegation of such matters to outside agents such as oyakata, but it was
also a recognition of the government's recent concern with political and
social unrest in Japan and its willingness to restrain such activities.

Finally, the document suggests that the owner-managers of the Noda
Shōyu Company were confident that the use of higher political authority to resolve the company's dispute was likely to be efficacious as
well as beneficial. This was not only a reflection of the standoff that had
rendered helpless both the company and the union, but it was also an
assumption that the resolution of the dispute would likely accrue more
to the benefit of the company than the union. The company, after all,
had not capitulated on its major goal: the implementation of the new
wage and work system. By contrast, the union could not claim any evidence of victory, save for its success in having the discharged workers
reinstated. Even this would be a moral victory for the firm, since the
discharged workers had to admit their offense in order to be reinstated.

On April 8 the company officers met with the governor at his offices
in Chiba City, returning to Noda the next day, when the strike group
led by Matsuoka left for its meeting with the governor. Matsuoka's
group returned at 9:50 in the evening. On April 10 Shiragami, head of
the Prefecture's Internal Affairs Office, arrived in Noda and immediately shuttled back and forth between the company and the union asking for their quick approval of his compromise plan. He left on the 5:40
P.M. train, but, as the following document testifies, his brief three hours
in Noda were successful.

Memorandum[9]

A mediation, as explained below, of the dispute between the
Noda Shōyu Company and the striking union has taken place.
This mediation has occurred for the further development of the
nation's industry and the welfare of both capitalists and workers.
The company and its employees are expected to honor the following stipulations in a spirit of mutual interdependence and harmony.

1. Employees will follow the hourly wage system as established
by the company, and it will be based on a workload which is stan-

dardized according to output on February 21, 1923. However, for a brief period, the standard workload will be based on output during March 12 and 13, 1923. Compensation will be based on output. When production is above the standard workload, compensation will be increased; when below, it will be decreased.

2. The wage system described in #1 above will be enacted by the end of May of the current year. Depending on output at that time, the company may want to revise the work system which it may do, but only after consultation with members of the committee of mediators listed below.

3. When employees have questions concerning important matters, such as the work system or the treatment of workers by the company, they are encouraged to talk to the mediators and to seek mediation with the company.

4. Workers who were discharged and now reappointed by the company will receive a substantial amount of money.

5. The company will treat those workers who were discharged and then rehired in the same manner that it treats all other employees. If, after a year of satisfactory performance, the reappointed workers wish to continue employment with the company, the fact of their discharges will not be allowed to affect their cumulative rank and privilege within the company.

April 10, 1923

Mediators: Saito Morikata, Governor of Chiba Prefecture
Honda Sadajirō
Fujita Shigeo
Kaneko Keijirō
Okawa Gobei
Sakai Sadahachi
Ukiya Gonbei
Ishizuka Seijirō
Takanashi Chūhachirō
Seda Fumitarō
Shoda Sadakichi
Shinoda Yatarō
Maeda Yusuke
Komazaki Zenzaburō
Itoh Kumajirō
Nakamura Kumajirō
Minami Torajirō
Mogi Rinzō

I recognize the above stipulations and I promise to respect the employees and interact with them honestly.

President, Noda Shōyu Co., Ltd., Mogi Shichirōuemon

We recognize the above stipulations and promise to perform our work with integrity.

Employee representatives: Okano Minoru
　　　　　　　　　　　　　 Wada Kiichirō
　　　　　　　　　　　　　 Furuya Sakuzo
　　　　　　　　　　　　　 Koiwai Sosuke
　　　　　　　　　　　　　 Yamaguchi Rokuichi
　　　　　　　　　　　　　 Matsuoka Komakichi
　　　　　　　　　　　　　 Yokoishi Shinichi

Finally, on April 12, a month after Taguchi Kamezō had arrived in Noda to take over negotiations for the local union employees, the dispute at the Noda Shōyu Company was formally resolved in a hand-clapping ceremony. The prefectural governor, the metropolitan police head, the board of directors, chief officers of the company, clerks, workers, and worker representatives gathered in front of the company headquarters at 2:00 P.M. A few speeches were made. Governor Saito, in an unprecedented action, pledged that he would resign if the mediation between the company and the workers proved unsuccessful, and he promised to continue to act as an intermediary for as long as he was in office. The afternoon air exploded with a thousand clapping hands in the traditional show of openhanded cooperation. Then, like two sumo giants preparing for the initial charge, the managers and workers wheeled and flowed toward their stations—managers to the corporate headquarters and the workers back toward the breweries.

The 1927–28 Dispute

The 1927–28 dispute was both similar to and different from the 1923 conflict. In spite of the prefectural officials' entreaties for good will and harmony, the company and the union had not learned to get along together in the intervening four years. The result was a strike, as it had been earlier, and although the process of dispute resolution proved remarkably similar in outline in both cases, the 1927–28 strike was far longer, more costly, and more politicized.

Another difference, less rooted in the disputes themselves than in the circumstances surrounding them, was the result of economic and political conditions. In 1923, even though the country was still mired in an economic trough following World War I, manufacturing output, exports of finished and semifinished goods, and agricultural production were increasing. But 1927 and 1928 were bad years economically. In 1927 the Bank of Taiwan and the Fifteenth Bank both failed from overlending, and the next year was one of extreme economic hardship in agriculture, which was still the major sector of employment in the economy.

The year 1929 was disastrous not just for Japan but for all industrialized nations. Yet Japan suffered more than most because of an ill-advised return to the gold standard that year, which intensified the economic extremity. The Seiyukai political party had regained its majority in the Diet in 1927, and an ex-Army general, Tanaka Giichi, had become premier. He reversed the more liberal policies of the Minseitō-Kenseikai cabinet: at home, unions, worker and agricultural tenant associations, and Socialist political activities were suppressed; abroad, military and diplomatic efforts to dominate China were redoubled.

The political and economic circumstances surrounding the 1923 and the 1927–28 disputes were quite dissimilar. The earlier period was a time of economic recovery, spirited union activism, and national optimism (save for the miserable Tokyo earthquake of that year). The later years were years of economic and financial loss as well as right-wing political ascendancy. These external factors greatly affected management-labor relations in Noda, as was evidenced by the dispute's main issues. Whereas the 1923 conflict erupted over the pace and structure of work, the 1927–28 difficulties were primarily over pay and benefits.

It would be a mistake, however, to focus solely on the articulated economic grievances, for beyond such economic issues lay a Gordian knot of unresolved questions concerning authority and legitimacy in the workplace. Although the brewery workers had become inured to management supervision in plants, restructured work groups, and the concept and reality of a standard workload, doubt remained about how fully they accepted such changes. Therefore, between 1923 and 1927 management attempted to indoctrinate workers on these matters as well as to educate them in a new philosophy of industrialism wherein managers and workers labored for mutual benefit. It proved to be easier to alter work habits than habits of mind, and the company had more success with changing how the rank-and-file worked than with transforming the reasons why they worked.

Work Environment

Part of management's new education effort involved defining the work environment. Surprisingly enough, although the company had been in existence for five years and the brewers of soy sauce had lived in Noda for much longer, no rules and regulations defined the boundaries and standards of job performance. An occasional document treated some aspect of production or operation, but these had always been proscriptive rather than prescriptive. During 1923–24 new rules and regulations, "Shanai Kitei" and "Kōin Kitei," defining duties and responsibilities for managers and workers alike were published and promulgated.[10] Worker education programs were initiated, not only to train workers for on-the-job advancement but also to further their primary school education. In February and in June of 1923, new boarding lodgings for workers were completed, and these offered in-house instructional facilities and opportunities.

The company offered other inducements. In 1924 a company-subsidized hospital was attached to one of the lodgings, and by 1926 the company provided health care and medical insurance programs at nominal cost. The company hospital was available to nonemployees also, but on a pay-as-you-go basis. In 1927 the company pioneered an employee cooperative association, one of the first of its kind in Japan. The coop used the membership fees of employees, greatly augmented by the company, to provide workers with a miscellany of benefits and services. Housed within the company and staffed with company personnel, the coop gave short-term unsecured personal loans and longer-term secured loans for real estate. When a worker was injured on the job, departed for military duty, married, had a child, or died, the coop gave the worker or surviving members of the worker's family small monetary gifts. Suggestions from workers that resulted in improved safety or production within the factories were rewarded monetarily. The coop also offered a bank savings program, government bond, and company stock-option purchase plans. Its final benefit was a retirement bonus calculated according to the number of years served with the company.[11]

In such ways the company sought to win over workers, to enlist their loyalty, and to make them company employees. Yet, at the same time that management was making such efforts, the Noda branch of the Sōdōmei was active as well. Like the company, the union sought not just to influence how work was done but also why it was done. Thus, the decade of the 1920s proved to be one of recurring conflict between the company and the union for the hearts, minds, and hands of the Noda soy sauce work force.

Education was a tool for the union as well as for the company. The Noda Labor School was established in June 1925, and union workers selected on a rotating basis were lectured on the history of socialism, the labor movement, economics, and politics. About a hundred a year attended the regular course of study, and hundreds more gathered informally to hear lectures and speeches by some of the best-known labor leaders in Japan.[12]

In addition to schooling workers in the history and philosophy of unionism, other efforts were exerted to build a strong local. Most important, union leaders built up enormous union and strike funds, so that when the next confrontation with the company occurred—something they assumed to be inevitable—the union would not have to ca-

pitulate for lack of money. Every member made regular monthly payments to the union treasury; in addition, regular collections for a separate strike fund were taken. Of this, 10 yen per month per thousand
local members was sent to the Kantō Regional Association as Noda's
contribution to the regional strike fund for Eastern Japan. Finally, each
local union in the Sōdōmei was encouraged to offer bank savings accounts for its members, who were more or less required to make deposits and discouraged from withdrawing them without the permission
of the local union leaders.[13]

Because the Noda Shōyu Company was one of the largest enterprises
in Japan at that time, and since all of its factories and subcontractors
within Japan were still located in Noda, the Noda branch of the
Sōdōmei union probably represented the largest concentration of
membership in Japan. The Kantō Brewery Labor Union contained
fourteen branches with 3,245 members in 1927, but the Noda branch
with 1,547 workers accounted for 48 percent of these![14] Given this
membership and the compulsory monetary contributions to the union,
the size of the union treasury in Noda soon became immense. By 1927
the union had reportedly accumulated the largest strike fund—100,000
yen by police estimate—in the land.[15] It was so large that during
1925–26 the Noda local gave 5,000 yen to the Sumitomo Besshi Dōzan
strike and 3,000 yen to the cotton textile workers in their Okaya dispute. Given this war chest and membership, the leadership of Sōdōmei
could ill afford not to win in Noda. Noda was the key to the success of
the Sōdōmei itself, yet in fact this reality would rupture the union, resulting in its fratricidal division.

During 1925 internal political struggles rent the Sōdōmei as two
principal factions contended for leadership. One, a more radical group
headed by Nosaka Sanzō and Asō Hisashi, pursued an openly anticap-
italist and antimilitarist program that would pit the Sōdōmei against
Japan's government-business-military establishment. This group favored "direct action" over political participation. The defection of these
leaders from the Sōdōmei in 1925 led to the formation of a rival union,
Nihon Rōdō Kumiai Hyōgikai (the Japan Council of Trade Unions),
which claimed thirty-two unions and a membership of 12,655 to the
Sōdōmei's thirty-five unions and 13,960 members.[16]

The other faction, a reform-minded but not revolutionary group,
sought to work within the so-called establishment in order to achieve
greater political power for the union and thereby change social and
economic conditions in Japan. Their vision was partially realized when
the Sōdōmei participated in the formation of the Social Democratic
Party (Shakai Minshūtō) on December 5, 1926. This political group included Suzuki Bunji and Matsuoka Komakichi, president and Eastern

regional director respectively of the Sōdōmei, who had been deeply involved with events in Noda from the start. Their interest in Noda was understandable: whoever controlled events in Noda, one of the prize territories of union activity, controlled one of the largest single blocs of unionized workers in Japan and, through them, the Sōdōmei, the country's biggest and most successful union organization. The competition was unbridled, and the Sōdōmei split again and again (in 1926, 1929, and 1939) over issues of union tactics and goals.

The labor strife in Noda was much more than a routine conflict between managers and workers in some industrial outcropping of Tokyo. For the company, control over workers and, even more important, accord with workers were fundamental to its strategy of mass production and mass distribution of Kikkoman shōyu in Japan. Without the active cooperation of workers, success would be impossible, for it was their labor that held together the company's increasingly capital-intensive, yet, at the same time, management-intensive processes of production and distribution. The lack of worker goodwill was as major a drawback in this endeavor as a lack of adequate investment in plant and equipment or in transportation facilities. For the union during the 1920s, control of the workers in Noda signified control of Sōdōmei itself. Suzuki and Matsuoka understood this and spared no effort to maintain and enhance their leadership in Noda. As for the workers, the sometimes forgotten constituent in the drive for power of company and union, their very livelihood, in its spiritual and material senses, hung in the balance.

The union probably held more of the workers' sympathy in this struggle than did the company. The union stood for the common man, or so it tried to appear, and it employed more of a grass-roots approach to gaining the affection of the workers. The company, from the workers' point of view, was distant and unapproachable. It dominated everything and everyone in the community in terms of size, wealth, and influence; it appeared calculating, formidable, and even fearsome in its power to alter fundamentally a poor man's life and livelihood. A worker might feel fortunate to be employed by this giant enterprise, but he could rarely feel comfortable in its keep.

Transportation Issues: Prelude to the Strike

How long and how far the company and the union would have continued in their institutional rivalry is uncertain, but events in 1925 and 1926 brought the two into a direct and final encounter. The issue involved the growing centralization and coordination of management within the company and the consequent absorption of functions that had once been carried on outside its institutional framework. As the company had internalized other functions earlier, such as keg-making and grain purchasing, in the mid-1920s transportation came increasingly under its direct control.

Before amalgamation and incorporation the larger breweries had owned some of the boats that carried their product to Tokyo. Independent carriers operated alongside the breweries' vessels in transporting part of the production of the larger factories and most of the output of the smaller plants. In 1920 the independent boatmen formed an unlimited partnership, the Noda Transportation Company, capitalized at 35,000 yen, to better manage their joint activities. But demand for their services was erratic, depending as it did upon the output of shōyu, their principal good of transport, and on the amount of shōyu carried by rail. Because of the greater reliability, speed, and ease of nationwide transportation by train, Noda Shōyu had shifted more and more of its distribution to the rails. A few years after its establishment, therefore, in September 1924, the Noda Transportation Company went bankrupt. The next month the Noda Shōyu Company took over the assets of the bankrupted partnership and joined them with two small wholesaling outfits that it owned in Tokyo to form the Noda Transportation Corporation, capitalized at 20,000 yen.[17]

It was this sort of predictable yet predatory behavior that precipitated the 1927–28 strike. In the course of taking over the scheduling and carrying of shōyu to market, the company disregarded the interest and traditions of the community in favor of its own. The Marusan Company, for example, was pushed aside by the Noda Shōyu Company in 1925 in favor of the Maruhon Transportation Company partly because many employees of the former were union members.

In 1900, when the cartel financed the building of the push-cart railroad in Noda to facilitate the movement of raw materials and finished goods between the breweries and the river banks, three families were allowed to run this rail service in return for a fee paid to the cartel for use of its equipment and facilities. These three families joined together in 1910 to form the Marusan Transportation Company as an unlimited partnership, and they continued to lease the equipment and facilities provided by the cartel until the Noda Shōyu Company was established in 1918. At that time the relationship between the companies changed. Noda Shōyu retained ownership of that part of the railroad's equipment and facilities that had been recently expanded and incorporated within the new steam engine line; now Marusan Transportation was paid by the soy sauce company for hauling its goods to the railroad dockings and to other local markets by cart or truck. The push-railroad tracks that bisected the town were no longer used, as the Hokusō line between Kashiwa and Noda made them obsolete. The Marusan Transportation Company remained essentially a carrier of soy sauce, but now it provided the means of transport from brewery to river bank or station, and for this was paid a fee. The relationship was thus reversed: the manufacturer now relied on the carrier, which operated its own carts, trucks, and other equipment rather than vice versa.

It is perhaps understandable that the Noda Shōyu Company, which had nurtured Marusan's business for twenty-five years, was upset when Marusan began to oppose company policy. First, Marusan employees did not wish to give up their status as independent contractors and rebuffed the Noda Shōyu Company's overtures to make them daily wage workers like their own employees. Second, once they became unionized in 1924–25, Marusan workers began refusing to handle the output of Factory 17 because it had no unionized workers. Although the other plants were unionized to varying degrees, Factory 17, the massive, three-story, ferroconcrete plant completed in July 1924, was wholly "open-shop," that is, closed to union members in this case. In order to be employed in Factory 17 workers reputedly had to pledge not to join the union.[18]

In response to Marusan's actions, the Noda Shōyu Company expanded the personnel of its container and purchasing departments (numbering twenty-two in 1926) and relied increasingly on two subsidiaries it owned: the Noda Transportation Corporation, formed in 1924; and the Maruhon Transportation Company, founded in 1925. These maneuvers allowed the company to handle whatever slack in transportation efficiency occurred because of the Marusan Company, but they represented responses and not solutions to the problem. Not unexpectedly, conflict over the refusal of the unionized transportation workers of Marusan to handle the output of the Noda Shōyu Company's largest and most efficient plant flared twice: in 1925 and in 1927. The first was handled easily by a few days of negotiation; the second brought on 218 days of strike, the ruin of the union, and the psychological conversion of workers to the company cause.

1927–28: An Overview

The 1927–28 strike has been described by many writers in more detail than I will attempt. My aim is to emphasize the significance of the strike, and in order to do so some of its details must be conveyed. This was the longest and one of the costliest, largest, and most important strikes in prewar Japan. Such superlatives are appropriate when one considers that upward of 3,500 individuals, directly and indirectly employed by the Noda Shōyu Company, were involved; that they were without work for three-fifths of a year; that the combined expenditures of company and union during the strike exceeded one million yen; that the failure of the strike may well have subverted the thrust of the Sōdōmei and other social democratic movements in prewar Japan; and that it ushered in an era of management-labor accord and enterprise unionism that continues in Japan today, more than fifty years later.

Enterprise unionism, about which more will be said later, is a form of union organization whereby workers are organized on a company rather than craft or industry basis. Although enterprise unions can be strong or weak in their dealings with the individual companies harboring them, they are almost always weak in terms of their wider affiliations. Cooperation rather than conflict typically characterizes the relationship between an individual company and an individual company union. This became especially true after 1940 when unions were coopted into the Industrial Patriotic Association, which mobilized labor for the war effort.

The 1927–28 strike was precipitated by the wage and work issue of old, namely, the refusal of a subcontractor (the Marusan Company) to come to terms with its major supplier regarding the structure of employment and the delivery of services. But the strike movement quickly shed these concerns in favor of the meat-and-potatoes issues of remuneration and fringe benefits within the Noda Shōyu Company itself. On April 10, 1927, the company was presented with six demands in a document signed "united employees" (*jugyōin ichidō*):

(1) A 10 percent wage increase for men and a 20 percent one for women;

(2) One day more every month to be added in calculating allowances for discharge, retirement, and resignation;

(3) Apprentice training for coopers in each plant;

(4) A minimum year-end bonus to be fixed at one month's pay;

(5) Promotion to skilled operative status (with certain rights of privilege and permanency in employment) to be fixed at four years;

(6) An extension of full coverage under the Employee Relief Provisions (*Kōin fujo kitei*) to part-time employees.[19]

The company seems to have been unprepared for these demands. Its belated response on April 20, after ten days of meetings with five elected representatives of the workers, was to reject (2) and (3), to agree to do its best to satisfy (4) and (5), to accept (6) without reservation, and to answer (1), the most important, with the following counterproposal: immediate increase in the company's contribution to the Health Insurance Plan, from 1.5 to 2.0 percent, and a decrease in the worker's contribution, from 1.5 to 1.0 percent; suggesting overtime as a means to raise compensation at that moment; and agreeing to take the workers' request for a pay raise into consideration at the appropriate time next year.

Negotiations continued throughout the spring and summer. At first the differences between employer and employee appeared irresolvable, but then signs turned hopeful. Immediately following the firm's response, the attitude of the union was to require financial proof of the firm's inability to meet the worker demands. In fact, the first week of May the workers formed committees in the hope of being able to review the company's financial ledgers and managerial decisions. The company utterly rejected such developments and on May 9 prepared for the worst by issuing a secret contingency plan instructing managers how to perform during the upcoming crisis. The plan counseled the dogged maintenance of the chain of command, an attitude of calm rather than panic, a thorough performance of duties, the establishment of a command post to evaluate developments quickly and issue orders promptly, and an attitude of trust and harmony within the managerial ranks. The wisdom of those preparations was not tested, however, and on May 11 the workers suddenly dropped their demands, and the company in another secret memorandum cautioned the managers against assuming an air of self-satisfaction over the workers' withdrawal. It counseled propriety and enforcement of regulations without arrogance, deceit, or distance.[20]

But, as the country sank further into economic depression, particularly in the countryside, production and morale plummeted. When production dropped below the standard workload and stayed there, the company lowered wages. The shop-floor workers responded with even less effort. Output and goodwill fell further. On September 16, 1927, some 1,350 workers, 65 percent, decided to go out on strike to secure the union's demands on wages and fringe benefits. On September 30 the company discharged 134 of those considered ringleaders: 34 for violations of Article 61, Clause 4, of the Factory Regulations, which prohibited strikes; the remaining 100 according to Article 19, which outlawed actions that incited workers to riot and lower productivity.[21]

Several warnings that more discharges would follow successfully dissuaded around 300 workers from continuing the strike. The company discharged another 950 strikers on December 20, 1927, which amounted to approximately half of the work force. By hiring 550 temporary workers and by running the more modernized plants (such as Factory 17) at full capacity, output reached 80 percent of prestrike production by the end of December. The next year, 1928, output soared to nearly 300,000 koku (14,280,000 gallons), the highest in the company's history to date.

With production at near normal levels, the company sat back to await the striking workers' retreat. It wanted more than a simple surrender by the workers, however. It sought a complete withdrawal of the demands of the strike group, an agreement that the original 134 discharged workers would not be rehired, and an eviction of those fired from company-owned housing within three months of the strike settlement.[22]

The workers had thought themselves well prepared for the strike. For several months they maintained their morale and gained national attention with such tactics as a boycott of school by the 564 children of the striking workers (a tactic first used in the 1923 dispute), mass marches to government offices in Chiba and in Tokyo (the latter were blocked by police), and social and religious gatherings to keep up their spirits (watched but not interfered with by local officials). After six months of this activity, a lone strike leader, desperate for success, even drafted a memorandum to the throne and tried to present it to the emperor directly. The effort was a failure, for the emperor's limousine sped by the prostrate figure.

The union had miscalculated its strength. The war chest that had been assembled was indeed formidable, but it would have had to be a magical treasure chest to support for long a body of 1,100 out-of-work laborers. The union expected at most a six-month strike—no more.[23] Yet the company, after the first few weeks, was running at nearly full

Workers' demonstrations during the 1927–1928 Great Strike; note the large number of police monitoring the march and in the crowd

capacity, and it had entered negotiations with the Yamasa and Higeta shōyu companies of Chōshi on a market and price-fixing agreement that would guarantee an outlet for that enormous capacity. In short, although the company had underestimated the union's resolve and determination, the union had seriously underevaluated the company's resources and market position. After the first month the outcome of the strike was never in doubt, although another six months of frustration and deprivation would have to be suffered by the workers until the matter could be settled.

On February 3, 1928, the Sōdōmei issued a self-serving and self-incriminating document, which admitted that the strike had gone on longer than hoped, that the strike group was exhausted financially as well as spiritually, and that the company had been able to outmaneuver the union by the simple fact of its continued, barely interrupted operation. In effect, the union admitted that it had taken out on strike a goodly proportion of Noda's able-bodied work force and that the action was ineffectual, poorly timed, and badly planned. Moreover, the Eastern Branch Headquarters of the Sōdōmei acknowledged that it was involved in a textile dispute in Shinshū that divided its efforts. The declaration closed with these words: "We pronounce to society that we are not engaged in a dispute for the sake of having a dispute, and we are prepared to accept any and all criticism." The declaration, signed by Matsuoka Komakichi, was an obvious signal to the Noda Shōyu Company that the union was ready to come to terms.[24] But unexpectedly, another group urged the Noda workers to defy the union.

During the winter months of 1928 the Noda workers found an unanticipated ally in the Communist Party, which in a few short months would be driven underground by an increasingly authoritarian government anxious to stamp out malcontents, subversives, and radicals of every stripe and hue. In a long and rather rambling declaration of support for the strike, the Kantō branch of the Communist Party came out against the cabinet of Prime Minister Tanaka Giichi, the oppressive Seiyūkai government, the company toadies who ran the town assembly in Noda, and the right-leaning leadership of the Sōdōmei (this was after the 1927 defection of the Japanese Council of Labor Unions and the League of Japanese Labor Unions, left-wing and centrist organizations respectively, from the Sōdōmei). The Communist Party called for a strike of all the Noda townspeople as well as the organizing of the railway and transportation workers into a strike group. Only by such coordinated and militant actions could the strike succeed. Although not acted upon, this declaration indicated the attention given to the Noda strike across the country.[25]

By early 1928, as in the 1923 dispute, outside pressure in the form of

political and civic organizations had begun to urge the two local parties—workers and managers—toward resolution. And, in all likelihood,
they themselves were convinced that the strike had gone on long
enough. By February there was no doubt that the strike group was exhausted financially, politically, and even morally. The company began
negotiations with Matsuoka Komakichi, the head of the Sōdōmei in
Eastern Japan, on February 2, 1928, to end the strike, but it was not
anxious to settle precipitately when it was so clearly in control. Matsuoka announced on February 2 that he had been solely empowered to
negotiate with the company and that he was withdrawing all strike demands as of that day. But in spite of this defeatist declaration, Matsuoka held on gamely for the reappointment of all discharged Marusan
and Noda Shōyu Company employees. He had no leverage to persist in
this position, however, and by the end of February he had given it up
completely. It was not all he had to give up, apparently, for during the
protracted negotiations for settlement with Namiki Shigetarō, Matsuoka admitted that, except for the strike, he would have run as a candidate for the national assembly from the Social Mass party in the general elections of 1928.[26]

By March Matsuoka was demoralized and humbled. Two events had
conspired to alter his attitude. A major strike at the Dai-Nippon Spinning Company had failed; and, during the same month, on March 15,
1928, the cabinet of Tanaka Giichi had permitted the mass arrest of
confirmed and suspected leftist radicals—an ill omen for the future of
an independent labor union movement in Japan. To this must be added
the economic distress of the strikers and their consequent dispirited
condition. Finally, the resolve of the company's officers not to give in or
compromise and their ability to remain unresponsive given the nearly
uninterrupted flow of soy sauce production combined to force the
union into an undignified and total surrender.

From the latter half of March until April 20, 1928, the details of the
strike settlement were worked out by the union, the company, and the
strike mediation committee. The addition of the strike mediation group
at this time seemingly prolonged the strike negotiations for the additional month. The group had not been involved in the early negotiations and had to be assembled and briefed in order to be brought into
the mediation process. Unlike its role in the 1923 dispute, the mediation committee in 1927–28 did not play an important part in bringing
the dispute to resolution. There was little need for mediation in fact,
except as a means for the union to save face. The company's victory
was so complete that high-level outsiders were not needed to placate
two evenly balanced foes.

On April 19 and 20 the final documents were prepared and publicized. The company agreed to rehire at its discretion 300 workers from the remaining strike group of 1,000 within ten days of the strike settlement and to pay 380,000 yen to those discharged. Those rehired received 100 yen each; those not rehired received varying amounts according to their category of dismissal. Within a year another 300 workers from the strike group were rehired by the company, which meant that nearly two-thirds of the striking workers ultimately returned to the Noda Shōyu Company.[27]

At the final ceremony of settlement on the morning of April 20, twenty-two individuals—eight from the mediation group, nine from the company, and five from the union—gathered in one of the reception rooms at headquarters of the Noda Shōyu Company. In a brief fifteen-minute ceremony Matsuoka as the representative of the union, Mogi Saheiji for the company, and Soeda Kiichirō for the mediation committee each gave a short address of congratulations on concluding their agreement. Matsuoka produced a wrinkled and already signed memorandum acceding to the company's terms, which Mogi Saheiji accepted. In that brief quarter of an hour, the 218-day strike was formally concluded. Informally, however, the ceremony of resolution continued until just before midnight. The twenty-two men ate, drank, and discussed away the afternoon and evening, recounting various incidents surrounding the dispute that had so completely altered their lives.[28]

Indeed, as a rite of passage and a ceremony of solemn consequence, the moment could not have been more profoundly marked than by the death the day before of Mogi Shichirōuemon, president of the company and leading shōyu manufacturer of Japan. It was coincidental, yet, like some tribal chieftain of old, Mogi Shichirōuemon died at the moment his work was done and when a new generation of leadership was needed to guide the company into an era of maturity.

Conclusion: Japanese Industrial Relations at a Crossroad

Labor unions came late to Japan. The Yūaikai, to become the Sōdōmei, did not begin until 1912, one or even two generations after the appearance of unions in the United States; it did not become powerful politically and socially until the 1920s. This difference in timing was critical for it allowed modern industrial enterprise to become well established in Japan without union interference or competition; it permitted big business to forge close ties to government without the political rivalry of an organized union movement that might have restricted what has become a hallmark of the Japanese business environment—namely, the willing cooperation of government and business; and it enabled companies to compete successfully with unions for the sympathy and support of workers as they became an increasingly significant force in the twentieth century.

Four reasons might account for the late-developing union movement in Japan. First, the industrial work force was relatively small until World War I, and what there was tended to be either female, as in the textile industry, or rural in location, as in the food and the cement-stone-glass industries. Neither condition was conducive to union activity. For women, industrial work involved generally a relatively brief period of three to five years; partly because of their youth, but mostly because of the adverse work conditions, they were closely supervised, and unions had little chance to organize them. Rural workers, although more male than female, were not any more disposed toward union organization. If they were locals they often had two jobs, one industrial and one agricultural; if not, like the females in the textile factories, they only worked several years before moving on. Local workers were too busy and perhaps too secure to care about the union; nonlocal workers had no reason to join a union if their employment was episodic and transitory. Unions succeeded, where they did, almost entirely in cities or industrial towns.

Second, the work force as a whole lacked a political consciousness that would incline it toward unionism. Shipbuilding and metal-working industries were the most organized and the most effective in articulating a new ideology for the workingman, but these were the exception. The prevailing political ideology—a mixture of Confucianism, imported Western ideas, and popular political thought without much sophistication—did not lend itself to the support of an autonomous labor movement rooted in assumptions of democratic pluralism, class conflict, or self-rule for workers.

A third reason for the late-developing union movement in Japan was that the nature of industrial organization before the 1920s did not easily support union activity. Most production was carried out in households or in shops organized according to householdlike principles of a patron-client relationship between a master craftsman and an apprentice. Work groups were small, work relationships were face-to-face, supervision was personal, and questions of workplace authority and legitimacy were practically nonexistent. Even in large factories the actual work was usually carried out by laborers organized into sections, teams, or gangs which were supervised by section heads, team leaders, or gang bosses. Work was decentralized and workers were not alienated by the vastness of factory organization or the complexity of the production process. The internal contracting system meant that work was limited in scale, personal in design, and simple in execution.

Finally, the lateness of union development was related to the effectiveness of police control of dissidents and dissident movements, among which were unionists, the labor movement, and political parties and groups which supported the labor movement. Given the impressive growth of the union movement in Japan in the decade following World War I, employers and government leaders alike feared the rise of a popular force beyond their control. This fear was translated into stepped-up police surveillance of unionists, their activities, and their supporters.[29]

In spite of these valid reasons for a late-developing labor union movement in prewar Japan, the longest and one of the most lamentable strikes in prewar Japan occurred at the Noda Shōyu Company—a company in the *countryside*, with a *poorly educated*, unsophisticated work force, organized into work gangs according to the system of *internal contracting!* What was different about Noda was the size of the work force—about 3,500 in a town ten times as large by the late 1920s—and the encrustation of the work system along household lines that had continued for several centuries. The inertia of this sizable investment in traditional patterns of work was challenged by two nearly irresistible forces: the political ambitions of the Sōdōmei leaders and the industrial ambitions of the Mogi-Takanashi managers of the Noda Shōyu Company.

The Sōdōmei union sought to organize the maximum number of workers in the shortest period of time. The largest group of industrial workers in Japan, the female operatives in the textile industry, were excluded; the food and beverage workers were the next largest group and the most promising for union organization. Its work force was large, overwhelmingly male, and minimally educated. In 1924, of the 1,510 factory workers surveyed by the Noda Shōyu Company, 93 percent were men, more than half of whom had four years or less of schooling.

With such an attractive prize, the efforts of the Sōdōmei in Noda were understandable and they were quite successful. The importance of the Noda branch to the Sōdōmei national was overwhelming: it accounted for 48 percent of the unionized food and beverage workers belonging to the Sōdōmei in Eastern Japan and for 11 percent of the union's overall membership. Thus, the Noda Shōyu Company was the linchpin to the Sōdōmei's political fortune in Eastern Japan in the 1920s.

But the political ambitions of the Sōdōmei were rivaled by the industrial ambitions of the owner-managers of the Noda Shōyu Company—the Mogi-Takanashi families. When the company began operations in 1918, it already enjoyed a 7 percent share of the national soy sauce market, but the owner-managers of the company were not content with that degree of success. They knew that the output per plant could be far greater if they invested enough capital to employ the latest mechanical, chemical, and microbiological techniques in a nearly continuous large-batch process of production.

Such processing required the introduction of a centralized, standard-ized, coordinated, and complicated organization of production, matched by an equally involved and interlocking organization of management. In an attempt to implement such a system the management of the Noda Shōyu Company upset the traditional patterns of employment, not only within its own factories but also within the scores of subcontracting en-trepreneurs in Noda that depended on the company. The Sōdōmei was quick to exploit the discontent and disorientation that resulted and, thus encouraged, took over the leadership of the local union move-ment.

In order to promote or prevent the changes that were affecting the nature of work from 1922 to 1928, the company and the union com-peted for the favor and loyalty of the Noda work force; each offered in-stitutional incentives. The union, which presumably stood for the com-mon man and employed more of a grassroots approach, won more support from the workers. To them, the company seemed distant and unapproachable.

Six years of rivalry between union and company were punctuated by several episodes of violence and strike activity, the worst occurring in 1923 and 1927–28. The latter proved to be the longest, and one of the largest and most expensive strikes in prewar Japan. The 218-day strike resulted in the discharge of 1,000 workers, the union's total destruction locally and general discredit nationally, and the emergence of a new pattern of industrial relations in Noda.

Traditional systems of manufacturing and of industrial organization based on the household model were replaced by a Western-inspired system of manufacturing, though not of industrial relations. Rather than Western-style unions, political parties, and industrial relations, the system of employment was characterized by so-called lifetime em-ployment, seniority-based compensation, internal (intracorporate) as opposed to external (intercorporate) labor markets, within-enterprise training, formal channels of mediation for labor-management dispute resolution, and a spirit of accord between workers and managers as well as between the company and the community. This pattern was re-peated elsewhere in the country as other companies also attempted to adjust to changing economic and technological conditions after World War I.[30]

The labor conflict at the Noda Soy Sauce Company marked a turning point in the company's history of industrial organization and industrial relations. But the experience was not unique except in the degree to which labor strife arose in the course of the transformation of the structure and process of work. Much the same sort of transformation took place elsewhere in Japanese industry—admittedly with less violence, but probably with less speed and a more prolonged catharsis as a result.

7.

Corporate Maturation

THE YEARS from around 1930, just after the Great Noda Strike of 1927–28, to 1955 or 1960, the close of what might be called the classical era of corporate paternalism, constitute a historical unit in that the basic character of the Noda Shōyu Company remained more or less constant in spite of impressive technological advances in shōyu fermentation and their translation into refinements of production, operation, and distribution. This was especially evident in four areas. First, a systematically devised company program of paternalism provided work and nonwork benefits to employees and residents of the town, although without giving them much voice in or responsibility for determining those advantages. The benefits of paternalism ranged from awards for job-cost reductions and bonuses for rites of passage, like marriages or births, to non-job-related considerations such as company-subsidized hospitals, libraries, and town halls. During these decades Noda became a company town, a small island of corporate paternalism, and the employees of Noda Shōyu like children in a far-reaching and all-consuming corporate policy of *in loco parentis*.

Second, corporate paternalism was based on employment practices that tended to favor continuous service with the company. Employees were paid relatively little at first, regardless of age and experience, and wages increased gradually in direct proportion to years of service. Noda Shōyu's employment policies were consistent with those of most large enterprises. In concert, they have come to be characterized as "the Japanese Employment System," which pivots around the well-known conventions of lifetime employment, seniority-based compensation, enterprise unionism, and within-enterprise training. These practices were related to circumstances of a controlled economy and of labor surplus. When, in the 1960s, the economy became less regulated and labor shortage rather than surplus became the rule, traditional employment policies at Noda Shōyu and elsewhere changed.

The third area of the company's constancy was a consistent strategy of business operation and organization: operations were based almost wholly on a single product, shōyu, and a single technology, soy and grain fermentation. The organization was designed as a two-tiered company structure wherein the Mogi-Takanashi lineages maintained family control and ownership at the apex of the enterprise, while gradually introducing and enforcing bureaucratic control and authority elsewhere in the organization. But by the 1960s the product line of the firm would no longer be confined to fermented grains, and the degree of family ownership and management in the firm was reduced in some measure.

Finally, this twenty-five- to thirty-year period forms an ideological whole in which the spirit of the company was paternalistic yet somehow egalitarian, and in which the family control of Noda Shōyu was linked ideologically with nationalistic symbols of Japan such as Family-Community-Nation. The continuance of this composition until the late 1950s underscores the lag in the countryside in fulfilling the goals of the Allied Occupation to democratize Japan and transform its industrial structure. Democracy as a moral force for change in the factories of Noda Shōyu and embodied in the activities and actions of a postwar union movement was not realized until at least the middle of the 1950s, long after Japan's defeat in World War II.

The continuity of a prewar ideological consciousness in the postwar period was related in part to the intentional overlapping of facilities for company and community and to the purposeful hiring of new Noda Shōyu Company employees from families that had, or had had, a member working for the firm. Such overlapping in facilities and personnel was a cornerstone of corporate policy from 1930 to 1960. These policies would not be seriously disturbed until residential turnover and new immigration into the community offset the ties that existed between company and community.

The New Paternalism

During the 1920s, particularly during the labor turmoil of that decade, the management of the Noda Shōyu Company realized that it would have to change both its attitude toward and treatment of labor. Actually, the company had been trying to do this for some time. From 1919 to 1928 it had attempted to alter the structure of material incentives to motivate workers to greater efforts. But better pay and benefits were in themselves not enough; more than materialistic reward was needed in order to impel workers to labor harder, better, and more conscientiously. Pay and benefits are, without doubt, great motivators, but their efficacy degenerates with time. Something more ideological, as well as more human, must be added to sustain a high level of work performance over a long period of time. Instead of the old platitudes about patriarchal authority, which had routinely been proffered as motivations for work and as justifications for management's control over workers, something more gentle yet more stimulating was needed. That new something was the family.

As before, when the cartel was superseded by the company, the family—or, at least a particular definition of the family—was employed for the welfare of the corporation. At that time it had been the family as defined by membership in one of the shōyu-brewing families of the Mogi-Takanashi lineages; now it was the family as defined by those working together in a spirit and structure of common industrial purpose. Whereas the former definition of family was biological-genealogical, the latter was strictly ideological.

The new definition of family and the new common purpose that joined labor and management were symbolized by the company ideal of "sangyō-damashii," the "spirit of industry" (spirit in the sense of animation and determination), which was coined and popularized within the company after the Great Strike.[1] "Sangyō-damashii" proclaimed a new social contract with labor, one rooted in a conviction that mutual respect and interdependence were required for management and labor to get along better in the future than they had in the past. If a sense of labor-management accord based on these feelings could be created, then employees (as opposed to workers) could be encouraged to change in ways favorable to the firm without the use of coercion. But employees needed to be convinced that their best interests and those of the company were one and the same. How better to effect this loyalty than to construct a familylike harmony that portrayed workers not as subordinate to managers, as in the days of patriarchal paternalism, but which presented workers and managers as employees and essential appendages of the same body.

To be effective, "sangyō-damashii" had to be more than a snappy slogan. The executives of Noda Shōyu sought to give the ideal a sense of something original and exciting in labor-management relations: it was to evoke a new philosophy for a new age. The framework for association would not be materialistic but personal, and labor-management relations would be carried out within a new atmosphere of trust, cooperation, and closeness that was *familylike*. It would be so personal in fact that distinctions between blue-collar and white-collar labor, while necessary to differentiate the various kinds of work to be done, would be unnecessary to connote social rank within the firm.

It is often suggested that a family style of management is a cultural given for the Japanese; in this one case at least, it was not. This management style was created and consciously crafted at the Noda Shōyu Company after the Great Strike of 1927–28. The new philosophy drew upon traditional values of family and the village of course. But the corporateness of a modern industrial enterprise and of an agricultural village are, upon even the most cursory reflection, quite different. Those who argue for the continuity of "village Japan" in "corporate Japan" ignore a sizable and growing literature that posits at least as much conflict as consensus in the agricultural communities of old as well as in the earliest manufacturing enterprises.[2]

Some may question the authenticity of a system of labor-management relations fashioned on a basis other than that of class relations. In the case of the Noda Shōyu Company, there can be little doubt that the new paternalism, once it took root, was genuine. The trauma of the Great Strike was too recent for anyone seriously to propose an antagonistic posture for either labor or management. Both sides wanted to forget the years of conflict. Also, even during the most contentious years of the 1920s, the overt support for the Sōdōmei leadership among the workers of the Noda Shōyu on the real bread-and-butter issues, like the general strike, involved not many more than half of the workers. So, after the most outspoken opponents of the company had been discharged and those remaining were sufficiently chastened by the failure and sacrifice of their seven-month strike, there was scant opposition, physical or psychological, to any reasonable company proposal.

Finally, it is doubtful that the conflict-based model of labor-management relations peddled by the Sōdōmei in Noda during the 1920s made much headway among the villagers of the region. Class differences were something that a rural Japanese schooled in Confucianism could understand, but class antagonism and class conflict were almost alien concepts. Class membership resulted in duties and obligations, not in rights and privileges. As a political philosophy, the Confucianism of the Japanese educational system emphasized social solidarity, community responsibility, a rational and responsible hierarchy of officialdom, and the effectiveness of bureaucratic benevolence.[3] These values, inculcated through education and reinforced through village tradition, worked to the company's advantage as it sought to convince villagers that the corporate good of both company and community was one and the same. In short, there was little to demand other than a just wage, and the Noda Shōyu Company did not pay substantially less than the going wage.

Conflict did not readily appeal to the villagers, nor did it offer an acceptable means of solving problems. Even during the strike, in spite of a lot of menacing posturing on both sides, there was little actual violence. Kimura's murder was so startling because physical conflict was generally eschewed. Although the Sōdōmei preached class conflict, it drew back from actually encouraging conflict because it sought to gain political power, which would have been impossible if it abetted industrial violence. Thus, since the most extreme principles of the union were never well accepted and the strike victory was so one-sided (and cathartic), it is understandable that a new philosophical basis and practical structure for labor-management relations was eagerly sought by both sides.

The choice of the "family" as the philosophical and practical idiom for institutional membership in the corporation was quite natural. Individuality would have been unnatural as a basis for recruitment and preferment. The family was an expression of the actual genealogical basis of ownership and management that undergirded the firm, as well as an expression of the ideal relationship that should obtain between employees. The flexibility of meaning given to the Japanese concept of family or ie was a convenience that all Japanese understood and accepted. What did not come naturally, however, were decisions about membership in the "family," that is, its working definition, and how to execute these decisions. Proof that the new paternalism was fashioned deliberately is provided by an explanation of whom it included and excluded, and the consequences of those choices.

Membership in the New Paternalism

The new paternalism involved several groups, each with differential access to the benefits of paternalism, although access was never defined clearly in terms of rights or degrees of favor. These groups could be described as the core group, the inner group, the outer group, and the outsiders. The core group was composed of the Mogi-Takanashi family members or their close associates who either owned stock in or managed the company (these were not mutually exclusive of course). Although the core group enjoyed legal and managerial prerogatives far in excess of anyone else in the company, these rights and privileges were never emphasized in the new paternalism. Instead, an attempt was made to minimize the sense of distance between the core group and the inner and outer groups. In this way the new paternalism was quite different from the old system, which consciously used social distance to inculcate obedience and respect.

The inner group included everyone else directly employed by the company but without the prerogatives of the core group. Even though their rights within the firm were not actually equal to those of the core group, their contribution—their labor—was portrayed as equal to that of anyone in the firm. In this way, everyone had a sense of equality within the company. Though it can be said that the father of a family has certain exclusive privileges and responsibilities of family headship, it is doubtful that on a psychological level he can be said to be more estimable than any other family member. What defined the inner group was this psychological sense of belonging and, as a result, a certain emotional egalitarianism lacking in the patriarchal Confucianism of former times. All employees were equal, even if, on closer inspection, certain employees were more equal than others. Such differences as there were, however, were not underscored even if they were acknowledged in the new paternalism.

The focus was on similarities rather than differences. All employees shared in the same medical, retirement, and bonus benefits. All could take advantage of the same bargains in company-operated retail cooperatives, travel clubs, housing units, and mutual savings and loan programs. Between 1923 and 1934 fifty-three different programs and policies in ten different benefit areas (injury and sickness, death, subsidies following natural disasters, marriage and birth, public service, travel, housing, retirement, health, and recreation) were implemented to provide a comprehensive and orderly structure of material as well as spiritual incentives to work long, hard, and well for the company. Again, their purpose was to create a sense of membership and identity that was all-encompassing and, it was hoped, all-fulfilling. If an employee identified completely with the company, problems of motivation would be eliminated, leaving the company to face the still formidable task of using corporate manpower efficiently.

Most important, after 1930 all employees were tied together in company committees designed to enhance intracorporate communication and decisionmaking. These committees were known as the *kōjō renraku kaigi*, and each factory elected a certain number of representatives to them depending upon the size of its work force. These representatives of production-line and supervisory employees then met with persons designated in each factory and in the company headquarters as liaison specialists to discuss matters of mutual concern. In 1935, for example, there were 28 liaison specialists in the main company office, 76 in seventeen different plant sites, and 232 liaison representatives out of 1,814 production personnel involved in the kōjō renraku kaigi procedure. They met regularly to discuss such matters as methods of improving productivity, health, sanitation, injury protection, recreation, welfare, employee education, employee morale, and company policy on death and bereavement among employees and members of employees' families.[4]

This system continued in the postwar period as the *rōdō-kyōgikai* program of consultation. In one eleven-year period, 1946–1956, this consultative body met eighty times to discuss 279 items ranging from wages and benefits to labor conditions (see table 19). In sum, through benefits and a participatory management structure, all employees—that is, all the members of the inner group within the umbrella of the new paternalism—shared a structure and a sense of togetherness that was entirely lacking in the orderly but categorically different roles for managers and workers under the old paternalism.

While such participatory structures were forging a closer association between production and supervisory personnel, the company was increasing the overall ratio of managers to workers in an effort to provide more effective coordination and centralization. If one compares this ratio before the Great Strike to that for the following quarter-century, the company became nearly 20 percent more management-intensive after 1929. Whereas from 1918 to 1926 there had been an average of 6.38 workers for every manager, after 1929 the ratio dropped to 5.27. So the employees of the Noda Shōyu Company were not only more intensively managed, but they were more involved themselves in the process of management. These developments were quite different, quantitatively as well as qualitatively, from the circumstances of the early 1920s.[5]

The outer group was the third ring, those indirectly yet substantially affected by the operations of the company. They could be wholesale customers, subcontractors, or, in a general sense, all those concerned with but not directly involved with the company. The most important component of this group was in fact the community of residents in Noda and surrounding villages and towns, but its heart—the community of the Noda Shōyu Company—was the families of company employees. Before the Great Strike lodgers and young locals made up the bulk of company workers; afterward, with increasing material and seniority-based benefits in place, workers were generally older, more settled, and usually married. By 1936 in fact almost 90 percent were married.[6] Most workers, married or not, lived in company-owned or subsidized housing within the twenty-eight villages located within twelve kilometers of the Noda city center. Such workers and their families formed a settled and stable nexus between company and community, which increasingly defined the quality and character of life in and around Noda after 1930.

Even without an intimate degree of association, the benefits of regular association with the Noda Shōyu Company were substantial. In Noda the railroad, bank, town hall and culture center, library, fire station, elementary school, hospital, and most of the athletic facilities and teams as well as the other recreational facilities and associations were all either company-owned and operated or company-sponsored and

TABLE 19. Topics and results of labor-management conference meetings, 1946–1956.

| Year | Labor representation | Number of meetings | Topics | | | | | | | | Results | | |
			Wages & salaries	Retirement	Welfare	Labor conditions	Treatment in general	Labor agreement	Others	Total	Agreement	Disagreement	Pending
1946	Noda Union	4	4	2	2	3	3	—	5	19	17	1	1
	Kansai Union	4	3	1	3	6	—	2	1	16	15	—	1
1947	Noda Union	9	7	6	5	2	5	6	1	32	30	—	2
	Kansai Union	11	15	5	2	6	5	3	1	37	21	1	15
1948	Noda Union	5	2	6	3	2	2	4	—	19	9	4	6
	Kansai Union[a]	5	3	4	3	1	7	3	—	21	12	—	9
	Amalgamated Union[a]	5	4	4	5	2	4	—	3	22	19	3	—
1949	Amalgamated	5	7	7	4	—	—	6	1	25	17	2	6
1950	Federated	4	9	1	4	—	—	2	—	16	15	1	—
1951	Federated	4	5	6	2	—	1	5	—	19	14	—	5
1952	Federated	5	6	4	3	—	—	2	—	15	15	—	—
1953	Federated	4	3	2	1	—	—	1	—	7	7	—	—
1954	Federated	4	3	—	2	—	—	1	1	7	7	—	—
1955	Federated	5	6	1	3	—	1	1	1	12	10	2	—
1956	Federated	6	6	1	4	—	—	1	—	12	11	1	—
total		80	83	50	46	22	28	37	13	279	219	15	45

Source: Kikkoman Company Archives, Company Statistical Tables—1918 to 1956 (Noda, 1956), unnumbered.
a. The Noda and Kansai unions were separate until August 2, 1948, after which time they amalgamated their efforts.

underwritten. A good deal of the town's water system was company-constructed, and much of the housing was company-built and mortgaged. From 1923 to 1956 the company water system never served a population of less than two thousand; by 1956, 1.75 million cubic feet of water was supplied by the company to the town annually. From 1918 to 1956, 252 houses of some 19,000 square meters' floorspace were built by the company in the town.[7] Company involvement in the water supply system and in housing was initiated for purely selfish reasons, so that the company could have a reliable supply of clean water for preparing the moromi during shōyu fermentation and in order that its employees could live inexpensively in town and thereby be more committed to their work and employer.

Such investments, conceived as by-products in the course of company development, had a way of becoming as much community as corporate property. The interests and activities of company and community had become so intertwined that it would have been impractical to attempt to separate them. Even the local Buddhist temples and Shinto shrines, the quintessential expression of community identity, were heavily subsidized by the company. They could not have operated on nearly the scale nor the affluence that they did without that subsidy. In 1934 a nonprofit foundation, the Kyōchokai, was set up to merge the interests of corporation and community in an institutional imitation of the same format on a national level (which had been established in 1919 by Shibusawa Eiichi, among others). In short, the company had invested substantially in the community in a number of ways, and the interests of the two had become more and more identical. Although some of this investment, such as the railroad and the bank, dated from the first decade of the twentieth century, most came during the second and third decades of the century.

A particularly good example of the company's investment in the community is the Kofukan, the community cultural center. Licenses to operate a nonprofit cultural center were requested of and received from the Ministry of Education and the Home Ministry in April 1929, almost a year after the settlement of the Great Strike. Within a half-year the Kofukan began to operate, supported at first with income donated by the Noda Shōyu Company and later with an endowment of Noda Shōyu securities contributed by the Senshusha.[8]

The Kofukan was begun in recognition of the fact that corporate welfare had become civic welfare in Noda, not only because the firm's employees had grown so numerous during the 1920s and thereby had come to occupy such an important segment of the gainfully employed local population, but also because since the 1923 strike civic, political, and industrial leaders had repeatedly pointed out that the shōyu industry was basic to the prosperity of the national economy. Given the importance of the soy sauce industry in Japan and the large and growing market share of the Noda Shōyu Company, the company had assumed a certain preeminence and with it a responsibility for the economic well-being of not only Noda but the nation as well. This was quite an undertaking for a company mired in the outback of Tokyo. Even though the company had become politicized in the union-management conflicts of the 1920s, Noda remained a country town, and Noda Shōyu company personnel were country people. Projects like the Kofukan reflected Noda Shōyu's acceptance of its new importance and quest for the cultural furnishings to accompany that prominence.

The company endowed the Kofukan handsomely. A sum of 150,000 yen was set aside as a building fund in the first year, and 50,000 yen were donated for each of the first seven years to establish an endowment for the center. Finally, 15,000 yen per year were given during the same period to underwrite the center's operating expenses. In sum, the company gave 605,000 yen to the Kofukan from 1929 to 1935. By the end of that period, the building to house the Kofukan foundation and its activities had been completed.[9] The four-story, ferroconcrete, Romanesque structure sat astride the main crossroad in town and towered over everything in sight, including the newly constructed headquarters of the Noda Shōyu Company. With an auditorium seating 850, a movie theater, a library, and forced-air heating on the first two floors, the building was an architectural as well as cultural triumph. More than the talk of the town, the Kofukan was the talk of Chiba Prefecture and Higashi Katsushika County. Thus, the company succeeded remarkably well in the effort to create a new image for itself both near and far. As a publication commemorating the opening of the building declared:

> The Kofukan was established to promote the cultural advancement of this area, and in doing so, to further the cultural destiny of our nation as well as to combine the strengths of both Eastern and Western civilizations. While preserving the beautiful customs of our race, the new cultural center enlivens the people and enables them to find a more satisfactory life through cultural and educational activities as well as through the welfare and recreational facilities of the center.[10]

In addition to the core group, the inner group, and the outer group, there was a group to which the benefits of association with the Noda Shōyu Company were not extended: the outsiders. Their exclusion was not accidental, but planned. Without the cost savings that accrued from excluding them, it is doubtful that those within the new paternalism could have been so blessed. A bargain, in effect, had been struck with employees of the inner group: they were increasingly well paid, well trained, well housed and fed, and they were consulted on a whole range of managerial issues while the company pressed for greater efficiencies in production and organization. All of this was possible because of the understanding that blue-collar workers were of the same family—the corporate family of the Noda Shōyu Company—as white-collar workers. They stood united, rather than divided, in opposition to those workers who were not part of the family.

Outsiders were irregular, temporary, and part-time workers. They had long fulfilled a necessary function of providing labor when demand exceeded the capacity of the regular work force. After the Great Strike, however, as regular workers become more and more privileged, irregular workers became increasingly distant from those privileges. After 1930 an irreversible and insurmountable division separated a new labor aristocracy (or, more accurately, a new lower middle class of regular workers) from an undereducated, overworked, and underprivileged class of temporary, part-time, and small-scale enterprise laborers.

Such workers enjoyed neither the material nor psychological benefits of employment in large companies with programs of corporate welfare. Instead, workers in small enterprises sweated in an atmosphere of often exploitative paternalism involving small-time bosses and insecure employment. Even if utilized in larger enterprises, they did not escape the petty paternalism of the old labor bosses because their employment was temporary and they labored most often under the direct supervision of their own superiors, not those of Noda Shōyu or some other large enterprise.

The segregation of workers into two groups—regular and irregular, or large and small enterprise—has become a feature of the Japanese economy and is usually referred to as economic dualism. Because of the advantages enjoyed by large firms, differences in productivity, capital investment, wages, and human resource development exist between them and smaller firms. These differences became substantial during the second and third decades of this century. Studies by Umemura Mataji, among others, have shown that there were only small differentials in wages associated with the size of manufacturing enterprise before World War I, but by 1932–33 they had become extremely wide and remained so into the postwar period.[11] The appearance of such wage differentials may well have occurred as a result of the introduction and adaptation in large factories of foreign technology that permitted a more intensive use of power, presumably resulting in higher productivity and higher wages.[12] The translation of higher productivity into higher wages did not always proceed well—witness the Great

Noda Strike—but once effected, it was nonreversible apparently since
economic dualism has characterized the Japanese economy from World
War I until today.

Economic dualism has led to the creation of a segmented labor market, with a minority of workers going into large firms with their advantages and a majority entering smaller enterprises. The differentials at
the time of initial employment become exaggerated with time because
of the inability of smaller enterprises to pay as well as larger concerns
and to train their workers as long or as well, which is ultimately reflected in a still greater wage differential. The higher wages paid by
large firms appear to be related to their price-controlling power in
product markets and their credit-rationing in capital markets, which
allow them to absorb the relatively higher wages.[13]

Paternalism and Patriotism

During the 1930s, as workers in Japan were increasingly segregated into
the "haves" (those with full participation in the corporate paternalism
of large enterprises) and the "have-nots" (those permanently excluded
from that membership), this division was reinforced by the political
turn of events. The efforts of Noda Shōyu to create a familylike sense of
belonging was strengthened on a regional and national level by patriotic campaigns undertaken by the government to promote productivity
and community among all Japanese.

The government's efforts to promote ideological identity through *institutional* membership had in fact begun much earlier with moral education in the schools and political lobbying in the countryside. One of
the best examples was the 1906 "Every Village a Family" campaign intended to consolidate the deities worshiped on the local level into one
shrine. Numerous other campaigns were promoted in the early twentieth century to create common purpose and definition among the Japanese people. Such efforts were accomplished through the mediation of
and membership in institutions. The outsiders just discussed, although
theoretically not excluded from the benefits of nationalistic and patriotic campaigns, were in practice denied such rewards through exclusion
from membership in the large intermediary institutions that channeled
the government message to their insiders.

This state of affairs resulted from not aiming the government's program of patriotic and ideological campaigns at the individual. At a
minimum, they were leveled at the family, but most often they were
aimed at the "community" of Japanese, however vaguely defined. Japanese who enjoyed a sense of wider community and wider institutional
membership, therefore, benefited most from the coincidence of the new
corporate paternalism with the advancing imperial autocracy. Perfor-

mance in the factory was tied to the performance of the national economy, and work became a patriotic duty. Thus, after the 1931 Manchurian Incident and the outbreak of conflict in China, which resulted in the formation of a patriotic front in Japan, factory work became an economic duty as well as a patriotic endeavor for those who belonged to a community united in common structure and spirit. "Sangyō-damashii" was no longer a company ideal but a national one. This fact was systematically enlarged upon in corporate efforts to indoctrinate (kyōka suru) employees, as in a 1938 company directive that outlined the structure and purpose of a newly formed committee on education that was consciously to link corporate performance to national success.[14]

The efforts of the Noda Shōyu Company to create a psychological sense of community among its employees after the Great Strike of 1927–28 corresponded with efforts of the Japanese government, beginning around the turn of the century but accelerating noticeably in the late 1920s and 1930s, to inculcate belief in a state, whose people were related to one another and to the emperor. This theory of the patriarchal state with the emperor as father, usually known as kokutai, was Japan's main ideological tenet from the inauguration of the Meiji Constitution in 1889 until its destruction in 1945.

In theory, all Japanese shared equally in kokutai. According to the thesis of Hozumi Yatsuka (1860–1912), generally credited as the chief expounder of kokutai, Japan was a patriarchal state because all Japanese were descended from Amaterasu Omikami, the Sun Goddess. The imperial family, particularly the emperor, as the most direct descendent of the goddess, stood in relation to the Japanese people as a father to his offspring. Because of that common descent, the imperial household and all other Japanese households were equivalent; state and household were biologically and, as a result, ideologically identical.

Officially this correspondence between state and household through the doctrine of kokka did not require any intermediary institutions such as corporations in order to be activated. Just being Japanese was enough. But as Maruyama Masao has argued, membership in intermediary institutions that could claim some degree of proximity to the emperor or, at least, the imperial purpose, could greatly augment one's sense of importance and power.[15] Thus, although all Japanese partook of some sort of institutional identity, be it family or village membership, and through that institutional identity participated in kokka and kokutai, membership in certain institutions was more potent than in others. Government officers, civil as well as military, were perhaps the most affected by a sense of psychological transference whereby their work became *the work* because of its importance to the emperor and the imperial mission in their eyes.

Two advantages helped the Noda Shōyu Company strengthen the

efficacy of proximity to the emperor that was gained through institutional membership in the firm. First, shōyu was essential in the Japanese diet; accordingly, the soy sauce industry was basic to Japanese life. By logical extension, the most important company in that industry was an important component of a strong national economy, and in fact regional and national officials of Japan expressed such a view of Noda Shōyu from the middle of the 1920s onward. Essential product equals important industry, which leads to national prominence. There was a second way in which Noda Shōyu's employees benefited from the connection between membership in the firm and a greater sense of participation in kokutai. Just as the kokka was predicated on the biological equivalence of the imperial household with all other Japanese households, so the existence of a core group within the Noda Shōyu Company—namely, the Mogi-Takanashi family members, who based their leadership of the firm on biological-genealogical as well as on legal-ideological grounds—mirrored the existence of a core group, the imperial family, within the universe of all Japanese families. In other words, the closed nature of the firm, predicated on an identity of ownership and management at the apex of the organization, paralleled the biological and ideological preeminence of the imperial family within the body politic of the Japanese.

The result of this combination of economic, political, and social features was that after 1930 the Noda Shōyu Company was able to create a new system of paternalism that wedded two seemingly unsuited partners: corporate welfare and corporate productivity. This appears to be a singular Japanese achievement; in the United States or Western Europe it was more often a choice between welfare capitalism and scientific management. Or, as Tamara Hareven has framed the choice in her study of the Amoskeag Company, a choice between wage benefits and playgrounds.[16] In Japan the choice was not between one or the other—at least, not if one enjoyed membership in the corporate family of a large enterprise. In such companies, through a combination of direct salary and wage benefits, seniority and performance incentives, and a carefully conceived spiritual purpose and solidarity, a singular business institution—the large corporation in prewar Japan—was created.[17] The strength of this institution was that it combined economic and emotional appeals; employees could experience a commitment that membership in Western corporations has never been able to provide.

This commitment and feeling of common purpose, however, was available to a minority of Japanese workers. The outsiders, the majority outside the institutional boundaries of large corporations, were less content in their work and were less well compensated. Differences in pay and benefits by size of firm and capital investment have given rise to the so-called dual economic structure. But it is doubtful that this term goes far enough in capturing the differences—social, psychological, as well as economic—that separate workers in large as opposed to small enterprises. The benefits of institutional membership in large enterprises were possible only because of the existence of these outsiders. It is no coincidence that as the new paternalism was institutionalized at the Noda Shōyu Company, a sizable and predictable body of part-time and irregular workers began to appear on the shop floor of the company's numerous breweries. From 1930 to 1956, 6.5 percent of the annual work force was temporary. If the most extreme year, 1939, is considered, over one-quarter of those working for the company were not regular employees. And they never entered the material and psychological community of success that enveloped the regular employees of the Noda Shōyu Company.

The success of Noda Shōyu was based on two elements. First, if the results of the famous Hawthorne experiments at the General Electric Company may be generalized cross-culturally, the conspicuous interest that the Noda Shōyu Company displayed toward its workers and in the workplace was reflected ultimately in greater performance and higher morale. Second, the talent of the company at tying work performance to small group interaction, both on and off the job, must be given a lot of credit for the company's success with industrial relations after 1930. Not only were workers made to feel and be part of a team, but this sense of togetherness was extended to the wider community through the physical and social expansion of the company into the town. Given the policies of reducing turnover and prolonging employment with the company, it was not long before sons and daughters of fathers and mothers employed at Noda Shōyu also entered its employ. This small group interaction within and outside the company transformed work groups into affective as well as effective work teams. It may have been the greatest achievement of the Noda Shōyu Company after 1930.

Two Features of the Japanese Employment System

It would be a mistake to assume that the success of the new paternalism was entirely or even largely ideological. Loyalty, commitment, hard work, and prolonged effort cannot be sustained on ideals and beliefs for long, but must be nourished by material reward and institutional recognition. The increasingly professional management of Noda Shōyu recognized the need for a combination of ideological incentives and material benefits, probably because they themselves enjoyed neither the emotional nor economic security that membership in the Mogi-Takanashi families provided. As a result, the company, through its Personnel Department, began to create a system of tangible rewards.

To understand the impact of these personnel policies on the company and to clarify their role within the new corporate paternalism, the personnel records for all white-collar males hired from 1918 to 1976 by Noda Shōyu were examined. The results, focusing on 1930 to 1960 are presented without the statistical tools of analysis used elsewhere. Readers interested in a longer and more technical treatment can refer to a previously published study.[18]

Records revealed the following general conclusions concerning employment and compensation at Noda Shōyu. First, the hiring of new employees at the managerial and production levels was highly irregular, except for an occasional period of consistency in the number of new men hired. This irregularity was seemingly dictated more by the circumstances of demand than supply, although the military draft and the wartime economy greatly affected the size and quality of the manpower pool before the war.

Second, the irregularity in recruitment was mirrored by a considerable disparity in the number of managerial employees who stayed with the firm for anything like "lifetime employment." Removing from consideration employees who died on the job or who were conscripted, three periods of persistency (measured by how many employees who were hired together remain in the firm's employ) can be isolated. In the early years, from incorporation to 1930, most managerial and supervisory employees stayed with the firm until retirement. None were recruited in 1931, but from 1932 to 1948 less than half of the newly hired or promoted managers stayed with Noda Shōyu twenty years, or for what might be considered most of a working lifetime. Much of the fluctuation in employment for this period, however, was attributable to wartime dislocation, for a man need not be drafted in order to experience war disruption of work and residence. From 1949 to the early 1960s persistency in employment climbs to its highest levels in the company's history.

Third, regardless of when someone was hired and how many were hired in the same year, education level was the primary criterion determining the initial remuneration of managerial employees; especially during an employee's first ten years with the company, pay was likely to be strictly by seniority. Thereafter, seniority-based compensation was tempered by what seems to have been a more subjective appraisal and reward based on performance, specialized knowledge, and service.

Interestingly, managerial employees with the highest levels of education followed the model of seniority-based compensation best, so that university employees, who were hired for managerial posts with increasing frequency after the Great Strike, adhered closest to the model of pay according to years of experience with the firm. This would make sense because other criteria of compensation, such as those just mentioned, become increasingly difficult to apply as one's work becomes more supervisory. University graduates, after a period of training and socialization when they might be involved in production, would be engaged almost exclusively in supervisory and other less mensurable duties.

The personnel records of Noda Shōyu, nevertheless, show that many managerial employees hired between 1930 and 1960 stayed with the firm for at least twenty years and were paid largely according to their experience. Lifetime employment and seniority-based compensation were the rule and apparently were effective policies both for keeping and for rewarding employees. Fluctuations in employment persistency and in the salience of experience as the prime component of wages did occur of course, but this is only natural and both economic and noneconomic causes might be adduced for such fluctuations.

Economically, prosperity and depression have considerable effect not only on one's desire to change employers but also on an employer's willingness to discriminate between employees through wage payments. Over the period in question at Noda Shōyu, persistency of employment apparently improved, as general economic conditions picked up and were translated into better wage benefits for more employees. Noneconomic circumstances affected employment and compensation as well, for as economic conditions bettered, a younger, more experienced, but less well educated employee was hired. Until the 1960s, the majority of persons who moved into managerial positions came from the countryside, and many were from the area around Noda. Company policy favored the hiring of country boys, especially locals, when possible, as they were thought to work harder and be more loyal than those from urban backgrounds. The most loyal employees—those who worked longest for the company and were paid more according to seniority than anything else as a result—were the younger, less educated managers from rural areas. Apparently, they fitted best into the company's new paternalistic programs and policies. This becomes apparent when the likelihood of leaving the firm is broken down by educational level (see table 20).

In addition to motivating employees toward long service with the firm, compensation by seniority brought other benefits to Noda Shōyu. The expansion of production facilities at home and overseas at a time when prices were fixed either by consensus among manufacturers or by military dictate allowed for the maximum investment in fixed costs, like plant and equipment, while variable costs, most importantly wages, could be minimized. Compensation by seniority allowed postponement of the brunt of labor expenses for almost the entire working life of those covered by such a system. An additional benefit of delaying full

TABLE 20. Likelihood of leaving firm by educational level, in percentages, 1918–1948 (n=584).

Years of education	Within 10 years	Within 20 years	Within 30 years
6	2.0	21.0	51.0
7	—	10.7	32.1
8	16.1	28.6	44.0
9	12.5	38.0	44.0
10	34.5	50.0	44.0
16	52.0	66.6	74.0

Source: Kikkoman Company Personnel Records, 1918–1976, my tabulation.

compensation was that productivity per unit of wages was higher, even though productivity per worker might be lower.[19] Although the number of workers paid more strictly according to seniority was small compared with those paid otherwise (because the group most affected by this compensation policy, university graduates, was a minority among managers before the war), their wages were considerably larger; thus, significant savings to the firm could be realized by paying this group low wages at first but rewarding them later for loyal service. Offsetting even a portion of labor costs greatly benefited a firm like Noda Shōyu which was engaged in the expensive process of modernizing not only the biochemical and mechanical processes of shōyu manufacture but also the methods and channels of distribution and sales.

The Prewar Employment System at the Noda Shōyu Company

A study of Noda Shōyu's employment practices shows generally moderate rates of employment persistency and seniority-based compensation for some managerial employees in the prewar period. Lifetime employment and seniority-based compensation as traditional practices, that is, as prewar, selective policies, were associated with the unity of ownership and control in management. This raises some crucial questions concerning the importance of household (ie) ideology and organization in Japan's business history.

Ie ideology is rooted in the protection, acquisition, and transfer of property. Those with property or destined to acquire it were educated to be dutiful and loyal to the corporate body or household in its material and human senses. For those outside the ie, loyalty to household and the enhancement of its prestige were neither expected nor needed. Because most traditional workers came from propertyless or essentially propertyless families and were not assimilated into positions of power in family-controlled economic enterprises, they were not particularly attracted to ie ideology.

This distinction is evident in the differential socialization of *fudai* and *genin* household members in the history of early Tokugawa agrarian relations.[20] Fudai members, who were expected to become full participants in the propertied household, were nurtured and educated as nascent "family" members. Genin were treated less well because they were not expected to become part of the "inner" organization—the ie or household in its corporate or propertied sense. John W. Hall and Thomas M. Huber have shown that what distinguished the "inner" warriors from the "outer" warriors of Okayama and Chōshū, respectively, was not only the size of their hereditary stipends but also the special roles, duties, and values that accompanied their closeness to the ruling lord and family.[21] Their role was to symbolize in their station and service the ideology of loyalty and tradition—not unlike the role of those compensated by seniority in the prewar managerial hierarchy at Noda Shōyu. By analogy to the "inner" warriors, we might consider the "inner" employees of the Noda Shōyu Company as a class of industrial retainers groomed to promote and protect the property and values of the families owning and operating the firm. By their service, they entered into the core group of the firm.

Too much can be made of such an ideological commitment, however. When employees stayed on the job, it was likely to be for pragmatic as much as paternalistic reasons. Robert Marsh and Hiroshi Mannari have found that Japanese stay with one firm for the same reasons Americans do—for cumulated pay, rank, seniority, and status.[22] In other words, paternalistic ideology does not create behavior consistent with the practices of permanent employment and seniority-based compensation, except perhaps for those at the propertied core of corporate groups. Nevertheless, companies cannot choose to ignore organizational spirit or ideology. Noda Shōyu articulated ie ideology as an alternative to unionism and as a vehicle of economic rationality. Workers were asked to produce more in the name of company loyalty and service.

Although the findings here are based on evidence from only one company, much of the argument undoubtedly holds for other Japanese enterprises as well because most prewar businesses, large and small alike, were family-owned and operated. Ie ideology, which joins kinship to property, is ideally suited for such enterprises. But it has become less and less appropriate since the war, with the breakup of zaibatsu-style industrial organization and the popularization of the egalitarian ideal, and since Japanese enterprises have expanded, diversified, merged, and moved into international markets. Paternalistic practices, where they exist, are no longer confined to particular groups within firms as an extension of the personality of owner-operators. Rather, in large firms they have become nearly universal, impersonal, and contractual.

The personnel system that existed in traditional firms before the war, with its different styles of reward and control, was a logical and effective system. Within it, forward-looking and profit-conscious innovation could be combined with the patrimony and prestige of a family-owned and operated firm. This approach to personnel management was successful in an important sense: persistency in employment was always moderate or better, even in the darkest days of the war. But it was unsuccessful in an important sense: those rewarded least according to ability, the better-educated employees, particularly the university graduates, left in large numbers.

The two-track approach to rewards was not unique with Noda Shōyu; it is a component of ie ideology and organization. Those closest to property are the core and cause of the process of segregating human resources; their status and power come from ties to property. The outer, secondary tier of personnel have separate processes of allocating status and reward. In such a system rewards for performance on the one hand and for loyalty on the other are not mutually incompatible for tradition and change are both accommodated.

The End of an Era

Although personnel records of the Noda Shōyu Company indicate a high degree of persistency in employment and a tendency toward seniority-based compensation among certain managers in the prewar period, neither lifetime employment nor compensation by seniority were the rule by any means. The company provided its employees with differential access to power, authority, and reward predicated on two constituent elements, one ideological and one organizational. Nonetheless, in spite of numerous internal divisions that derived from these two features, Noda Shōyu was remarkably successful in fostering an attitude of harmony and purpose not only within the corporation but also within the wider community of Noda and its environs.

Part of this success can be traced to the new model of corporate paternalism and to the dedicated efforts of workers and managers to rebuild the company in the image of that model after the Great Strike. The other part can be attributed to forces outside the firm, such as the government's growing involvement in the economy after 1930, which coincided nicely with the company's efforts to restructure the firm. As the emerging military government in Japan began to control credit, to limit access to and prices of raw materials, and to interfere in labor markets through civil and military conscription, companies like Noda Shōyu were encouraged to move increasingly toward practices like life-time employment and seniority-based compensation, whenever practical, as a way of minimizing variable costs in an uncertain and unpredictable economic environment. Such practices, not coincidentally, structured costs to the advantage of investment rather than short-term gain; they also won the loyalty and dedication of regular workers who were more secure than ever in their employment. Of course the draft and wartime circumstances meant that such practices were extended to a smaller and smaller proportion of the prewar labor force, as part-time laborers and female workers grew in number at Noda Shōyu.

The increase in nonpermanent employees allowed for the continuation of an extremely high rate of dividend payments to company shareholders, the most important of whom were the officers of the holding company Senshusha. From 1929 through 1945 the average annual dividend equaled 60 percent of the total disposable income minus legal reserve requirements (see table 21).

The achievements of Noda Shōyu from the 1930s to 1960 were remarkable. The closely held ownership of the firm was maintained while the production and operation of the firm was thoroughly modernized by the application of the latest chemical, mechanical, and managerial techniques; Western-style unions and political associations were rejected and workers were educated to accept and respond to a new corporate paternalism; and "tradition" and "modernity" were both accommodated in the organizational as well as ideological life of the corporation. This remarkable synthesis worked reasonably well for the generation in question. It allowed the company to expand its market share from a low point of 5.1 percent in 1923 (during the first major strike) to two or three times that figure from the 1930s through the 1950s (see figure 12 and table 22).

This growth in market share coincided with Noda Shōyu's shift away from barrels to bottles and cans during the period in question. Although a small amount of shōyu had been bottled from the early 1910s, the first factory built exclusively for bottling soy sauce did not open until March 1930. Thereafter, the percentage of soy sauce shipped in bottles as opposed to other containers, principally barrels, rose rapidly, reaching 40 percent by 1934 and 54 percent by 1941. After the outbreak of war, however, bottle production fell sharply and did not recover to the 40 percent level until 1949–50. Since the 1950s bottles and, more recently, plastic containers have become so common that the company no longer manufactures or even uses the soy sauce kegs that were syn-

TABLE 21. Average annual dividend rate
(percentage), 1929–1945.

Period	Dividend rate
1929 first 6 months	69
second 6 months	65
1930 first 6 months	62
second 6 months	67
1931 first 6 months	20
second 6 months	61
1932 first 6 months	65
second 6 months	73
1933 first 6 months	79
second 6 months	86
1934 first 6 months	73
second 6 months	75
1935 full 12 months	71
1936 full 12 months	70
1937 full 12 months	57
1938 full 12 months	66
1939 full 12 months	63
1940 full 12 months	61
1941 full 12 months	55
1942 full 12 months	54
1943 full 12 months	40
1944 full 12 months	41
1945 first 6 months	44
second 6 months	31

Source: Kikkoman Company Archives, Company Statistical Tables—1918 to 1956 (Noda, 1956), unnumbered.

onymous with shōyu for so long. The use of materials other than wood, such as glass, metal, and plastic, for storing and shipping shōyu was closely related to the growth in market share for the company. Bottles, for example, were cheaper to make, easier to store and distribute, more durable than the easily split and warped wood, more reusable, and more sanitary. The willingness of the Noda Shōyu Company to shift an ever-larger share of its production to such alternative containers, when other manufacturers were reluctant to do so, is another illustration of its innovative management and industrial leadership.

Market share grew in other ways as well. Through direct investment abroad and acquisitions at home the company steadily expanded capacity and production. On December 31, 1936, for example, with an

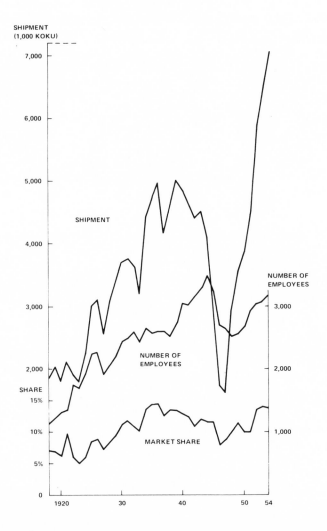

FIGURE 12. GROWTH OF EMPLOYMENT, SHIPMENT,
AND MARKET SHARE, 1918-1954

SHIPMENT
(1,000 KOKU)

7,000

6,000

5,000

SHIPMENT

4,000

NUMBER OF
EMPLOYEES

3,000   3,000

NUMBER OF
EMPLOYEES

2,000   2,000

SHARE
15%

10%   1,000

MARKET SHARE

5%

0

1920   30   40   50 54

SOURCE: KIKKOMAN COMPANY ARCHIVE, COMPANY STATISTICAL TABLES — 1918 TO 1956 (1956).

TABLE 22. Noda shōyu shipments (in koku) and market share, 1918–1954.

Year	Shipments	National output	Company share (percent)
1918	184,909	2,639,498	7.0
1919	204,324	2,940,133	6.9
1920	181,736	2,796,277	6.5
1921	211,643	3,215,663	9.6
1922	191,439	2,268,641	5.9
1923	177,859	3,470,563	5.1
1924	224,682	3,661,453	6.1
1925	300,087	3,519,382	6.5
1926	309,674	3,530,922	8.8
1927	256,486	3,504,229	7.3
1928	311,439	3,648,697	8.5
1929	343,316	3,629,944	9.5
1930	370,851	3,311,469	11.2
1931	375,727	3,188,459	11.8
1932	365,193	3,300,578	11.1
1933	324,056	3,197,835	10.1
1934	443,477	3,247,919	13.7
1935	475,193	3,313,894	14.3
1936	494,010	3,395,542	14.5
1937	416,063	3,284,474	12.7
1938	462,461	3,384,087	13.7
1939	498,306	3,670,642	13.6
1940	486,562	3,814,596	12.8
1941	501,562	4,063,702	12.3
1942	440,931	4,016,826	11.0
1943	452,061	3,782,704	12.0
1944	409,742	3,489,044	11.7
1945	271,459	2,365,694	11.5
1946	174,706	2,221,432	7.9
1947	165,292	1,868,005	8.8
1948	291,117	2,830,047	10.3
1949	356,183	3,059,242	11.6
1950	385,538	3,830,204	10.0
1951	455,386	4,590,045	9.9
1952	565,871	4,170,438	13.6
1953	645,593	4,567,038	14.1
1954	706,676	5,109,874	13.8

Source: Kikkoman Company Archives, Company Statistical Tables—1918 to 1956 (Noda, 1956), unnumbered.

investment of 1 million yen, the Manshu Noda Shōyu Company was established to manufacture Kikkoman soy sauce and Homare miso in the Japanese colony of Manchuria. (This factory complemented the Nihon Shōyu Company, which had been operated by Noda Shōyu in Korea since 1918.) In April 1937 the Noda Shōyu Company purchased 80 percent of the outstanding 70,000 shares of the Higeta Soy Sauce Company of Chōshi city in Chiba Prefecture.

One of the oldest and largest brewers in Eastern Japan, Higeta had been unable to secure a large enough share of the market to pay for the modernization of plant and equipment that it had undertaken during the late 1920s and early 1930s. These modernization efforts had occurred at a time when government regulation of the economy and market-sharing agreements among manufacturers made it doubly difficult—indeed, unlikely—that a medium-sized brewer (large compared to most brewers but small in comparison to Noda Shōyu) could secure enough return to amortize new investment in plant and equipment. Yet without new investment in the mass production and mass distribution technology pioneered by Noda Shōyu, makers like Higeta Shōyu were doomed to a lingering but inevitable failure. Higeta attempted to remain viable through new investment in expanded capacity; when this failed in 1937, one of Noda Shōyu's oldest rivals was absorbed into the Noda brewery's expanding empire.[23]

Noda Shōyu purchased three more breweries in 1938–39, all smaller than Higeta Shōyu: Yamayama Shōyu (another Chōshi firm), Showa Shōyu, and Kamibishi Shōyu.[24] Surprisingly enough, this policy of horizontal integration allowed the company to maintain but not enlarge the 10- to 15-percent market share it had come to enjoy. This resulted from the difficulties of increasing market share in the military-dominated economy. Especially after 1936, when the All-Japan Industries Association (Dai-Nippon Sangyō Hōkokukai, Sampō for short) was established, the military masters of the country rationed credit, disrupted manpower, limited raw material purchases, fixed prices, and generally made it impossible to plan for and implement policies of market expansion. It was difficult then even for large manufacturers like Noda Shōyu to secure sufficient raw materials of adequate quality at reasonable prices to take advantage of the economies of scale and speed that it enjoyed. In spite of the purchase of four manufacturers between 1937 and 1939, the Noda Shōyu Company was unable to do better than hold its own at home, even if overseas sales, particularly those to the military, picked up considerably (see tables 23 and 24). Yet it would not be fair to minimize its sales performance: in spite of the difficulties of the domestic market, Noda Shōyu maintained its leadership in the face of the failure of rivals and the unpredictability of a military-command economy.

TABLE 23. Sales of shōyu by the Korean branch of Noda Shōyu, 1912–1944 (in taru).

Year	Kikkoman	Kikkoryū	Total[a]	Military sales
1912		36,573		
1913		28,756		
1914		25,086		
1915		27,934		
1916		36,225		
1917		31,971		
1918		36,738		
1919		50,517		
1920		45,941		
1921		26,122		
1922		46,954		
1923		44,856		
1924		55,687		
1925	7,749	53,425	61,174	
1926	23,680	57,302	80,982	
1927	22,144	63,932	86,067	
1928	28,745	57,757	86,502	
1929	29,860	56,001	85,861	
1930	47,128	44,312	91,440	
1931	80,857	41,692	122,549	
1932	76,065	43,362	119,427	
1933	76,663	43,986	120,649	
1934	122,538	54,514	177,052	16,570
1935	144,341	70,720	215,061	27,900
1936	143,798	53,943	197,741	12,000
1937	176,141	85,510	256,651	16,518
1938	220,706	152,131	372,837	59,877
1939	185,173	120,865	306,038	42,009
1940	99,160	120,806	219,966	36,634
1941	75,934	152,167	228,101	111,060
1942	7,298	175,429	182,727	67,669
1943	4,649	149,162	153,811	32,353
1944	5	146,352	146,357	46,775

Source: Kikkoman Company Archives, Company Statistical Tables—1918 to 1956 (Noda, 1956).

a. Includes military sales to 1934.

TABLE 24. Sales of miso paste in Fengtien, China, and Korea (in kan).

Year	Fengtien		Korea		Total	
	Total[a]	Military sales	Total[a]	Military sales	Total[a]	Military sales
1912			83,855			
1913			102,134			
1914			102,147			
1915			110,722			
1916			208,329			
1917			251,830			
1918			317,463			
1919	42,994		304,587		347,581	
1920	148,826		265,580		414,406	
1921	157,802		268,801		426,603	
1922	181,565		340,208		521,773	
1923	220,967		388,836		609,803	
1924	250,489		406,693		657,182	
1925	248,900		394,469		643,369	
1926	256,700		410,538		667,238	
1927	232,410		406,636		639,046	
1928	199,963		428,866		628,829	
1929	199,103		459,278		658,381	
1930	205,516		436,269		641,785	
1931	193,986		398,403		592,389	
1932	226,768		452,789		679,555	
1933	211,444		480,691		692,135	
1934	247,604		588,812		836,416	
1935	240,101		617,948		858,049	
1936	257,122	40,000	600,125	0	857,247	40,000
1937	320,829	40,820	755,632	115,268	1,076,461	156,088
1938	548,569	183,206	988,462	323,236	1,537,031	506,442
1939	572,269	81,942	938,341	716,820	1,510,610	798,762
1940	488,615	67,076	880,537	151,624	1,369,152	218,700
1941	505,367	105,856	1,041,917	246,530	1,547,284	352,389
1942	695,505	314,078	1,380,688	607,943	2,076,193	922,021
1943	490,514	94,828	1,205,191	113,721	1,695,705	208,549
1944	454,662	181,358	1,848,274	355,051	2,302,946	536,409

Source: Kikkoman Company Archives, Company Statistical Tables—1918 to 1956 (Noda, 1956), unnumbered.

a. Total includes military sales.

Given this creditable performance, it may be inappropriate to question the apparent success of Noda Shōyu. Yet it would be remiss not to point out that the company's achievements had been accomplished without overhauling its core: the executive boardroom from which the Mogi-Takanashi owners managed the firm. This unchanging core, in the face of so much apparent success, would become a major obstacle to the growth of the enterprise and to the most efficient allocation of resources already acquired.

The Limits of a Family Firm

For three hundred years, 1661 to 1960, the basis for the growth of the soy sauce industry in Noda was, in one form or another, the family. Because of the flexibility of the Japanese definition of ie, the family could always be adapted, rather than rejected, in the various stages of enterprise development. The family defined the critical employees in nascent breweries, determined the circle of kinsmen for pooling resources and information as factories grew, and supplied the analogue for both the structural and ideological statement of the joint-stock company eventually established in Noda. Nevertheless, however defined, the family cannot accommodate all changes. There is a limit to which any innovation—and the family model of enterprise growth as it developed in Noda was a major innovation—will allow change. Once the family was established as the rule of enterprise transformation in Noda, change was confined to that paradigm of structure and function.

As a result, the rural zaibatsu forged at Noda was constrained in ways that the larger urban zaibatsu were not. In those giant combines enterprise size and geographical dispersion, as well as industrial variety within the enterprise group, forced modernization of management style and business organization that was not experienced in Noda. In the Mitsubishi, Sumitomo, Yasuda, and Mitsui combines, professional managers had long ago taken over the leadership of the enterprise groups from the men who founded them. This revolution in management occurred around the turn of the twentieth century, when the size and complexity of these mammoth businesses made them too much for one family, no matter how talented, to manage. Yet, because of the general reliance on debt rather than equity financing in Japan, in the period before World War II great zaibatsu families did not normally lose ownership over their growing empires, even if they had to allow a larger role to be played by banks and other financial institutions in the overall control and coordination of member firms in an enterprise group. Nevertheless, ownership was separated from management, and this allowed the juxtaposition of a class of highly educated professional managers between owners of enterprises and the enterprises themselves, giving companies like the Mitsui Trading Company and Mitsubishi Heavy Industries Company an entirely different flavor and form from that of the Noda Shōyu Company.

In Noda the prevalence of family ownership as well as control meant that the number and capabilities of Mogi-Takanashi heir-apparents in the firm determined company strategy and structure. The need to find appropriate positions for family members affected job recruitment and appointment. That the status of one's family could define one's career in the firm is revealed by examining the careers of various Mogi-Takanashi managers before 1960. Of the forty-two Mogi, Takanashi, Nakano, and Horikiri family members who entered the firm between 1918 and 1960, the chaff were quickly sorted from the wheat. Those whose families did not belong to the original eight households that forged the firm were never accorded more than a middle-level position. Those who made it to the top came from five families: three Mogi, one Nakano, and one Takanashi. Scions of these households invariably achieved high rank in the company. Most often this was because of attitude and ability—but not always.

When the necessity of matching family status to company appointment was multiplied by the half-dozen high appointments needed to fill all the positions sought by Mogi-Nakano-Takanashi claimants from two different generations, the overall direction of the firm was fixed in considerable measure by the limits of the family model, which defined the essence of the enterprise. Carried to an extreme, concern with family could greatly affect the possibilities for growth and change available to a firm.

There is a large body of literature in economic and business history that relates the lack of entrepreneurial daring to the salience of family values in business organizations. French business from the eighteenth to mid-twentieth century is frequently considered a case in point. It is argued that the mentality of a family firm is such that security and stability are valued more than growth and innovation. A steady source of income to preserve family status could be best obtained through conservative business practices that do not risk its dynastic fortunes.[25] This point of view might be even more valid to the degree that a large number of family members sought position within the framework of a family firm: the need to secure a livelihood for a larger rather than smaller group of claimants would put strict limits on how much might be risked and on what degree of experimentation with enterprise form and function would be allowed.

There is little doubt that the family character of Noda Shōyu from 1930 to 1960 was both a cause of the firm's success and a reason for its lackluster performance. Although the family provided stability and continuity of leadership and a moral force and ideological rationale for enterprise development, its nexus contributed to a notable lack of imagination in business, which confined activity to a narrow range of products and organizations subordinate to the family-dominated holding-company structure. As a result, the need to fulfill the logic of familialism did not always end with the best people achieving the top positions or in the most efficient allocation of the enterprise's resources. This was most true in the first and second decades of this century when family rank and connections, and little else, determined power and position first within the cartel and later within the company. From the third through fifth decades, family rank, then education, became the primary determinants of careers. More recently, promise and the maturing of promise into performance must be added to family rank and education in order to reach the top of the corporate hierarchy.

Although family concerns appear to have been paramount in deciding business strategy and structure for perhaps three decades before World War II, and for maybe another decade following that watershed, the family model was not so overwhelming or incapacitating as to lead to entrepreneurial failure in the case of the Noda Shōyu Company. The family model of business organization in Japan is unusually resilient, and, from the 1930s to the 1950s, all Japanese companies, family-dominated or not, have had to operate in a market environment circumscribed by first one military government and then another. In such circumstances, the conservative character of a company's management can be ascribed to external factors as well as to family control.

Nevertheless, the nature of ownership and management of the Noda Shōyu Company must be blamed, in part at least, for the unimaginative if effective piloting of the firm's course from 1930 to 1960. If one examines the background of its last seven presidents, it is not surprising to discover that the first four of them, who directed the company from 1928 to 1962 and maintained a conservative strategy of horizontal integration, were all natural sons. Only two of the four had a university education. Since 1962, however, two of the last three presidents, who moved the company toward product diversification and forward integration into a much stronger marketing position, were adopted sons, and all three were educated in economics or law at prestigious universities.

Natural sons and adopted sons are equally esteemed in the performance-conscious Japanese household system; but natural sons, because they have been reared and groomed in the environment of a family business, are perhaps too well informed and too well trained to take chances, to do things differently from their forebears, and generally to experiment with alternate products and processes. Adopted sons, by contrast, may be less reluctant to try something new; indeed, they may be anxious to prove their value with new ideas and innovative schemes. The two adopted sons who have been presidents in the postwar era were not adopted until after they had completed their university training. Their formative years and training were passed entirely outside the influence of a family firm.

In sum, the limits of the family model of organization and ideology are tied to the character and quality of family members who join the firm. The performance of the Noda Shōyu Company from 1930 to 1960 was tied to the careers of the Mogi-Takanashi managers who took over the firm in the aftermath of the Great Strike and steered it through the uncertainty and anguish of the interwar and war years. The company's performance in the past two decades, however, has depended on a cohort of new family leaders who have responded to a much different business environment. In their attempts to respond to that new environment, these men have significantly altered the definition of a family firm.

A Corporate Coming of Age

The period from 1928 through the 1950s was a time of measured growth for the Noda Shōyu Company. After its production processes were secured in the wake of the Great Strike and its prices and markets were insured by agreements among manufacturers and distributors in the following year (1929), company attention turned to the creation of a stable and loyal work force in Noda and to the gradual expansion of its business empire at home and overseas.

The company managers skillfully designed channels of cooperation between the company and its employees as well as the larger community. Participatory management structures brought all regular employees into the organizational life of the company, and promotion and compensation were geared to reward faithful, dedicated employees. Noda Shōyu supported the town by investing in the railroad, schools, company housing, and in other civic buildings and functions. By the middle of this century the interests and interactions of company and community had become so intertwined that they could not be separated easily.

Company and community were interrelated ideologically as well. In the course of the nationalistic crescendo in Japan before World War II, the common Japanese identity and cause were trumpeted near and far. This type of propaganda was especially effective when intermediary institutions such as corporations could moderate between the august majesty of the emperor and the common citizen. The Noda Shōyu Company utilized the patriotic fervor of prewar Japan to its advantage as it socialized workers in its programs of employee education and training, and as it sought greater efficiencies in production during an era when raw materials were increasingly hard to acquire and when domestic markets were not very profitable.

With markets set and workers in order, the Noda Shōyu Company enjoyed several decades of steady if unspectacular growth in sales and market share. From about 1930 to 1960 it exemplified a successful, well-managed and well-respected, if conservatively piloted, Japanese corporation.

8.

Democratization and Internationalization

ALTHOUGH the overall aims and outcomes of the Allied Occupation of Japan (1945–1952) have been debated for some three decades now, there have been few attempts to trace in detail the results of Occupation policy for a single business institution. Yet only by doing so for corporations as well as for a whole range of other institutions will a realistic portrait of the Occupation emerge. Moreover, through such an examination one can assess and evaluate the degrees of continuity and discontinuity in the prewar and postwar institutional history of modern Japan.

In analyzing the effects on Kikkoman, as Noda Shōyu was renamed after the war (first, as the Kikkoman Shōyu Company in 1964, and, in 1980, as the Kikkoman Corporation), we find that among the major policies of the Occupation—land reform, demilitarization, economic deconcentration, and democratization—democratization had a major effect and deconcentration, only a minor one. The apparent impact of these—principally, democratization—proved to be so great that Kikkoman was noticeably transformed as a result. However, the changes introduced by the Occupation, rather than representing a rupture with past practices, advanced a number of interrelated development that appeared long before the Occupation and that continue to affect the course of Kikkoman's development even today.

The Course of Democratization

The transformation of business under the Occupation did not occur suddenly, since what constituted democratic behavior was not always apparent to the Japanese or, even more surprisingly, to the victorious Allies. Especially after the so-called "reverse-course" was inaugurated in 1947–48, Occupation authorities reversed so much of their earlier handiwork that a set of consistent and coherent policies was hard to discern. As a result of this vacillation as well as a wholly understandable reticence on the part of the Japanese, the impact of democratization was not immediately or openly apparent. Unlike a century earlier during the *yonaoshi* incidents (a sort of combined agrarian and millennial epiphenomenon) when Japanese took the streets chanting, "Ee ja nai ka" (it's all right, isn't it?), Occupation-period Japanese did not celebrate the delights of democracy in any such obvious and kinetic ways.

Ideological excess, except among certain Communist groups, was conspicuously absent from the forced democratization of Japan after World War II. Familiarity may have had something to do with this, for democratic concepts and practices had been known for roughly half a century before the Occupation. But the earlier experiences with democracy were largely personal, experienced on one's own, while the hallmark of democratization after the war was the institutionalization of democratic concepts and practices for the first time on a large scale among the general population.

It was in this process of institutionalization, rather than in the rhetoric or ideology of democracy itself, that democratization would have such a considerable effect on the Kikkoman Corporation. Yet the full effects of any process require time to take hold, and it would be some years—in fact, not until after the Occupation officially ended in 1952—before the full force of democratization on Kikkoman would be felt. Further, the process of institutionalizing democracy was not an isolated action but was telescoped within a visibly greater force for change in postwar Japan: the internationalization of business planning and activities.

Democratization affected the company structure in three ways. First, it altered the legal definition of the family in Japan and, as a result, refined the concept and utility of the family form as it was employed for business purposes among the soy sauce brewers of Noda. Democratization changed the family from an institution designed to control business activities in a variety of ways to an institution that was separate and distinct from, and increasingly subordinate to, the firm in the control and manipulation of assets. Accordingly, the congruence of family and firm and the identity of family control with family management that had characterized the enterprise for three centuries were upset. With time, the requirements of successful corporate management outstripped the foreshortened resources and finite nature of the newly defined democratic family in Japan, thereby drastically curtailing the number of family-owned and operated firms among Japan's largest industrial companies.

Second, the Occupation inspired a Western-style labor union movement, which finally gained momentum in Noda during the 1950s, resulting first in labor strikes and the rise of an autonomous and active labor union movement that was beyond the company's control, and then in the labor union's support of the election of a series of Socialist party representatives to county, prefectural, and national assemblies as well as to the mayoral office in Noda. All of this had the effect of severing the close ties that had been maintained between Kikkoman and the town of Noda for half a century.

The third effect of democratization came in the form of anti-monopoly hearings called to investigate the reasons for Kikkoman's overwhelmingly large share of the soy sauce market, its price-fixing and market-sharing agreements with other manufacturers, and certain of its selling arrangements with wholesalers and retailers. These hearings prompted the company to reorganize its sales and marketing practices, internationalize its operations, and diversify its product line.

Democratization of the Family

The Japanese stem family is a patrilineal household organized for perpetuity around common property, genealogy, and ceremony. Stem families were encouraged legally in Japan by repeated government pronouncements, beginning in 1675, as a preventative measure against land fragmentation.[1] The result was that lineages based on the access, use, and preservation of common resources became frequent after the seventeenth century. Common ownership of resources meant realistically that the main or head household controlled most of the land, tools, and technology required for farming or for other property-based endeavors, and that branch households, when they were permitted to form, were allowed some degree of access to and use of the lineage's "common" resources. Over time there appears to have been an almost inevitable attenuation of the power of the main household and, therefore, of its exclusive ability to dispose of the lineage's common resources. Particularly able household heads could arrest the relaxation of a main household's control, however; under such men the authority of the main house was reinforced and even expanded over and against that of subordinate households.

This process of household division of resources, on the one hand, and household consolidation or delegation of power and authority, on the other, was repeated with unrecorded frequency in Japan until the end of World War II and the Occupation. The Allies, which meant primarily the Americans, sought to undo the absolute legal authority of the household head and the age-related as well as sex-related biases that were part of the prewar family system. In the Occupation view of Japanese culture, the ie system allowed household heads an unwarranted amount of civil and moral authority over their children, other household members, and relatives.

Just as this authority tended to be absolute within a lineage group organized around a system of common property, so too the same authority was extended to the emperor of Japan in his assertions of headship over all Japanese. His claims were based upon the nationalization of land that occurred in the name of the emperor after the Meiji Restoration of 1868. As a result, the entire country was united under the emperor, who was both landowner and householder over everything and everyone. Propaganda in schools and in the military inculcated a belief in the common identity of all Japanese, based in part on theories of racial superiority and in part on assertions of common household origin emanating from the imperial headship.

Such assertions were reinforced in the Civil Code of the Meiji Period (1868–1911). For example, families with specific farming plots were identified through the land tax law. These families were responsible for much more than the payment of taxes on their holdings. They were legally responsible as householders and landholders within the imperial sovereignty for the public as well as private behavior of anyone who happened to be on their soil. Viewed this way, families were much more than single institutions of civil society: they were the cornerstone of a society in which civil as well as moral responsibility and authority were combined, and they were wholly incorporated, at least in theory, within the apparatus of the imperial state in prewar Japan. Thus, families were omnibus institutions that spliced the natural and powerful claims of parents over their offspring with the customary authority accorded to a household head in a land-based lineage system. These parental claims were buttressed, in turn, by political and economic rights under the civil code. By consolidating the authority of a household head in this way and by aligning this authority with the absolute power of the emperor, the family system can be fairly said to be a crucial foundation of society and state in Japan before World War II.

The use, by analogy, of such family-based authority within industrial enterprises of prewar Japan was common. After the Great Strike of 1927–28, the Noda Shōyu Company practiced a familylike management ideology and style. The domination of the top positions in the firm by members of the Mogi-Takanashi families helps account for this. Even more important than this organizational rationale for family authority were the efforts of the Mogi-Takanashis to articulate consciously an ideological function for the company within the overarching imperial mission. In the end, such a family-owned and operated enterprise as Kikkoman could expect and did receive outstanding performance from its workers, in large measure because of the close conjunction of structure and ideology.

The Occupation changed all that by making equality and not hierarchy the basis of society. The individual rather than the household became the locus of legal responsibility. Male-centered inheritance and family headship were eliminated, and this removed much of the institutional inequality in the status and rights of women. By abrogating the household-centered ideology of the preceding three-quarters of a century, an end could be brought to the provision of successors to households (conceived as enduring corporate structures) through such practices as temporary headship (*inkyo*) and adoption (*yōshi*), rather than through the transfer of property to individuals, most often one's natural descendants. In such ways the absolute power of the household head was replaced by parental obligation and a much reduced civil authority of parent over child. Occupation authorities essentially legislated a transition from what might be called the institutional-imperial family of prewar Japan to the companionate family of the postwar period.[2] Hereafter, only a few spheres of family life would be regulated by law.

These changes were imposed, not evolved from within. The resistance and occasional lack of cooperation of government officials, as well as private citizens, to Occupation policies (or, more precisely, to their implementation) made it doubtful that the practical intent of the law often took precedence over the actual letter of the law. But in terms of the written law at least, the moral basis or foundation of the former family system was expunged and the practices and concepts underlying that system were outlawed.

There is no doubt that with time the new democratic family began to take root, especially among younger Japanese. A public opinion survey conducted by the Office of the Prime Minister in September 1956 shows a weakening of support for the old-style family, especially with regard to the institutional devices by which the prewar family had been able to muster absolute legal, political, moral, and emotional authority over its members. To the question of whether one supported the traditional stem family as an institution, varying degrees of support were discovered among different age groups in the population (see table 25).

Before World War II the family system provided Noda Shōyu not only heirs and successors to manage corporate resources (93 percent of which were closely held either by the Mogi-Takanashi families directly or by these same families indirectly through a holding company), it also allowed for the patriarchal and paternalistic supervision of the company's employees by top management. The democratization of the family changed this in three principal ways. First, holding companies

TABLE 25. Support for the traditional household (ie) as an institution (percent in support of certain propositions shown), 1956.

Age group	Continuity of the household	Concentration of power in selected family members	Maintenance of property through successive generations
20-year-olds	56	13	18
30-year olds	69	16	27
40-year-olds	81	26	34
50-year-olds	85	32	40
60 years & older	91	32	44

Source: Morioka Kiyomi and Yamane Tsuneo, eds., *Ie to Gendai Kazoku* (Tokyo: Baifukan, 1976), p. 282.

were outlawed. (Actually, the Occupation policy of what is generally called "zaibatsu-busting" was largely responsible for the dismembering of holding companies, but this policy would not have had much effect without the parallel policy to democratize the family. This was necessary in view of the way that families, by use of the laws of household succession and inheritance, were able to hoard corporate resources separately from those manipulated through a holding company.)

In the case of the Senshusha holding company, which controlled a majority of the assets of Kikkoman before the war, Imperial Edict 567 of 1946 froze and eventually forced the liquidation of the Senshusha's nearly two-thirds share in the company, while new family inheritance and successor laws interdicted the undivided accumulation of the almost one-third share by the designated heirs of the Mogi-Takanashi families. Imperial Edict 567 required those enterprises designated as "restricted concerns"—in effect, all companies with a capitalization of 5 million yen or more—to divest themselves of shares in other companies.[3]

Second, the aspirations and actions of members of the Mogi-Takanashi families changed as a result of the Occupation policy of democratization. Lineage and household heads no longer enjoyed unquestioning obedience. They could no longer decide on career choices, marriage partners, and patterns of succession for their offspring. They could no longer pass on an undivided estate to a single heir in the interest of preserving and concentrating capital, nor could they exclude women from inheritance and succession. In short, they had lost much of their power to husband the family's resources and manage them as if the family were a firm—a corporate entity in which property counted for more than people.

The declining ability of a household head to control family resources was matched by the changing values of family members, especially by their rising sense of egalitarianism. In particular, younger family members, those educated after the war and not socialized into the traditional family system, were reluctant to accept the dominance and submission that it demanded. Not surprisingly, the frequency of interlineage marriage and adoptions, by which the Mogi-Takanashi families had been able to control succession and maintain the continuity of management personnel and power within the lineage system, dropped remarkably. Only two cases of interfamily marriage or adoption have been recorded in the postwar period, in contrast with forty-six such events between 1738 and 1938 (one every four and a third years). The sharp break with past practice is indisputable. In the new era of the democratic family, the kinship system has been directed away from the promotion of social and economic solidarity, the protection of property, and the continuity of family enterprise—the primary concerns of the stem family during most of the prewar years.

Yet the demise of the stem family and the rise of the egalitarian family has not signaled, at least in the one short generation since 1945, a loss of managerial talent flowing from the Mogi-Takanashi families to Noda Shōyu. Because these families still retain one-quarter ownership in the firm (shares that were held separately from the Senshusha, see table 26) and because a fast-track career within Kikkoman is more attractive than an otherwise slow promotion into Japan's geriatric leadership, the scions of the Mogi-Takanashi families in Noda still enter the company in reliable fashion. There, by virtue of birth alone, their chances for success are good.

Not content with such odds, however, most of these sons (daughters

TABLE 26. The top ten shareholders in Kikkoman in 1955.

Name	Number of shares	Percent of total shares
Mogi Saheiji	695,200	4.35
Takanashi Koichirō	550,000	3.44
Mitsubishi Trust Bank	500,000	3.13
Senshusha Company	500,000	3.13
Mogi Katsumi (Kashiwa head)	484,300	3.02
Mogi Shichizaemon	410,000	2.65
Noda Institute of Industrial Science	368,550	2.56
Kofukan Foundation	360,000	2.25
Meiji Mutual Insurance Co.	300,000	1.87
Mogi Yuri (Kashiwa spouse)	238,000	1.48
total	4,406,050	27.88

Source: *Kikkoman Annual Report to Shareholders*, 1955.

are still excluded from significant managerial careers outside of the family) add a graduate degree in business or economics at the best Japanese and American universities to their already impressive undergraduate educations in Japan. Because of the large number of Mogi-Takanashi families connected with the firm, achievement must be added to the lineal status of sons in order to ensure them an opportunity at a top position. The combination of ascription and achievement has resulted in rapid promotion for the continuity of family management at Kikkoman in spite of the greatly reduced degree of family ownership since the war.

Doubt remains over how long family control of ownership and management can persist. The demand for outside capital to finance Kikkoman's ambitious diversification efforts and possible reluctance of the current crop of Mogi-Takanashi adolescents to follow the time-honored but conventional path to management blazed by some dozen generations of ancestors raise questions about the viability of Kikkoman as a family firm in the twenty-first century.

A third way in which democratization of the family in postwar Japan has affected management policies lies in the manner that it induced an ideological revolution of sorts in large enterprises' supervision and motivation of employees. Obedience to hierarchy and a quiet dedication to productivity were hallmarks of employee performance at the Noda Shōyu Company from 1930 to 1945. But these were predicated on patriotic zeal in view of the ideological connection between work in the breweries of Kikkoman and Japan's imperial mission in East Asia. Loyalty to the company was equated with loyalty to country.

Since the war, the entire ideological scaffolding on which the country's remarkable prewar performance was based has been dismantled. Demythologizing the emperor removed the final and essential element in a national hierarchy of loyal Japanese. The household head, be he the emperor, the corporate chief executive officer, or the patriarch of a lineage association, no longer claims or exerts legal and moral authority over those beneath him. Although patriarchal attitudes (and policies) may not have disappeared altogether, their absolutistic basis has been removed and an egalitarian ethic is relentlessly replacing it.

Unionization—Within and Without the Noda Factories

The first labor unions formed at Kikkoman after the war were instituted in January 1946 at the Kansai plant in Western Japan and the following month at the Noda plants in the hinterland of Tokyo. Neither was aligned with the other nor identified with any larger union movement. In October 1949 a liaison committee between the two unions was formed, and in 1957 a single unified union representing soy sauce workers in all the Kikkoman plants was forged.

The top-down democratization of Japan encouraged the labor union movement, among other programs, to open up economic opportunity and to liberalize the economic structure. In 1946, with the encouragement of the Supreme Command of the Allied Powers (SCAP), the Japanese government passed three laws that provided a powerful legal basis for the formation and function of unions: the Labor Union Law; the Labor Standards Law; and the Labor Mediation Law. Under such patronage, the early union movement flourished, as did the Socialist and Communist parties. By the end of December 1945, 509 labor union associations had formed, claiming 380,677 members. A year later the figures stood at 10,700 unions and 4,900,000 members.[4]

The two most powerful unions were the General Federation of Labor, or Sōdōmei, a revival of the prewar Yūaikai-Sōdōmei under Matsuoka Komakichi, which had ties to the right-leaning Social Democratic Party; and the National Congress of Industrial Labor Unions, or Sanbetsu (Zen-Nippon Sangyōbetsu Rōdō Kumiai Kaigi), which had an association with the Communist Party. In 1946 the Sōdōmei claimed 1,699 unions with 855,399 members; the Sanbetsu listed only 111 unions but with 1,550,961 members.[5]

The Noda unions were affiliated with neither the Sōdōmei nor Sanbetsu at first; but by August 1947 they had joined the former. The Sōdōmei's strength was in prefectural union associations and light industry, while Sanbetsu was strongest with government workers, miners, and laborers in heavy industry. In the beginning three different groups of workers within Kikkoman contended for control of the union in Noda. Significantly, two of the three were composed of supervisory workers (foremen and section leaders), and only one of production line personnel. After considerable discussion and bickering, the groups agreed to form a single labor association, even if it would be initially and rather overwhelmingly under the control of supervisory workers.

When the Noda Shōyu Labor Union was formed on February 9, 1946, it claimed 1,813 members—80 percent of the blue-collar work force. In its first formal statement, the union stated the following goals: we will be independent; we will work for everyone's benefit; we will shed destructive ideas and nourish a mutually beneficial ideology; we will unite and work together.[6] Within two weeks of its establishment the union negotiated and won major concessions on ten demands concentrated in three areas: wages; participation in management; and union prerogatives in matters of hiring, firing, and work conditions. By these negotiations, wages were immediately increased by 45 percent, with an additional 8⅓ percent salary increment for food, and two labor-management committees were formed, one for sharing information relating to economic and business conditions and one for mutually resolving matters of work conditions. The latter included an agreement that required the union's consent for layoffs and dismissals.[7] There was little doubt that working conditions for soy sauce workers improved in Noda as the labor union movement spread and intensified.

In spite of these impressive gains, union leadership in the formative period of the union movement can hardly be described as typical. Umeda Isao, the first leader of the local, held a Ph.D. in Agricultural Sciences and was director of the corporation's research and development laboratory. Okada Shirō, his almost immediate successor, lacked a university education but had been plant manager of several soy sauce breweries in Noda. Under Okada, the local avoided Sanbetsu efforts to organize the Noda labor association as an industry-based union within the national foods industry. Yet even as Noda rejected Sanbetsu's overtures, the local garnered its first political victory when one of the candidates it backed won a seat on the prefectural assembly, seven more were elected to the Noda City Council, and sixteen out of twenty to the Regional Township Association. It was not until June 1949, and the election of Yokozeni Jukichi to the headship of the Noda union, that the atypical character of the union's leadership changed. Barely an elementary school graduate, Yokozeni possessed a political savvy and skill that any politico would envy. He had worked his way up through the ranks of the blue-collar work force at Kikkoman by a combination of a gritty effort while on the job and by taking advantage of the educational courses offered to employees by the company after work hours.

Yokozeni worked quickly to consolidate his control over the union and to secure the place of the local union within the larger political arena. In February 1949 he had joined the Socialist Party and by March had been elected one of its representatives to the Prefectural Assembly. In August 1949 the Association of Labor Unions in Chiba Prefecture was formed and Yokozeni was elected its deputy head. That same month membership criteria in the Noda Shōyu Labor Union were clarified; section heads and assistant section heads in offices and factory foremen and assistant factory foremen in the breweries were excluded from membership. This swung the balance of power within the union to nonsupervisory personnel for the first time. In October the union associations representing Kikkoman employees in Eastern and Western Japan merged with Yokozeni as the head of the amalgamated association. Finally, in November 1949, Yokozeni was appointed as the head representative of the Sōdōmei in Chiba Prefecture. In less than a year he had been elected to the Prefectural Assembly, had taken over the Noda Shōyu Labor Union, had become the second-in-charge of the

Consolidated Labor Union Association of Chiba Prefecture, had organized the All Kikkoman Labor Union and then become its head, and had been appointed the chief representative in the prefecture of the largest federation of combined unions in the country.

In the course of the next year (1950–51), Yokozeni successfully led a campaign for the equal treatment of union and nonunion regular employees in matters of wages and fringe benefits. This campaign, called "Shakō Ipponka" (Normalization of White- and Blue-Collar Employment), exerted pressure on the company to pay all employees according to a combination of seniority and experience and to equalize health, retirement, and fringe benefits. The campaign coincided in timing and content with similar union efforts nationwide that resulted in significant gains for unions throughout Japan.

Even for a man of Yokozeni's ambition and talents it took some time to digest these gains, and it was not until 1953 that he actively pursued new offices. That year the union advanced him as a candidate for the national assembly (a bid that eventually failed, mostly because of the lackluster support he received from the Socialist Party in Chiba Prefecture). In March 1954 Yokozeni moved from the mainstream to the left-wing faction of the Socialist Party. He then pulled the Kikkoman union out of Sōdōmei and joined it with the independent National Food and Beverage Workers Union, which had been established one year earlier by the United Beer Workers Union. Upon executing these maneuvers—securing an independent political base within the newly found Food and Beverage Workers Union and taking this power with him to the left wing of the Socialist Party—Yokozeni ran successfully as a Socialist Party candidate from Chiba Prefecture for the National Assembly in 1954.

In the February General Elections of 1955, however, the Noda Shōyu union, along with the unions of Nihon Kentetsu, Kawasaki Seitetsu, and Nihon Parupu (all in the First District of Chiba Prefecture), were implicated in a voting fraud scandal. As a result, Yokozeni, along with the assistant head and union secretary, resigned and a new group of union officers were appointed.

Effect of Unionization upon the Company

The emergence of an independent and active labor union within the Noda Shōyu Company had two immediate and fundamental results: the formalization of rules to run the organization; and a higher total wage cost to the company than would otherwise have been the case. Both of these were well foreshadowed in the *Labor Agreement* of 1950 between the union and company.[8] Article 4 of this document stated that "the company in exercising these actions and responsibilities (the rights of management) will attempt to reflect as much as possible the will of the members of the union." Yet, because as Article 9 stipulated, the company had become a "union-shop," not open to employment for nonunion members, "reflecting the will of the members of the union" meant reflecting the will of all employees below the level of assistant department and section heads. Thus, the company was required to seek the formal approval of most employees, represented by the union, in order to exercise the rights of management.

Admittedly, some sort of tacit and informal bond already existed between the company and its regular employees and thereby limited the degree of freedom that management enjoyed in exercising its decisions. Since the Great Strike of 1927–28 the company had labored to inculcate not only feelings of reciprocity between nonsupervisory and supervisory employees but actual cooperation through participatory labor-management committees as well.

The postwar difference was the extent of formalization with which that bond or compact was expressed. The circumstances of cooperation were standardized in a way that was previously inconceivable. This was revealed most strikingly in the workings of the Labor Council. Article 16 of the *Labor Agreement* established a Labor Council composed of thirty persons, half from the company and half from the union. Its purpose was to discuss alterations of working conditions in the company and negotiations of disputes over those alterations. According to Article 18, fundamental matters relating to the welfare of the union members fell into the domain of the Labor Council as did "any matters deemed appropriate for discussion by the Labor Council." Article 37 enjoined the company to discuss in advance with the Labor Council any disciplinary action of an employee, and any employee who objected to his/her treatment by the company would raise an objection through the offices of the union that would find its way back to the Labor Council.

After 1950 all areas and matters of employment within the company were subject to specification as well as to negotiation, a far cry from the prewar company-dominated consensus of management and labor. The legalization of the labor union, the drafting of a *Labor Agreement*, the formation of a Labor Council within the company, and the formalization of all aspects of employment were all new initiatives. The total effect of such formalization went beyond mere organizational change: how an employee thought, behaved, and, most important, believed changed as well. Formalization exaggerated the tendency toward egalitarianism within the company. Egalitarianism was not new, but its motive was.

Prewar egalitarianism was noneconomic. Its intent was not to equalize the economic interests of company employees—although that did occur to a degree—but to widen membership in the firm's corporate character. The work-related contributions of regular employees, regardless of value and rank, were cloaked in the idiom of family service. The firm became like a family in spirit, and all its employees, like all the members of a family, shared equally in its success. But postwar egalitarianism was and is different, installed as it was by Occupation fiat and derived as it is from Western political theory. It is part of the great historical tradition of what is called enlightened self-interest, and it is the very juxtaposition of self-interest between the company and the employee that distinguishes prewar and postwar working attitudes.

Self-interest in the abstract has little meaning, but self-interest as expressed in rules, codes, and codicils to labor agreements takes on concrete meaning. When a worker learns that he or she, through the union, can change the company's hours of operation to suit his or her needs better (Article 59), that is self-interest. Or when an employee is able to influence the company to provide recreational or educational facilities for workers that would otherwise not be available, that, too, is self-interest. Self-interest in postwar Japan is defined as that frame of mind wherein employees weigh in a very conscious manner what they receive in the way of compensation and promotion against what they give in the way of their work, dedication, and spirit of labor. Self-interest of this sort did not define prewar employment at Noda Shōyu after 1930 but has become a noticeable feature of employment since World War II.

The other major impact of the union on the company was to increase the total cost of labor. The company was required to establish and staff committees, divert personnel, build nonproductive facilities, and generally to invest resources where it would have been otherwise unlikely to do so. More specifically, the *Labor Agreement* permitted up to nine company employees who were concurrently union officers to devote themselves full-time to union business while on the company payroll (Article 12). Various buildings, equipment, and other tangible resources owned by the company could be used by the union without charge (Article 13). The union could object to the employment of anyone hired by the company (Article 24); it had to be consulted when anyone was to be discharged (Article 26). The company was required to reemploy most persons who had been on leave, even for a long time, and could not terminate the employment of someone who accepted an appointment in the public sector (Articles 33 and 34). The company was compelled to continue the employment of those reaching retirement age for up to an additional two years if the employee so desired (Article 42). Female employees over eighteen years of age were forbidden to work excessive hours or on holidays (Article 65). In these articles and in many other areas the company was constrained in its employment practices in the postwar period in ways never known before.

In retrospect, the Yokozeni period of leadership of the Noda Soy Sauce Workers Union from 1949 to 1955 was an era of remarkable accomplishment. What had been essentially a loose association of supervisory and nonsupervisory workers under the uninspired leadership of Umeda and Okada was transformed into a labor union movement of political claw and economic sinew. If the Occupation policy to democratization had meaning for workers, it was realized through labor unions that gained important wage, work, and fringe benefit concessions from companies, catapulted people into office who were more than sympathetic to the interests of labor, and provided leverage to compete with big business and big government, both of which had been long entrenched in power since before the war. If political pluralism was a desired manifestation of democracy, then the labor union movement at Kikkoman, a product of the Occupation policy of democratization, granted power and position to a large segment of the population that had been previously excluded from their exercise.

The most compelling examples of the union's growing power, however, occurred long after the Occupation. In 1959–60 the union found itself strong enough in Noda and secure enough within the newly established Churitsurōren (Federation of Neutral Labor Unions) to resort first to work slowdowns and next to strikes to force the company to grant concessions. During the 1960s three main types of concessions were sought: level of compensation, retirement benefits, and age of retirement. Although the company and union bickered over these matters, the differences were more matters of degree rather than of kind. Company and union had reached a sort of compromise where each recognized the existence and strength of the other. This tacit compromise, however, probably owed as much to a prolonged period of high annual rates of growth in per-capita income and per-capita national product as it did to any eagerness of company and union to get along with one another.

Company and Community after 1962

If company and union seemed to be on the road to peaceful coexistence, company and community did not. In 1962 the Spring Labor Offensive (a fairly routine annual spring "struggle" wherein one or another of the larger labor federations demonstrates for pay increases and larger summer and year-end bonuses) coincided with the local Noda township elections. Through the efforts of the Kikkoman union, Shinmura Katsuo (who had been the *sonchō*, or district headman, of nearby

Fukuda Village) was elected mayor of Noda. Shinmura's victory was the first of a half-dozen or so mayoral seats to go to the Socialist Party in Chiba Prefecture during that decade. He was also the first mayor of Noda in the twentieth century who had not been a Kikkoman employee.

In the April elections of 1966, of the twelve Socialist candidates for city council (six of whom were from the union), eleven were elected (five from the union), thereby strengthening Shinmura's position. The domination of city government since 1966 by members of the Socialist Party drove a wedge into what had been a nearly inseparable association of company and community for almost half a century. Some might argue that the relationship had been one of company dominance and community dependence, but no one would deny its closeness. After 1966, however, Shinmura, perhaps partly to repay the company for its opposition to his election and perhaps in part because of his conviction that modernization of the town's politics required the separation of corporation and community, undertook a course of action designed to wean the community from reliance on the Kikkoman Shōyu Company. The waterworks, built by the company in 1923, was taken over as a municipal public utility, as were the community library and maintenance of the dikes protecting the town from the Tone and Edo rivers. The company discontinued operation of its own fire station unit at this time. More of the upkeep of the local temples and shrines was assumed by the town. A city-backed nursery and day-care center was opened, albeit on land owned by the Mogis. The town's major hospital and park, more expensive to take over and to operate, were left in the hands of the company or the Senshusha.

Perhaps the best example of the schism between company and community that developed while Shinmura was mayor was the decision to build a new 1,500-seat civic auditorium and cultural center on the outskirts of Noda. The erection of this cultural palace was more symbolic than anything else, since an entirely adequate and well-loved cultural center, the Kofukan, already stood in the center of town—a gift from Kikkoman in 1929 and still subsidized by the company through a combination of endowment funds and outright grants for over 90 percent of its operating budget. The Kofukan housed civic meetings, provided space for the town library, was regularly used by twenty-three civic and cultural groups, and engaged extensively in the education of the young through an in-house private foundation that provided scholarship programs, tutorials, and block grants to schools.[9]

The Socialist government in Noda, however, thought it was bad for the town's image to be so reliant on Kikkoman or institutions closely identified with the firm. Shinmura was embarrassed that so many activities that would normally take place in public town halls and institutions free of private attachments, in Noda were held in buildings and programs supported by a private—and what was worse, capitalist—company. Hence, the town's new civic and cultural center was built at great expense and maintained at considerable annual deficit to the municipal budget. Fortunately (or unfortunately) for the image of Noda, use of the old but more convenient downtown cultural center has not fallen off while the new suburban center seems to be gradually establishing its own position and role in community affairs. Now, instead of being identified exclusively with soy sauce, Noda is beginning to be thought of as a town of polish and education.

Antitrust and Business Strategy

Just as the question of democratization raised concerns over the excessive concentration of corporate power in Noda Shōyu's relations with Noda, so too the same sorts of concerns were at issue when Kikkoman's predominant market power became a focus of antitrust inquiries in 1951, 1954, 1957, and several occasions in the 1960s. In the 1950s price fixing among competitors was at issue, and during the 1960s Kikkoman's position as a price leader for the industry and the company's efforts to move more directly into the marketing of its products were construed as evidence of excessive market power.

In all of the actions against the Noda Shōyu Company the Japanese Fair Trade Commission (FTC) was guided by the Occupation policy of democratization. The Americans wished to create an open, competitive market with reasonable opportunity for entry into all of the product markets of a modern industrial economy. The primary method for doing this was to break up the concentration of ownership of the means of production that had, in the American view, characterized Japan's prewar, zaibatsu-centered economy. Deconcentration of ownership was in itself not a guarantee of free and open markets. Both deconcentration and democratization of markets were essential for Occupation policies to succeed. The deconcentrating of economic power among a handful of zaibatsu families was carried out during the Occupation itself, while the guaranteeing of free and open markets was left to the Japanese FTC for enforcement as a legacy of the Occupation period.

Both of these legal programs found their justification in laws passed by the Japanese Diet in 1947 with the encouragement of the American Occupation government: the Antimonopoly Act (Shiteki Dokusen no Kinshi oyobi Torihiki no Kakuho ni kansuru Hōritsu, or Law Concerning the Prohibition of Private Monopolies and the Maintenance of Fair Trade, and the Deconcentration Law (Kado Keizairyoku Shūchū Haijohō, Law for the Elimination of Excessive Concentration of Economic Power). If vigorously enforced, the democratization law could have dismembered the large combines of Japanese enterprises. Not surprisingly, it was repealed in 1955, a scant three years after the American Occupation ended.

In January 1951 the price of soy sauce, subject to government regulation by the Price Control Board, was allowed to rise to 56 yen per shō (1.8 liters) on the retail market. Noda Shōyu Company and three other major makers (Yamasa, Higeta, Marukin) met to discuss the adequacy of this price and, finding it wanting, petitioned the Price Control Board to raise the price to 80 yen per shō. The Board was unwilling to go so far, but it did allow a price of up to 75 yen per shō to be charged for the best-quality soy sauce and an average price of 70 yen per shō for soy sauces of lesser quality. These four makers advised their wholesalers and retailers to raise their prices accordingly. Thereafter, the manufacturers checked periodically to ascertain the price at which their soy sauce was sold in the marketplace. The Soy Sauce Manufacturers Association, following the lead of the big four, established a policy outlining maximum but not minimum price levels and suggesting a maximum price of 75 yen per shō for the best-quality soy sauce.[10]

In June 1951 the three other makers came to Noda for a meeting with Kikkoman where it was agreed that their average price to wholesalers should be 61 yen per shō and their average price to retailers and consumers should be 64 yen and 75 yen per shō, respectively. They maintained this agreement until October of the same year when they were told to desist by the Japanese Fair Trade Commission.

The four largest manufacturers, including Kikkoman, did not deny that they had fixed prices, but they did deny that it was done to the detriment of the consumer. They claimed their agreement was to set maximum prices for their products. Antimonopoly regulations had been developed, they argued, to protect consumers from manufacturers who overcharged; such manufacturers fixed minimum prices. The big four makers asserted that their actions could not harm competition in the marketplace because it was already restricted by the 75-yen maximum price suggested by the Price Control Board. The soy sauce producers, while not repudiating their collusive agreements, denied that a deleterious effect resulted from them. The intent of their agreements was not to overcharge customers, but to prevent precisely that.

The Japanese FTC parried the manufacturers' arguments by insisting that the monopolistic power needed to fix maximum prices was the same as that necessary to set minimum prices. Excessively concentrated economic power was undesirable in whatever form it took, and interference with the market mechanism, no matter its nature, was unjustified. The FTC assumed, therefore, that the companies in question, if they acted cooperatively, exercised undeniable and undesirable power over the soy sauce market. It produced statistics showing that the big four enjoyed a cumulative market share of over 20 percent in 1949, which was considered the point above which excessive market power became evident. (The same statistics showed, however, that the market share of the four major producers had in fact declined in the postwar as compared to the prewar period. See table 27.)

The FTC felt that the involvement of the Price Control Board in the setting of appropriate price levels with the advice of the soy sauce manufacturers did not justify their collusion on the matter of prices. The Board's administrative guidance was not law, not a substitute for antitrust legislation, and not a justification for makers to fix prices. At the close of 1951 the FTC found Kikkoman and the three other soy sauce manufacturers guilty of sharing information concerning the costs of production and of distribution, of establishing pricing agreements among themselves, and of sharing information that affected the pricing of soy sauce for the consumer market. They were ordered to stop such practices.

The 1954 antimonopoly probes were directed more at Kikkoman than the other major producers, since the Noda Shōyu Company was the only manufacturer with enough market power to influence nationwide prices for soy sauce through the example it set as the industry price-leader. The FTC held that it was absolutely disadvantageous for the other makers to have their prices higher or lower than Kikkoman's. They could neither outproduce Kikkoman and thereby enjoy a cost per unit advantage, nor could they afford to price their product lower and therefore advertise to the public that their soy sauce was inferior to the Kikkoman brand. Brand, price, and quality were so completely intertwined in the public's mind that no producer was willing to price its goods lower than Kikkoman and risk having its soy sauce considered inferior.

In addition to price leadership, the FTC found that Kikkoman's ability to affect the resale price of its product in the retail market was extreme and absolute. This was because manufacturers assumed the freight costs of sending soy sauce from the factory to the station nearest its exclusive wholesalers in various cities and towns. Consequently, price to wholesalers was nationally uniform regardless of the distance of markets from factories. In the postwar period in Tokyo, for example, the twelve wholesalers that handled the four major brands had formed the Tokyo Shōyu Wholesalers Association (a continuation of the prewar body by the same name). Under the wholesalers in Tokyo, were twenty to thirty jobbers. The main work of the wholesalers and jobbers

TABLE 27. Market concentration in the soy sauce industry, 1937 and 1949.

Rank	Company name	Production[a]	Market share (percent)	Accumulated market share (percent)
		1937		
1	Noda Shōyu	412	12.6	12.6
2	Yamasa Shōyu	139	4.2	16.8
3	Choshi Shōyu (Higeta)	108	3.3	20.1
4	Marukin Shōyu	80	2.4	22.5
5	Tatsuno Shōyu	70	2.1	24.7
6	Shoda Shōyu	27	0.8	25.5
7	Kinoene Shōyu	24	0.7	26.2
8	Funayama Shōyu	22	0.7	26.9
9	Chokai Shōyu	22	0.7	27.6
10	Tsuboya Shōyu	22	0.7	28.2
	total national production	3,285		
	total number of producers	7,000		
		1949		
1	Noda Shōyu	372	10.9	10.9
2	Marukin Shōyu[b]	156	4.6	15.5
3	Yamasa Shōyu	98	2.8	18.3
4	Choshi Shōyu	82	2.4	20.7
5	Tatsuno Shōyu	29	0.9	21.6
6	Shoda Shōyu	28	0.8	22.4
7	Funayama Shōyu	26	0.8	23.2
8	Nihon Chomiryō	21	0.6	23.8
9	Wadakan Shokuryō	18	0.5	24.3
10	Nihon Shōyu	18	0.5	24.8
	total national production	3,426		

Source: Kōsei Torihiki Iinkai Chōsabuhen, *Nihon ni okeru Keizairyoku Shūchū no Jittai* (Tokyo: Jitsugyo no Nihonsha, 1951).

a. Unit = 1,000 *koku* or 47,600 gallons.

b. Chemically manufactured rather than naturally brewed soy sauce, using amino acids and hydrolyzed fats.

in fact was not the distribution of shōyu in Tokyo but the collecting of orders and of payments for deliveries from the city's more than five thousand main retail outlets for soy sauce. These were for the most part wine and liquor stores, some department stores, and food shops. In 1953, 95 percent of Kikkoman and 90 percent of all major brands were sold in this way; only 5 to 10 percent was sold through specialty shops selling miso, seaweed, or other such items.

Although the Tokyo wholesalers placed orders with manufacturers, makers shipped directly to retailers. Because the price of shōyu was uniform no matter the distance of markets from factories, and because manufacturers shipped from 90 to 95 percent, depending on the brand, of their product directly to retail outlets in Tokyo, the retail price suggested as appropriate by manufacturers became in effect the selling price for shōyu to the nation's housewives. Thus, price leadership became price control.[11]

The FTC averred that Kikkoman was well aware of the way its actions affected the market for soy sauce and that it acted accordingly. In other words, in setting its prices, Noda Shōyu determined the prices not only for its own but also for all other manufacturers. The company was aware of this if for no other reason than because several of its employees were engaged continuously in visiting retailers in Tokyo to check, among other things, on the prices they charged. Thus, the FTC found that Kikkoman enjoyed what amounted to a private monopoly in the Tokyo area.

The FTC findings in 1954 and 1957 were clear enough, but the means of correcting excessive market control were less certain. Little changed in Kikkoman's relations with other makers and with distributors until the next decade, and even then, the changes were less the result of antimonopoly law than a shift in Kikkoman's corporate strategy.

Although nothing was said about them during the FTC hearings in the 1950s, the soy sauce manufacturers harbored other, and to them more compelling, reasons for their collective behavior. The many varieties of soy sauce were a result of the widespread availability of acceptable raw materials, the ease of manufacture, and the array of local, regional, and even occupational taste preferences. In addition, chemically made unfermented soy sauces had proliferated during and after the war because of the difficulty of obtaining large quantities of good raw materials (soybeans, wheat, and salt) and the advantages of more rapid and less expensive production of soy sauce through the use of such techniques. For these two reasons, the big-four makers of fermented and semi-fermented soy sauces felt justified in making price-fixing arrangements.

Both Kikkoman and the Occupation were responsible in large part for the changes in the nature of soy sauce manufacture during and after the war. After 1939 the Japanese government controlled the price of shōyu in the marketplace, and after 1940 it required that defatted soybeans be substituted for whole ones in the manufacturing process. Once the traditional raw materials for manufacture became almost impossible to obtain in large quantity, makers began to experiment with alternative substances and methods.

Kikkoman led the way. At the end of the war it developed New-style Shōyu No. 1 (Shinshiki Ichigo Shōyu), which substituted copra presscake for soybeans. In 1948 Noda Shōyu introduced its semichemical shōyu (shinshiki shōyu). The company had felt compelled to develop and to popularize these newer methods because Occupation officials, as an answer to crop shortages, had recommended that soy sauce producers give up fermentation altogether in favor of the faster and less expensive process of mixing hydrochloric acid and hydrolyzed vegetable protein (HVP). This product, known in Japan since the 1920s, was not very common before the war because it lacked the satisfying flavor, aroma, and taste of naturally fermented shōyu. In 1945, in its ignorance, the Occupation had instructed that all soy sauce would henceforth be made using HVP and hydrochloric acid in the interest of conserving grains and of speeding up the processing and distribution of food seasonings.

By the 1950s, however, more traditional soy sauce makers were returning to fermentation as the principal process of producing good quality shōyu, the price of which had been deregulated by the Price Control Board in 1950. Brewers could hope to recover the expense of preparing a more time-consuming and better quality product by selling it at a higher price. Thus, price-fixing arrangements were justified as the only means whereby they and the consumer could be protected from poor imitations of their product. By guaranteeing a good quality shōyu of uniform taste at reasonable prices, the major makers believed they could repel the recent advances of chemical soy sauces and of local, miscellaneous brands. Because so much of the cost of fermented shōyu depended on the volatility of commodity markets for grains, especially during a period of rapid inflation of food prices in Japan, the big-four manufacturers believed their efforts to stabilize markets and prices were defensible.

In private, Kikkoman argued that if it had solely its own interests at heart, and not those of the industry and consumer, it would not have made public various major technological advances in soy sauce manufacture that it had pioneered between 1944 and 1951. These, like New-style Shōyu No. 1, were all proprietary discoveries involving fermentation, microbiological, and enzyme technology that had been developed in the Noda Shōyu research laboratories. The fact that these discoveries were freely published by Kikkoman was evidence that the company was as interested in furthering the general quality of soy sauce manufacture in Japan as with increasing profits.

That was the 1950s. During the 1960s the thrust of the FTC's investigation of Kikkoman changed. In these hearings the company's efforts at forward integration or moving into marketing and distribution outside of Tokyo by encouraging distributors to handle their products exclusively were held to be illegal. These hearings provide one of the clearest, yet in a way most inappropriate, examples of the Occupation legacy of democratization in the antitrust area.

The hearings involved the Kikkoman-Kai, an association of distributors (tokuyakuten) in the Osaka area who handled Kikkoman products exclusively, and in 1966 accounted for 31 percent of sales in the metropolitan area. In September 1967 Kikkoman told the group that it was raising the price of its product from the factory and asked them to raise the prices of the Kikkoman products they sold. In January 1968 Kikkoman further advised the distributors to increase the prices charged to their subsidiary jobbers for handling Kikkoman products.[12]

The FTC found in this case that Kikkoman had interfered in the pricing and marketing policies of an association of distributors who were not part of the corporation itself. This was in contradiction to Article 8, Clause 1, of Japan's antitrust laws, which prohibit any manufacturer from involvement in the pricing and marketing activities of an unrelated association in the distribution sector. If Kikkoman had owned the distribution network in question in Osaka—that is, if the company owned and operated the plant and equipment associated with the exclusive distribution of its products in Osaka—this would not have constituted a violation of antitrust regulation. Since Kikkoman-Kai was not part of the Kikkoman Corporation, however, the company's attempts to set prices and policies for the resale of its products on the wholesale and retail markets were illegal. If the Kikkoman-Kai had decided to raise prices, that was another matter; such a decision was within its appropriate economic functions and entirely legal.

The Kikkoman-Kai handled a large but not dominant share of Kikkoman's products in Osaka's metropolitan area. Because of this, it was not possible to accuse Kikkoman of using either a closed territory system (sole distributors with clearly defined territories) or a designated wholesaler system (where retailers purchase the manufacturer's product from only designated wholesalers)—practices that inhibited competition. Instead, what the FTC found objectionable was that the dominant manufacturer in the industry through the use of exclusive outlets was reducing the competition among distributors of their product in a presumed effort to keep prices high, and advising, if not informing, distributors of the appropriate wholesale/retail prices for their products. For a distributors' association to set uniform prices was in itself illegal, just as it was illegal to exclude other products from distribution (although both practices were quite common). For a manufacturer to abet and participate in such agreements was likewise a violation of antitrust policy. Accordingly, both the Kikkoman-Kai and the Kikkoman Corporation were reprimanded and ordered to stop such practices.

These examples of the Occupation policy of democratization as applied to antitrust regulation of monopolistic business practices seem simple enough. Kikkoman did not deny either its price-fixing activities with other manufacturers in the 1950s or its pricing and marketing agreements with distributors in the 1960s. In both cases the activities in question were not conceived or carried out covertly. Quite the contrary: the Noda Shōyu Company publicly revealed its intention of gaining some measure of control over the pricing and marketing of its products. Herein lies the inappropriateness of the FTC's rulings in these cases: it overlooked entirely the historical circumstances surrounding the distribution of most consumer products in Japan. These circumstances were quite different from those of the United States, which provided the context for the development and evolution of antitrust policy.

Background to Marketing Development

Kikkoman's efforts to develop a strong marketing network with uniform pricing policies can be traced back to the early efforts of the Noda soy sauce brewers to develop their own urban sales and distribution organization, independent of the powerful tonya associations that controlled marketing in most urban areas. The Noda associates' first efforts, the establishment of the Tokyo Shōyu Company in 1881, failed in bankruptcy caused by the excessive costs of setting up an entirely separate system of urban distribution as well as by opposition by the entrenched association of distribution agents. After this failure in 1889 an accommodation between the Noda brewers and the Tokyo wholesalers was reached, but it was never entirely satisfactory for the soy sauce makers, who realized that it was necessary to manage production as well as distribution of their product if they were to coordinate and control them effectively.

The opportunity to do both did not appear until the 1930s, when Noda Shōyu, along with the Yamasa and Higeta Shōyu companies, reached an agreement among themselves as well as with the Tokyo tonya group for a common pricing and marketing policy in which the producers, not the distributors, determined the prices and quantities of products to reach the market. By the 1960s Kikkoman and Yamasa in

Eastern Japan (the largest two makers in the country) had been co-operating on matters of price as well as distribution for three decades. This experience involved the other major maker in Eastern Japan as well, since Kikkoman had taken over Higeta soy sauce in 1936 and, although required to divest itself of this acquisition in the postwar period, has continued to market Higeta products through its own distribution network since 1966. In short, Kikkoman has long sought to avoid the monopoly over urban distribution enjoyed by the various wholesaling associations. Just when the company would appear to have gained some margin of success in this endeavor, however, the historical and cultural biases against an association between separate manufacturing and marketing enterprises—long evident in American antitrust regulation—prevented Kikkoman from realizing its long-held historical goals in this area.

Curiously enough, the failure of the Noda Shōyu Company to guarantee retail price maintenance for its soy sauce has had more of a detrimental effect on its rivals than on itself. This was because of Kikkoman's ability as the price and market-share leader in the industry to finance simultaneously a vigorous sales and marketing campaign for its soy sauce and to inaugurate a series of new ventures in a move to diversify its product line. Other Japanese soy sauce makers were not able to attempt that then nor are they able to do so now.

The Growth of Internationalization

Americans like to believe that the Occupation was successful. How else can one explain Japan's prosperity and prominence in the world today—just a short generation following what must be considered one of the most totally devastating physical and psychological defeats in modern history. Democratization has come to be recognized as the policy goal that guided and supported this radical transformation of the political, economic, and moral values and institutions of Japan.

The policy of democratization transformed the Noda Shōyu Company. With regard to firm and family relations, the Mogi-Takanashi families that have directed Kikkoman from the beginning lost both leverage and control within the firm. When the traditional stem family lost its legal and political prerogatives, its usefulness as an institution to manage family inheritance, succession, and power deteriorated. This undermined the ability of the Mogi-Takanashi families to control Kikkoman and the Senshusha holding company. Besides disallowing these institutional features, the democratization of the family required that a new ideological rationale be developed for Kikkoman—one that would provide incentives on the basis of equality rather than of hierarchy.

One measure of the difficulty encountered by the firm in the course of this conversion of the family was the emergence of an independent labor union movement. By the 1960s Kikkoman shared political and economic power with the union and the community to a degree unimaginable before World War II and the Occupation of Japan. Power was shared as well as diffused in new ways, and all of this acted to democratize both lifestyle and livelihood in Noda.

Effect of Exogenous Factors on Kikkoman

For all the apparent success of the Occupation of Japan and the democratization of Kikkoman, the question remains as to what difference these exogenous factors had on the company in the long run. The effect of the policy of democratization depends on which yardstick is applied. The question to be asked, it would seem, is what would have happened to Kikkoman without this Occupation policy. The answer, I think, is that very much the same sort of transformation of the company would have occurred—perhaps not as quickly or as completely, but nevertheless with the same overall direction and content. My belief is based not so much on conjecture as on empirical inference drawn from evidence of change already under way or likely to occur at Kikkoman. These changes appear to be part of a process of the internationalization of business practices worldwide.

In the area of family and firm there had been an obvious and growing separation of ownership and management at Kikkoman since 1925. Even before that time the trend could be discerned, but with the establishment of the Senshusha holding company in 1925, it became more clearly visible. Several things were happening at once. The growing size of the company—from roughly 1,000 employees in 1918 to 2,000 in 1925, to 3,000 in 1940, and to 4,000 in 1966—resulted in a reduction in the need for managerial resources and influence drawn from the Mogi-Takanashi families. At the same time, the increasing sophistication in managerial skill and experience represented in the growing ranks of middle- and upper-level company employees indicated a decreased need for family expertise. The appearance of new institutions other than family and lineage—such as cartel, corporation, and holding company—to carry out specialized economic functions signaled a decline in Kikkoman's dependence on the Mogi-Takanashi households. The involvement of such outside institutions as banks and investment firms also resulted in a contraction of what was required of the family.

The lessening of family function was paralleled by a reduction of family size, not only among the Mogi-Takanashi but across the country as well. The coresident nuclear household of a husband and wife living together on their own has become the norm in all economically advanced countries. Even in Japan, where the nuclear household accounted for just half of all households in 1900, by 1970 it represented three-quarters of the total.[13] In short, since the early twentieth century the control and especially the management of Kikkoman has been gradually but progressively transferred from familial to nonfamilial forms of organization. In this sense, the Occupation merely speeded up a process already well under way.

Much the same argument might be aimed at the issue of unions. Every advanced capitalist nation today has an industrial relations system in which unions play a large part and in which industrial relations law is based on positive rights guaranteed either to individual or to collective bodies. Although it is possible that such rights might not have been accorded individuals in Japan without the Occupation interlude, it is highly unlikely that collective bodies would have failed eventually to receive recognition of such rights. Indeed, something much like that already had occurred in prewar Japan when large companies established a system of permanent tenure for regular employees.

Regular employees of major Japanese corporations were so called because they enjoyed a range of benefits. These included the expectation of permanent employment with a firm (barring bankruptcy or some such catastrophe) and of a compensation scheme weighted heavily toward monetary reward calculated according to years on the job. Although these expectations never attained the status of legal rights in the prewar period, they did acquire a degree of entitlement among regular employees so that they were the equivalent of law—at least, customary law in large corporations. In effect, these entitlements represented a kind of contract—a compact or covenant, if you will—that an employer could break only with the greatest consequences.[14]

The Allied Occupation of Japan did little more than formalize these traditions for the regular employees of large firms. Regular workers in large corporations account for roughly 30 percent of the privately employed work force in Japan, and, not surprisingly, about 30 percent of Japanese workers are unionized. Moreover, 80 percent of these belong to so-called enterprise unions wherein employees are not organized on an industry or craft basis but instead on a company basis. Such unions are private in that they are not closely affiliated with any labor group outside of the company; since they enlist both shop and office workers, they are fairly inclusive within the enterprise, but they are definitely exclusive as well, refusing membership to all but an elite corp of workers—that is, the regular workers of large firms. In short, democratization speeded along the unionization of an already privileged minority of industrial employees.

Whether in the postwar or prewar period, benefits such as lifetime employment, seniority-based compensation, and extensive on-the-job training were possible only within periods of rapid economic growth for large corporations. Employment entitlements and economic advancement were irrevocably related to one another, and the correlation had little direct relationship with Occupation policy. Democratization has simply allowed the better-off workers in large firms to legalize their superior position in Japan's so-called dual economy or dual economic structure of large and small firms.

The extension of such entitlements to regular workers and then the subsequent imperilment of them in Noda can explain a good deal about postwar difficulties between company and community. At the end of the 1950s the production at Kikkoman underwent a basic change from what was essentially a large-batch, mechanically interrelated process to a nearly automated, continuous process technology. In this newer, more fluid process of manufacture, the basis for the special relationship of company and community was discarded: the mutual interdependence of the company's jobs and the community's skilled labor was broken.

In the current kōji incubation process, several tons of roasted wheat kernels and soybean grits are made into kōji semi-automatically in forty-eight hours' time in special, sealed culture rooms without the aid of human workers. Since 1966 one plant, Factory 7, has maintained thirty such kōji incubation process rooms. After germination the kōji is moved automatically by conveyor and elevator to the brewing vats for mash fermentation. Factory 7 has 2,100 fermentation vats, each producing 10,000 large bottles (1.8 liters) of soy sauce every eight months. Using the latest hydraulic presses, 90 percent of this is converted to either shōyu or shōyu oil, while the remaining 10 percent is sold as soymeal cake. As late as 1955 the conversion efficiency was 70 and not 90 percent.[15]

Besides these mechanical advances, the microbiological side of shōyu manufacture changed dramatically. Three changes were most notable: a high-temperature, short-duration method of cooking soybean flakes was developed, which not only was more economical and efficient but also resulted in 15 percent higher yield of protein in the final product (as measured by the total nitrogen utilization ratio); new, pure-culture strains of kōji molds and new lactic acid bacteria and yeasts to enhance brine fermentation were developed, which accelerated and improved the quality of fermentation; an increase in the use of defatted soybean flakes (in place of whole soybeans) reduced costs, speeded fermentation, and streamlined production (by decreasing shōyu oil as a by-product of the manufacturing process).

The overall effect of these and other innovations was a reduction in the inflation-adjusted cost as well as the fermentation period for shōyu production, while the percentage of nitrogen recovered in the shōyu from the breakdown of the raw materials reached 90 percent by 1975 (as compared to 60 percent in the 1930s and 75–80 percent in the 1960s).[16] This was accomplished without increasing the size of the work force. These advances, the result of scientific investigation and its application to fermentation, not only reduced the company's need for labor in the absolute sense but also lessened its dependence on skilled workers—those most attuned to the art rather than the science of shōyu production.

Because of these technological changes the company's need for manpower declined and its need for outside skilled labor (jukurenkō) dropped drastically relative to the demand for such workers in the previous three-quarters of a century. Not surprisingly, as the company's requirement for local manpower, both skilled and unskilled, declined, relations between company and community deteriorated, allowing for further estrangement under the series of Socialist mayors first elected in 1962.

The difference in timing between the rise to power of the union within the company and the rise to power of the Socialist Party within the community has been critical to the company's continued successful operation. Had the company faced a simultaneous barrage from both within and without, the continued 10 to 15 percent compound annual growth rate in sales achieved since the 1950s would have been highly unlikely. As it was, the emergence of the union in the 1950s was related to the appearance of candidates from the Socialist Party in the 1960s, but the two phenomena, though related, are only disjointedly linked. Through automation and other capital-intensive investment, the company was able to reduce its dependence on an outside skilled labor pool before the Socialists had captured control of a majority of local political offices. The disjunction in timing allowed the company enough leeway to hold blue-collar employment in soy sauce manufacture at roughly 2,500 persons since 1951, even though production has tripled.

It should be emphasized, however, that while blue-collar employment in the company stabilized, a good deal of in-company training raised the skill level of those remaining employees. But these skills were highly company-specific; that is, they were related to the particular technology of fermentation employed by Kikkoman and in their own way illustrate once again the nature of the particularistic bond between Noda Shōyu and its regular employees. The company is willing to invest money in these workers, but not in temporary or part-time workers. Thus, while one set of workers has remained stable in size but has grown in skill, another has grown in size but failed to advance in terms of skill or entitlement to employment. This is one cause of political friction between company and community—at least, for some members of the community.

The recognition of a union within the company can be seen as an extension of the entitlements gained by regular workers before the war, while the separation of company and community in a political sense since the 1960s can be understood as part of the process of technological modernization and resultant worker redundancy. Neither development owes much to the Occupation policy of democratization, and both can be observed in other industrially advanced nations.

The effect upon Kikkoman of democratizing the economy and preventing companies with concentrated economic power from monopolizing product markets must be considered. It is ironic that Noda Shōyu, rather than numerous larger corporations, should be taken to task. The zaibatsu operating companies escaped deconcentration in large part because the effect of the Occupation was to dismantle holding companies, interlocking directorates, securities and personnel interlocks, while leaving zaibatsu power in different product markets largely untouched. This was apparently because of the Occupation belief that little could be done about this concentration and that most zaibatsu shared markets as oligopolists rather than dominating them as monopolists. As a consequence, medium-sized but highly specialized firms like Kikkoman got snared in the antitrust net that far more economically concentrated companies avoided.

There is little doubt that the FTC hearings in 1951 caught Kikkoman by surprise. Until then the company had escaped scrutiny, and although the Senshusha holding company had been forced to sell its holdings in Kikkoman, this liquidation of assets was carried out categorically as part of a policy that required deconcentration of all holding companies with more than 5 million yen in assets, rather than construed as something enacted specifically against Kikkoman. Furthermore, the involvement of the Price Control Board in setting shōyu prices in 1950 gave Kikkoman the mistaken impression that the government abetted price agreements among manufacturers. This misunderstanding foreshadowed a continuing postwar contest between the FTC and other Japanese governmental agencies, such as the Ministry of International Trade and Industry (MITI), over the role of government advisement of industry or what is often called administrative guidance (gyōsei-shidō).

Development of a New Business Strategy

After 1951 the company set in motion a number of efforts that resulted eventually in a new business strategy for the firm that owed very little to the FTC. The basic problem facing Kikkoman in the 1950s and 1960s was less the threat of antimonopoly hearings than of declining per-capita consumption of soy sauce in Japan. This menace to corporate fortune emerged for two reasons. First, the demand for food and food-related products is mostly inelastic—that is, as society becomes more affluent and as individuals find themselves with more disposable income, they spend less and less of it, as a proportion of the total, on foodstuffs. Second, because of their exotic, nutritional, or otherwise perceived value, postwar Japanese have switched increasingly from traditional to Western foods that do not require soy sauce as a seasoning. Thus, soon after the Occupation the executives at Kikkoman faced a deteriorating per capita soy sauce market, a market that had accounted for 85 percent of sales in 1953.[17]

One response to this was to try to gain an ever-larger share of a declining market and to do so by taking market share away from traditional rivals. The price-fixing agreements with other makers that were so attractive immediately following the war were no longer so attractive, and one response to this changing market environment was the effort to establish exclusive distributors to handle Kikkoman products. These distributorships, tied closely to the company until the FTC hearings in the 1960s, have developed into an arm's-length association with the company. But Kikkoman would be an unimaginative company if it allowed its newly found mission to sell more at others' expense to halt there. It has continued to rely on traditional channels of distribution through tonya to market some of its goods, while it has created a new network of wholly owned distributors to run in tandem with the now at-arm's-length network. Most important, the company has spent some of its considerable revenues on advertising and an ambitious consumer education program.

Beginning in 1955–56, Kikkoman plunged into the world of advertising and product promotion, exploring questions that it had neglected since its rise to dominance some three decades earlier. The amount and fluctuation of demand were studied. Research teams explored how best to advertise and to expand sales. Trademark brand patterns and colors were specified and then publicized across the land. A planning and research department to coordinate these efforts was founded in 1957–58. A house-to-house education program was launched to teach consumers, especially housewives, the advantages of soy sauce, how to cook with it, and how to prepare savory delicacies with it. Kikkoman provided free shōyu to the innumerable cooking classes taken by young Japanese women preparing for marriage. Television was used extensively; the company sponsored such programs as the "International Cooking College for Housewives" in which international dishes using shōyu were prepared. The goal of most of this was to make an old product seem new and Western—to create a new image for shōyu.

The company broke away from the old distribution channels and began to sell to supermarkets and to chain and department stores. Repeating a pattern begun before the war, Kikkoman used its sales offices in smaller cities as direct delivery outlets. Beginning in 1951 with an office in Fukuoka, it set up wholesale offices (with some direct distribution functions) in such cities as Nagoya, Yokohama, Hiroshima. In 1973 a subsidiary company, Kikkoman Merchandising Center, was established to coordinate sales activities around the country and to respond quickly to whatever requests were raised by sales offices and outlets within Japan. Various sizes and sorts of shōyu containers were test marketed, and the most popular, such as the Mann-Pack which combined a number of different Kikkoman products, were sold nationwide.[18] Kikkoman was immensely successful in this sales and marketing campaign, raising its market share in Japan from 14 percent in 1952 to double that—28 percent—in 1965, and to one-third in 1980.

Fortunately for Kikkoman, this blitzkrieg into sales and distribution was undertaken at just the right time not only to shore up the company's position in the declining market for soy sauce in Japan but also to permit the company to sell all of its increasing production from the newly automated and highly efficient factories. By the end of the 1950s the challenge was no longer whether enough soy sauce could be made, but whether it could be sold. Increased production was related to increasing expenditures on research and development and increasing numbers of patent applications. (see table 28).[19]

Internationalization

Given the volume of production achieved by the company (45 million gallons annually by the end of the 1950s), it was natural that it would begin to look overseas for markets. Once the forecasting, sales, and marketing tools developed for the home market were perfected, it was logical to apply them outside Japan. So what had begun as a defensive

TABLE 28. R&D expenditures and patent applications, indexed, 1961–1970.

Year	R&D domestic expenditures	Year	Patent applications		
			Domestic	International	Total
1961	100 index no.	1961	100 index no.	+ 0	100
1963	201	1968	500	+ 62	562
1967	250	1969	512	+ 363	875
1970	397	1970	412	+ 263	675

Source: Kinugasa Yōsuke, "Takokuseiki Kigyō e no Senryaku," p. 11.

measure to prop up soy sauce sales in a declining home market became an offensive maneuver to internationalize the outlook and operations of the Kikkoman Corporation.

The company had already acquired some international experience before the war, when in the late 1930s one-tenth of its production was exported. But half of that went to countries in the yen currency bloc (largely Manchuria and North China, excluding Korea and Taiwan), and most of the remainder went to Hawaii and America's West coast with their considerable Japanese and Japanese-American population. The postwar internationalization has been far different, as Kikkoman attempted to serve a North American and Western European market of primarily non-Japanese descent. Fortunately, a good deal of what the company had learned in its consumer education and television promotion efforts in Japan after 1955 was applicable overseas in the 1960s and 1970s.

The assault on the international market can be conveniently, if somewhat artificially, dated from the American presidential elections of 1956 when Kikkoman bought air time in the midst of the election coverage in the United States to advertise its products to the wholly non-Japanese audience tuning in to the television broadcast. Shortly thereafter, certain Safeway stores began to carry Kikkoman soy sauce. In June 1957 Kikkoman International Incorporated was established and was soon rooted in San Francisco. Ten years later, after a decade of 20 to 30 percent rates of increase in annual sales, Kikkoman contracted on a commission basis with Leslie Food Company, a subsidiary of Leslie Salt Company in Oakland, California, to bottle Kikkoman Soy Sauce and to bottle and blend Barbecue Marinade (teriyaki sauce) shipped in bulk from Japan. This relationship continued from 1968 to 1972, after which Kikkoman began producing shōyu at its own plant in Walworth, Wisconsin (which had a 2.5-million-gallon capacity in the initial year of operation). Transportation costs from Japan to the United States of brewed soy sauce were roughly one-fourth of production costs, while transportation and other expenses of carrying raw materials to Japan were between 5 and 20 percent of preproduction costs.[20] Both were substantially reduced by the opening of the Wisconsin plant.

The timeliness of the decision to open the North American factory was reinforced by the American embargo on the sale of soy beans to Japan in 1973, a year after the Walworth factory opened. In the balance of that decade, sales in North America continued to climb at a 10 to 15 percent annual rate of increase—a rate that was not as rapid as it had been earlier but one that was calculated in terms of an expanded market and a larger market share. A good deal of this accomplishment must be credited to Kikkoman's North American marketing strategy, which was and is to sell soy sauce as an all-purpose, international seasoning rather than one limited to Oriental cookery.

Diversification

Kikkoman's success in multiplying sales and market share in Japan and abroad represents only half of its response to the declining per-capita market for soy sauce in Japan. The other part of the company's plan to cope with this disheartening development was to diversify its product line so as to lessen its dependence on one product.

In 1949 Noda Shōyu Company produced seven branded products: Kikkoman Soy Sauce, Kikkoman Sauce, Manjō branded Sake, Kikkoman Tsuyu and Kikkoman Memmi (soup bases for noodle dishes), Manjō Shōchū (vodkalike potato spirits), and Manjō Whiskey (brewed by Kikkoman, but never marketed extensively or for long). Today Kikkoman sells more than three dozen branded food and food-related products (table 29 identifies most of them) through a network of parent and subsidiary companies; in addition, it invests in restaurants, pharmaceuticals, food importing and exporting, and food processing machinery.

All these new products and ventures are logical extensions of market positions and management know-how that were in Kikkoman's possession at the start of its diversification effort. Many, such as the bewildering variety of sauces and juices, are products that, although unsophisticated in terms of the technology of manufacture, must compete with a variety of similar goods. Here, Kikkoman's channels of marketing for its traditional products as well as its recently enhanced advertising outlays give it a great advantage over its rivals.

Kikko Foods Corporations was founded as a packer of fruit and vegetables in 1961. Two years later a joint venture, Japan Calpak Co., Ltd., was established with Kikkoman Shōyu Co., Ltd., Mitsui & Company, and Del Monte Corporation (the California-based packing company) to sell Del Monte brand products in Japan. Kikkoman also packs Disney brand juice and nectar as well as a variety of Kikko brand canned goods. By the 1970s its Del Monte- and Disney-branded tomato and fruit juice products enjoyed a 30 percent share of a very large Japanese market.

There are some new products that derive from the company's traditional strengths in research and development in the areas of fermentation, brewing, and enzyme technology. The Mann's wine product line—the name of which is itself a shortened version of Kikkoman—and the digestive aid preparations of Seishin Pharmaceutical Company are outstanding examples. Given its strengths, Kikkoman can be ex-

TABLE 29. Kikkoman's main products and product lines, 1981.

Kikkoman brand products
  shōyu
  mild shōyu (lower salt content, 8%)
  light color shōyu (usu-kuchi)
  teriyaki barbecue marinade and sauce
  Worcestershire sauce
  tonkatsu sauce
  memmi and tsuyu (soup bases)
  sukiyaki sauce
  instant soy soup mix
  instant osuimono (clear broth soup mix)
Manjō brand products
  mirin (sweet rice wine)
  shōchū
  plum wine
Yomonoharu brand products
  sake
Del Monte brand products
  tomato ketchup, juice, puree, paste
  chile sauce
  Mandarin orange juice
Disney brand products
  fruit juice (orange, pineapple, grape)
  nectar (peach, orange)
Mann's brand products
  wine and sparkling wine
  brandy
Higeta brand products (marketed but not made by Kikkoman)
  shōyu
  tsuyu
  Worcestershire sauce
Ragu brand products
  spaghetti sauces
Kikko Tomato Ketchup brand
Monet Cognac brand

Source: The Kikkoman Corporation, *Kikkoman Product and Pricing Brochure* (Tokyo?, 1981).

pected to branch out into new products, such as industrial enzymes, food engineering (amino acids, yeasts, and other micro-organic matter), and perhaps genetic engineering. Finally, there are new product areas based on technologies related to those historically employed by the company; they include soft drink (Coca-Cola and Fanta) bottling, certain aspects of restaurant operations, and machinery for processing food.

Although the revenues of Kikkoman still depend heavily on the sale of shōyu—62 percent of sales in 1981—the company has moved away from an almost complete reliance on soy sauce in the 1950s to a point where, by the close of the 1980s, soy sauce sales will account for no more than half of all sales.[21] One could say that Kikkoman began its diversification program somewhat late compared to several of its competitors, such as the Suntory and Aji-no-moto corporations, and that its efforts, because of their reactive rather than active character, have been somewhat halfhearted. As a result of the tardiness and tentativeness of Kikkoman's diversification, its principal products other than shōyu play second fiddle to larger competitors: the Kagome Company leads in tomato products and fruit juices; Sanraku Ocean (Mercian brand), in wines. Nevertheless, Kikkoman has diversified extensively while greatly enlarging its share of the home and international market for naturally brewed shōyu. Food manufacturing and processing companies are not highly diversified in their product line, and this seems especially true in Japan. By any measure, Kikkoman is highly prosperous and well positioned for future growth.

Since the 1950s and the realization that the future market for shōyu in Japan was not auspicious, Kikkoman has emphasized sales and marketing within Japan to considerable success, developed a worldwide outlook and operating capacity, and broadly diversified its product line by relying on the marketing and technical strengths of the firm. Much of the individual credit for overseeing these changes must go to Mogi Keizaburō, head of the Planning Department when it was decided to return to a naturally fermented shōyu, to promote that product's distinctiveness both domestically and internationally, and to diversify the firm's non-shōyu product line. Mogi Keizaburō, an adopted son, shepherded these strategic developments through the firm during his tenure (1962–1974) as sixth president. Keizaburō's eldest son, Yuzaburō, presently heads the company's international division.

Democratization versus Internationalization

Although the Occupation policy of democratization had undeniable impact on Kikkoman for the first decade following World War II, it has had increasingly less importance since that time. By the mid- to late-

1950s the closed ownership of the company had been reversed and shares were widely held and traded. This development owed relatively little to democratization. The dilution of family ownership was tied directly to Kikkoman's diversification strategy and the internationalization of its operations and activities, and the need to raise capital for them forced the liberalization of ownership. Internationalization rather than democratization has had the greater effect on reducing family control. Nevertheless, the Mogi-Takanashi families still retain the largest single bloc of shares in the company (about 20 percent), and friendly enterprises (Nihon Seimei Insurance Company and two Mitsubishi banks) hold another substantial share (about 20 percent). As a result, the Mogi-Takanashi families remain securely entrenched in the top management positions. There has been relatively little democratization of ownership and top management even if the company has been internationalized in outlook and effort.

The internationalization of Kikkoman's circumstances helps explain the accommodation of company and community, for everyone inside as well as outside the corporation has come to realize that Noda is no longer interdependent with a company characterized by worldwide assets and ambitions. Although dissatisfaction with the company is sometimes still apparent, reflected especially in local and regional elections, major antagonisms have not divided company and union or even company and community for nearly two decades.

Critics of the company do exist, but some are merely jealous of its prosperity, others are angry about its limited employment opportunities for regular workers, and still others are annoyed by the inescapable and not wholly pleasant smell of soy sauce that permeates the town. As more and more newcomers and Tokyo commuters swell Noda's population, criticisms may simply indicate ignorance of the company and its efforts.

Kohei Homma of Rikkyo University, in a 1979 survey of the residents of Noda, found a surprising ignorance of the Kikkoman Corporation's past and present accomplishments as well as a general lack of understanding about the nature of the relationship between Kikkoman and the community of Noda. Over half of the five hundred persons queried felt that there was no relationship between improving productivity for the company and improving circumstances in the town. A majority felt that there was little benefit to the town from the company's cultural and welfare activities.[22]

Nonetheless, company, union, and community have accommodated one another since the Occupation period, and it is difficult to judge how much of this has been inspired by the ideal of democratization. One hesitates to qualify, much less quantify, such matters. Most of this process of adjustment, however, has come in the late 1960s and 1970s, the era of internationalization, rather than in the 1950s and early 1960s, the period when democratization was pronounced.

The FTC's imprint on Kikkoman in 1951 was to deny it a close relationship with distribution networks not owned by the company. But although this avenue of advancement was blocked, Kikkoman's new sales and marketing promotion carried it to a greatly enhanced market share and a noticeably broader product line. The impact of democratization in the 1950s, which was to negate price and market agreements among major manufacturers, became an undisguised blessing in the 1960s when Kikkoman could deploy its vastly superior financial and technological resources to crush its rivals in the marketplace in a completely legal and "democratic" manner. This, too, is in keeping with the worldwide business trend, wherein manufacturers in order to maintain sales in an increasingly competitive international environment have turned to an enterprise orientation noticeably more geared to marketing.

The continuity of ownership and management in the firm, the formalization of company and union interdependency, the accommodation of the company and the wider community to each other, and the declining relevance of antimonopoly legislation for Kikkoman in its newer market strategy make one chary of the efforts of government, domestic no less than foreign, to influence strongly the nature of business enterprise and to control the direction of its evolution. The circumstances of enterprise growth within a particular historical and cultural context as well as the incessant need for economic accountability seem to determine the nature of business growth in Japan as well as in the Western world.

The crucial distinction between democratization and internationalization was the degree to which either was voluntarily conceived and carried out. Democratization was an imposed system of Western values which often lacked resonance with Japanese ideas and institutions. Its effects were evident to the degree that either past practices or current beliefs of the Japanese were compatible with the goals of the Occupation. This was especially true after the 1947–48 change in Occupation policy, which emphasized Japanese recovery at the expense of the institutionalization of a particular idealized vision of a postwar democratic Japan. In Kikkoman's case, democratization appeared to accelerate but not to alter various changes already under way.

Internationalization was a voluntary process of bringing specific features of Kikkoman's business practices more in line with what was being done in large corporations in other advanced countries. The effort was more focused and less formal and lacked most of the pedantic character of democratization. Another difference between democratization and internationalization is illustrated by the familiar function-and-form dichotomy. The Occupation's efforts to democratize Japan were based on a belief that function follows form. The conception of a democratic Japan was embodied in legal definitions and specific institutional features: the individual and not the household as the basis of society; universal suffrage for women as well as men; a more equitable distribution of farming land; a different sort of industrial relations system. From such concrete conceptions, the Occupation proceeded to design and encourage specific institutional changes, and from such institutional changes, particular ideological and organizational outcomes were expected.

Internationalization, however, is a much less precise concept than democratization, and there is little agreement in the context of a single institution, such as a corporation, of what it should mean. As a result, the stress is on functionalism rather than on formalism. Functionalism, in the case of international business, is anything that will work, be effective, and be profitable. Because of the free-form character of internationalization, a variety of organizational devices and styles are effective, and form usually follows function rather than vice versa.[23]

There is an evident willingness on the part of Kikkoman to experiment with new products, production techniques, management styles, and operational forms in the international arena. There is even the hope that a new American seasoning—an indigenous shōyu, so to speak—will be realized from the company's efforts in Wisconsin and elsewhere in North America. The internationalization of Kikkoman is epitomized by the openness with which the company approaches the international market today, and the range of options it considers. It is in this open-ended strategy of adaptation to the international business environment rather than in the closed-in character of specific institutional manipulation that the contrast between internationalization and democratization is most apparent in Kikkoman's case.

Conclusion

FOR THREE CENTURIES the Kikkoman Corporation and its business fore-bears have been conspicuously successful in giving the world shōyu, an all-purpose seasoning of unusual value, versatility, and history. The excellence of Kikkoman shōyu is clear from the fame it has attained as the sole branded product of traditional Japanese manufacture to have succeeded worldwide. The Kikkoman Corporation is the oldest manu-facturing enterprise among the two hundred largest industrials in Japan today, and it is the largest soy sauce producer in the world. An unbro-ken continuity of management can be traced through ten generations of Takanashis and eight generations of Mogis since the seventeenth and eighteenth centuries. This remarkable continuity must be considered in combination with other notable qualities of Kikkoman's manage-ment—its durability and creativity.

Prosperity has not continued automatically, however; the Mogi-Takanashi brewers have responded to many changes and opportuni-ties. The first and most seminal decision in the firm's development can be traced to the establishment of the first family for the exclusive man-ufacture of shōyu in Noda in 1768. The Kashiwa house was founded four years after the marriage of the second son of Takanashi Hyōzae-mon, descendant and namesake of the first Takanashi to brew shōyu in Noda in 1661, to the daughter of Mogi Shichizaemon, patriarch of all Mogi families in Noda. The marriage in 1764 was contracted as an adopted son-in-law, mukō-yōshi, marriage in order to satisfy the tradi-tional Japanese preference for patrilineal descent and primogeniture. When in 1768 the couple established a separate branch household to engage exclusively in the manufacture of shōyu, they unknowingly founded a dynasty which would guide the fortunes of the shōyu indus-try in Noda and in Japan for the next two centuries.

The Kashiwa house soon became the largest and most advanced independent brewer in Noda. Not only were its material resources devoted single-mindedly to one product and one manufacturing process, thereby raising the technical quality and efficiency of shōyu fermentation far beyond what it had been, but also the human resources of the family could be concentrated in the acquisition and refinement of knowledge concerning the production and distribution of shōyu. Mogi Shichirōuemon VI, head of the Kashiwa house from the late nineteenth to early twentieth centuries, was the embodiment of the benefits of family specialization. Specialization, the key to progress, led to the application of science and the scientific method to the art of fermentation, the mechanization of production, and the successful management of both.

After 1887, when the local brewers formed a cartel, the head of the Kashiwa house was normally its chief officer. In 1917, when eight Mogi and Takanashi families formed a company, the first president of the Noda Shōyu Company, Limited, was Mogi Shichirōuemon. Since then, four of the company's seven presidents have come either directly from the Kashiwa family or indirectly from one of its branches. Mogi Katsumi, current head of the Kashiwa line and president of the Kikkoman Corporation since 1980, maintains the two-century legacy of continuity, ingenuity, and resiliency of the Kashiwa house in the Noda shōyu industry.

Important as the Kashiwa house was and is for the history of the Kikkoman Corporation, one household does not make or break a corporation. Especially after the formation of a cartel in 1887, the limits of the family form of enterprise organization as the basis for shōyu production were superseded. This was significant because, during a time when economies of scale in manufacture were unknown, the logical way of expanding capacity was to increase the number of producers. This was accomplished in Noda by bringing together nearly two dozen local shōyu manufacturers for a period of some thirty years.

In the United States the cartel is often treated as an undesirable economic institution which impedes free competition by promoting cooperation rather than competition among manufacturers. Yet the Noda shōyu brewers were ideological and institutional innovators. Beginning with joint purchase of raw materials and the common shipping and distribution of finished goods, the cartel associates developed a sense of mutual purpose and action. They invested large sums in new plant, equipment, and infrastructure, while they gave away impressive grants for charitable and patriotic causes.

In 1900 the cartel founded a bank in Noda to finance the growing capital needs of an enlarged association of brewers and their burgeoning activities. In 1904 a research and development laboratory was constructed to facilitate the mechanical and biochemical aspects of shōyu production. In 1911 a railroad line between Noda and Kashiwa, the main transportation hub in central Chiba Prefecture, was constructed largely at the expense of the cartel. After 1911, with the introduction of steam boilers into production and the rapid appearance of mechanical and microbiotic aids to shōyu fermentation, the cartel began to transform the essence of shōyu manufacture from that of a small-batch, brewmaster-controlled production process to a large-batch, organization- and science-centered fermentation system.

This growth in capacity and production was matched by the development of a national sales and distribution network made possible not only by the transporting of Noda shōyu nationwide over the Japanese railway system but also by the shifts in consumer preference for various kinds of soy sauce and for the amounts and containers in which it was sold. The cartel sent shōyu as far away as Hokkaido and Hawaii, while new avenues of distribution in Tokyo and in the countryside around Noda were pursued. The first bottles of Kikkoman shōyu appeared during the cartel era.

The full potential of the economies of scale in production and the economies of speed in distribution was realized only after the creation of a much more centralized and integrated structure of shōyu manufacture than that provided by the Noda Shōyu Brewers' Association. In 1918 the Noda Shōyu Company, Limited, was begun in an attempt to coordinate, allocate, and monitor through a well developed managerial hierarchy the increasingly complex processes involved in manufacturing and distributing for a national shōyu market in Japan. Earlier methods of operation for the shōyu cartel had required only a rough consensus on matters of purchasing, sales, and investment. Such a loose form of collaboration, however, could not withstand the pressure of large-scale investment in new plant and equipment and of heightened managerial control which investment on that order would require. Surprisingly, the rallying point for the new post-cartel business organization was that most traditional yet malleable and motivating of all institutions: the family. Unlike the cartel, with its emphasis on locale and occupation, the new corporate enterprise focused primarily on family. But these families were interrelated genealogically and experienced in the growing sophistication of the shōyu industry. Seven Mogi families, out of the twenty-two families that had belonged to the cartel on one occasion or another, joined with Horikiri Monjirō and Takanashi Hyōzaemon (a direct descendant of the Takanashi Hyōzaemon who brewed shōyu in 1661) to form the Noda Shōyu Company, Limited, in December 1917. Once the new corporation was in place, it required less than seven years for its executives to transform the enterprise from a local shōyu maker into a rural zaibatsu, a family-based, holding company conglomerate, with interests in banking, railroads, shipping and storage companies, and in domestic as well as foreign manufacture of a variety of food and food-related products.

The Noda Shōyu Company, or the Kikkoman Corporation, has been a unique expression of the energy and the entrepreneurship of the Mogi-Takanashis because it has been family-owned and operated since the start. Few family firms have done so well for so long and remained family firms, but the Mogis have been willing to risk everything—name, property, and position—on the belief that they could brew a finer shōyu in larger amounts than anyone else. Their daring has been recognized and rewarded.

Major change is rarely accomplished without major cost, and incorporation in 1917–18 was followed by a decade of labor difficulties culminating in the Great Noda Strike of 1927–28. The strike and the turmoil leading up to it were caused to a considerable degree by the incorporation of the Noda Shōyu Company, which was motivated by the opportunity for an expanded market made possible by advances in production and distribution technology. Such advances, unfortunately, far outstripped the methods of labor organization then prevalent in the shōyu industry.

Most factory workers before the twentieth century were seasonal, leaving the farm for temporary work during the winter; a minority of workers labored full-time in the breweries for a limited number of years. By the turn of the century, as factories became larger, more complex, and more year-round in operation, most workers were no longer farm boys looking for a few days' wages. Work gangs or crews were hired on year-long contracts by labor recruiters and supervised by labor bosses. The resulting system called internal contracting meant that the design and pace of work and the supervision of workers were entirely separate from the ownership and nonmanufacturing management of an enterprise.

The Mogi-Takanashi brewers, who had begun corporate operations in 1918, were forced to confront the problem of labor organization by 1919. What they proposed was revolutionary. Their plan was to transform the short-term, decentralized, and piecemeal character of labor organization into something more permanent, centralized, and systematic. This was to be accomplished by converting independent labor recruiters into company employees and by coopting labor bosses into factory foremen, by rewarding workers with better pay schemes and with more opportunity for promotion, by studying the system of production and rationalizing its flow, and by setting standards and incentives for work performance. In short, the company officers sought to restructure the nature of factory work and the character of the employment system, and through these their relationship with the local work force and the community of Noda. Many workers, seeing a total reforging of their livelihood and lifestyle, rebelled.

Labor troubles had appeared in Noda as early as 1921, but the real difficulties surfaced in 1923 and in 1927–28. Then many but not all of the workers of the Noda Shōyu Company, as well as laborers from ancillary shops and enterprises in town, struck the company under the leadership of the Yūaikai, later the Sōdōmei or General Federation of Labor in Japan. The Sōdōmei had been losing ground in Japan since the end of World War I when the economic downturn had discouraged workers from joining the union and when ideological differences within the union movement itself had sapped the union's spirit and organization. In an effort to revive its momentum and regroup its failing leadership, the Sōdōmei made Noda Shōyu a major target after 1925. This led to the longest strike on record in prewar Japan and the near destruction of the Sōdōmei union. The Noda Shōyu Company by its victory was able to centralize and streamline the work process and to monitor as well as reward workers for their performance. The market share of the company, which had never exceeded 8.8 percent before 1926, had become, by 1936, 14.5 percent. Moreover, a closer and more compatible association of company and workers as well as a highly interdependent and mutually rewarding relationship between company and community resulted. From 1930 to 1960 company and community enjoyed a mutuality of involvement and dependence, an era of paternalism never equaled before or since. The new pattern of industrial relations at Noda Shōyu has generally been referred to as the "Japanese system of employment." The history of Kikkoman demonstrates how the corporate paternalism that evolved at this time was a rational and economic response, more than a cultural and historical one, to the financial, managerial, and organizational needs of Japanese companies in the middle of the twentieth century.

With the combining in 1925 of nearly a dozen manufacturing and nonmanufacturing concerns into a centralized holding company, and with the settling of the Great Strike in 1928, the Noda Shōyu Company turned to the expansion of production at home and overseas. The world's largest shōyu plant was opened near Kakogawa in 1929; by 1939 four smaller shōyu makers, including Higeta Shōyu, had been acquired by Noda Shōyu. In 1936 the Manshu Shōyu Company was established in Manchuria to brew Kikkoman shōyu and Homare miso for markets in China. Noda Shōyu had been operating in Korea since 1918 when it had amalgamated the assets of the Nihon Shōyu Company, owned by Mogi Yūuemon, into the new corporate structure. By 1939 roughly 10 percent of the company's output was exported; just over half went to East Asia, while approximately one-fifth shares each went to Hawaii and to North America. In 1939, 99 percent of the shōyu exported to the United States, some 2,375 metric tons, carried the Kikkoman trademark.

While the Noda Shōyu Company profited handsomely in the United States before World War II, it suffered as a result of that country's antitrust policy following the war. The American-led Occupation sought to undo the cooperation on matters of output and prices which characterized many industries, including the shōyu industry, in Japan. Noda Shōyu and four other major makers were forced to relinquish their collusive practices. This prompted the company not only to expand aggressively its shōyu market share in Japan at the expense of its former colleagues but also to diversify its product line to include tomato and fruit juice products, wine, soft drinks, pharmaceuticals, food processing machinery, and restaurants. Meanwhile, left-wing politics in Noda and "modern" ideals of marriage among the younger generation of the Noda shōyu brewing families have meant that Kikkoman could no longer depend on community and clan to buttress the company in Noda.

In the late 1950s Noda Shōyu began to reapply the advertising and marketing lessons learned during the course of its domestic expansion to the North American market. New distribution channels to supermarkets, chain, and department stores have been opened, and an ambitious consumer education program has been launched. In 1957 Kikkoman International Incorporated was established in San Francisco; more recently, controlling interests in the Japan Food Corporation, the largest importer and exporter of Oriental foods in the United States, and in the Tokyo-based Pacific Trading Company, another leading food importer-exporter, were acquired. Having secured sources of supply and integrated distribution channels, Kikkoman soon became America's best-selling soy sauce, passing Chung King in supermarket sales in 1971 and La Choy in 1976. Opening its own shōyu production plant in Wisconsin in 1973 (with a 6,000 kiloliter capacity in the first year of operation), Kikkoman was able to double its production capacity in the United States by the end of the decade. Ten years after its opening, the Wisconsin plant is now approaching an annual output of 30,000 kiloliters. Shōyu sales in America were reaching $100 million annually and per capita consumption was up to ten tablespoons (as compared to 2.65 gallons per capita consumption in Japan) by 1981. In many ways Kikkoman's plant in the farming fields of Walworth, Wisconsin, has metaphorically returned the company to its origins in the rice fields of Noda. In Wisconsin, as in Noda three centuries ago, manufacturing is combined with the rhythms and pulses of the agricultural cycle, and the local Wisconsin natives, factory hands as well as farmers, wear their Kikkoman uniforms in good-natured ignorance of the Japanese symbols on their backs.

As the company has prospered in Wisconsin and overseas, its ties with the community of Noda, by contrast, have weakened. This is the result not only of internationalization but also of the modernization of the production process, the lessening of the company's dependency on local skilled labor, the electoral dominance of Noda and much of Chiba Prefecture by political leadership opposed to big-business, and the diversification of the company's product line. Nevertheless, for Kikkoman, company, clan, and community will continue to be inseparable at some level; they will continue to represent a remarkable interaction of product, lineage, and locale for decades to come.

Appendices

Notes

Glossary

Index

Ie and the Shōyu Industry

IE, the Japanese stem family, is a descent group that is considered to endure forever, whereas the nuclear family, known as *setai* or *kazoku*, is limited in size, scope, and space/time. Ie embody past and future generations and persist by virtue of the continuity of property and genealogy through current family members. A *dōzoku* is a large line of descendants or clan members composed of several ie and characterized by a main household (*honke*) and a number of branch households (*bunke*) in which descent from the main house is traced through males.[1]

According to Robert Smith, a leading expert on Japanese kinship, the residential unit of the ie

> consists of a senior married couple and a married child with his or her own spouse and children. Such a family unit may include as many generations as are alive, but there can be only one married couple in each generation . . . Among the sacred duties of the head, who controlled the destiny of its living members, was that of preserving the descent line unbroken. He was responsible for passing on, enlarged if possible, the goods and property that he had inherited, and it was his task to see to the proper veneration of the ancestors.[2]

The ie is not the family most Western Europeans and North Americans are familiar with. Contemporary American households are not formed primarily to preserve continuity of property and genealogy. Marriages are based on affection and implicit (sometimes explicit) contractual obligations to share in housework, childrearing, and breadwinning. In Japan, however, the family relationship is not necessarily a volitional or even contractual alliance. As most often conceived, the family is a kin-based unit where property ownership and descent relationships are paramount and exclusively male-centered, and where power and dignity are enjoyed predominantly by male heads of household. The ie apportions obligations and concentrates authority hierarchically, by sex and descent.

This characterization is clouded by the existence of family members in the ie who are not biologically related to the household head. The distinction between kin and nonkin, often so important in the Chinese and Western family, is not always emphasized in the Japanese stem family. Nonkin and fictive kin, most often the adopted, frequently constitute a substantial part of the total household membership. Rather than adhere to a strict genealogical definition of family, ie boundaries are often determined by who contributes to the economic welfare of the group. Kinsmen, in the genealogical sense, usually constitute the nucleus of such economic groups, but kinship is neither the absolute nor exclusive criterion of membership. Logically the ie is not purely a kinship unit but is often an economic organization dressed up in family trim.[3] It is useful to conceive of the ie in terms of concentric circles of "kinsmen": there is an inner core of consanguines where genetic descent is presumed and an outer core of consanguines where genetic descent is implied but not required.

Such variations in the composition and structure of ie and dōzoku is reflected in a continuing debate among social scientists over whether kinship in ie and dōzoku should be defined primarily by descent or by contributions to corporate property, tools, and knowledge. This debate further confuses the issue of the family-firm analogy, for not only must the Western family be distinguished from the Japanese stem family but the ie itself must be understood according to two separate but related criteria: genealogical and economic membership. Most often, ie and dōzoku are viewed as patrilineal descent groups in which economic ties have frequently overshadowed genealogical relationships.[4] Some scholars, however, have emphasized genealogical relationships, arguing that households come together typically in times of crisis and emergency and do so on the basis of kinship.[5] One well-known Japanese social scientist has taken the extreme view that ie and dōzoku are not patrilineal descent groups at all, but groups based solely on residence and locality.[6] Examples of households organized around common residences and occupations may be found in traditional Japan, but they are the exception more than the rule.

Most social scientists recognize the importance of both genealogical relationships and economic ties in defining ie and dōzoku, although one concept is generally emphasized over the other in practice. Both views are valid, depending on what part of rural Japan is studied. The northeast is noted for a strong economic content in kinship relations—so strong in fact that genealogical ties are sometimes created to buttress established economic dependencies. The northeast is also an area of limited economic resources, single rice cropping, and skewed personal income. The southwest, by contrast, is characterized by a more highly developed commercial economy, double rice cropping, agricultural land reclamation, and more evenly distributed personal income. Here the kinship relationship normally overshadows the economic content of household composition and structure.

Origins of the Stem Family

Economic geography helps to distinguish the two facets of membership in Japanese stem families. The Japanese household can be both a descent and a corporate group, with one generally emphasized. The concept of the corporate relationship has many origins, most of which are lost to historical documentation. During the thirteenth to seventeenth centuries Japan passed through a period of internecine warfare and economic disruption. A soldier could expect a violent and early death. The prospects for a cultivator were not much better, given the dangers of malnutrition, epidemics, and tyrannical government. Among warriors and peasants alike, a rule of primogeniture, or in some cases modified primogeniture, evolved as a means of preserving family and property.[7] However small an inheritance might be, chances for family survival and perhaps for the eventual accumulation and transmission of property to future generations were enhanced when the inheritance remained intact and was passed to and through the head of the household, the socially and legally designated heir.

Often in such turbulent times inheritances must have gone unclaimed. There was no established means for property to pass in an orderly fashion between parties, whether related or unrelated. To amend this, the position of household head was linked to a kind of office, whose functions of maintaining continuity and inheritance rights outlasted the individual occupant. Over many years of civil and military turbulence the idea of the household as a corporate group, distinct but not necessarily different in personnel from the household conceived as a kinship group, became linked with the concept of the position of household head. In this case, the ie and dōzoku are corporate entities managed by a household head who is nominated to that office on the basis of merit and promise rather than descent. The head is usually referred to by the title of "household head"; this position, and indeed that of membership in the corporate household itself, can exist without any current incumbents.[8] The household, in this sense, is a legal invention—one that requires an executor or head to carry out its corporate functions: the maintenance and continuity of property, genealogy, and household ritual.

The Case of Kikkoman

If kinship in the ie or dōzoku is to be determined principally by descent, a number of anomalies immediately appear in the case of those families most closely associated with Kikkoman or its antecedent enterprises. Although traditional Japanese households practiced single-son inheritance, it was not always the eldest or even the natural son who inherited. Adoption was widely practiced in order to provide male heirs when none existed, to substitute a more promising male heir when one's own did not measure up, or to attract a husband for a nubile daughter. In this last case, it was common to adopt a son for the combined purposes of marrying one's daughter as well as providing a household successor. Such "sons" took their adopting family's surname.

Given the flexibility of recruitment and membership in households that adoption provides, it is accurate to say that in the case of households and lineages associated with Kikkoman economic considerations sometimes overwhelmed kinship considerations. This can be seen most clearly when households divided or branched for the purpose of initiating a new economic venture. Branching was a device wherein a main household established a separate, branch household with its own genealogical and corporate identity. In only one of six cases of adopted son-in-law marriages in figure A-1 did the adoption and marriage coincide with a household branching for the purpose of founding a new shōyu enterprise (shown here by a dotted line connecting the households involved). In the five other cases, however, adopted son-in-law marriages sustained the continuity of family ownership and control in a soy sauce brewery. In the case of male adoption and marriage, therefore, economic considerations, namely, the founding and organizing of branch households in the shōyu business, appear to have directly dominated kinship decisions involving household division only about 17 percent of the time (one out of six cases of adopted son-in-law marriages). Where household division was not the concern, but household maintenance and continuity in shōyu manufacture were, 83 percent of son-in-law adoptions were linked to economic matters (five out of six cases of adopted son-in-law marriages).

In this one example of adopted son-in-law marriage, kinship considerations—the maintenance and preserving of property through time—seemingly overshadowed economic concerns. In another instance the marriage coincided with the establishment of a branch household for

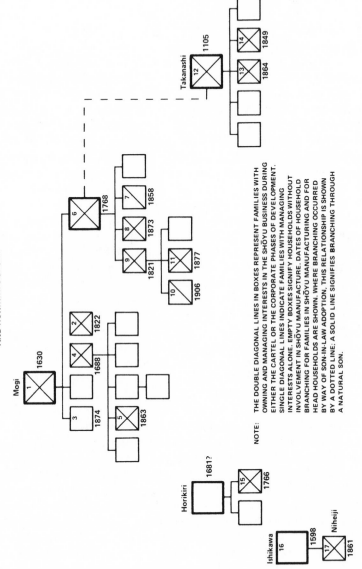

FIGURE A-1. BRANCHING RELATIONSHIPS IN MOGI, TAKANASHI, ISHIKAWA, AND HORIKIRI DŌZOKU

NOTE: THE DOUBLE DIAGONAL LINES IN BOXES REPRESENT FAMILIES WITH OWNING AND MANAGING INTERESTS IN THE SHŌYU BUSINESS DURING EITHER THE CARTEL OR THE CORPORATE PHASES OF DEVELOPMENT. SINGLE DIAGONAL LINES INDICATE FAMILIES WITH MANAGING INTERESTS ALONE. EMPTY BOXES SIGNIFY HOUSEHOLDS WITHOUT INVOLVEMENT IN SHŌYU MANUFACTURE. DATES OF HOUSEHOLD BRANCHING FOR FAMILIES IN SHŌYU MANUFACTURING AND FOR HEAD HOUSEHOLDS ARE SHOWN, WHERE BRANCHING OCCURRED BY WAY OF SON-IN-LAW ADOPTION, THIS RELATIONSHIP IS SHOWN BY A DOTTED LINE; A SOLID LINE SIGNIFIES BRANCHING THROUGH A NATURAL SON.

the purpose of founding a new shōyu brewery. This was clearly a case of subordinating kinship to the inauguration of a new manufacturing venture. Such cases were rare: one in six, if examples of adopted son-in-law marriage are considered, and perhaps ten in fifty, if all examples of marriage, adoption, and branching among the soy sauce brewers of Noda are examined.

Figure A-2 represents a large input-output table that delineates kin exchange within seventeen families that were in one way or another involved in the Noda soy sauce business between 1688 and 1978. (Actually twenty-two families had been involved with soy sauce brewing, but some of them did not last long or were not local.) More than half of these events are female-centered. Combining marriages and adoptions (adoptions are actually a form of early betrothal) by sex, we find twenty-seven such events involving women and only nine involving men. This difference in frequency is highly significant statistically, indicating that the imbalance was planned and not accidental.[9] That the imbalance should be so striking is intriguing. The reasons for it, I believe, have to do with political and economic considerations in the exchange of kinsmen for enterprise development.

Why would families choose to record female-centered events in a ratio of three to two and female-centered marriages and adoptions in a ratio of three to one? The answer lies in the fact that a marriage of a daughter involved neither power nor property in a formal or institutional sense. Power—that is, the capacity to decide issues of family membership, ritual, and property—in a patriarchally organized society, was a privilege of men. Because property was concentrated, in the hands of men, female marriages risked neither power nor property and so were ideally suited to the initiation and maintenance of family alliances. Therefore, we find a preponderance of female-centered events.

Other types of family-to-family interactions might be examined to see if kin exchange involved the transfer of property and power as well. The result of this analysis is shown in Table A-1. Of fifty events, fourteen occur between "clans," nineteen within the extended Mogi clan, three within the Takanashi, and only one in the Ishikawa. Thirteen events occur within subclans of the Mogi lineage and do not involve the main Mogi house of Mogi Shichizaemon. Reviewing the frequency of these events reveals that as a rule main houses of clans and subclans send out more household members for marriage and adoption than they take in; in effect, they implant their offspring in subsidiary houses. The same rule applies between clans. The number of women that a house is able to offer for marriage may be interpreted as a measure of its dominance over another house, as gauged by the genealogical rank-order of donor and recipient households and the frequency of in- and

FIGURE A-2. KIN EXCHANGE, 1688-1978

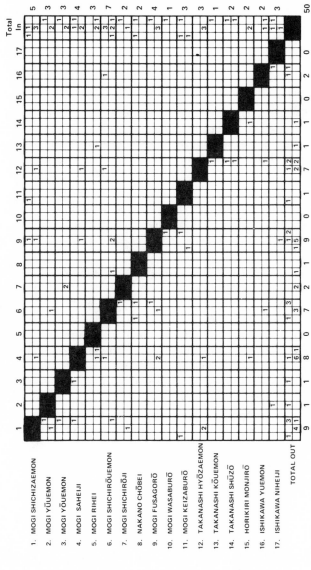

TABLE A-1. Household development and kin exchange, Noda Shōyu Brewers, 1868–1978.

Type of interaction	property	power
25 daughter marriages	no	no
11 son branchings	yes	yes
6 son marriages	no	yes
3 son adoptions	no[a]	yes
3 daughter branchings	yes	no
2 daughter adoptions	no	no

Source: Unpublished family records of major shōyu manufacturers in Noda.

a. In the case of son-in-law adoption, although he brought little property with him, he soon became the heir-apparent in the house into which he was adopted and married. This is a case of delayed property transfer.

out-marriages. This may be related to the desire of main houses to keep their children close to home and the willingness of subordinate houses to accept family members from genealogically older and therefore socially superior households.

Within clans or lineages, male rather than female placement in subordinate households assumes importance. This makes sense in view of the desire of main houses to control the timing and number of minor houses established within their own line—principally through branching, and secondarily through marriage. Branchings normally involve "sons," marriages, "daughters." Thus, the role of biology in family and enterprise development is paramount and may be construed as evidence of the degree to which kinship dominated economic concerns, or the degree to which the family may be understood as an analogue of the firm. The following epigram summarizes the evidence from this section and captures the essence of the place of biology in family development:

> It's better to give than receive,
> Between clans, dispatch daughters,
> Within clans, secure sons.

Family Strategies

The Kashiwa branch house of the Mogi clan, founded by Mogi Shichirōuemon in 1768, has been conspicuous in executing the strategy outlined above, and its power and position in the Noda soy sauce business have not been equaled since the mid-nineteenth century. The success of the Kashiwa house must be viewed in perspective, however.

Since different development strategies, within and without the Noda soy sauce industry, have been pursued by other clans, the wisdom of these other investment choices should be weighed against the probable success in manufacturing and marketing shōyu at earlier times. Until the early nineteenth century soy sauce manufacture was only one of several possible ventures for investment and did not appear to be any more attractive than several other local enterprise possibilities.

The subclan headed by Mogi Saheiji, for example, diversified into local commercial and professional endeavors. Although the main house of the Mogi Saheiji clan continued to work within and to be successful in the soy sauce business, subhouses moved into such occupations as cereal commodity sales, pharmacy, optometry, jewelry, and watchmaking. These endeavors have been less financially rewarding than management in the shōyu enterprise, but working within the local communities of Noda and the surrounding towns has provided economic security, civic respectability, and personal satisfaction for many members of the Mogi-sa clan (the lineage descendant from Mogi Saheiji).

The Takanashi clan's move into the Tokyo warehousing and distributing business is another example of diversification that, on the whole, has compared favorably with the economic success of Kikkoman. A considerable portion of the canned food as well as the alcoholic and carbonated beverages destined for and moving within Tokyo were and still are handled by Takanashi branch households. Shōyu producers located in Chōshi, another well-known site of shōyu manufacture in Chiba Prefecture, have diversified in much the same manner. One of the two Hamaguchi households making shōyu in Chōshi also established a branch household in Edo (Tokyo) in 1645 for wholesaling shōyu and marine food products. This branch of the Hamaguchi family, along with the Tokyo branch of the Takanashi family from Noda, account for a large share of the shōyu sold and distributed in Tokyo today.

The success and failure of any family strategy of either diversified or concentrated investment depends in large part upon luck, and it was bad luck, in the form of two disastrous fires in 1871 and 1908, that was responsible for the declining fortunes of Mogi Shichizaemon, head of the Mogi clan and once the principal investor in the Noda soy sauce industry.[10] Such misfortune was not unique. Earlier in the mid-nineteenth century, for example, bad luck that included successive years of poor harvests, declining business, and famine between 1836 and 1838 had reduced the number of soy sauce breweries in Noda from eighteen to eleven.[11]

Aside from bad luck, human failings could affect diversification. It would be a mistake to assume that family alliances were always easily entered into or maintained, even in Japan. The Terada family, a leader in the spinning industry, is a case in point. This was a local family of some industrial prominence, located near Nagoya and blessed with numerous offspring. But when the many children and stepchildren of Terada Jiyoshige, the family innovator in the field of cotton spinning, could not agree on matters of family succession and therefore of family control of the business, two separate manufacturing ventures (making the same product) with separate and independent holding companies and boards of directors were created. The companies competed vigorously for several decades at the turn of the twentieth century until one branch was finally forced out of the textile business. What might have been a perfectly natural business alliance between two related families ended instead in economic disaster for one and enmity for both.[12]

Recent research has shown that not only the idea but also the form of the family in nineteenth-century Japan varied a great deal according to economic class. As there was no preordained form or function for the family, families had to be aware of their resources and opportunities in order to make the best of what they had. A network of cooperating kinsmen could be a great help in this regard, but cooperation could not always be assumed.[13]

There were other reasons for a network of cooperating kinsmen. In an era when raw material availability, the fermentation process, and even transportation were to a considerable degree dependent on weather, climatic fortune was a crucial factor in enterprise success. The unpredictability of weather, harvests, commodity markets, and consumer demand cautioned against too great an investment in any one line of endeavor, like shōyu manufacture. Yet the costs of making shōyu were considerable, and they were for the most part fixed in the form of fermentation tanks, brewing and extracting equipment, and storage and shipping facilities. The fixed nature of this large investment in plant and equipment did not permit a rapid throughput of product or a quick turnover in the marketplace. Fermentation required eighteen to twenty-four months, and urban market sales were controlled by a system of wholesaling and distributing which denied manufacturers direct access to consumers. Accordingly, Noda shōyu manufacturers were presented with an investment decision of great complexity and uncertainty: how much to invest in manufacturing capacity, given the uneven pattern of investment and the unpredictability of supply and demand markets. Too little invested might result in insufficient capitalization to take advantage of a rise in prices, whereas too much invested might lead to an inadequate return in a poor market and possible bankruptcy as a result.

In this context, the advantages of a large kinship network to support business activities become immediately obvious. In addition to opportunities for sharing information concerning raw material costs, labor availability, and production know-how, the Mogi-Takanashi group enjoyed the decided advantage of kin support in financing shōyu manufacturing and shipping facilities. By the end of the eighteenth century, not only did the members of the Mogi-Takanashi families aid each other in the establishment of enterprises, but they frequently sold and traded all or part of their operations to each other. They also stood ready to purchase the facilities of nonkinsmen in the Noda area. Although such financial dealings were not handled in a formal sense by the combined Mogi and Takanashi families until the days of cartel and incorporation in the late nineteenth and twentieth centuries, informally such deals were struck often between the head and branch households of a single genealogical line. Where intermarriage and adoption may have created strong ties between households of different lines of descent, moreover, close business dealings could be expected to develop over time.

Further examination of the pattern of marriages, adoptions, and household branchings within the four main Kikkoman lineages (Mogi, Takanashi, Horikiri, and Ishikawa) reveals another way in which the organization of economic relationships and the promotion of social solidarity provided a rationale for the kinship system. The histogram or bar graph (figure A-3) that summarizes the frequency of kin exchange between and within these dōzoku discloses that the frequency of such events increased regularly until the end of the nineteenth century, at which point a noticeable drop occurs. In the twentieth century interlineage alliances almost disappear.

The decline in frequency coincides directly with the formation of a shōyu manufacturing cartel in 1887 and the founding of the Noda Shōyu Company, Limited, in 1918, the precursor of the Kikkoman Corporation. Once the organizing and regularizing of economic relationships and activities could be handled by formal institutions designed for such purposes, the kinship system essentially gave up such functions. The promotion of social and economic solidarity, the protection of property, and the continuity of family enterprise were turned over to the cartel and eventually to its corporate successors. As a result, noneconomic matters became more salient for descent groups; children could marry out of the business; natural offspring, and not adopted scions, could assume family headships; affection and attraction could play a greater part in courtship and marriage. Families could be less concerned with economic affairs and cultivate more personal and emotional matters.

FIGURE A-3. HISTORICAL FREQUENCY OF MARRIAGES, ADOPTIONS, AND
HOUSEHOLD BRANCHINGS WITHIN THE FOUR MAIN KIKKOMAN LINEAGES, 1688-1978

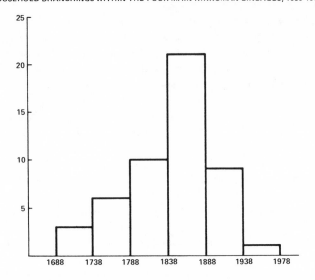

Change in the Function of Kinship and
Development of Specialization

Although interlineage allliances in the form of clan-based marriages, adoptions, and household branchings no longer play a dominant role in the organization and operation of Kikkoman, ie as opposed to dōzoku membership continues to count for a great deal. Since the establishment of the company in 1918, kinship has been employed not for interfamily cooperation but for interfamily rivalry. Household membership has become all-important in determining access to the upper reaches of corporate power. Consider the following statistics on family membership and corporate power and privilege. Of the twenty-eight main and branch households in the three Mogi, Takanashi, and Horikiri dōzoku (see figure A-1), the percentage of households by lineage is as follows: Horikiri, 11; Takanashi, 21; Mogi, 68; the percentage of households that engage in shōyu manufacture: Horikiri, 13; Takanashi, 50; Mogi, 53.

Clearly the Mogi clan has spawned the largest number of households and spurred the highest rate of participation in the soy sauce business, but within the overall Mogi clan one main and two branch households contend. The importance of the subdivisions within the Mogi clan is revealed by the fact that, although all eight of the company presidents to date have been Mogis, within the greater Mogi lineage 63 percent of the company presidents can be traced to the Kashiwa branch household of Mogi Shichirōuemon, 25 percent from the Mogi-sa group of Mogi Saheiji, and only 12 percent from the main house of Mogi Shichizaemon. Household hegemony was reflected as well on the first board of directors, with 67, 22, and 11 percent representation for the households of Mogi Shichirōuemon, Saheiji, and Shichizaemon, respectively.

The shifting strategies of the Mogi, Takanashi, and Horikiri families raise an important point. The diversification of family interests and the movement of particular families from one business to another over the years reveal another dimension of the family-firm analogy. Families were primarily concerned with the continuity of genealogy and property through time and less concerned with the preservation of a particular form for doing so. They moved willingly among farming, manufacturing, land and commodity speculation, moneylending, and combinations of these, in order to maintain the family line unbroken. Security was valued more than specialization.

In time the balance would shift for a number of reasons. A newly formed family's concern with survival diminishes over the years. As one generation blends into two, and then three or more, status, prestige, and, therefore, specialization become increasingly important. Also, as other families grow, develop, and diversify, the fields of opportunity within a particular geographical area may lessen, and it may no longer be so easy to redirect a family's livelihood. If a family happens to do particularly well in a certain line of endeavor and is well known in the community for that specialization, it is reluctant to shift to another area. Eventually the continuity not only of household but of a particular form of household may assume overwhelming personal, genealogical, and community importance. In this way, the maintenance of a specific line of endeavor, such as soy sauce manufacture, can come to dominate a family's current and future efforts, and, as a result, business strategy can overwhelm family and kinship consideration.

This process of specialization within soy sauce manufacture was especially evident among families of the Kashiwa branch of the Mogi lineage. Their gain, however, was at the expense of other families. Opportunities to diversify into soy sauce manufacture were progressively reduced during the latter half of the eighteenth and all of the nineteenth centuries, so that by the twentieth century no new Mogi families—or any other families from Noda for that matter—were able to enter the business. The preeminence of Kashiwa lineage in soy sauce manufacture can be traced back to its specialization in this activity since 1768. But the Kashiwa families' specialization and subsequent success have been helped along the way by "vassal" families.

Vassal families were the bantō of the Kashiwa lineage. To use a feudal term, bantō were the hereditary retainers or the trusted assistants of

Mogi headmen who through long and loyal service became indispensable to their employers. Bantō made the concerns of Mogi families their own. In a time when the Mogis themselves knew little about the detailed operation of the enterprises that they funded, bantō often provided the requisite detailed supervision and oversight.

In Noda, because of the large number of Mogi families involved in soy sauce manufacture, bantō never succeeded to ownership in the industry. Elsewhere in Japan, however, where the number of kinsmen was not sufficient to guarantee competent successors to a family's corporate endeavors, bantō frequently married into or were adopted into their employer's family in order to maintain the line of succession. In Noda, bantō daughters occasionally married Mogi scions, but there is no record of any bantō son succeeding to the headship of a Mogi family. Numerous documents, however, attest to the continuing loyalty and service of bantō families in Noda to their employers. Bantō families became surrogate families of the employers in many ways. Even if they could not actually succeed to the headship of a Mogi family, they could identify in spirit as well as in labor with the Mogis. The tasks of preserving the continuity of Mogi family property and genealogy through time became their tasks as well, and Mogi and bantō families were joined for generations in rising and falling fortunes.

Indeed, the intimacy of their association continued in the next life: just as the ie of any Mogi family was conceptualized as an unending descent group in which the actions and possessions of the current generation were linked with past and future generations, so too the bantō family conceived of its unending destiny in relation to the family of its employer. Loyalty in death as in life was the ideal. Such loyalty in reality may have been exceptional, since the uncertainties of life were unlikely to permit such a sustained and close relationship for a long time, but in Noda the gravesites of nine bantō families alongside the headstones of the member families of the Mogi Kashiwa lineage bear silent testimony to their fealty and dedication (see figure A-4). No better evidence of the use of kinship for the ends of enterprise could be offered.[14]

Thus, if one looks at the three dōzoku—those of Mogi Shichirōuemon, Mogi Saheiji, and Takanashi Hyōzaemon—that were most directly associated with Kikkoman or its antecedent enterprises, the premodern interdependency of family and firm helps explain the priority sometimes given to social and economic cooperation for enterprise development within the kinship framework. This was most true in the eighteenth century when, in the absence of other devices, the family was institutionalized as a social and economic control group in the management and maintenance of shōyu manufacture. Since that time

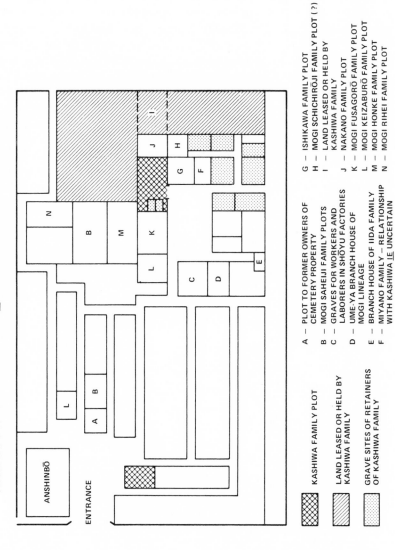

FIGURE A-4. GRAVE SITES OF THE KASHIWA IE AND ITS RETAINERS AT ANSHINBŌ TEMPLE

ANSHINBŌ

ENTRANCE

KASHIWA FAMILY PLOT

LAND LEASED OR HELD BY
KASHIWA FAMILY

GRAVE SITES OF RETAINERS
OF KASHIWA FAMILY

A – PLOT TO FORMER OWNERS OF
    CEMETERY PROPERTY
B – MOGI SAHEIJI FAMILY PLOTS
C – GRAVES FOR WORKERS AND
    LABORERS IN SHŌYU FACTORIES
D – UME-YA BRANCH HOUSE OF
    MOGI LINEAGE
E – BRANCH HOUSE OF IIDA FAMILY
F – MIYANO FAMILY – RELATIONSHIP
    WITH KASHIWA IE UNCERTAIN

G – ISHIKAWA FAMILY PLOT
H – MOGI SCHICHIRŌJI FAMILY PLOT (?)
I – LAND LEASED OR HELD BY
    KASHIWA FAMILY
J – NAKANO FAMILY PLOT
K – MOGI FUSAGORŌ FAMILY PLOT
L – MOGI KEIZABURŌ FAMILY PLOT
M – MOGI HONKE FAMILY PLOT
N – MOGI RIHEI FAMILY PLOT

the interdependency has become less and less evident as individual families have come to pursue social and economic advancement within the framework of the corporation.

Since the 1930s and especially since World War II, employment and promotion within the firm for family members are no longer considered patriarchal duties and rights. Families have had to become more frankly competitive with each other within the context of the corporation in order to secure employment and promotion. By agreement, only one son—usually the eldest—from each family in each generation has been allowed to join the company in the postwar period. (Two out of nine families, both of the Kashiwa lineage, have managed to circumvent this rule.) As a result, families carefully groom that scion, for its corporate fortune rests firmly on his future.

Since the Pacific War, the firm is no longer an extension of family property and pride. Instead families have come full circle to rely upon it for purpose and direction. In this way, they follow the firm now, while before the twentieth century, there was a noteworthy tendency for enterprise development to follow the contours of the family. In its most extreme form, a branch household with its own independent business was created in order to support an heir. In this century the proposition has been reversed: what is good for the family is subordinated to what is good for the firm.

APPENDIX B

Scroll from Mogi Fusagorō with Preface by Mogi Keizaburō to Shoda Bunuemon on the Founding of a Shōyu Brewery, 1872[1]

Directions: Mix together

First year, January	2 koku (95.2 gallons) of the *best* quality grains
First year, April	2 koku
First year, October	2 koku
Second year, March	2 koku

Ferment the above mixture for an average of 16½ months from January of the first year and press before November of the second year.

Alternatively

First year, July	2 koku of *better* quality grains
Second year, June	3 koku
Second year, November	3 koku

Ferment this mixture for an average of 15 months from July of the first year.

Alternatively

First year, July	2 koku of *good* quality grains
Second year, June	6 koku

Ferment for an average of 10 months from June of the second year.

Alternatively

First year, July	4 koku of *good* quality grains
Second year, July	4 koku

Ferment for an average of 19 months from July of the first year.

Instructions: Depending on the recipe used and the fermentation time required, the amount of mash to be prepared is based on the shipping rate desired at the end of the summer. For example, if beginning in January and continuing until July, 500 kegs (4.3-gallon taru) per month are shipped, this would equal a semi-annual production of 271 koku (12,900 gallons). If during this same period, 300 kegs per month were shipped, then 2,100 kegs for seven months or 190 koku (9,044 gallons) would be the production figure.

Cost calculations: (for 1,200 kegs of the best quality shōyu)

raw materials—good quality soybeans, 50 koku	250 ryō
wheat, 50 koku	167 ryō
akaho salt, 200 hyō	67 ryō
subtotal	484 ryō

307

	grand total (add 5 percent for loss & waste)	505 ryō
	kegs and labor—kegs	171.5 ryō
	miscellaneous (including labor, laborers' room & board, transport and other incidentals)	200 ryō
	Total costs	876.5 ryō

Revenue
calculations: (for 1,200 kegs of the best quality shōyu)

1,200 kegs at market price	1000 ryō
shōyu kasu (press cake residue)	40 ryō
Total revenue	1040 ryō

Profit
calculations:

Total revenue	1040 ryō
Total costs	876.5 ryō
Difference	163.5 ryō
Profit as a percent of costs	163.5 ryō/876.5 ryō or, 18.65 percent profit

Rules and Regulations of the
Noda Shōyu Brewers' Association[1]

To: Ei Funakoshi, Governor of Chiba Prefecture
Request to form the Noda Shōyu Brewers' Association

Noda Township, Higashi Katsushika County, Chiba Prefecture. Representatives of the Noda Shōyu Brewers' Association: Mogi Saheiji, Takanashi Hyōzaemon, Mogi Shichirōuemon

We, the above stated representatives, in accordance with the Prefectural Edict No. 106, issued in 1884, having the agreement of more than three-quarters of the parties involved, allowing for the established tradition of our industry, do hereby present articles of association asking for the establishment of a manufacturing cartel.

June 1887

>Mogi Saheiji, Takanashi Hyōzaemon, Mogi Shichirōuemon
>Miyano Sangorō Headman, Noda Township
>Okada Takanosuke, Headman, Imagami Village
>Nakamura Shigetoshi, Headman, Nagareyama Township
>Ōtsuka Toheita, Headman Umahashi Township
>Tanaka Genshichi, Headman, Kami-Hongō Village

According to Prefectural Edict Number 106 of 1884 concerning the establishment of manufacturing cartels, the following statutes have been fixed and agreed upon:
  I. The Organization and Name of the Association
    1. The members of the association are those involved in the manufacture of shōyu in the town of Noda, District of Shimōsa and Higashi Katsushika County, and the surrounding area.
    2. The name of the cartel will be the Noda Shōyu Brewers' Association.
  II. The Location of the Association and Its Headquarters
    3. The association will operate within Chiba Prefecture, Shimōsa County.

4. It will include the following villages: Noda, Kami-Haniwa, Nakano-dai, Imagami, Nagareyama, Shinsaku, Nemoto.

III. Purpose and Method

5. The purpose of the association, based on mutual trust and harmony, is to promote the management of individual, family-based breweries as well as the association as a whole.

6. The members of the association will conduct themselves honestly and avoid selling imperfect goods which will destroy our good reputation.

7. If in their dealings, our brokers prove to be not trustworthy, then upon reaching unanimous agreement, we shall repudiate them and thereby protect our profit.

8. The following regulations concerning employment shall be made known to all workers and employees. If any employee is dismissed, the circumstances of the dismissal shall be investigated by the association president and reported to the association.
   a. the orders of the owners shall be carried out by the tōji, the factory foremen,
   b. there shall be no violent demonstrations.

9. Anyone reported committing a violation under Article 8 above, will no longer and hereafter be employed by the association.

IV. The Selection of Association Officers and Their Authority

10. There shall be a president and three assistants, that is, secretaries.

11. The president will be elected by members of the association, and the three assistants shall serve by rotation from within the association membership.

12. The president shall manage all the ordinary affairs of the association and direct the financial performance of the association.

13. The secretaries shall assist the president in the management of the affairs of the association and represent the president of the association whenever the occasion arises.

14. The following duties shall be the exclusive prerogative of the president of the association:
    a. the calling together of meetings of the association,
    b. the determination of the agenda for both regular and extraordinary meetings of the association,
    c. the obligation to communicate information on changing market conditions and prices to members of the association,
    d. the right of expenditure of up to 10 yen on any one occasion on matters affecting the association,
    e. a careful accountancy of the association's expenses.

15. Members of the association are not paid for conducting business, but expenses incurred while on association business shall be reimbursed.

16. Secretaries of the association shall have one year appointments. The president shall be elected annually at the spring meeting, and if re-elected, consecutive terms may be served.

17. Unless the president elect has a legitimate excuse, he must accept the

office of president of the association. If he has already served three terms, however, he has the right to refuse a fourth term.

V. Meetings of the Association

18. There will be regular and extraordinary meetings.

19. The regular meetings will be held on January 8 and June 20.

20. Members of the association should make all efforts to attend the meetings. If, however, the meeting cannot be attended for some legitimate reason, an alternative representative may be sent. Persons absent from the meeting have no right to question or criticize the decisions reached by those attending the meeting. If one is not able to attend, an explanation for the absence must be sent to the association with all haste.

21. To be officially convened, meetings require a quorum of half of the membership.

22. Regular meetings should be convened by the president of the association. In the case of extraordinary meetings, however, a temporary president may be selected.

23. The place, date, and time of the meeting should be announced on the agenda for the meeting, which must be circulated at least one day in advance of the meeting.

VI. Entering the Leaving the Association

24. When someone wishes to join the association, he will be required to read the rules of the association and to place his seal on a copy of the rules of the association under the association president's name. The entrance of a new member to the association will be reported to all current members.

25. When someone wishes to withdraw from the association, he will inform the president of the association of his reasons for withdrawal. The president will communicate this request to those responsible for reviewing such matters. In the case of a withdrawal, the person concerned will be held responsible for his share of the expenses of the association up to and including the day of withdrawal from the time the person joined the association.

VII. Regulations Regarding the Levying and Collecting of Expenses

26. Expenses incurred during meetings of the association as well as by joint decision of the association will be assessed upon the members of the association.

27. Emergency expenses may be approved upon consensus of those attending an extraordinary meeting.

VIII. Savings

28. In order to carry out our functions, once every year in January each member of the association will pay to the association an amount of money equal to one yen for every 100 koku of production in the immediately prior year. The amount of production for the prior year must be reported to the president of the association by January 10.

29. All matters relating to the collection of annual dues from the membership will be supervised by the president of the association or his assistants.

30. The dues collected by the association should not be used for the next ten years. When this period expires, the principal should be divided and returned to the membership but the interest on the principal should be retained by the association. If, however, an emergency arises and some of the principal must be expended, this decision must be made with the consent of the entire membership.

31. Those who withdrew from the association will have their dues (principal) and interest on their dues returned to them.

IX. Default

32. Those found in error of the 6th, 7th, or 9th Article of this agreement or those who conceal the amount of their production must pay a penalty of between 5 and 30 yen, to be decided by the rest of the membership.

33. Any member of the association who is fined more than three times under Article 32 above must be reported in the newspaper as well as fined again.

34. Those who fail to attend a meeting announced in advance must pay a fine of one yen; those who are late must pay a fine of 50 sen [half a yen].

35. All of the money collected by fines will become part of the treasury of the association.

36. If this agreement needs to be revised, it must be revised in the course of a meeting of the association and consent in favor of the revision must be reached among the membership.

The following persons attest to the accuracy of the above agreement:

Mogi Shichirōuemon, Noda-chō
Mogi Saheiji, Noda-chō
Takanashi Hyozaemon, Kami Hanawa-mura
Takanashi Kōuemon, Kami Hanawa-mura
Mogi Shichizaemon, Noda-chō
Mogi Yūuemon, Noda-chō
Mogi Rihei, Nakano-dai-mura
Tobe Yashirō, Noda-chō
Yamashita Heibei, Noda-chō
Akimoto Sanuemon, Nagareyama-mura
Horikiri Monjirō, Nagareyama-mura
Asami Heibei, Nagareyama-mura
Takeuchi Kiyosaburō, Shinsaku-mura
Shimamura Katsusaburō, Nemoto-mura

Higashi Katsushika-gun, Shimosa-gori, Chiba-ken

Appendix D

Noda Shōyu Brewers' Association
Income and Expenses, 1888–1918 (yen)

Period	Income	Expense	Running balance
1888: 1887 reserve fund—reserve carry forward[a]	380.		
89: 1888 reserve—carry forward	460.		
90: 1889 reserve—carry forward	508.		1,348.
91: interest on 1888–90 reserve	49.40		1,397.40
91: 1890 reserve—carry forward	367.		
92: 1891 reserve—carry forward	391.		
93: 1892 reserve—carry forward	453.		2,608.40
93: interest on 1891–92 reserve	175.796		2,784.196
94: interest on 1893 reserve	174.331		
94: 1893 reserve—carry forward	466.		3,424.527
94: Takanashi Kōuemon reserve withdrawal		138.	
94: Takanashi Kōuemon interest on reserve withdrawal		21.45	
94: Takanashi Shuzō reserve withdrawal		17.	
94: Takanashi Shuzō interest on reserve withdrawal		2.642	
94: Shimamura Katsuzaburō reserve withdrawal		8.00	

Period	Income	Expense	Running balance
94: Shimamura Katsuzaburō interest on reserve withdrawal		1.243	3,236.192
95: 1894 reserve—carry forward	523.		
95: 1894 interest on reserve fund	176.70		3,935.892
96: 1895 reserve—carry forward	541.		
96: 1895 interest on reserve fund	236.017		4,712.909
97: 1896 reserve—carry forward	585.		
97: 1896 interest on reserve fund	282.775		5,580.684
98: 1897 interest on reserve funds	334.840		5,915.524
98: Horikiri Monjirō reserve withdrawal		237.	
98: Horikiri Monjirō interest on reserve withdrawal		74.188	
98: Akimoto Sanuemon reserve withdrawal		163.	
98: Akimoto Sanuemon interest on reserve withdrawal		51.023	
98: Asami Heibei reserve withdrawal		83.	
98: Asami Heibei interest on reserve withdrawal		25.981	
98: Takeuchi Kiyosaburō reserve withdrawal		72.	
98: Takeuchi Kiyosaburō interest on reserve withdrawal		22.538	5,186.794
98: 1897 reserve—carry forward	486.		5,672.794 (sic)
98: Lumber expense for new amusement park		139.828	5,532.972
99: 1898 reserve—carry forward	534.		
99: 1898 interest on reserve fund	385.		6,451.972
1900: 1899 reserve—carry forward	583.		
00: 1899 interest on reserve fund	394.898		7,429.870

Period	Income	Expense	Running balance
01: 1900 reserve—carry forward	657.		
01: 1900 interest on reserve fund	537.570		
01: 1901 half-month (January) interest	34.930		8,659.370
01: 1901 tax on residential property		225.	
01: 1901 tax on plant and equipment		279.060	8,155.310
02: 1901 reserve—carry forward	713.		
02: 1901 interest on reserve fund	593.800		
02: Payment on Noda Push-Trolley shares		1,025.	8,437.110
03: 1902 reserve—carry forward	748.		
03: 1902 interest on reserve fund	598.030		9,783.140
04: 1903 interest on reserve fund	681.430		
04: Building expense amusement park		1,500.	
04: Plant and equipment, research lab		2,839.930	
04: 1903 reserve—carry forward	1,574.00		7,698.640
04: Payment to Mogi Shichirōuemon for land		698.640	7,000.000
05: 1904 interest on reserve accumulated	505.		
05: Entrance payment from Horikiri Monjirō	200.		
05: 1904 reserve—carry forward	1,718.		9,415.000
05: Payment to Mogi Shichirōuemon		1,045.020	
05: Compensation to head of research lab		200.	
05: Compensation to laboratory assistant		50.	8,119.98
06: 1905 interest on accumulated reserve	529.700		
06: Dividend from push-trolley	25.00		

Period	Income	Expense	Running balance
06: Income from sale (of one) trolley share	12.50		
06: Dividend from push-trolley	15.00		
06: Expenses at research lab (for 1905)		895.100	
06: 1905 reserve—carry forward	1,974.00		9,781.880
07: 1906 interest on accumulated reserve	586.860		
07: Dividend from push-trolley	30.00		
07: 1906 reserve—carry forward	1,904.00		12,301.940
07: 1906 expenses at research lab		1,549.624	
07: 1906 land rent for research lab		31.10	10,721.216
08: 1907 interest on accumulated reserve	643.270		
08: Dividend from push-trolley	30.		11,394.486
08: 1907 reserve—carry forward	2,000.00		13,394.486
08: 1907 expenses at research lab		2,105.	
08: 1907 land for research lab		40.906	11,248.580
09: 1908 interest on accumulated reserve	564.570		
09: 1908 dividend on push-trolley	30.00		
09: 1908 reserve—carry forward	1,912.00		13,755.150
09: 1908 expenses for research lab		590.00	
09: steel girders (6)		148.00	
09: lumber (unseasoned)		4.10	
09: Payment Mogi Fusagorō		26.23	
09: Salary and extras for Mr. Suzuki, head of laboratory		156.375	
09: Retirement compensation, Suzuki		150.000	
09: Medical payments for the sick, infirmed		190.190	
09: Rent for research lab (for land)		31.10	

Period	Income	Expense	Running balance
09: One month's salary for Suzuki		30.	
09: Miscellaneous expenses at laboratory		4.270	12,424.885
09: Interest to Yamashita Heibei	187.500		12,612.385
10: 1909 interest on accumulated reserve	857.620		
10: Dividend from push-trolley	30.00		
10: 1909 reserve—carry forward	2,224.00		15,724.005
10: Expenses for research lab		1,385.676	
10: Payment to Kojima		29.00	
10: Land rent to Umebayashi		31.10	
10: Dividend from push-trolley	30.00		14,308.230
11: 1910 interest on accumulated reserve	914.570		
11: Dividend from push-trolley	15.00		
11: 1910 reserve—carry forward	2,325.00		17,558.800
11: Expenses—research lab		1,526.428	
11: New construction—research lab		550.	
11: Gas generator		350.	
11: Appurtenances for the generator		136.	
11: Supply pump for generator		72.	
11: Chemical equipment and supplies		398.	14,530.370
12: 1911 interest on accumulated reserve	1,020.840		
12: Dividend from push-trolley	30.		
12: Presentation from Tokyo brokers	50.		
12: 1911 reserve—carry forward	2,546.		18,177.210
12: Expenses for research lab		1,855.276	
12: Expense for land at proposed railroad station		584.427	15,737.507
13: 1911 interest on accumulated reserve	980.560		
13: Dividend from push-trolley	15.		16,733.070
13: Expense for land at Noda railroad station		1,101.760	

Period	Income	Expense	Running balance
13: Expense for storage—railroad station		1,534.330	
13: Expense for drainage & excavation at station		37.600	
13: Expense for storage construction at research lab		1,445.032	
13: Expenses for research laboratory operation		2,534.598	10,079.750
13: 1912 reserve—carry forward	2,899.		
13: 1911 reserve funds from (Kikkosho?)	60.		13,038.750
14: 1913 interest on accumulated reserve	867.400		
14: Dividend from push-trolley	25.		
14: 1912 reserve from Horikiri Monjirō	27.		
14: 1913 reserve—carry forward	2,761.		16,719.150
14: Railroad station—storage and drainage		218.865	
14: Expense for research lab operation		4,247.981	12,252.300
15: 1914 interest on accumulated reserve	651.400		
15: Dividend from push-trolley	12.50		
15: Railroad station—storage/land income	543.700		
15: 1914 reserve—carry forward	3,039.		16,498.900
15: Expenses for operation of research lab		556.400	15,942.500
16: 1915 interest on accumulated reserve	1,033.250		
16: Dividend from push-trolley	37.500		
16: Railroad station—storage/land income	396.300		
16: 1915 reserve—carry forward	3,041.00		20,450.550
16: Expense for research lab operation		2,048.664	
16: Purchase—28 shares push-trolley (24 yen/share)		700.	17,701.890

Period	Income	Expense	Running balance
17: 1916 interest on accumulated reserve	953.840		
17: Railroad station—storage/land income	425.300		
17: 1916 reserve—carry forward	3,563.00		22,644.030
17: Expense for operation of research lab		1,910.514	20,733.516
18: 1917 interest on accumulated reserve	1,164.610		
18: Railroad station—storage/land income	425.300		
18: Expense for research lab operation		790.520	21,532.910

Source: Kikkoman Company Archives, "Noda Brewers' Association Ledger" (n.p., 1918).

a. All bookkeeping calculations were reported in January of the year following the transactions.

Property Held by Mogi-Takanashi Families Joining Noda Shōyu Company Inventory Taken November–December 1917

Paid-in Captial: Family	Yen	Shares
Mogi Saheiji	1,990,000	19,900
Mogi Shichirōuemon	1,890,000	18,900
Takanashi Hyōzaemon	990,000	9,900
Mogi Shichizaemon	840,000	8,400
Mogi Fusagorō	500,000	5,000
Mogi Keizaburō	140,000	1,400
Horikiri Monjirō	101,000	1,010
Mogi Kumazō	100,000	1,000
Mogi Sadanosuke	100,000	1,000
Nakano Chōbei	70,000	700
Mogi Shinichi	50,000	500
Mogi Yūuemon	50,000	500
Ishikawa Niheiji	40,000	400
Nakano Eizaburō	30,000	300
Mogi Shichirōji	30,000	300
Takanashi Nisaburō	13,000	130
Takanashi Masanosuke	10,000	100
Takanashi Hideo	10,000	100
Takanashi Shōichirō	10,000	100
Mogi Junzaburō	10,000	100
Mogi Shiichirō	10,000	100
Mogi Michizō	8,000	80
Mogi Junichirō	6,000	60
Mogi Shinsaburō	2,000	20
Total	7,000,000	70,000

Additional Capital Accounts   290,156.80

BREAKDOWN

Land Holdings

4th factory (2,411.4 tsubo)	bought from Mogi Fusagorō	10,851.300 yen
4th factory (425.7 tsubo)	Mogi Saheiji	1,915.200
5th factory (2,191.4 tsubo)	Mogi Fusagorō	9,861.300
6th factory (3,192.2 tsubo)	Mogi Shichirōuemon	10,054.800
6th factory (559 tsubo)	Mogi Saheiji	1,760.400
7th factory (4,486.7 tsubo)	Mogi Shichizaemon	14,132.700
8th factory (3,436.2 tsubo)	Noda Shōyu Gōshi Co.	10,823.400
9th factory (7,897.7 tsubo)	Mogi Saheiji	24,876.900
9th factory—Imperial Household area and attached land (4,220.2 tsubō)	Mogi Saheiji	11,767.500
10th factory (10,905.5 tsubo)	Mogi Shichirōuemon	34,350.300
12th factory (6,602.6 tsubo)	Takanashi Hyōzaemon	20,798.100
12th factory (3,344.8 tsubo)	Takanashi Hyōzaemon	10,535.400
14th factory (3,774.1 tsubo)	Mogi Shichirōuemon	11,888.900
14th factory attached area (1,859 tsubo)	Takanashi Hyōzaemon	5,055.400
15th factory (3,796.5 tsubo)	Mogi Saheiji	11,958.300
15th factory attached area (1,446 tsubo)	Takanashi Hyōzaemon	4,554.900
16th factory (2,442 tsubo)	Mogi Keizaburō	7,692.300
Warehouse (1,077 tsubo)	Mogi Shichirōuemon	3,392.100
Tax Officers' residences (278.6 tsubo)	Mogi Saheiji	877.500
Total		207,945.900

Buildings and Plant

Main office building	bought from Mogi Shichirōuemon	3,022.200 yen
1st factory	Mogi Shichizaemon	54,025.200
2nd factory	Mogi Shichirōuemon	57,323.700
3rd factory	Mogi Saheiji	42,755.400
4th factory	Mogi Fusagorō	35,159.400
5th factory	Mogi Fusagorō	25,486.200
6th factory	Mogi Shichirōuemon	26,769.600
7th factory	Mogi Shichizaemon	47,718.900
8th factory	Noda Shōyu Gōshi Co.	30,536.800
9th factory	Mogi Saheiji	154,831.500
9th factory	Mogi Saheiji	31,322.700
10th factory	Mogi Shichirōuemon	86,170.500
11th factory	Takanashi Hyōzaemon	15,759.900
12th factory	Takanashi Hyōzaemon	72,153.900
13th factory	Takanashi Hyōzaemon	40,011.300
14th factory	Mogi Shichirōuemon	44,711.100

15th factory	Mogi Saheiji	69,504.300
16th factory	Mogi Keizaburō	26,779.500
17th factory	Horikiri Monjirō	22,748.400
18th factory	Mogi Fusagorō	5,760.000
Warehouse	Takanashi Hyōzaemon	4,174.200
Warehouse	Mogi Saheiji	8,473.500
Tax Officers' housing	Mogi Saheiji	2,359.800
Warehouse	Mogi Shichizaemon	8,991.000
Warehouse	Mogi Shichirōuemon	8,154.000
Warehouse	Mogi Fusagorō	
Total		931,032.000

Machinery

1st factory, 17 pieces	bought from Mogi Shichizaemon	23,022.900	yen
2nd factory, 21 pieces	Mogi Shichirōuemon	14,876.100	
3rd factory, 3 pieces	Mogi Saheiji	1,791.000	
4th factory, 12 pieces	Mogi Fusagorō	9,994.500	
5th factory, 13 pieces	Mogi Fusagorō	10,560.600	
6th factory, 13 pieces	Mogi Shichirōuemon	8,208.000	
7th factory, 14 pieces	Mogi Shichizaemon	18,036.000	
8th factory, 14 pieces	Noda Shōyu Gōshi Co.	7,904.700	
9th factory, 24 pieces	Mogi Saheiji	49,731.300	
10th factory, 31 pieces	Mogi Shichirōuemon	33,300.000	
11th factory, 12 pieces	Takanashi Hyōzaemon	8,887.400	
12th factory, 12 pieces	Takanashi Hyōzaemon	8,946.900	
13th factory, 15 pieces	Takanashi Hyōzaemon	18,321,300	
14th factory, 16 pieces	Mogi Shichirōuemon	16,235.100	
15th factory, 13 pieces	Mogi Saheiji	18,405.000	
16th factory, 17 pieces	Mogi Keizaburō	9,139.500	
17th factory, 9 pieces	Horikiri Monjirō	1,966.500	
Total		258,526.800	

Fermentation Vats

1st factory, 7 large tanks	bought from Mogi Shichizaemon	30,969.000	yen
2nd factory, 10 large tanks	Mogi Shichirōuemon	36,149.400	
3rd factory, 7 large tanks	Mogi Saheiji	16,184.700	
4th factory, 5 large tanks	Mogi Fusagorō	28,210.500	
5th factory, 8 large tanks	Mogi Fusagorō	17,401.500	
6th factory, 6 large tanks	Mogi Shichirōuemon	12,744.000	
7th factory, 6 large tanks	Mogi Shichizaemon	29,673.000	
8th factory, 7 large tanks	Noda Shōyu Gōshi Co.	16,011.000	
9th factory, 6 large tanks	Mogi Saheiji	76,491.000	
9th factory, 2 large tanks	Mogi Saheiji	10,549.000	
10th factory, 10 large tanks	Mogi Shichirōuemon	60,249.600	

11th factory, 6 large tanks	Takanashi Hyōzaemon	7,956.000
12th factory, 6 large tanks	Takanashi Hyōzaemon	35,424.000
13th factory, 6 large tanks	Takanashi Hyōzaemon	31,329.000
14th factory, 5 large tanks	Mogi Shichirōuemon	31,115.700
15th factory, 6 large tanks	Mogi Saheiji	33,246.000
16th factory, 8 large tanks	Mogi Keizaburō	14,124.600
17th factory, 5 large tanks	Horikiri Monjirō	13,500.000
Total		509,328.000

Trademark and Other Intangibles

Kikkoman trademark	bought from Mogi Saheiji	246,572.600 yen
Manjo Mirin	Horikiri Monjirō	5,846.400
Total		252,419.000

Business Expense

Real estate registration fee for incorporation	35,000.000 yen
Total	35,000.000

Local Accounts Payable

Mogi Shichirōuemon	206,413.000 yen
Mogi Saheiji	99,016.000
Takanashi Hyōzaemon	65,000.000
Mogi Shichizaemon	65,832.000
Mogi Fusagorō	55,000.000
Noda Shōyu Gōshi Co.	43,013.000
Total	534,274.000

Moromi Mash

51,549 koku	bought from Mogi Shichirōuemon	873,997.200 yen
54,847 koku	Mogi Saheiji	947,325.600
30,227 koku	Takanashi Hyōzaemon	512.199.900
22,808 koku	Mogi Shichizaemon	386,371.800
17,733 koku	Mogi Fusagorō	298,113.300
6,902 koku	Noda Shōyu Gōshi Co.	111,812.400
5,880 koku	Mogi Keizaburō	95,356.800
3,390 koku	Horikiri Monjirō	53,432.100
Total		3,278,609.100

Raw Materials

7,282 koku of soybeans	bought from Mogi Shichirōuemon	97,101.000 yen
3,338 koku of soybeans	Mogi Saheiji	46,230.300
2,880 koku of soybeans	Takanashi Hyōzaemon	39,315.600

3,200 koku of soybeans	Mogi Shichizaemon	41,145.300
1,859 koku of soybeans	Mogi Fusagorō	24,786.000
670 koku of soybeans	Noda Shōyu Gōshi Co.	8,613.900
548 koku of soybeans	Mogi Keizaburō	7,785.000
50 koku of soybeans	Horikiri Monjirō	642.600
14,224 koku of wheat	Mogi Shichirōuemon	196,947.000
10,681 koku of wheat	Mogi Saheiji	147,896.100
6,793 koku of wheat	Takanashi Hyōzaemon	94,063.500
5,481 koku of wheat	Mogi Shichizaemon	75,898.800
4,096 koku of wheat	Mogi Fusagorō	54,891.000
1,994 koku of wheat	Mogi Keizaburō	14,652.000
1,704 koku of wheat	Noda Shōyu Gōshi Co.	23,598.900
512,800 kin of salt	Mogi Shichirōuemon	13,845.600
231,120 kin of salt	Mogi Saheiji	6,239.700
259,620 kin of salt	Takanashi Hyōzaemon	7,009.200
186,200 kin of salt	Mogi Shichizaemon	5,027.400
113,500 kin of salt	Mogi Fusagorō	3,064.500
10,000 kin of salt	Noda Shōyu Gōshi Co.	270.000
15,400 kin of salt	Mogi Keizaburō	415.800
6,000 kin of salt	Horikiri Monjirō	162.000
Total		909,601.200

Kegs

3,273 new kegs	bought from Mogi Shichirōuemon	7,511.400 yen
67 new kegs	Mogi Shichirōuemon	144.000
4,013 old kegs	Mogi Shichirōuemon	14,418.000
4,616 old kegs	Mogi Shichirōuemon	4,702.500
1,548 large kegs	Mogi Shichirōuemon	1,638.900
3,203 new kegs	Mogi Saheiji	7,352.100
9,594 new kegs	Takanashi Hyōzaemon	22,023.900
old kegs	Takanashi Hyōzaemon	9,557.100
2,143 new kegs	Mogi Shichizaemon	4,919.400
old kegs	Mogi Shichizaemon	15,697.800
1,291 new kegs	Mogi Fusagorō	2,962.800
old kegs	Mogi Fusagorō	10,063.800
old kegs	Noda Shōyu Gōshi Co.	3,115.800
519 new kegs	Mogi Keizaburō	1,192.500
old kegs	Mogi Keizaburō	3,240.000
2,140 old kegs	Horikiri Monjirō	2,889.000
Total		111,429.000

Soy Sauce

soy sauce	bought from Noda Shōyu Gōshi Co.	6,068.700 yen
Total		6,068.700

Rice

489 koku of rice	bought from Mogi Shichirōuemon	10,122.300 yen
93.2 koku of rice	Mogi Saheiji	1,928.700
179 koku of rice	Mogi Shichizaemon	3,915.900
Total		15,966.900

Lumber

225,910 board shaku	bought from Mogi Shichirōuemon	126,057.600 yen
55,720 board shaku	Mogi Saheiji	86,891.400
11,000 board shaku	Takanashi Hyōzaemon	6,138.000
22,000 board shaku	Mogi Shichizaemon	11,276.000
15,400 board shaku	Mogi Fusagorō	8,593.200
Total		239,956.200

SUMMARY BY CATEGORY OF INVENTORY

	value (yen)	*value (percent)*
Land Holdings	207,945.900	2.85
Buildings & Plant	931,032.000	12.77
Machinery	258,526.800	3.55
Fermentation Vats	509,328.000	6.99
Trademark & Intangibles	252,419.000	3.46
Business Expenses	35,000.000	0.48
Accounts Payable	534,274.000	7.33
Moromi Mash	3,278,609.100	44.97
Raw Materials	909,601.200	12.48
Barrels	111,429.000	1.53
Shōyu	6,068.700	0.08
Rice	15,966.900	0.22
Lumber	239,956.200	3.29
Total	7,290,156.800	100.00

Source: Kikkoman Company Archives, Property Inventory at the Time of Incorporation, (n.p., 1917).

New Wage and Work Proposal, Noda Shōyu Company, 1919[1]

I. Issues for Improving the Conditions of Factory Workers

1. Based on the annual year-end accounting, a fund for the welfare of factory employees as well as for their medical and retirement benefits will be established from the company's profits.
2. In order to increase the welfare of the workers, a mutual aid association consisting of laborers as members will be formed.

   The expenses for the mutual aid association will be paid from capital and interest held in the fund mentioned above. (The aims and regulations of the mutual aid association are provided separately.)
3. Wages for factory and warehouse workers will be paid on a daily basis and the system of yearly wage contracting will be established.
4. Pay days will be twice a month, on the 14th and on the second from the last day of the month.
5. In order to prevent turnover during busy times of the year, a bonus will be paid according to the following schedule:
   (a) Allowance for no absenteeism:

   25 days without an absence—2 days' salary

   30 days without an absence—3 days' salary

   The above will be computed every month and will be paid once at the end of the work year. (Holidays will be included in the number of work days calculated.)
   (b) Bonuses for continued service:

   one-year service—10 days' salary

   two-year service—12 days' salary

   three-year service—15 days' salary

   Three days' bonus will be added to the computation for every year of service.
   (c) Bonus for responsibility:

   A worker who is engaged in a responsible position which is carried out faithfully will receive in addition 5 days' salary.

   Items (b) and (c) above will be paid to the workers at the end of the year.
6. One day's salary in the case of (a) means one day's wage averaged over

the month; (b) and (c) represent one day's wages averaged over the year.

7. Community and Housing: Commuters complain more and they are more absent than those who live in the company dormitories. For these reasons, commuting expenses will be provided for those who commute to work.

8. Factory employee classifications:
   1st class (*honnin*), 2nd class (*chūnin*), 3rd class (*yamadashi*) are the three classes of workers. The daily wage differs depending upon the classification.

9. Payment arrangements for medical and retirement benefits will be set up. Persons who are ill or injured or about to retire will be paid such benefits.

II. *Outline of Regulations for the Mutual Aid Association for Workers*

1. Purpose: This association is established to increase the happiness of the laborers of the Noda Shōyu Company, Ltd., to harmonize the interests of the capitalists and the workers, and to increase the productivity of labor.

2. The name of the association: This association will be named the Noda Labor Mutual Aid Association.

3. Members: There are two kinds of members—special members and official members. Official members are those who work at the company: the company board of executives, tōji, office and factory workers; special members are those who have been specially appointed or those who have contributed money to the association.

4. Chairman: The chairman is the president of the Noda Shōyu Company, Ltd.

5. Advisers: The company's board of executives will be the advisers of the Association.

6. Managers: The managers of the Association are the heads and two representatives from each factory who have been selected by the other workers.

7. Standing Committee: Three of the factory foremen and three of the worker representatives will be selected. In addition to these, the chairman and three company managers will be appointed to the Standing Committee.

8. Business of the Association:
   (a) When a demand for a raise or other labor-related issues come up, a meeting of managers and workers will be held and negotiations between the two sides will take place.
   (b) Once every year a celebration of thanks for the efforts of the laborers will be held.
   (c) Workers whose contributions to the business were outstanding or those who were inspirations for other workers will be commended.
   (d) Lectures on religious and other spiritual matters will be held.
   (e) In order to encourage an attitude of thrift among the workers, certain provisions will be established for them at the bank to encourage savings.

9. Budget: Expenses for the association will be paid from the interest of a fund established for the betterment of the workers as well as from contributions given to the Association.

The above items as essential points in the regulations of the association will be provided.

III. *Solving Problems in the Factories*
1. Wages for the Workers: The yearly wage system will be abolished and a daily wage system established in its place. The practice of paying cash advances will be stopped and wages will be paid either two or three times per month. The previous yearly wage system made it difficult to move workers during busy periods. Furthermore, halfway through the year, illness, military service, and other unforeseen circumstances, along with other inconveniences, such as the difficulties of redeeming advance payments or canceling back payments, made this system quite troublesome. The substitutes found to replace workers were often poor. They disturbed work and prevented increases in work productivity. Under a daily wage system, the abovementioned abuses will not be concerns. Furthermore, by commending those workers who are dedicated to the company, we hope to reduce turnover.

[The recommendations in this article were approved by over 60 percent of the factory managers, tōji, and workers]
2. Commuting and Costs: Electricity, bedding, charcoal, and other expenses of daily life are provided free in company dormitories. Therefore, price increases in various commodities do not affect lodgers in the dormitories, and winter or summer temperatures are not a concern for them. In contrast to this, commuters are responsible for all their own expenses and because of commodity price increases, the complaints of commuters are frequent. They struggle to survive by taking extra jobs. As a result, requests for salary increases are more likely to come from commuters than lodgers although the company would like to treat both groups with fairness.
3. Concerning Workers' Classifications, Honnin, Chūnin, Yamadashi: Although there are differences among the honnin, or most experienced workers, their wage has been the same since olden times. Thus, there is no wage difference between the devoted and the lazy among them. The company wants to keep advanced and competent workers, while weeding out superannuated ones; and the company would like to have four basic grades for workers (*kō, otsu, hei,* and *tei*) rather than two or three. The company wants to eliminate all of the old and private considerations which were part of the traditional wage system.
4. Recognition for Workers: The company wants to give bonuses as well as recognition to those workers whose service is long, meritorious, and a model for others. On the other hand, those who are frequently absent, idle, and sick are to be reprimanded, discharged, or otherwise discouraged.

5. To establish a time of rest and relaxation for workers, there will be 9 full days and 43 half-days of vacation during the year. Musical instruments may be used for the workers' enjoyment, and recreational facilities for the benefit of both the lodgers and the commuters will be established.

6. Old Age Pension and Savings Plan: Those who have been serving the company diligently for several years have contributed to an important degree to this business. Such workers must prepare themselves for retirement, but the company would like to instruct and encourage them in a plan for their security during old age. This will be part of the favorable treatment which the company shows to its devoted workers.

7. Lectures on religion and other subjects to instruct workers in a positive way: In general, workers are lacking in religious conviction and their moral sense is not developed. They are unlikely to think independently and they tend to follow things blindly. Once or twice a month appropriate teachers will be selected, and their lectures and teaching will give direction and purpose to the thinking of the workers.

8. As for demands for an increase in wages, the company would like to cultivate a sense of duty and responsibility among workers. Although there are requests for raises, responsibility seems to be lacking and productivity is not increasing. What can be done to improve this situation? Although we have been thinking about it constantly, no solution presents itself. There are considerable wage differences among factory workers, carpenters, plasterers, boiler operators, and other positions. These differences seem to affect the workers and, as a result, those who should be devoted to the company seem lacking in spirit.

9. Tōji are the head representatives of each factory and they work to have satisfactory performance in each plant. In the past, tōji were the most skilled workers and they were able to unify the workers; most tōji are old now and it is difficult for them to keep up with the younger workers.

At this time we would like to suggest the need for improvement in the selection of tōji and in their leadership and supervision of the workers.

10. The districts from which oyabun recruit workers need to be unified and they should check on the background of the workers they find. After they represent the workers at the time of contract negotiations for employment, their function is completed. Accordingly, they have nothing to do with accidents that might occur during the year or with workers who transfer from one factory to another. Because of the distance of the oyabun from the work itself, good workers are not likely to be selected, and poor workers are not motivated to do better. On this occasion all recruiting functions are to be unified and the backgrounds of all of the workers will be checked. In this way it is hoped that the high rates of turnover, absenteeism, and transfer, which have caused much hardship, will be reduced.

August 27, Taishō 8 (1919)
All the Factory Managers and Foremen

Notes

Introduction

1. Roman numerals following a name indicate the number of generations in the family line. For a detailed discussion of the Japanese family system, see Appendix A.

2. Anonymous, *Noda Shōyu Kumiaishi* (n.p., 1919?), pp. 16–19.

3. Ibid., pp. 11, 19.

4. W. Mark Fruin, "The Japanese Company Controversy," *The Journal of Japanese Studies,* 4 (Winter 1978), 267–300.

5. The emperor became involved, in part, because Kikkoman had been a supplier of shōyu products to the Imperial Household.

6. Peter Duus, *The Rise of Modern Japan* (Boston: Houghton Mifflin, 1976), p. 118.

7. Johannes Hirschmeier and Tsunehiko Yui, *The Development of Japanese Business, 1600–1973* (Cambridge, Mass.: Harvard University Press, 1975), pp. 206–211.

8. Koji Taira, *Economic Development and the Labor Market in Japan* (New York: Columbia University Press, 1970), pp. 184–203.

9. The official definition of what constitutes a small- and medium-sized enterprise in Japan has not remained constant. Before World War II a firm with less than 100 employees fell into that category; from 1945–1965 the cutoff grew to 300; and since 1966 the upper limit has been raised to 500. For a delightful description of the family character of much of the small industry in Japan, see Lawrence Olson, *Dimensions of Japan* (New York: American Universities Field Staff, 1963), pp. 13–33. For figures on the importance of family members in small- and medium-sized enterprises, see Tokyo Metropolitan Government, *Minor Industries and Workers in Tokyo* (Tokyo: Dai-Nippon, 1972), p. 40.

Thomas Rohlen's study *For Harmony and Strength* (Berkeley and Los Angeles: University of California Press, 1974), documents this position for a modern, medium-sized bank in Central Japan.

1. Factories in the Fields

1. See Thomas C. Smith's masterful treatment of this theme in "Pre-Modern Economic Growth: Japan and the West," *Past and Present*, 60 (August 1973).

2. Ando Seiichi et al., "Yuasa Shōyugyō no Kenkyū," part of a series on important industries of Wakayama Prefecture, Wakayama Daigaku Keizaigakubu, March 1954, 29 pages.

3. Ichiyama Morio, *Noda no Shōyu* (Noda: Noda City Local History Museum, 1973), p. 19.

4. Kawakoshi Kenji, ed., *Shashi—Choshi Shōyu Kabushiki Kaisha* (Tokyo: Toppan, 1972), pp. 41–46.

5. Ichiyama Morio, ed., *Noda Shōyu Keizaishiryō Shusei* (Noda: Noda Shōyu Research Department, 1955), p. 1.

6. Ichiyama Morio, *Noda no Rekishi* (Nagareyama: Ronso, 1975), p. 38. See also Gilbert Rozman, *Urban Networks in Ch'ing China and Tokugawa Japan* (Princeton: Princeton University Press, 1974).

7. Ichiyama Morio, ed., *Noda Shōyu Kabushiki Kaisha Sanjugonenshi* (Tokyo: Toppan, 1955), p. 69.

8. Ichiyama Morio, ed., *Noda Shōyu Kabushiki Kaisha Nijunenshi* (Tokyo: Toppan, 1940), pp. 122–123.

9. I am indebted to William Shurtleff for much of this information on the biochemistry of shōyu fermentation. See especially two works by William Shurtleff and Akiko Aoyagi: *The Book of Miso* (Ballantine ed., 1976, App. C), and their forthcoming work, "A History of Soybeans and Soyfoods," The Soyfoods Center, 1984.

10. Thomas C. Smith, "Ōkura Nagatsune and the Technologists," in Albert M. Craig and Donald H. Shively, eds., *Personality in Japanese History* (Berkeley: University of California Press, 1970), pp. 127–154.

11. Kim Choshi, *Shōyu Enkakushi* (Tokyo: Tokyo Tsukiji, 1913), p. 36.

12. Ichiyama Morio, ed., *Kikkoman Shōyu Shi* (Tokyo: Toppan, 1968), pp. 120–121.

13. This discussion of traditional brewing technology and its changes was drawn from Ichiyama, ed., *Kikkoman Shōyu Shi*, pp. 118–129, 148–186.

14. Aburai Hiroko, "Chōshi Shōyu Jōzōgyō ni okeru Kōyō Rōdō," *Kinsei*, 4 (February 1980), 24–40.

15. *Gumma-ken Yuraku-gun Shi* (Tokyo: Meicho, 1973), p. 48; Kawakoshi, ed., *Shashi*, p. 68.

16. Kikkoman Company Archives, *Ippaku Hikaechō* (n.p., 1885).

17. Aburai, "Chōshi Shōyu," pp. 33–34.

18. Kawakoshi, ed., *Shashi*, pp. 68, 107–110.

19. Ichiyama, ed., *Noda Shōyu Keizaishiryō Shusei*, pp. 12–14.

20. Anonymous, *Noda Shōyu Jōzō Kumiai Shi* (n.p., 1919?), p. 92.

21. Aburai, "Chōshi Shōyu," pp. 35, 36.

22. In 1911, according to national census records, Noda and the surrounding five villages had a population of 26,993.

23. Interviews, September 9 and 11, 1976, with Nakano Eizaburō, former president of the Noda Shōyu Company and employee of the company from 1918 to 1958.

24. Yoshida Tōru, "Honpō Shōyu Kōgyō Rōdō Jijō," *Shakai Seisaku Jihō*, 62 (November 1925), 127–130.

25. Ichiyama, ed., *Noda Shōyu Keizaishiryō Shusei*, pp. 117–125.

2. Clan and Cartel in Meiji Japan

1. See Kozo Yamamura, "The Development of *Za* in Medieval Japan," *Business History Review*, 47 (Winter 1973), 438–465.

2. Kawakoshi Kenji, ed., *Shashi-Choshi Shōyu Kabushiki Kaisha* (Tokyo: Toppan, 1972), p. 72; Ichiyama Morio, ed., *Noda Shōyu Kabushiki Kaisha Nijunenshi* (Tokyo: Toppan, 1940), p. 100.

3. Ichiyama Morio, ed., *Kikkoman Shōyu Shi* (Tokyo: Toppan, 1968), p. 323.

4. Kawakoshi, ed., *Shashi*, p. 72.

5. Ibid., p. 74.

6. Ibid., p. 73; Ichiyama, ed., *Kikkoman Shōyu Shi*, pp. 272–273.

7. Ichiyama Morio, ed., "Regulations of the Tokyo Shōyu Company (1881)," *Noda Shōyu Keizai Shiryō Shūsei* (Noda: Noda Shōyu Research Department, 1955), pp. 88–91.

8. Kawakoshi, ed., *Shashi*, p. 74.

9. Ibid., pp. 74–75; Ichiyama Morio, ed., *Noda Shōyu Kabushiki Kaisha Sanjugonenshi* (Tokyo: Toppan, 1955), pp. 82–85.

10. In just two years, for example, production had jumped 30 percent between 1887 and 1889. See annual production totals as listed in Figure 4.

11. Anonymous, *Noda Shōyu Jōzō Kumiai Shi* (n.p., 1919?), pp. 56–57.

12. Ibid., pp. 47, 107, 144, 253–258, 300. The fluctuations in wages were sometimes considerable and rather frequent.

13. Ibid., pp. 276–279.

14. Ibid., pp. 86, 149.

15. Kawakoshi, ed., *Shashi*, pp. 81–82.

16. *Noda Shōyu Jōzō Kumiai Shi*, pp. 158–159.

17. Ibid., pp. 159–160.

18. Kikkoman Company Archives, "Report on Activities, 1921–1922" (1922), mimeographed, 6 pages.

19. The information on Western scientific studies of shōyu fermentation and how these research efforts affected a whole generation of Japanese scholars comes from William Shurtleff and Akiko Aoyagi's chapter on "Soy Sauce, Shōyu, and Tamari," in "A History of Soybeans and Soyfoods," forthcoming, The Soyfoods Center, 1984.

20. *Noda Shōyu Jōzō Kumiai Shi*, p. 328.

21. Ibid., p. 333.

22. Ibid., p. 344.

23. For a complete discussion of the historiographical and economic debate over the nature of entrepreneurial motivation during the Meiji Period, see W. Mark Fruin, "From Philanthropy to Paternalism in the Noda Soy Sauce Industry—Pre-corporate and Corporate Charity in Japan," *Business History Review* 61 (Summer 1983), pp. 168–191.

24. Gustav Ranis, "The Community Centered Entrepreneur in Japanese

Development," *Explorations in Entrepreneurial History,* 13 (1955), 466; Johannes Hirschmeier, *The Origins of Entrepreneurship in Meiji Japan* (Cambridge, Mass.: Harvard University Press, 1964), p. 158; *Meiji Taishō Zaisei Sōran* (Tokyo: Tōyō Keizai Shinpōsha, 1926); *Noda Shōyu Jōzō Kumiai Shi.*

25. *Meiji Taishō Zaisei Sōran,* pp. 678–679.

26. Shinshima Jisuke, *Kozō kara Mita Rakudō* (Tokyo, 1929), pp. 4, 9.

27. Ibid., p. 8.

28. There is only one discussion in English of what is known as "the Great Noda Strike." George O. Totten's discussion of this calamitous event relies heavily on the account of Matsuoka Komakichi, one of the leaders of the strike, later turned politician. Totten presumes that the precorporate and early corporate policies of paternalistic management at Noda Shōyu were a major cause of the strike. Paternalism, in Totten's use of the word, is a pejorative term. My research, by contrast, finds that new work rules rather than paternalistic policies were the cause of the strike and that paternalism benefited rather than harmed the workers on the whole. Moreover, paternalism became a systematic company policy only after and not before the strike. See Totten's "Japan's Industrial Relations at the Crossroads: The Great Noda Strike of 1927–28," in Bernard S. Silberman and H. D. Harootunian, eds., *Japan in Crisis—Essays on Taisho Democracy* (Princeton: Princeton University Press, 1974), pp. 398–436.

29. For a full discussion of the creation of a system of lifetime employment and seniority-based compensation, two features of the so-called Japanese system of employment, see my article based on documents from the Noda Shōyu Company: W. Mark Fruin, "The Japanese Company Controversy: Ideology and Organization in a Historical Perspective," *The Journal of Japanese Studies,* 4 (Summer 1978), 267–300.

30. Johannes Hirschmeier and Tsunehiko Yui, *The Development of Japanese Business, 1600–1973* (Cambridge, Mass.: Harvard University Press, 1975), p. 178; Ryōichi Miwa, "Nihon no Karuteru," in Hidemasa Morikawa, ed., *Nihon no Kigyō to Kokka* (Tokyo: Nihon Keizai Shinbunsha, 1976), p. 171.

3. From Cartel to Corporation and Beyond

1. Johannes Hirschmeier and Tsunehiko Yui, *The Development of Japanese Business, 1600–1973* (Cambridge, Mass.: Harvard University Press, 1975), p. 178.

2. Leslie Hannah, "Mergers," in Glenn Porter, ed., *Encyclopedia of American Economic History* (New York: Scribner's, 1980), p. 643.

3. William W. Lockwood, *The Economic Development of Japan* (Princeton: Princeton University Press, 1954), pp. 113–117.

4. Kikkoman Shōyu Company Archives; my translation.

5. Ichiyama Morio, ed., *Noda Shōyu Kabushiki Kaisha Nijunenshi* (Tokyo: Toppan, 1940), pp. 139–141.

6. Ichiyama Morio, ed., *Noda Shōyu Kabushiki Kaisha Sanjugonenshi* (Tokyo: Toppan, 1955), pp. 125–130.

7. Kikkoman Company Archives, Accounts Ledger, 1918–1919, pp. 1–24.

8. "The 200 Largest Industrial Firms in Japan for 1918," compiled by W. Mark Fruin and Yui Tsunehiko in 1982.

9. Kikkoman Company Archives, Executive Attendance Record, 1918.

10. Kikkoman Company Archives, Minutes of the Meetings of the Sales Committee, 1919–20.

11. Kikkoman Company Archives, Minutes of the Meetings Research Committee, beginning June 28, 1919.

12. Ibid., p. 8, September 28, 1919; p. 3, July 28, 1919.

13. Ibid., p. 6.

14. Kikkoman Company Archives, Survey of Local Barrel Makers, 1919.

15. Kikkoman Company Archives, Survey of Blue-Collar Workers, January 1918.

16. Kikkoman Company Archives, Minutes of the Meeting of the Research Committee, Sept. 28, 1920, p. 26. Phrase attributed to Mogi Shichizaemon.

17. Kikkoman Company Archives, Company Personnel Records, 1918 to 1923.

18. Kikkoman Company Archives, Minutes of the Meeting of the Second Day of the Month Group, begin Sept. 2, 1919.

19. Ibid., Nov. 2, 1919, p. 6.

20. Ibid., pp. 6–7; April 2, 1920, pp. 17–18.

21. Ibid., December 2, 1921, p. 56.

22. As early as 1920 the minutes of the various committees record implicit as well as explicit statements to the effect that efficiency in the workplace is connected to lifestyle outside of it. The connection was made more clearly and forcefully in succeeding years.

23. Kikkoman Company Archives, Outline of Housing Available for Workers—The Noda Soy Sauce Company, 1924, 4 pages.

24. Kikkoman Company Archives, Minutes of the Meetings of the Research Committee, Apr. 28, 1922, p. 47. The Yamazaki Iron Works were acquired to facilitate the mechanization of the production process undertaken at this time. Ichiyama, ed., *Noda Shōyu Kabushiki Kaisha Nijunenshi*, p. 209.

25. Ichiyama, ed., *Noda Shōyu Kabushiki Kaisha Sanjugonenshi*, p. 134.

26. Fruin and Yui, "200 Largest Industrial Firms."

27. Ichiyama Morio, ed., *Kikkoman Shōyu Shi* (Tokyo: Toppan, 1968), pp. 484–486.

28. Morikawa Hideo, *Nihon Zaibatsu Shi* (Tokyo: Kyoikusha, 1978), p. 176.

29. Kikkoman Company Archives, Accounts Ledger, 1919.

30. For more background on the zaibatsu, see Shigeaki Yasuoka, "Overview," in Shigeaki Yasuoka, ed., *Nihon no Zaibatsu* (Tokyo: Nihon Keizai Shinbunsha, 1976), pp. 10–40; Morikawa, *Nihon Zaibatsu Shi*.

4. A Loyal Retainer's Farewell

1. I take primary responsibility for this translation, although the help of Inouye Mariko with the formal Japanese of the Meiji-Taishō periods was invaluable.

2. Much of the following discussion of Confucian-inspired management is derived from Robert H. Silin, *Leadership and Values: The Organization of Large-Scale Taiwanese Enterprises* (Cambridge, Mass.: Harvard University Press, 1976), esp. pp. 34–39.

5. Prelude to Turmoil

1. My description of the homicide and that of George O. Totten, the only other one in English, vary considerably, in detail and in interpretation. See George O. Totten, "Japan's Industrial Relations at the Crossroads: The Great Noda Strike of 1927–28," in Bernard S. Silberman and H. D. Harootunian, eds., *Japan in Crisis—Essays on Taisho Democracy* (Princeton: Princeton University Press, 1974), pp. 398–436.

2. Kikkoman Company Archives, Minutes of the Meeting of the Research Committee, Oct. 28, 1921, p. 42.

3. This was taken from the report of the Research Committee on November 28, 1922. Totten writes that the first members in the union were from Factory 15, followed soon by all of the workers in Factory 16 (p. 412). Because this is not verified by reference to any source, I have chosen to follow the report of the Research Committee, which was understandably concerned and careful in such matters.

4. Ichiyama Morio ed., *Kikkoman Shōyu Shi* (Tokyo: Toppan, 1968), pp. 236–238.

5. Yoshida Tōru, "Honpō Shōyu Kōgyō Rōdō, Jijō" *Shakai Seisaku Jihō*, 62 (November 1925), 128–129.

6. Ibid., pp. 127–130.

7. Koji Taira, *Economic Development and the Labor Market in Japan* (New York: Columbia University Press, 1970), p. 154.

8. Interviews with Nakano Eizaburō, former president of the Kikkoman Corporation and an employee of that company from 1918 to 1958, Sept. 9 and 11, 1976.

9. Alfred D. Chandler, Jr., *The Visible Hand: The Managerial Revolution in American Business* (Cambridge, Mass.: Harvard University Press, 1977), pp. 271–277. In most instances in the United States, internal contracting had been abandoned by World War I.

10. Oliver E. Williamson, *Markets and Hierarchies: Analysis and Antitrust Implications* (New York: Free Press, 1975), pp. 96–97.

11. Kikkoman Company Archives, Biroku Jūyakushitsu (n.p., 1919), pp. 1–4.

12. In 1919 the average daily wage for men in the food industry was 1.64 to 1.81 yen. Ohkawa Kazushi et al., *Estimates of Long-Term Economic Statistics of Japan Since 1868—Prices, Bukka*, Choki Keizai Tokei, no. 8, rev. ed. (Tokyo: Tōyō Keizai Shinpōsha, 1968), pp. 248–249.

13. Yoshida, "Honpō Shōyu," p. 128.

14. George O. Totten, "Labor and Agrarian Disputes in Japan Following World War I, *"Economic Development and Cultural Change*, 9 (October 1960), 187–212.

15. Anonymous, *Honsha Sōgi Taikan* (n.p., 1928), p. 3.

16. Stephen S. Large, *Organized Workers and Socialist Politics in Interwar Japan* (Cambridge: Cambridge University Press, 1982), p. 118.

17. Unpublished list of the two hundred largest industrials in Japan in 1918, compiled by W. Mark Fruin and Tsunehiko Yui in 1980 and updated in 1982.

18. Stephen S. Large, *The Yūaikai, 1912–1919* (Tokyo: Sophia University, 1972), p. 154.

19. *Honsha Sōgi Taikan*, pp. 19, 21, 32, 49, 56.

20. My summary is based on: Anonymous, *Honsha Sōgi Taikan*; Matsuoka Komakichi, *Noda Dairōdō Sogi* (Tokyo: Kaizō, 1928); Noda Shōyu Kabushiki Kaisha, *Noda Sōgi no Ketsumatsu* (Tokyo: Tokyo Asahi, 1928).

21. *Honsha Sōgi Taikan*, pp. 22, 32, 33.

22. Ibid., p. 28.

23. Kikkoman Company Archives, Jōzōkō Heikin Hitori Sagyō Bunryōhyō (n.p., 1929?), 3 pages.

6. The Noda Strikes: 1923 and 1927–28

1. Anonymous, *Honsha Sōgi Taikan* (n.p., 1928), p. 3.

2. Ibid., p. 49.

3. Ibid., p. 50.

4. Ibid., p. 53.

5. Ibid., pp. 53, 54, 56, 61.

6. Ibid., pp. 63–65.

7. Ibid., p. 66.

8. Ibid., p. 71.

9. Ibid., pp. 72–73.

10. Kikkoman Company Archives, "Shanai Kitei," mimeographed, 1923–1945; Kikkoman Company Archives, "Kōin Kitei," mimeographed, 1923–1945.

11. Kikkoman Company Archives, "Kyōzaikai Kiyaku," mimeographed, 1927.

12. George O. Totten, "Japan's Industrial Relations at the Crossroads: The Great Noda Strike of 1927–28," in Bernard S. Silberman and H. D. Harootunian, eds., *Japan in Crisis—Essays on Taisho Democracy* (Princeton: Princeton University Press, 1974), pp. 416, 425.

13. Oi Hitotetsu, ed., *Noda Kessenki* (Tokyo: Nihon Shakai Mondai Kenkyūjo, 1928), pp. 22–23.

14. Totten, "Japan's Industrial Relations," p. 413.

15. Shihōshō Keijikyoku, "Noda Sōgi ni Tsuite," mimeographed, marked secret (1928), pp. 3–4.

16. Stephen S. Large, *The Yūaikai, 1912–1919* (Tokyo: Sophia University, 1972), p. 195.

17. Ichiyama Morio, ed., *Noda Shōyu Kabushiki Kaisha Nijunenshi* (Tokyo: Toppan, 1940), pp. 659–661.

18. Mogi Keizaburō, *Watakushi no Rirekisho* (Tokyo: Nihon Keizai Shimbunsha, 1971), p. 22.

19. Totten, "Japan's Industrial Relations," p. 403. In some versions of these demands, there was the specification of 12 coopers per factory to be trained; see, for example, Matsuoka Komakichi, *Noda Dairōdō Sōgi* (Tokyo: Kaizō, 1928), pp. 111–112. The company archives contain a broadsheet of the worker demands without that specification. It is signed "united employees" and dated April 10, 1927. I have followed this version.

20. *Kikkoman Company Archives, Shanai Kunshu—Showa Nisannen Sōgi ni Kansuru* (Noda, 1927–28), pp. 1–7.

21. Totten, "Japan's Industrial Relations," p. 405. The names of those discharged and the reasons for their dismissal (according to the Company Rules Manual) were published by the company in a 9-page mimeographed document, entitled "Kaiko Riyū" (Reasons for Dismissals), undated.

22. Kikkoman Company Archives, *Namiki Kōjō-Kacho to Matsuoka Komakichi-Shi to no Taiwa Yōyaku* (n.p., 1928), pp. 3–4.

23. Matsuoka Komakichi, "Showa Sannen Nigatsu Mikka yoru Hatsugen," statement to reporters, 1928, 4 pages. Matsuoka admitted as much to Namiki during their talks: see Kikkoman Company Archives, *Matsuoka Komakichi to Kaiken Kiroku* (n.p., 1928), p. 10.

24. Matsuoka Komakichi, "A Declaration Concerning the Noda Labor Strike," Feb. 2, 1928, mimeographed, 3 pages. Four days later Matsuoka announced personally the surrender to Namiki. Kikkoman Company Archives, "Matsuoka-Shi to no Kaiken ni Tsuite" (n.p., Feb. 6, 1928), 2 pages.

25. The Japanese Communist Party—Kantō Executive Committee, "Brave Brothers of the Dispute Group in Noda," March 1928, mimeographed, 4 pages.

26. Kikkoman Company Archives, *Matsuoka Komakichi to Kaiken Kiroku* (see note 23), p. 19.

27. Yoshimura Akira and Sato Yoshiya, *Sangyō Damashii* (Tokyo: Nihon Nōritsu Kyōkai, 1976), p. 41. Of the original 1300 strikers 700 were discharged ultimately; 200 withdrew from the strike before it was settled.

28. Namiki Shigetarō, "Sōgi Kaiketsu Oboegaki Seishiki Chōin Jōkyō" n.p., 1928, mimeographed, 8 pages.

29. Stephen S. Large, *Organized Workers and Socialist Politics in Interwar Japan* (Cambridge: Cambridge University Press, 1982), p. 119.

30. In a recent book Hazama Hiroshi discussed the introduction of many of these changes around the country although he fails to treat the story in Noda. See Hazama Hiroshi, *Nihon ni okeru Rōshi Kyōchō no Teiryū* (Tokyo: Waseda Diagaku Shuppanbu, 1978).

7. Corporate Maturation

1. Ichiyama Morio, ed., *Noda Shōyu Kabushiki Kaisha Sanjugonenshi* (Tokyo: Toppan, 1955), pp. 619–624.

2. See Thomas C. Smith, *The Agrarian Origins of Modern Japan* (Palo Alto, Calif.: Stanford University Press, 1959); Koji Taira, *Economic Development and the Labor Market in Japan* (New York: Columbia University Press, 1970); Hugh Patrick, ed., *Japanese Industrialization and Its Social Consequences* (Berkeley: University of California Press, 1976).

3. Roderick MacFarquhar, "The Post-Confucian Challenge," *The Economist,* Feb. 9, 1980, pp. 67–72.

4. Kikkoman Company Archives, "Noda Shōyu Kabushiki Kaisha ni okeru Rōdō Jijō" (Noda, 1936), p. 12.

5. Kikkoman Company Archives, Company Statistical Tables—1918 to 1956 (Noda, 1956).

6. "Noda Shōyu Kabushiki Kaisha ni okeru Rōdō Jijō," p. 3.

7. Kikkoman Company Archives, Company Statistical Tables—1918 to 1956 (Noda, 1956).

8. Kofukan Zaidanhōjin, *Kofukan Yōran,* rev. ed. (Noda: Tachibana, 1957).

9. Ichiyama, ed., *Noda Shōyu Kabushiki Kaisha Nijunenshi* (Tokyo: Toppan, 1940), pp. 667–673.

10. Kofukan, *Kofunkan Yōran,* p. 1; translation mine.

11. Umemura Mataji, "Chingin Kakusa to Rōdō Shijō," in Tsuru Shigeto and Ohkawa Kazushi, eds., *Nihon Keizai no Bunseki,* vol. 2 (Tokyo: Toyo Keizai, 1955).

12. Yasuba Yasukichi, "The Evolution of the Dualistic Wage Structure," in Patrick, ed., *Japanese Industrialization,* pp. 265–269.

13. Ibid., p. 253.

14. Kikkoman Company Archives, "Shanaiki," No. 69, Dec. 26, 1938, mimeographed.

15. Maruyama Masao, *Thought and Behavior in Modern Japanese Politics* (London: Oxford University Press, 1963).

16. Tamara Hareven, *Family Time & Industrial Time* (Cambridge: Cambridge University Press, 1982).

17. In 1936 indirect benefits as a share of the compensation (all salary, wages, and benefits) paid to Noda Shōyu Company employees came to 25 percent of total wage costs. "Noda Shōyu Kabushiki Kaisha ni okeru Rōdō Jijō," p. 27.

18. The part of this chapter dealing with lifetime employment and seniority-based compensation was published previously in more detail in the *Journal of Japanese Studies* (Summer 1978). Reprinted by permission.

19. Peter F. Drucker, "Economic Realities and Enterprise Strategy," in Ezra Vogel, ed., *Modern Japanese Organization and Decision-Making* (Berkeley: University of California Press, 1975), p. 240.

20. Thomas C. Smith, *The Agrarian Origins of Modern Japan* (Palo Alto, Calif.: Stanford University Press, 1959).

21. John W. Hall, "The Ikeda House and Its Retainers in Bizen," John W. Hall and Marius B. Jansen, eds., *Studies in the Institutional History of Early Modern Japan* (Princeton: Princeton University Press, 1968), pp. 79–88; Thomas M. Huber, "Choshu Activists in the Meiji Restoration," paper presented at Center for Japanese and Korean Studies, University of California, Berkeley, March 9, 1977.

22. Robert Marsh and Hiroshi Mannari, "A New Look at 'Lifetime Commitment' in Japanese Industry," *Economic Development and Cultural Change,* 20 (July 1972), 611, 622; Konosuke Odaka, "The Structure of Japanese Labor Markets," *Riron Keizai-Gaku* 18 (June 1967), 31, 40–41.

23. Ichiyama, ed., *Noda Shōyu Kabushiki Kaisha Nijunenshi*, pp. 677-680.

24. Ichiyama, ed., *Noda Shōyu Kabushiki Kaisha Sanjugonenshi*, pp. 164, 166, 168.

25. See David Landes, "French Entrepreneurship and Industrial Growth in the Nineteenth Century," *Journal of Economic History,* 9 (May 1949), and "Social Attitudes, Entrepreneurship, and Economic Development: A Comment," *Explorations in Entrepreneurial History,* 6 (May 1954).

8. The Democratization and Internationalization of Kikkoman

1. Tamaki Hajime, *Kindai Nihon ni okeru Kazoku Kōzō* (Tokyo: Shui Shoten, 1956), pp. 14-15.

2. Kawashima Takeo, *Ideorogi to Shite no Kazoku Seido* (Tokyo: Iwanami Shoten, 1957), pp. 13-15.

3. Eleanor Hadley, *Antitrust in Japan* (Princeton: Princeton University Press, 1970), pp. 73-74.

4. Editorial Committee for the 30-Year History of the Kikkoman Labor Union, *Kikkoman Shōyu Rōdō Kumiai Sanjunenshi* (Noda: Kikkoman Shōyu Rōdō Kumiai, 1977), pp. 22-23.

5. Ibid.

6. Ibid., p. 29.

7. Ibid., pp. 31-32.

8. The Noda Shōyu Company, Limited, *Labor Agreement* (in Japanese); (Tokyo: Yoshida Shuppansha, 1950), pp. 1-50.

9. Interview with Ishige Toshiji, director of the *Kofukan,* July 11, 1979.

10. Details of this anti-trust case are drawn from *Besshi Juristo*, No. 53 (January 1977), a Japanese legal periodical devoted to summarizing and explicating legal decisions rendered in Japan. See *Bessatsu Juristo*, no. 53 (January 1977), pp. 14-15, 28-29.

11. "In re Noda Shōyu Kabushiki Kaisha, 7 FTC 108 (FTC Decision, December 27, 1955)," *Fair Trade,* 1 (1956), 18-27.

12. Ibid., p. 110.

13. Morioka Kiyomi and Yamane Tsuneo, eds., *Ie to Gendai Kazoku* (Tokyo: Baifukan, 1976), p. 287.

14. See Frank K. Upham's use of these terms in his unpublished paper, "Patterns of Violence, Litigation, and Social Change in Japan," presented at the Midwest Regional Seminar on Japan, Evanston, Ill., Mar. 7, 1981.

15. Unpublished interview of Mogi Saheiji by Tsuchiya Takao in Noda, March 1974.

16. I owe much of my information on the modernization of fermentation technology in the manufacture of shōyu to William Shurtleff and Akiko Aoyagi. See their *The Book of Miso,* Ballantine ed., 1976, esp. pages 523-524, and the chapter on "Soy Sauce, Shōyu, and Tamari," in the forthcoming "A History of Soybeans and Soyfoods," The Soyfood Center, 1984.

17. Yamaichi Securities Co., Ltd., *Japanese Corporations Yearbook—1955* (Tokyo: Okamura Publishing Co., 1955), p. 115.

18. Kinugasa Yōsuke, "Takokuseiki Kigyō e no Senryaku—Gendai

Nihon Kigyō Bunseki: Kikkoman Shōyu Kabushiki Kaisha," *Kikkoman Shōyu Kabushiki Kaisha Hanbai Shiryō,* 694 (August 1974), 12. Reprinted from *Keizai Jurai,* 4 & 5 (July–August 1974).

19. Kinugasa, "Takokuseiki Kigyō," p. 11.

20. Noda Shōyu Kabushiki Kaisha, *Annual Report—1949,* January 1950.

21. Tōyō Keizai Shinpōsha, *Kaisha Shikihō* (Tokyo: Tōyō Keizai Shuppan-sha, 1982), p. 128.

22. Kohei Homma, "Kikkoman Jūgyōin Shimin Siekatsu Chōsa," September 1979, *Rikkyo Daigaku Shakaigaku Kenkyūshitsu,* 39 pages.

23. See W. Mark Fruin, "How 'Japanese' are Japanese Manufacturing Enterprises in the United States," *The Asia Record* (August 1981), 26–27.

Appendix A. Ie and the Shōyu Industry

1. Harumi Befu, *Japan: An Anthropological Introduction* (San Francisco: Chandler, 1971), pp. 38–46. Probably the best historical work in Japan on the changing structure and function of ie over time is being done by Akira Hayami of Keio University in Tokyo. For a seminal study of Japanese lineage and enterprise development, see Takashi Nakano, *Shōka Dōzokudan no Kenkyū* (Tokyo: Miraisha, 1974). Most students of ie and dōzoku emphasize patrilineal descent, but Keith Brown does not. He argues for cognate, not agnate, descent; see his "Dōzoku and the Ideology of Descent in Rural Japan," *American Anthropologist* 68 (1966), 1129–1151.

2. Robert J. Smith, *Kurusu* (Stanford: Stanford University Press, 1978), pp. 45–46.

3. Harumi, *Japan: An Anthropological Introduction,* p. 39.

4. Kizaemon Ariga, "Introduction to the Family System in Japan, China, and Korea," *Transactions of the Third World Congress of Sociology,* 4 (1956), 199–207; Michio Nagai, "Dōzoku: A Preliminary Study of the Japanese Extended Family Group and Its Social and Economic Functions," *Interim Technical Report No. 7* (Columbus: Ohio State University Research Foundation, 1953).

5. Seiichi Kitano, "Dōzoku and Ie in Japan: The Meaning of Family Genealogical Relationships." R. J. Smith and R. K. Beardsley, eds., *Japanese Culture: Development and Characteristics* (Chicago: Aldine, 1962); Keith Brown, "Dōzoku and the Ideology of Descent in Rural Japan," *American Anthropologist,* 68 (October 1966), 1129–1151.

6. Chie Nakane, "Analysis of Japanese Dōzoku Structure," *Toyobunka Kenkyūjo Kiyō,* 28 (1962) 133–167.

7. Primogeniture was modified to the degree that, although one son and only one son inherited, he was not necessarily the eldest son or even one's natural son.

8. I owe a great deal of my thinking on the office of the household head and on Japanese households more generally to an unpublished paper by Laurel Cornell, "Patterns of Succession to Household Headship in Japan," Oct. 20, 1976.

9. Using a chi-square test, the difference in frequency was significant at the 99.99 confidence level. The tallies were taken from family tablets main-

tained at local Buddhist temples and were kept to record family relationships that were considered significant to the ie in either its genealogical or corporate manifestation.

10. Morio Ichiyama, *Kikkoman Shōyu Shi* (Tokyo: Toppan, 1968), chronological appendix, pp. 3, 5.

11. Morio Ichiyama, *Noda no Rekishi* (Nagareyama: Ronso, 1975), p. 41.

12. Fujita Teiichirō, "Chihō Zaibatsu Seisei no Shojōken—Terada Zaibatsu o Megutte," in Yasuoka Shigeaki, ed., *Zaibatsushi Kenkyū* (Tokyo: Nihon Keizai Shimbunsha, 1979).

13. See my article on peasant migrants from landed and landless families in nineteenth-century Japan to get some feeling for the differences that economic class had for family function and form. W. Mark Fruin, "Peasant Migrants in the Economic Development of Nineteenth Century Japan," *Agricultural History* (April 1980), 261–277.

14. The opportunity to remain with one's enterprise in the next life is not an anachronistic impulse apparently. Kyoto Ceramic Company, one of Japan's leading electronic firms, opened an employee cemetery in 1982. A company spokesman commented, "We are all members of one family, so it is natural to stay together after we die." *The Wall Street Journal*, Dec. 7, 1981, p. 34.

Appendix B. Scroll from Mogi Fusagorō with Preface by Mogi Keizaburō

1. Shoda Shōyu Company Archives, Scroll from Mogi Fusagorō, 1872.

Appendix C. Rules and Regulations of the Noda Shōyu Brewers' Association

1. Anonymous, *Noda Shōyu Jōzō Kumiai Shi* (Noda, 1919?), pp. 5–15; translation mine.

Appendix F. New Wage and Work Proposal, 1919

1. Kikkoman Company Archives, "Shokkō ni kansuru Kaizen Mondai" (Noda?, 1919), 12 pages.

Glossary

bakufu   the central government structure during the Edo or Tokugawa Period
(1603–1868); also known as shōgunate
bantō   hereditary retainers, trusted assistants
bantō-gashira   office manager
bunke   branch household
chokkatsuchi   territory administered by the central government
dōzoku   a lineage or clan composed of several ie
fudai   hereditary vassal or tenant family
fukoku kyōhei   "rich country and strong army" national movement
furoshiki   large square of cloth used for wrapping
fusuma   sliding door or screen
genin   agricultural servant
go   a board game, somewhat similar to chess and checkers
gyōsei-shidō   government advisement of industry
hakama   a pleated skirt worn with kimono
han   a domain or territory ruled by a lord
hiroshiki   worker dormitory
honke   the main household in a lineage
honnin   workers with experience
ie   stem family, descent group
igusa   reed used for woven matting
ikka   united (one) family
inkyo   a kind of regency office for persons considered unsuited to assume the
office of household head
inkyo-bantō   a senior bantō
jigara   foot-powered machinery
jinrikisha   man-powered buggy
jūgyōin ichidō   united employees
jukurenkō   skilled workmen or craftsmen

kabu nakama   guildlike association
kaizō   reconstruction
kakushin   reform
kama-ya   kettle-tenders
kashira   functional foremen
kasu   shōyu residue cake left after squeezing
kazoku   nuclear family
kemari   a type of soccer popular among courtier families in Kyoto
kigyo-ikka   "the enterprise as family"
kishukusha   company-built or company-subsidized housing
kobun   child, or apprentice
koi-kuchi   dark soy sauce
kōji   mixed wheat and soybeans, heated, without brine
kōji-katsugi   a person charged with moving the mixed soy beans and wheat
     before they are mixed with brine or that process
kōjō renraku kaigi   company committees designed to enhance intracorporate
     communication
kokka   theory of kokutai that identifies the state and household
koku   47.6 gallons; shō = 1.8 liters (1.92 quarts)
kokutai   theory of the patriarchal state with the emperor as father
komeya   cereals merchant
kozō   apprentice
kyōka suru   to indoctrinate or to socialize
mirin   sweet sake
miso   fermented bean paste
moromi   mash composed of wheat, soybeans, and brine
moromi-kaki   stirring of the moromi during early stages of fermentation
mugi-iri   wheat roaster
mujin-ko   mutual-aid society
muko-yōshi   adopted son-in-law
muromae   a person responsible for mixing soy beans with wheat before they
     are cultured or that process itself
nagaremono   seasonal or temporary workers
naya-seido   system of internal labor contracting
nenkō joretsu   compensation and reward according to seniority
ongaeshi   repaying one's debts to society
oyabun   labor recruiters (Noda)
oyabun-kobun   a master and an apprentice
oyakata   labor recruiters
rakugo   a comic story often told by professional storytellers
rōdō-kyogikai   a council for discussing labor-capital issues
ryō   monetary unit in gold
sake   fermented rice wine
samurai   a member of the warrior class
sangyō-damashii   "spirit of industry" slogan
sen   100 sen equals 1 yen; unit of monetary measure
setai   nuclear family

skikakegama   large metal kettles sheathed in wood
shinnin   workmen without experience
shinshiki shōyu   postwar shōyu using some HVP in fermentation
shō   1.8 liters (1.92 quarts)
shōgun   the supreme authority within the Bakufu government
shōyu   soy sauce
shōyu-abura   shōyu oil
shūshinkoyō   lifetime or long-term employment with one employer
sonchō   district headman or village mayor
sumō   wrestlers
tabi   socks
tamari   thick, dark food seasoning made from soy beans
taru   barrel of 4.3-gallons measure
taru-koshirae   making of soy sauce barrels
tatami   reed matting in large woven sections
tenryō   territory administered by the central government
tōji   factory foremen
tokuyakuten   association of distributors
tōnya   government-licensed middlemen who receive and distribute products
tsubō   measurement of 3.31 sq. meters (3.95 sq. yds.)
usu-kuchi   light soy sauce
wakashū   junior clerk
wakashū-gashira   senior clerk
yonaoshi   a combined agrarian and millennial movement of the eighteenth
    and nineteenth centuries
yōshi   technique of adopting persons into the family to advance the family
    fortune
za   guild association
zaibatsu   groupings of interrelated enterprises
zōri-tori   servant who takes care of shoes and sandals

Index

HARVARD STUDIES IN BUSINESS HISTORY